Marine bugler sounds Church Call at dedication of first permanent
Marine chapel in Korea.

The History of the

CHAPLAIN CORPS

UNITED STATES NAVY

VOLUME SIX • DURING THE KOREAN WAR
27 June 1950-27 June 1954

NAVPERS 15936

United States Government Printing Office
Washington : 1960

970

"On behalf of the American public, I want to congratulate our chaplains on the fine work they are doing and the service they are performing. Today, as our country has joined the other United Nations in the struggle which has given us the greatest chance for lasting peace this generation has had, military chaplains are performing their services at home, on foreign shores, in ships at sea, and in the front lines of the Korean battlefield.

"The military chaplain is a man who braves many dangers as he does his work serving God and the young men defending the nation's spiritual traditions."

President HARRY S TRUMAN

TABLE OF CONTENTS

NORTH KOREAN AGGRESSION
27 June–2 November 1950

THE INCHON-SEOUL OPERATION
13 September–7 October 1950

COMMUNIST CHINESE AGGRESSION
3 November 1950–24 January 1951

FIRST UNITED NATIONS COUNTEROFFENSIVE

25 January–21 April 1951

CHINESE COMMUNIST SPRING OFFENSIVE

22 April–8 July 1951

UNITED NATIONS SUMMER-FALL OFFENSIVE

9 July–27 November 1951

SECOND KOREAN WINTER

28 November 1951–30 April 1952

KOREAN DEFENSE—SUMMER-FALL 1952

1 May–30 November 1952

THIRD KOREAN WINTER

1 December–30 April 1953

KOREAN DEFENSE

Summer and Fall 1953

ARMISTICE AFTERMATH

27 July 1953–27 July 1954

Rear Adm. George A. Rosso, CHC, USN Chief of Chaplains.

FOREWORD

This is the sixth volume of *History of the Chaplains Corps, United States Navy*. The first volume published in 1949 presents a narrative account of the development of the Corps from the Revolutionary War to the declaration of a state of emergency on 8 September 1939.

The second volume continues the narrative history of the Chaplains Corps from 8 September 1939 to the spring of 1949. The next three volumes are biographies of Navy chaplains.

The present volume narrates the history of the Chaplains Corps during the Korean Conflict from 27 June 1950 to 27 June 1954. It primarily concerns the chaplains in combat. Therefore, naval chaplains who were assigned to the 1st Marine Division and supporting units are most often mentioned. The latter category would include the 1st Marine Air Wing where chaplains worked with replacements and wounded brought from the front and still found time to do relief work. It also refers to the chaplains who were assigned to ships which were involved in surface and air action, and those who served aboard hospital and MSTS ships giving needed aid and support to all United Nations troops in Korea. There were others who served in more secondary but important billets.

There is always a danger in the composition of a history that almost assuredly some "unsung heroes" will fail to receive recognition for their accomplishments. Every attempt has been made to "let the chaplains speak". Much of this volume will record their own accounts of what took place.

The History of the Chaplain Corps, United States Navy, volume VI, has been the product of three chaplains working successively. As a result there was the situation of "planting, watering, and reaping." The last writer has attempted to retain much of the structure and planning to which he fell heir.

Chaplain Clifford M. Drury (retired), formerly the Chaplain Corps historian and writer of the first four volumes, started this history. Chaplain Paul S. Sanders continued the collection of material and organizing the book. Special tribute should be given to Reserve Chaplain W. Ivan Hoy, associate professor of religion at the University of Miami, who was the final writer of the text. He successfully followed the pattern set by previous writers, coordinated the loose details, and completed the volume for publication.

This volume has evolved from the plans to publish a volume of the history treating with the period from the spring of 1949 until the present. One chapter was to have dealt with the Korean Conflict. It became apparent that one chapter of reasonable size in a volume of this type would not do justice to the activities of the chaplains in Korea. It was, therefore, determined that a separate volume on Korea be produced. This was to be followed with the publication of the other material in an additional volume. Because of this decision some of the material from Formosa, Japan and other Far Eastern areas has not been included. It was decided that the present volume should deal for the most part with chaplains immediately concerned with the conflict. It is to be desired that all material not directly concerned with Korea, but dealing with the Orient, be considered in the volume yet to be produced.

In these pages you will find the thrilling and inspiring service of Navy chaplains. Their dedication to God and their country should go down in the annals of our great nation. As the present Chief of Chaplains I look back at the Corps during those fateful Korean War days and proclaim that I am proud to be associated with such a dedicated group of clergymen. They answered a call to serve and they did so in an outstanding manner.

GEORGE A. ROSSO,
Rear Admiral, CHC, USN,
Chief of Chaplains.
November 1959.

INTRODUCTION

TO HALT AGGRESSION

On 25 June 1950 North Korean forces crossed the 38th Parallel and began an invasion of South Korea.[1] Two days later the Security Council of the United Nations condemned this act of aggression as a breach of world peace and requested its members to come to the assistance of the Republic of Korea. The same day President Harry S. Truman announced that he had ordered United States naval and air forces to give the South Koreans "cover and support." A blockade of the entire Korean coast was instigated.[2] Japan-based Air Force units were authorized to bomb specific military targets north of the 38th Parallel. Gen. Douglas C. MacArthur, Supreme Allied Commander of Far Eastern Occupation Forces, with headquarters in Tokyo, was made the Commander in Chief of the United Nations Command. On 29 June the President authorized him to employ certain supporting U.S. ground forces in Korea.

Neither moral suasion nor economic sanctions had been sufficient in the years preceding the outbreak of World War II to prevent or halt the aggression of Japan, Italy, and Germany. The League of Nations, helpless before naked power, had been effectively destroyed as the agent of international order. Now the United Nations Security Council (with Russia voluntarily absent and Yugoslavia abstaining) determined not only to condemn but also to combat aggression. Fifty-three nations (excluding only the U.S.S.R. and her satellites Poland and Czechoslovakia of the entire United Nations membership) approved the decision of the Security Council and pledged military, medical, and economic assistance. A remote Asiatic peninsula, whose very location was unknown to many Americans, thus became, before the end of the year, the scene of the fourth most costly war effort in American history, both in blood and money.[3]

When hostilities began the Marine Corps had two divisions, both seriously understrength. Even with most of the men of the 2d Marine Division transferred to the 1st Marine Division at Camp Pendleton, Calif., the combined strength was still so low that Reserves had to be called to active duty to build the 1st Division up to full wartime strength. The mobilization of the Marine Corps Reserve was ordered by President Truman with the sanction of Congress on 19 July.[4] Maj. Gen. Oliver P. Smith assumed command of the 1st Division, consisting of the 1st, 5th, and 7th Marines (infantry regiments) and the 11th Marines (an artillery regiment), together with the usual supporting battalions (Headquarters, Ordnance, Medical, Supply, etc.). Reserve units hastily assembled at Camp Pendleton were integrated into the Division. Only a cadre had been left at Camp Lejeune, N.C., around which to rebuild the 2d Division, largely of Reserves. A reinforced battalion of some 900 men (3d Battalion, 6th Marines, 2d Marine

---

[1] For background on Korea and events leading up to the North Korean invasion, see L. M. Goodrich, *Korea: A Study of U.S. Policy in the United Nations* (New York, 1956), chs. I–IV. Chap. V deals with the United Nations response to the armed attack upon a free republic.

See also: Lynn Montross and N. A. Canzona, *U.S. Marine Operations in Korea, 1950–53;* vol. I, *The Pusan Perimeter* (Washington, 1954), chs. I, II and the beginning of ch. III. *Ibid.;* vol. II, *The Inchon-Seoul Operation* (Washington, 1955), ch. I. Also M. W. Cagle and F. A. Manson, *The Sea War in Korea* (Annapolis, 1957), ch. I.

The North Koreans invaded the Republic of Korea at 0400, Sunday, 25 June 1950. Since Seoul is 14 hours ahead of eastern standard time, that was 1500 in New York and Washington (then on daylight time), Saturday, 24 June 1950. Dates in this book are those of the place under discussion.

The U.S. State Department received official notice of the invasion from Ambassador Muccio shortly past 9 p.m. on the Saturday night. By 3 a.m. of the Sunday morning Secretary General Trygve Lie of the United Nations was given the news at his home. The United States asked for a meeting of the Security Council, which met at 2 p.m. on Sunday. With the Russian delegate voluntarily absent and Yugoslavia abstaining, the Security Council put the blame for aggression directly upon North Korea and ordered a withdrawal of its troops from the South.

[2] A lively account of the 7th Fleet's involvement from the beginning is Walter Karig, M. W. Cagle and F. A. Manson, *Battle Report;* vol. VI, *The War in Korea* (New York, 1952), chs. 1–5.

On the Navy's blockade and bombardment missions, from the beginning to the end of the Korean War, see Cagle and Manson, *op. cit.,* ch. 9.

[3] Montross and Canzona, *op. cit.,* vol. I, p. 1.

[4] *Marine Corps Gazette* (September 1951). E. H. Giusti, "Minute Men—1950 Model: The Reserves in Action." Also Montross and Canzona, *op. cit.,* vol. I, ch. III; vol. II, ch. II.

Division) attached to the 6th Fleet in the Mediterranean was sent around the world through the Suez Canal; arriving in Kobe, Japan, on 7 September it would be assimilated into the 7th Marines and dispatched to Inchon.

A Marine division in World War II had an allowance of 16 chaplains. Following the war, the Tables of Organization of the Marine Corps were revised to call for 26 chaplains to a division, plus any additional who might be assigned to attached units. The increase in chaplain strength was partly the result of the enlargement of the total strength of a Marine combat division; it was in part also a recognition by the Marine Corps of the fine work done by Navy chaplains serving with Marines in World War II.

At the time of the outbreak of hostilities in Korea, 21 Naval Reserve chaplains, on inactive duty, were attached to various Organized Marine Reserve units scattered throughout the country. When these units were activated the chaplains concerned were also called to active duty. The fact that they had received compensation for their service with Organized Reserve units was taken by the Bureau of Naval Personnel as an indication that they had already volunteered for active duty. Three of the twenty-one were released to inactive duty shortly after reporting. Among those recalled who served with the 1st Marine Division in Korea in the opening months of the conflict were Chaplains William N. Lyons, Preston D. Parsons, and Robert L. Patton. Chaplain Godfrey J. Reilly had returned to active duty in June 1950 shortly before the North Korean invasion.

In answer to General MacArthur's request for at least a Marine Regimental Combat Team, there was assembled at Camp Pendleton the 1st Marine Provisional Brigade; activated on 7 July, it sailed from San Diego on 14 July some 6,500 strong.[5] A combined ground-air team, the Brigade's ground forces consisted of the 5th Marines, at that time the only Marine infantry regiment of approximate combat strength, the 1st Battalion, 11th Marines (artillery), and company-sized support units. Air support was Marine Aircraft Group 33, consisting primarily of three fighter squadrons. Orlando Ingvoldstad, Jr., was the Brigade chaplain, and there were three others with the ground units: Bernard L. Hickey,

[5] Montross and Canzona, *op. cit.,* vol. I, pp. 49ff. A lively account may be found in Andrew Geer, *The New Breed* (New York, 1952). Ch. I is entitled "A Fire Starts; the Fire Brigade Is Called."
See appendix B(1) of this present volume for comments regarding chaplain activities on Troop Transports, in Chaplain Orlando Ingvoldstad's Battle Report of 14 July–12 September 1950.

William G. Tennant, and Otto E. Sporrer. John H. Markley was chaplain for the aircraft unit.

So hastily were the Marines hustled aboard transports for Korea that there was no time to check them aboard. A head count was made after the ships were at sea. On one the results showed plus 12! Gen. Randolph McC. Pate, when afterward as Commandant of the Marine Corps he recounted this story to a Navy League convention, commented that the 12 were "read off" publicly, commended privately, and the matter closed.

The main body of the 1st Division sailed from San Diego 10–22 August and completed debarking at Kobe, Japan, on 3 September.[6] Chaplain Joseph G. Power, in his reply to a questionnaire distributed by the Chaplains Division in March 1954, commented on the work of chaplains in the trans-Pacific crossing:

I remember the services in the GENERAL M. C. MEIGS on the way to Japan, with four Protestant chaplains holding Divine Services in different parts of the ship simultaneously. Each service must have had well over 200 Marines in attendance.

Roman Catholic chaplains were also affording a spiritual ministry to the men of their faith. Navy chaplains were again observing a phenomenon frequently noticed during World War II—an increased interest in religion on the part of men facing grave danger. The old proverb was illustrated anew, that "man's extremity is God's opportunity."

The duties of chaplains serving with Marines were outlined in the U.S. Marine Corps Staff Manual, 1948, paragraph 241, as follows:

Chaplain:
a. Advises the commander and staff in religious and moral activities of the command.
b. Supervises the spiritual welfare of the command.
c. Conducts religious services, including funerals.
d. Gives spiritual ministrations to the sick and wounded.
e. Corresponds with relatives of deceased personnel.
f. Coordinates the religious work of the various welfare agencies.
g. Supervises and coordinates the assignment, training, and work of the chaplains of subordinate units.
h. Prepares estimates and allotments of funds for religious activities not specifically charged to other agencies of the command.

Naturally the duties of a chaplain can never be fully reduced to writing. How can official regulations define the inspiration which flows forth from daily exemplary living? Or how can one adequately describe the ministry of giving spiritual aid and comfort to individuals on the battle line or in the hospital? No

[6] Montross and Canzona, *op. cit.,* vol. II, pp. 74ff.

manual can ever encompass the intangibles which are most vital in every chaplain's ministry.

By Executive Order No. 10179 the President of the United States on 8 November 1950 established the Korean Service medal to commemorate the service of members of the Armed Forces of the United States during operations in the Korean theater; the inclusive dates were eventually set as 27 June 1950 to 27 July 1954.[7] It was awarded for land service in Korea, air service over Korea and service within waters adjacent to Korea, within prescribed boundaries, or in such other areas as Commander, Naval Forces, Far East, should designate as having directly supported the military effort in Korea.

Engagement stars were eventually authorized for ten separate periods, ending with the signing of the armistice agreement at Panmunjom on 27 July 1953. Each of the following rated a battle star on the Korean Service ribbon.

K–1   North Korean Aggression, 27 June–2 November 1950.

K–2   Communist China Aggression, 3 November 1950–24 January 1951.

K–3   Inchon Landing, 13–17 September 1950.

K–4   First United Nations Counteroffensive, 25 January–21 April 1951.

K–5   Communist China Spring Offensive, 22 April–8 July 1951.

K–6   United Nations Summer-Fall Offensive, 9 July–27 November 1951.

K–7   Second Korean Winter, 28 November 1951–30 April 1952.

K–8   Korean Defense, Summer-Fall, 1952, 1 May–30 November 1952.

K–9   Third Korean Winter, 1 December 1952–30 April 1953.

K–10   Korea, Summer-Fall 1953, 1 May–27 July 1953.

This scheme of periodization will provide the basic outline of the following account of Navy chaplains during the Korean War, with some adjustment. It will be noted that the official code given above numbers the Inchon landing third and awards a battle

[7] *U.S. Navy and Marine Corps Awards Manual.* NAVPERS 15,790; revised 1953 and further revised by current Official Change Memoranda.

star only for the 5 days 13–17 September; this short period is therefore chronologically comprehended within the first period, 27 June–2 November 1950. In order to follow the action of the 1st Marine Division more closely, our first chapter will deal mainly with the Pusan Perimeter operation, followed by a second chapter on both the Inchon landing and the Seoul operation, covering the period 13 September–7 October 1950. Chapter 3 will deal mainly with the Chosin Reservoir campaign, which fell within the K–2 dates; the Marines were in their Masan rest camp by Christmas 1950.

Beginning with chapter 4 our account will follow precisely the dating of engagements listed in the code. Following the chapter dealing with K–10, chapter 11 will be occupied with chaplains in Korea following the Panmunjom armistice agreement. The 1-year period 27 July 1953–27 July 1954 rates the award of the Korean Service medal, but does not carry with it any engagement star.

Inevitably the larger share of attention is devoted to chaplains serving with the 1st Marine Division and the 1st Marine Aircraft Wing. There were others on board the larger ships in Korean waters, as well as "circuit riders" serving smaller vessels on rotation schedules. On occasion casualties were received as the result of enemy fire from shore, or from mines; the larger number were sustained by Navy and Marine flyers operating from carriers. In addition to other duties, chaplains aboard such ships ministered to the wounded and officiated at the last rites paid the dead. Still other "padres" were attached to various units under Commander Naval Forces, Far East, mostly based in Japan. Those aboard transports carrying troops to and from combat areas, as well as those on hospital ships, found many opportunities to minister to the physical and spiritual welfare of Navy and Marine Corps personnel.

For all these, as also for those chaplains only indirectly involved in the Korean War, this present volume of *The History of the Chaplains Corps, U.S. Navy* may serve as a memorial to their devotion to the service of God and man.

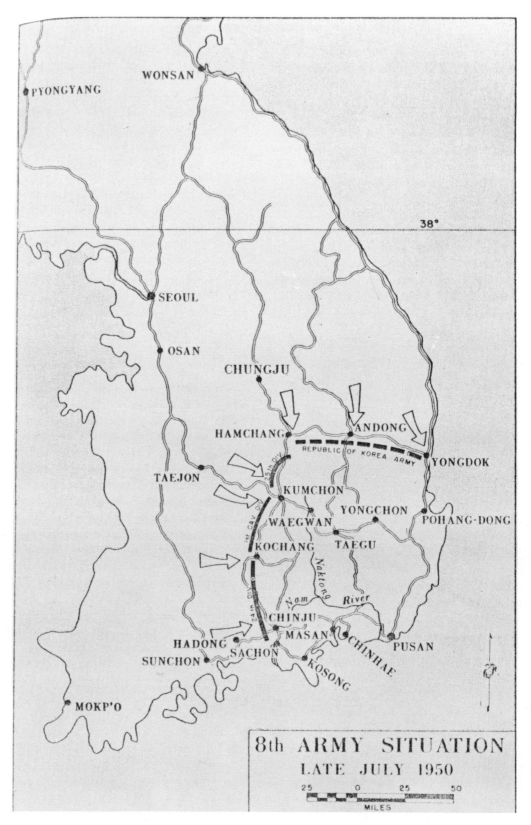

8th ARMY SITUATION
LATE JULY 1950

Reproduced by permission from *U.S. Marine Operations in Korea.*

— 4 —

CHAPTER 1

NORTH KOREAN AGGRESSION

27 June–2 November 1950

The forces of the Republic of Korea (frequently referred to as ROK) proved unable to stem the offensive of the better-trained and better-equipped troops from the North. General MacArthur drew upon all available men from the occupation forces located in Japan and elsewhere.[1] Three U.S. Army divisions (24th, 25th, and 1st Cavalry), then on a peace-time basis, psychologically and physically unprepared for actual combat, were grouped as the 8th Army under Lt. Gen. Walton H. Walker and hurriedly sent to Korea. Even such reinforcements were unable to stem the steady southward advance of the North Korean soldiers who, indoctrinated with a fanatical zeal, pressed onward confident that complete victory was within their immediate grasp. By late July four battered ROK divisions and the three U.S. Army divisions had been driven back to within some fifty miles of the vital supply port of Pusan. The rim of defense around the last remaining free area of the Republic of Korea, about 120 miles long, was called the Pusan Perimeter. Into this critical situation General MacArthur was throwing every possible reinforcement in order to keep a toe-hold in Korea for future retaliatory action.

The Pusan Perimeter

On 2 August the ground forces of the 1st Marine Provisional Brigade landed at Pusan.[2] With the exception of a small Marine legation guard at Seoul, it constituted the 1st Marine land force to fight in the Korean War. Four chaplains were attached to the ground units—Orlando Ingvoldstad, Jr., and William G. Tennant (Protestants) and Otto E. Sporrer and Bernard L. Hickey (Roman Catholics). Writing

aboard the transport on 2 August, just before the Marines disembarked at Pusan, Chaplain Sporrer commented on his work in a letter to Chaplain Daniel F. Meehan, Assistant Director of the Chaplains Division.

We had great numbers every day at Mass and confessions every night. The morale is wonderful and if ever the Marines did a job we will do it. I am very proud and happy to be with them. I will never cease to thank you for this duty. Please don't separate me from these men until you absolutely have to, and then let me stay with the Marines until this war is over.

On 7 August the Marines went into action in defense of Hill 342, southwest of Masan; the first casualties were received and Navy chaplains were once again under fire. At this time the chaplains were assigned as follows: Chaplain Hickey, 3d Battalion, 5th Marines; Chaplain Sporrer (artillery), 1st Battalion, 11th Marines; Chaplain Tennant, "B" Medical Company, at Masan; and Chaplain Ingvoldstad, Rear Echelon, at Pusan. Hickey and Sporrer covered the forward aid stations, Tennant the evacuation center and the cemetery at Masan, and Ingvoldstad the Army evacuation hospital at Pusan through which all patients passed on their way to hospitals in Japan. This engagement in the Chindong-ni-Kosong-Changchon area lasted 7–13 August.[3] Chaplain Ingvoldstad offers many valuable comments on this period based upon his personal experience.

First Naktong

On 17 August, having been regrouped at Miryang, well within the Perimeter, the Marines were again committed to action, assaulting Obong-ni Ridge, in what became known as the First Battle of the Naktong (River).[4] During this day Chaplains Ingvold-

---

[1] Montross and Canzona, *op. cit.,* vol. I, ch. III (esp. pp. 43ff.) and ch. IV (esp. pp. 68ff.)

See also: Cagle and Manson, *op. cit.,* ch. 2. Karig *et al., op. cit.,* chs. 6–13. A preliminary Army account of the first 6 months of the Korean War is entitled *Korea, 1950* (Department of the Army: Office of the Chief of Military History, 1952). Ch. II deals with the first frantic efforts to stem the Red advance.

[2] Montross and Canzona, *op. cit.,* vol. I, ch. V.

[3] *Ibid.,* chs. VI–VIII. For a journalistic, but useful account of the early Pusan Perimeter battles, see Geer, *op. cit.,* chs. II and following. Also *Korea, 1950* (Department of the Army), ch. III.

[4] Montross and Canzona, *op. cit.,* vol. I, chs. IX, X.

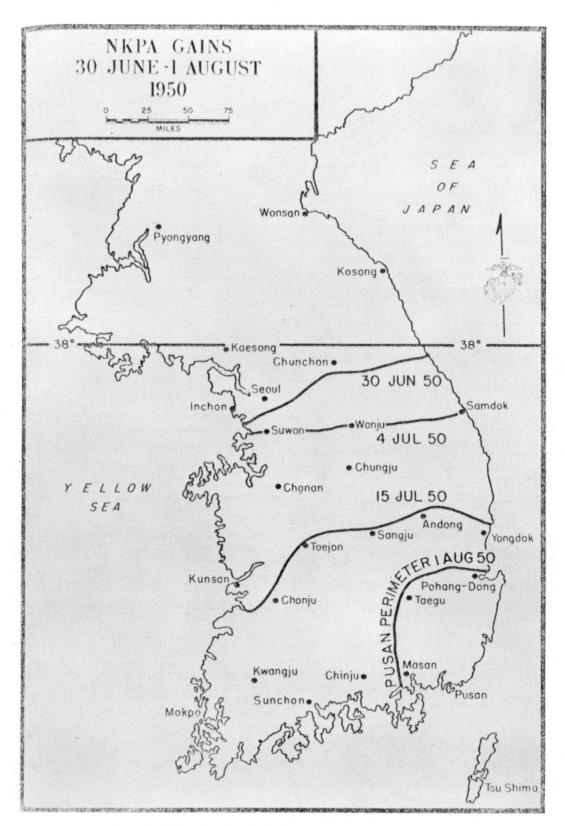

Reproduced by permission from *U.S. Marine Operations in Korea.*

Improvisation.
A camp cot is used as the base of the altar by Chaplain Otto Sporrer as he holds mass for the 11th Artillery in a field behind the battlelines in South Korea.

Memorial Services.
Squadron members bow their heads as Chaplain John H. Markley conducts a memorial service for fliers who were shot down by North Korean antiaircraft fire on a night-fighter mission.

United Nations Cemetery, Masan.
Flags fly at half-mast where fallen marines and fellow comrades find their last resting place.

stad and either Sporrer or Hickey were in the forward aid station, while Tennant was at the regimental collecting and clearing station. The chaplains were constantly on the move. As far as possible it was planned to have a Protestant and a Roman Catholic chaplain available at forward aid stations all the time.

On 18 August, with each of the 5th Marines battalions engaged, the chaplains operated as follows: Ingvoldstad visited the forward aid station of the 1st Battalion, 5th Marines, then that of the 3d Battalion, then held a Protestant Service at the artillery unit, and finally moved on to the 2d Battalion's aid station for the night. Sporrer celebrated Mass at the artillery unit and likewise moved from one battalion aid station to each of the others. Tennant remained all day and night with the regimental collecting and clearing station, while Hickey visited all the aid stations, though staying mostly with that of the 3d Battalion.

The Naktong objective was secured on 19 August and the Marine Brigade ordered into Eighth Army reserve. Its bivouac area from 21 to 31 August was a bean patch near Masan, from which the Marines

Memorial Services.

Chaplain Orlando Ingvoldstad, Jr., is shown holding memorial services at the Army-Marine Corps Cemetery in South Korea at Masan on 24 August 1950.

Burial Service.

Chaplain William G. Tennant conducts a graveside service. Photographs of such services were sent to the next of kin.

would fight their way around the peninsula and complete their circuit five months later (following the withdrawal from Chosin) to the identical bean patch.[5]

The chaplains were now able to conduct funeral and memorial services for the men killed in the first action, that of 7–13 August. Upon the suggestion of the Brigade commander, Brig. Gen. Edward A. Craig, an individual picture was taken of each grave with the appropriate chaplain standing by in benediction. These pictures were sent to Headquarters, Marine Corps, in Washington, and after casualty notices had been sent to next of kin, many requests were received from bereaved families for the pictures.

On 22 August Chaplain Ingvoldstad wrote to Chaplain Stanton W. Salisbury, Chief of Chaplains:

As I'm writing I'm sitting under a shelter in a bean field; it's hot, sticky, and dusty. Shooting is going on in the hills around us, but the activities of our camp are normal, as we are in reserve right now. Shortly we'll probably be in it again.

Sporrer is with the Artillery battalion, but also gets up into our aid stations . . . Hickey, Tennant and I have been

working the battalion aid stations, Hickey usually with 3rd Bn., Tennant and I between 1st and 2nd. Then we also shift around as the need is. Our battalion aid stations are as close as 100–150 yards from the fighting and at times under fire. I can truthfully say none of our wounded have left the zone of action without being seen by a chaplain.

Second Naktong

The Marines were involved in a third engagement, 3–5 September, in the same Naktong River area, repulsing a desperate Communist attempt to breach the Pusan Perimeter.[6] Beginning at midnight on the fifth, the Brigade was withdrawn to Pusan, where staging began for what would be the Inchon amphibious landing. In 1 month the air-ground team had fought 3 difficult battles, suffering 902 casualties, including 9 missing in action, 163 deaths and 730 wounded. In addition to the ministry rendered the dead and wounded, the chaplains had faithfully maintained Divine Services. On Sunday, 27 August, for instance, the four chaplains conducted eight services. But, as Ingvoldstad wrote, "We've been holding services regardless of days, whenever

---

[5] *Ibid.,* pp. 207f.

[6] *Ibid.,* chs. **XI, XII.**

we stop long enough. Had around 300 this morning at 0700."

Chaplain Otto E. Sporrer was awarded the Army Bronze Star with Combat "V" for heroism in the Pusan Perimeter campaign. The citation reads as follows:

As a member of the 1st Battalion, 11th Marines, 1st Provisional Marine Brigade for heroic achievement on 7 August 1950 at Chindongni, Korea. On 7 August 1950 Lieutenant Commander Sporrer was in the vicinity of an artillery battery position which was undergoing heavy enemy counterbattery fire. The enemy scored a direct hit on a gun position causing many casualties. Without regard for his own personal safety, Lieutenant Commander Sporrer voluntarily exposed himself to the heavy fire in order to assist the wounded. Heedless of the heavy fire, he administered effective first aid and assisted in evacuating the wounded to a place of safety. The heroism displayed by Lieutenant Commander Sporrer on this occasion reflects great credit on himself and the naval service.

Each of the other Navy chaplains who took part in the defense of the Pusan Perimeter received the Bronze Star for acts of heroism and valor in later campaigns. Chaplain Sporrer was also awarded the Army Silver Star for another act of heroism which took place on 18 August in the battle for Obong-ni Ridge. This second citation reads in part:

On this date Lieutenant Commander Sporrer in his capacity as Catholic Chaplain visited the forward aid station of the Fifth Marines, then in attack on enemy positions ot the ridges west of the Naktong. Learning that a number of wounded were on the ridges awaiting evacuation, Lieutenant Commander Sporrer organized a litter-bearing team of Korean civilians and showing a high degree of courage and skill led them through heavy small arms, automatic weapons and mortar fire. By his leadership and example Lieutenant Commander Sporrer encouraged the litter-bearing team to continue even after they had been pinned down by enemy fire. He then succeeded in evacuating a number of seriously wounded to the Aid Station.

MAG 33

The Brigade's air support, Marine Aircraft Group 33, had arrived in Kobe, Japan, on 31 July. Since Korean land-based operations were impossible, the planes were flown to nearby Itami for maintenance and testing and returned to the carriers SICILY and BADOENG STRAIT, from which the two fighter squadrons operated during the initial months of the war.[7] The night-fighter squadron was based in Japan. The helicopters included in Marine Aircraft Group 33 were the first such to be formed into a unit for combat service overseas.[8] They, together with the observer squadron and the Air Support section, were ferried to Korea and came under direct Brigade control.

With Marine Aircraft Group 33 was one chaplain, John H. Markley, a Methodist. Subsequently, when the main body of the 1st Marine Aircraft Wing arrived in September, Chaplain John P. Murphy, a Roman Catholic, came out with them from El Torro, Calif., Marine Air Station as Wing Chaplain. On 14 September he wrote from Itami, Japan, to the Chief of Chaplains that he and Markley would cover Marine Aircraft Group 33, by then partly shore-based in Korea, leaving the Wing headquarters to be covered by a Protestant Air Force chaplain and two American missionary priests. It was planned that Marine Aircraft Group 12, on arrival, would be carrier-based and therefore covered by ship's chaplains. Adding that an aircraft group numbered about 3,000 personnel, Murphy asked for a Protestant and a Roman Catholic chaplain for each group, in addition to himself as Wing Chaplain.

Marine air power was early engaged in the attempt to block the enemy's advance. Before the Brigade's ground forces became operative, already on 3 August eight Corsairs of VMF–214 operating from the SICILY had made the first Marine air strike in defense of the Pusan Perimeter.[9] On succeeding days, joined by VMF–323 operating from the BADOENG STRAIT, the Brigade's air arm continued to pound enemy concentrations north of Eighth Army's defensive lines. During Marine ground operations the three squadrons of Marine Aircraft Group 33 provided outstanding close air support, vindicating the Marine Corps' doctrine of ground-air teamwork.

Aboard the SICILY as chaplain was Cornelius O. Sullivan, a Roman Catholic. His counterpart in the BADOENG STRAIT, Chaplain Oswald B. Salyer, was a Methodist. Both men ministered to the Navy crews of their ships and the embarked Marine air personnel as well. The first Marine pilot killed in Korea was Capt. V. M. Moses, of Jewish faith. No Jewish chaplain was available, and it fell to Salyer, a Methodist, to conduct a service for the captain on 13 August. Fittingly the chaplain was able to read the first part of the service in Hebrew.

Writing to the Chaplains Division, Salyer described a helicopter highline routine which enabled Sullivan and himself to extend their ministry. At 0800 on Sunday, Salyer conducted Protestant service aboard the BADOENG STRAIT, Sullivan celebrating Mass

---

[7] Ibid., pp. 89f.
[8] Ibid., p. 50. See also Montross, Cavalry of the Sky (New York, 1954), an account of the development and early use by the Marines of combat helicopter squadrons.

[9] Montross and Canzona, op. cit., vol. I, pp. 98f. Cagle and Manson, op. cit., pp. 61–67.

aboard the SICILY. At 0900 the chaplains would be exchanged by the BADOENG STRAIT's helicopter, so that at 0915 there would be Mass in that ship and Protestant service in the SICILY. Afterward each chaplain transferred by highline to one of the ships of the destroyer screen for a third service, returning to his home ship by highline again. Thus both Protestant and Roman Catholic worship was held in each of the two carriers every Sunday, and in each destroyer once a month.

Seventh Fleet

The two senior naval commands in the Far East were 7th Fleet and Commander Naval Forces, Far East. Seventh Fleet, commanded by Vice Adm. Arthur D. Struble, though dispersed in the Philippines and at Hong Kong, was within fast cruising range of Korea. Its main force, Carrier Division 3, consisting of the VALLEY FORGE and embarked Air Group Five, the cruiser ROCHESTER, and eight destroyers, under Rear Adm. J. M. Hoskins, was fortunately in a state of readiness, even though the ships' peacetime mission had been largely "showing the flag" around the Orient.[10]

Vice Adm. C. Turner Joy, Commander Naval Forces, Far East, had his headquarters in Tokyo. In the interval between World War II and the Korean War the chief mission of ComNavFE had been assisting the recovery of Japan. Besides supervision of the naval stations at Yokosuka and Sasebo, and helping to rebuild the Japanese merchant fleet, ComNavFE utilized a support force (Cruiser Division 5) consisting of the cruiser JUNEAU, four destroyers, and six minesweepers, under Rear Adm. J. M. Higgins, in clearing Japanese waters of leftover mines, Chinese pirates, and Japanese and Korean smugglers.

U.S. naval forces, with 7th Fleet under operational control of ComNavFE, were made available to General MacArthur, Commander in Chief, Far East, on 26 June. The first surface action occurred on 2 July, when the JUNEAU destroyed several North Korean motor torpedo boats encountered north of Kangnung on the east coast. But the enemy had, of course, next to no naval power; the missions of United Nations naval forces were chiefly ship-to-shore bombardment and the launching of bombing strikes against the airfields and rail facilities of the North Korean capital of Pyongyang and, later, the Wonsan oil refinery.

From midnight of 24 July, when elements of 7th Fleet weighed anchor for the east coast of Korea, naval close air support began to be furnished the ground forces of 8th Army.[11] Coordinated through 5th Air Force, the squadrons of VALLEY FORGE and, after 1 August, PHILIPPINE SEA lent their support to the beleaguered defenders of the Pusan Perimeter. The arrival of the cruisers HELENA and TOLEDO in late July strengthened the blockade effort; and in early September this would be further strengthened by the organization of Task Force 95, the United Nations Blockading and Escort Force, composed of ships of 10 nations.[12]

The final naval contribution to the Pusan Perimeter duel was the rescue during the night of 16 August of the ROK 3d Division, which had ably held fast to allow inland units to withdraw but was now itself in danger of isolation and being cut to pieces. Supported by the HELENA and destroyer escorts, 4 LSTS removed 5,830 military personnel, 1,260 civilian refugees, and 100 military vehicles from the beach near Yonghae.[13]

ComNavFE

As the Navy girded itself for a war it had not been led to expect, Admiral Joy's command expanded to furnish the United Nations Command the strongest possible naval striking power. Japan-based naval activities expanded to provide service and support of every sort for the ships and aircraft of 7th Fleet, the amphibious force, and the elements of Fleet Marine Force, Pacific, operating in the war theater.

The main center at first was Commander, Fleet Activities, Yokosuka (Navy #3923). Two chaplains were aboard, Thomas V. Edwards, Roman Catholic, and Henry J. Beukema, Reformed. On the Fourth of July Beukema wrote to Chaplain Salisbury:

We are now in Condition II. We see huge convoys of tanks and trucks. Ships are being feverishly loaded with war supplies. Today, normally a holiday, is become a work day. We anticipate the arrival of approximately one thousand officers and enlisted men to man the destroyer escorts recently returned by Russia. . . . All available ships in the area have sailed for Korea. . . . What the picture will be within the next thirty days is difficult to state. We hope that once the North Koreans are pushed behind the 38th Parallel normalcy will ensue. . . .

On 11 July Beukema wrote concerning Fleet Activities, Sasebo:

The normal complement is seventy enlisted men and five officers. How many men will be eventually assigned to Sasebo is not known; no doubt the base will serve our Korean task forces. Consideration should be given the placement of a chaplain at that activity, if only temporarily.

[10] Cagle and Manson, *op. cit.*, ch. 2, esp. pp. 30–47.

[11] *Ibid.*, pp. 47–61.
[12] *Ibid.*, pp. 288–298.
[13] *Ibid.*, pp. 69f.

One interesting pause in the midst of feverish war activity deserves noting. On 15 July a ceremony was held in front of the Perry Monument at Kurihama, Yokosuka, to commemorate the 98th anniversary of the landing of Commodore Matthew G. Perry in Japan. Chaplain Edwards gave the opening prayer and Chaplain Beukema a benediction.

On 22 July Chaplain James E. Reaves reported as relief for Beukema; both men wrote the Chaplains Division asking that Beukema be allowed to remain for at least several months. On 28 July Reaves wrote "the Chief":

> Yesterday I made the ward rounds at the dispensary and found it impossible to get away under 3 hours. The patient load is increasing there daily, and the senior medical officer indicated to me that they expect it to mushroom out of all proportion to its present size.

As the buildup continued and casualties began pouring in "in a flood," the chaplains found their energies taxed to the limit. The Chaplains Division advised that the chaplains consult their command with reference to the establishment of additional chaplain billets as it was the responsibility of the latter to initiate a request of this nature. Chaplain Beukema was detached, and Edwards and Reaves carried on.

Chaplains in the Fleet

Large carriers were entitled to two chaplains. Harold E. Meade had reported aboard the PHILIPPINE SEA in July as Roman Catholic Chaplain. The same month Chaplain Charles W. Nelson, an Episcopalian, who had been serving in the ship since January, was hospitalized and ordered stateside for treatment. Chaplain John E. Zoller, attached to Commander Service Force, Pacific, whose regular duties carried him throughout the Pacific Fleet visiting auxiliary vessels too small to rate a chaplain, was temporarily on board from 11 July to 7 September. Ernest R. Barnes reported for duty as the ship's Protestant chaplain on 6 September. And thereby hangs a tale.

Barnes had been serving as Camp Chaplain, Marine Barracks, Camp Lejeune, N.C. He had been issued orders the middle of June to 3d Naval District where, in September, he expected to begin duty under instruction at Union Theological Seminary, New York. The beginning of the Korean War, however, caused the cancellation of the postgraduate study program and Barnes was ordered instead to the PHILIPPINE SEA. Detached from Camp Lejeune on 7 August, before the arrival of his relief, Chaplain Abbot Peterson, Barnes spent the next month trying to catch up with his ship. Finally, on 9 September, he wrote the Chief of Chaplains from Sasebo, Japan, where he had managed to report aboard.

> I shared your concern about getting to the ship as rapidly as possible. By keeping in touch with the Command people I was able to avoid the mistakes which several of the local Air-Traffic Control officers were about to make in routing me, thus arriving in Sasebo just 2 hours before the ship dropped anchor. Had I not kept in touch with the high echelons, I would have missed the ship, inasmuch as the traffic people were going to route me to Okinawa.

Later on, when Chaplain Barnes was assigned in May 1951 as Wing Chaplain, 1st Marine Aircraft Wing, Chaplain Zoller would again be temporarily aboard the PHILIPPINE SEA, from 15 April to 3 June. Meanwhile he had served temporarily aboard the cruiser ROCHESTER (7 October–3 November 1950) and the oiler KASKASKIA (3 November–25 November 1950) while those ships were operating in Korean waters. From 8 December 1950 to 9 January 1951 Zoller was temporarily attached to the U.S. Naval Hospital at Yokosuka, Japan. The shortage of chaplains and the exigencies of sudden war had made necessary many expedients, not the least useful of which was the attempt to supply as widespread a ministry as possible by means of such "circuit-riding" activities.

Of one of his experiences, when assigned for a brief time to a fleet tug, Zoller wrote as follows:

> One Sunday, in extremely heavy seas, it seemed impractical to try to hold Divine Service. However, this was the crew's first experience of having a chaplain on board and . . . they had particularly requested Holy Communion.
>
> It was almost impossible to stand upright unassisted. . . . To ask the men to come forward for the Sacrament would be impossible by reason of [limitation of] space and the ship's movement. Further, the coordination of eye and muscle involved in serving by intinction seemed unattainable under the circumstances. Yet I felt that to deny them the Sacrament would be a grave error.
>
> The solution was to prepare strips of bread approximately one-half inch square and 2 inches long and to fill the chalice one-fourth full. At the appropriate time [after the elements were consecrated], the men were instructed to take a strip of bread as I passed among them, if they desired to receive Holy Communion. Following this, I passed among them again with the chalice and each man dipped one end of his bread into the cup. . . .

He concluded: "It was a bit awkward, and surely unorthodox, but the service was solemn throughout and the men spoke later of the blessing they had received."

Aboard the VALLEY FORGE were Chaplains Abner R. Cook (Methodist), who had reported in March, and Paul J. Knapp (Roman Catholic), who reported in May. The cruisers normally carried only one

Worship at Sea.

A weekday mass is held aboard the HELENA while in Korean waters. The officiating chaplain is John J. McGowan, Jr.

chaplain. John J. McGowan, Jr., was relieved in the HELENA by Chaplain Jerome J. Sullivan in September. Chaplain Benjamin J. Davis served in the JUNEAU from March 1949 to March 1951, 2 years being the normal tour of ship-board duty.

Chaplain Barnes sent to Chaplain Salisbury further information concerning naval activities in the Far East. He wrote:

At Yokosuka the buildup is like a mushroom; something like 7,000 there now, and to go higher. Supply is bringing in staff to serve 10,000. The dispensary is now a hospital, the wings [formerly] occupied by dependents being rapidly reconverted to wards. By the end of September they expect to have a 2,000-bed capacity. There were 431 casualties there the day I arrived.

He continued:

At Sasebo the harbor is full of ships. It looks like Pearl [during] the last war. Chaplain McGann called a meeting on his ship the 7th. There were nine of us in attendance: McGann, Cook, Vaughan, Knapp, Wolf, Curry, Zoller, Meade, and myself.

Chaplain Francis L. McGann, then Assistant Fleet Chaplain on the staff of Commander Service Force, Pacific Fleet, was in the Far East area on temporary duty with Commander Service Division 31. Matthew A. Curry was aboard the cruiser WORCESTER, being detached shortly thereafter. Robert A. Vaughan and August J. Wolf were both in destroyer tenders, the DIXIE and the PIEDMONT respectively.

Barnes concluded his letter to Chaplain Salisbury: "Shortly the ship will put to sea again on further operations. I will keep in touch with you and Chaplain [Edward B.] Harp [Fleet Chaplain, Commander Service Force, Pacific Fleet] as opportunity to get mail off is afforded." The fleet too was getting prepared for the next move: Inchon.

Chaplain SOP

After each combat engagement Marine line officers write a Battle Report, which is afterwards closely studied in order to improve the Corps' fighting efficiency. Such reports were of course mandatory for the line but were not regularly asked of staff components. Although they had accompanied Marines in many engagements, chaplains had apparently never made an official Battle Report. At the conclusion of the Marines' involvement in the Pusan Perimeter campaign, and while aboard ship en route to the Inchon landing, Chaplain Ingvoldstad compiled a summary of the work of the Brigade chaplains from their departure on 14 July from San Diego through operations down to 12 September 1950. (See appendix B(1) of this present volume.) The value of chaplains thus incorporating their experiences and activities into official records is revealed by the events which followed.

As the Battle Reports of the 1st Provisional Marine Brigade were being forwarded to Marine Corps Headquarters, Chaplain Ingvoldstad's report of the work of chaplains received special attention. On 24 October 1950 Lt. Gen. Lemuel C. Shepherd, Jr., Commanding General, Fleet Marine Force, Pacific, wrote to Chaplain Salisbury (Chief of Chaplains), saying in part:

I have recently read the report of Chaplain O. Ingvoldstad, Jr., on the operations of the 1st Marine Brigade in Korea from 14 July to 12 September, and consider it outstanding. If this report has not been brought to your attention, I suggest you read it and I am sure you will agree with me that the advice obtained therein should be passed on to all chaplains operating with Marines in the field.

It is the first time that I have ever seen anything in writing relative to what chaplains should do in combat and I think the notes jotted down by Chaplain Ingvoldstad may well be reproduced in pamphlet form to be included in instructions for young chaplains, especially those going to duty with Marines.

In his letter of acknowledgment of 30 October, Chaplain Salisbury called Ingvoldstad's report "an excellent piece of work" and stated that "it is our plan to have it reproduced for use by chaplains going into such combat."

On 29 October the Division Chaplain, Robert M. Schwyhart, sent a letter to all regimental chaplains attached to the 1st Division requesting each to com-

with the purpose of preparing a Standing Operating pile facts and information based upon experience, Procedure (referred to as SOP) for chaplains. The material gathered was edited by Chaplain Schwyhart and submitted as a recommendation to the Force Chaplain, FMF Pac, for approval. The result was Fleet Marine Force, Pacific, General Order 19, dated 28 March 1951; Subject: "Standing Operating Procedure for the Chaplain Service of the Fleet Marine Force, Pacific." This order extended over eight mimeographed pages and spelled out in detail the duties expected of a Navy chaplain serving with the Marines. (See appendix C.) A similar order was subsequently drawn up for Marine chaplains serving in the Atlantic, which appeared as Fleet Marine Force, Atlantic, General Order 41, dated 31 July 1951.

Letters of Condolence

One section of the SOP for chaplains, FMF Pac, read as follows:

When practicable an individual picture of each grave with the appropriate chaplain standing by in benediction should be taken, so that families may secure copies if desired.

This was done as far as possible throughout the

Division Chaplain's Headquarters.
The division chaplain was located in this tent which is at the command post of the division.

Korean War, having been begun with the burials of those killed in the Pusan Perimeter operations. Under the outline of duties expected of chaplains in combat operations were the following:

Duties on Conclusion of Landing and Assault Phase:

(1) At the close of operations, unit chaplains will prepare letters of condolence to next of kin of those lost in action. These letters will be properly channeled through the command. The office of the Division Chaplain can assist a unit chaplain by looking up the following information relative to each person deceased:

(a) Name, rank, serial number.
(b) Date of death, place of burial, and religion.
(c) Name and address of next of kin.
(d) Name of officiating chaplain at burial.

(2) At the close of an operation, the Division Chaplain, with the approval of the Commanding General, should arrange for a memorial service to be held at the Division cemetery or in other cemeteries where Division dead are buried.

Such letters of condolence were faithfully written by individual chaplains and, judging from the responses received from bereaved families, were deeply appreciated. Memorial services were held periodically throughout the Korean War, both on division level and also in smaller units.

Mission Completed

On 13 September the 1st Provisional Marine Brigade was deactivated and reabsorbed into the 1st Marine Division, its components resuming their old unit designations and embarking from Pusan to join the main body of the Division being embarked from Kobe. For its "outstanding and heroic performance of duty on the field of battle during the period 2 August 1950 to 6 September 1950" the Brigade was awarded a Presidential Unit Citation by Syngman Rhee, President of the Republic of Korea. It was also given a Presidential Unit Citation by the President of the United States "for extraordinary heroism in action against enemy aggressor forces in Korea from 7 August to 7 September 1950."

On the eve of the Inchon assault, the following 28 Navy chaplains were attached to the Division:

Division Chaplain—Robert M. Schwyhart.
Headquarters Battalion—Garson Goodman and William N. Lyons.
Division Troops—Howard H. Groover, Ernest A. Ham, William M. Hearn, Aarne J. Juntunen, Patrick A. Killeen, Preston D. Parsons, Robert L. Patton, Charles S. Pigott, Joseph G. Power, William A. Rennie, Eugene I. Van Antwerp, and Lawrence R. Phillips.
Regimental Units:
1st Marines—Glyn Jones (Regimental Chaplain), Kevin J. Keaney, and James W. Lewis.
5th Marines—Orlando Ingvoldstad, Jr. (Regimental Chaplain), Bernard L. Hickey, and William G. Tennant.
7th Marines—John Craven (Regimental Chaplain), Cornelius J. Griffin, and Kester M. Hearn.
11th Marines—Otto E. Sporrer (Regimental Chaplain), Robert A. Bonner, Barker C. Howland, and Godfrey J. Reilly.

Goodman was of the Jewish faith. Griffin, Hickey, Keaney, Killeen, Reilly, Sporrer, and Van Antwerp were Roman Catholics. The others were Protestants. Chaplain Ernest A. Ham was left with the Administrative Rear Echelon at Camp Garver, near Kobe, Japan, primarily for the purpose of giving assistance to Marine casualties in the hospitals at Kobe, Osaka, and Kyoto. Among those left behind were also some 500 17-year-old Marines, who by order of the Secretary of the Navy had been removed from the troop list just before the Division embarked for the Inchon amphibious landing.[14]

---

[14] Montross and Canzona, *op. cit.,* vol. II, p. 76.

CHAPTER 2

THE INCHON-SEOUL OPERATION

13 September–7 October 1950

Military strategy called for a surprise landing in the rear of the North Korean Army. Inchon, on the west coast, about 20 miles from Seoul, was selected for several reasons. It was the port of the capital city. Its capture would permit the United Nations forces to cut the enemy's supply and communications lines. Moreover, because of the unusual tides in the area, it seemed to General MacArthur that the enemy would be expecting his counterattack elsewhere. The X Corps, commanded by Maj. General Edward M. Almond, was given the task of taking Inchon and advancing via Kimpo airfield to the Han River and the capital. X Corps included, besides the 1st Marine Division and the attached 1st Marine Aircraft Wing, the 7th Infantry Division, an understrength occupation-duty division whose complement would be filled out with South Korean soldiers.

The operation had been planned even before the 1st Marine Division was fully organized.[1] Because of the wide range of high and low tides, the assault would have to made at just the right time, else the vessels would be stranded on mud-flats. Unless Inchon could be taken by the middle of September, the operation would have to be postponed, and probably abandoned. Time was running out. The Division was embarked from Kobe on 11 September, minus the 7th Marines, not yet fully reorganized, and joined at a predetermined rendezvous point by its newly reintegrated elements which had constituted the 1st Provisional Marine Brigade.

Victory Over Time and Tide

The first objective was the island of Wolmi-Do, just offshore in Inchon harbor. Aerial bombardment began on 10 September as Marine fliers started "soft-ening up" Wolmi-Do; they were joined by planes from Task Force 77 operating from the VALLEY FORGE, the PHILIPPINE SEA, and the BOXER.[2] This last ship had arrived from the States only within the last few days, having fought Typhoon Kezia in its last laps before reaching Sasebo. Preliminary bombardment was begun on 13 September by the cruisers TOLEDO and ROCHESTER, in company with the British cruisers KENYA and JAMAICA.

Early on Friday morning, 15 September, the 3d Battalion, 5th Marines landed on Wolmi-Do and an hour before sunset the remaining Marine units assaulted Inchon itself on the evening tide.[3] Within 24 hours the seaport of some 250,000 inhabitants was taken. The Marines suffered only moderate casualties as the attack took the enemy by surprise and the prelanding bombardment had wiped out most of his prepared defense positions.

At the same time naval forces headed by the battleship MISSOURI, rushed to Korea from Norfolk, Va., shelled Communist troop concentrations; and the 8th Army, under Lt. Gen. W. H. Walker, launched a sudden movement designed to break out from the Pusan Perimeter.[4] By 26 September elements of 8th Army had effected a linkup with the 7th Army Division working its way southeastward from Inchon. By the end of the month organized NKPA resistance in the south had begun to collapse.

Liberation of Seoul

Within 48 hours after the initial landing the 5th Marines took the important Kimpo airfield, and other

---

[1] Montross and Canzona, *op. cit.,* vol. II, Chs. III–IV. See also Cagle and Manson, *op. cit.,* ch. 3. Karig *et al., op. cit.,* Chs. 14–21.

[2] Montross and Canzona, *op. cit.,* vol. II, pp. 85–87. Also Cagle and Manson, *op. cit.,* pp. 91–94.
[3] *Ibid.,* pp. 94ff. Montross and Canzona, *op. cit.,* vol. II, chs. V–VII, beginning on p. 87.
[4] *Korea, 1950* (Department of the Army) sketches the movements of other UN forces in the South while the Marines were occupied in the Inchon-Seoul area. See pp. 147–150.

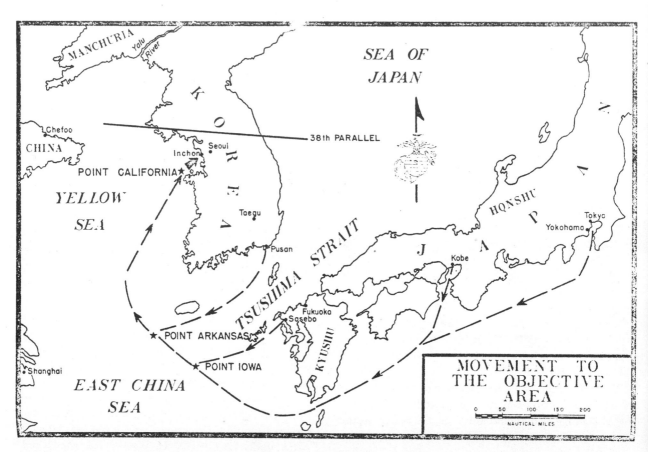

Reproduced by permission from *U.S. Marine Operations in Korea.*

The chart shows the rendezvous pattern for the elements making up the Inchon attack force. Wide dispersal of units, the importance of surprise, and the absolute necessity of making the assault on the high tide made planning more than usually difficult. The imminence of Typhoon Kezia in the East China Sea and Tsushima Strait complicated planning immeasurably more, since it was expected to arrive just in the path of the outloaded attack force. The main body of the 1st Marine Division embarked from Kobe, the former 1st Provisional Marine Brigade from Pusan. (See Montross and Canzona, *U.S. Marine Operations in Korea,* Vol. II, pp. 79ff.)

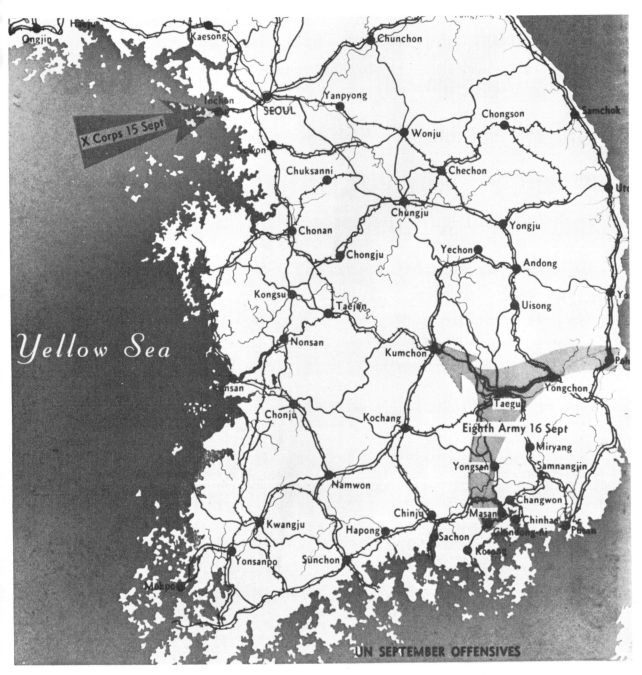

Ongjin Haeju Kaesong Chunchon

X Corps 15 Sept Inchon Yanpyong Chongson Samchok

SEOUL Suwon Wonju Uto

Chuksanni Chechon

Chungju Yongju

Chonan Yechon Andong

Chongju

Kongsu Taejon Uisong Yo

Yellow Sea Nonsan

Kumchon Yongchon Poh

Ansan Taegu Eighth Army 16 Sept

Chonju Kochang Miryang

Yongsan Samnangjin

Namwon Masan Changwon

Chinju Chinhad

Kwangju Hapong Sachon Kumdong-nim Pusan

Yonsanpo Sunchon Kosong

Makpo

UN SEPTEMBER OFFENSIVES

Reproduced by permission from the *Marine Corps Gazette*.

units pressed forward towards the Han River.[5] Seoul, the capital, built around the base of tree-covered South Mountain, was enveloped from two directions by Army, Marine, and ROK Marine troops of X Corps. Supported by artillery and close air support, the operation at first met light resistance. It was even thought possible the city might be spared heavy destruction. But the North Koreans were determined, and it was only after intensive street fighting during 25–28 September, advancing yard by yard, even foot by foot, that the city was at last secured.

According to Marine Corps records, total casualties in the Inchon-Seoul operation included 415 killed in action or dead from wounds, 6 missing, and 2,029 wounded.[6] About two-thirds of these were sustained in the hill battles on the outskirts of Seoul and in the bitter house-to-house and barricade-to-barricade street fighting which took place within the capital city. According to official records, the enemy's estimated casualties numbered 13,666 plus 6,492 prisoners. Throughout the Korean War, the number of casualties inflicted on North Korean and Chinese Communist forces would be many times greater than that sustained by the United Nations forces.

The Inchon amphibious assault was rated a separate engagement, and service during the period 13–17 September rated an individual battle star on the Korean Service ribbon. For its action in the Inchon-Seoul operation, the 1st Marine Division (reinforced) was awarded a Presidential Unit Citation covering

On to Inchon.

Marines and sailors embarked and on the way to Inchon for the invasion take time out to attend divine services led by Chaplain Hickey. 13 September 1950.

Inchon Harbor.

This photograph was taken a few days after the invasion. 19 September 1950. The area pictured is west of Wolmi-Do Island.

[5] Montross and Canzona, *op. cit.*, vol. II, chs. VIII and following. XIII details the fight for Seoul and the final chapter (XIV), the remaining Marine efforts around Seoul before being relieved by Army units on 7 October.
[6] *Ibid.*, appendix J, p. 333.

the dates 15 September–11 October 1950, and a Korean Presidential Unit Citation for the period 15–27 September 1950.

On 8 October a Memorial Service was conducted at the cemetery established by the 1st Marine Division at Inchon, in honor of the United Nations personnel who lay buried there. Some 3,000 Marines from the Division and the 1st Marine Aircraft Wing were present. Chaplains representing the three major faiths—Protestant, Roman Catholic and Jewish—took part, with Maj. Gen. Edward M. Almond, USA, as the main speaker.

Chaplain Casualties

Three chaplains—Ingvoldstad, Tennant, and Bonner—were wounded in the Inchon-Seoul operation. Chaplain Ingvoldstad was slightly wounded in his right arm by shrapnel from an exploding missile which killed two men and wounded eight others. He received treatment at the 5th Marines Aid Station and was able to maintain an uninterrupted duty status.

Chaplain William G. Tennant, also in the 5th Marines, was wounded by mortar fire on 22 September while in the act of aiding wounded personnel. Writing on 27 September from a Naval hospital base in Japan to Chief of Chaplains, S. W. Salisbury, Chaplain James E. Reaves gave the following account of the incident:

> You may have gotten word that Chaplain Tennant has been wounded. Last Friday afternoon he tangled with a 120-mm. mortar shell. He will have to have an operation on his left arm for the removal of fragments and possibly some repair work, but so far we have no word as to how long a convalescence period he will have. He lost a great deal of blood from a facial wound but is doing very nicely. His men tell me that he did a magnificent job there on the front at Seoul. A sergeant by the name of O'Sullivan told me that Tennant was up with a man who had been badly hit when he (the sergeant) began yelling for him to get down and crawl back to where he was dug in. He said Tennant ignored him and continued to help the man who was down. About that time one shell fell and got Tennant and the next got the sergeant. At that time his outfit had 29 wounded and 7 killed outright. Every officer and man I've talked with has praised Tennant to the skies.

Chaplain Tennant was air-evacuated the following day to Fukuoka, Japan. His wounds required treatment in a hospital for about a month. Chaplain Lawrence R. Phillips was transferred on 23 September from the 1st Combat Service Group to the 5th Marines as Tennant's relief.

For heroic achievement during operations against the enemy in the fight for the Pusan Perimeter and in the Inchon Landing, Chaplain Tennant was awarded the Bronze Star. His citation reads in part:

> Without regard for his own personal safety, he repeatedly exposed himself to the enemy fire to administer solace and spiritual guidance to the wounded and dying. Courageously and with no regard for personal fatigue, he constantly moved among the assault units to assist in the evacuation and care of wounded Marines. Although warned to take cover, he remained with the assault unit helping to care for and give spiritual ministration to the wounded Marines until he was wounded by enemy mortar fragments and evacuated. His actions throughout this period were an inspiration to all members of the regiment.

The third chaplain to be wounded in the Inchon-Seoul campaign was Robert L. Bonner. On 27 September Bonner was riding in a jeep near Seoul when it ran over a land mine. The resulting explosion inflicted second and third degree burns on his face and lacerations on his wrists, and impaired his hearing. Within 3 hours he was received at the Division Hospital and the same day air-evacuated to Fukuoka. Chaplain Bonner later received the Silver Star medal "for conspicuous gallantry and intrepidity in action against the enemy while serving as a chaplain with a Marine artillery regiment in Korea from 15 September to 27 September 1950." The following quotation from the citation gives additional information about the incident:

> Lieutenant Bonner, though not required to do so, regularly visited elements of his regiment attached to front line units, courageously exposing himself to enemy small arms and mortar fire in order to encourage and minister to the men. While returning to his regiment after one visit he was seriously wounded when the vehicle in which he was riding struck a land mine. With the vehicle in flames, he risked his life to remove three wounded comrades. Despite his own severe burns and painful wounds he then walked more than half a mile to a battalion aid station to obtain medical assistance for his comrades. Only then would he consent to treatment for his own wounds. His courageous conduct and disregard for personal safety combined with his constant concern for the officers and men in his spiritual keeping were an inspiration to all who served with him.

Combat Ministry

Some 3 weeks following the landing at Inchon on 15 September were spent in combat. The chaplains found it necessary to adapt their ministry to the existing circumstances.[7] For the most part, large gatherings of men for religious services could not be held. Chaplain Ingvoldstad mentioned, in his answer to the Chaplains Division questionnaire, holding as many as seven religious services in one day for small and sep-

---

[7] See Chaplain O. Ingvoldstad's report of chaplain activities in one regiment, from 30 August to 7 October 1950; app. B(2) of this present volume.

Memorial Services, Inchon.

Chaplain Otto Sporrer offers the requiem prayers.

First Marine Division holds memorial services for its fallen heroes at Inchon. Conducting services are chaplains representing the various faiths. These shown are (from left to right) Chaplains John Craven, Orlando Ingvoldstad, Jr., Glyn Jones, Garson Goodman, Bernard L. Hickey, and the Division Chaplain, R. M. Schwyhart.

Chaplain Glyn Jones reads the service.

Chaplain Robert M. Schwyhart, USN gives the closing prayer.

arated units prior to the Han River crossing. Once he held a service below an embankment while enemy bullets whistled through the trees overhead.

Chaplain John H. Craven, a Southern Baptist, baptized three men by immersion in evaporator tanks of the troop transport the day before they landed at Inchon on 21 September. Following debarkation five more men were baptized in collapsible rubber water tanks used by the Combat Engineers in Inchon. Craven was Regimental Chaplain of the 7th Marines, newly organized in Japan and composed of officers and men from the former 6th Marines, 2d Marine Division, including its 3d Battalion, which had been in the Mediterranean at the outbreak of the war, and others drawn from posts and stations in the United States, plus nearly 2,000 recalled Reserves deemed combat-ready.[8]

Chaplain Barker C. Howland in his questionnaire contributed the following story:

Baptizing a man could be a problem if done strictly according to the tenets of my denomination. One baptism, in particular, I remember which was held right outside of Inchon after the successful conquest of Seoul. The man had gone to a Church of Christ church in Texas. The medical officer attached to our regiment recommended that I not baptize the man down by the shore because he felt the water was polluted. Several of the men in the regiment came through in the pinch and constructed for me a tank made out of galvanized iron which they had scrounged. Water was heated for it was in October and there in that tank I baptized this Marine.

(The word "scrounge" had become a common word in the vocabulary of U.S. troops during World War II. No onus was attached to "scrounging." It meant simply getting by other than official means something that was needed.)

Chaplain Joseph G. Power wrote in his questionnaire reply: "On the morning of 15 September 1950, while the preliminary bombardment of the Inchon coastal defenses was in progress, I served Communion to almost an entire Marine infantry company, and baptized 16 men." Chaplain Craven reported that it was his custom to offer Communion at almost every service. Many of the Protestant chaplains carried individual communion sets so that the Sacrament could be administered to small groups or even to but one man. The Chaplains Division would later develop a combat communion kit, but this was not made generally available to the chaplains in Korea until after the cease-fire order of July 1953.

On 1 October 1950 all Protestant chaplains connected with the 1st Marine Division observed World Wide Communion Sunday. Among the services held was one at the Division Hospital at Inchon where

Chaplain William A. Rennie was assisted by a choir from a local Korean Methodist Church. At Seoul Chaplain Robert M. Schwyhart preached in the Chodong Presbyterian Church at the invitation of the pastor, the Reverend David Chung. This congregation met amidst the ruins of its former church. Meetings of chaplain and service personnel with Korean Christians were an inspiration for all, and often gave to the Americans convincing evidence of the results of missionary work.

As in World War II, chaplains ministering to Marines under combat conditions adapted themselves to existing circumstances and held Divine Services under diverse and often adverse circumstances. Chaplain Craven in his reply to the Chaplains Division questionnaire summed up the experience of all of his fellow chaplains who saw service in Korea when he wrote:

Conducted Divine Services under all sorts of conditions: in Korean houses, drug stores, nail factory, city hall, enclosed courtyards, barns, warehouse, railroad stations, theatre building, school building of a Benedictine Monastery, creek beds, rock quarries, shell holes, tents, reverse slopes and open country. The altar was rigged on ox carts, jeep hoods, ammunition crates, metal spools for communication wire and stretchers. I also set up the portable altar set on Korean porches, tables and desks. Many times, of course, services were conducted without setting up the portable altar set.

A most unusual setting for Christian worship was provided on 28 September when both Protestant and Roman Catholic services were held in front of the Presidential Palace in the city of Seoul. Chaplain Bernard L. Hickey celebrated Mass and Chaplain Lawrence R. Phillips led a Protestant service, both for the 5th Marines. On the same day, near the city of Seoul, Chaplain Garson Goodman conducted a Jewish service. On the following day, 29 September, General MacArthur, President Syngman Rhee, and other high ranking dignitaries met in a solemn ceremony within the capitol building in recognition of the liberation of the city.

Heroic Service

For heroic or meritorious achievement during the Inchon-Seoul operation, the following eight Navy chaplains were awarded the Bronze Star medal: Division Chaplain Robert M. Schwyhart; Regimental Chaplains Glyn Jones, John H. Craven, and Orlando Ingvoldstad; and Chaplains William G. Tennant, Patrick A. Killeen, Godfrey J. Reilly, and John H. Markley.

Mention has already been made of the citation

---

[8] Montross and Canzona, *op. cit.,* vol. II, p. 33.

Services at the Governor's Palace.

Chaplain L. R. Phillips conducts services for Protestants on the steps of the governor's palace scarred and blackened by shell fire.

Catholic services are conducted by Chaplain Hickey for marines who participated in the capture of Seoul. Services are held on the palace steps.

awarded Chaplain Tennant. The citation accompanying the medal given to Chaplain Schwyhart notes that he had traveled with front line units on numerous occasions while they were subjected to enemy fire and that he had administered solace and spiritual comfort to wounded and dying Marines.

"His advice to the Commanding General in religious and morale activities of the command was of immeasurable assistance to the success of the Division," the citation concludes.

The citations for Chaplains Jones (1st Marines) and Craven (7th Marines) were identical. Both were for the period 23 September to 1 October. The citations read in part:

Acting as regimental chaplain [he] fearlessly and courageously exposed himself to the intense enemy small arms, machine gun and mortar fire to visit and encourage the members of the front line units during the attack. His complete disregard for his own personal safety and personal interests shown during his constant moving among the assault troops and the wounded was an inspiration to all personnel of the regiment.

Since Chaplain Craven had received a Bronze Star during World War II, he was awarded a gold star in lieu of a second Bronze Star.

Chaplain Ingvoldstad (5th Marines) was cited for "heroic service" performed during the period 15–27 September. "Displaying outstanding professional ability," the citation states, "marked courage and confidence in the performance of duty, Lieutenant Commander Ingvoldstad rendered distinguished service in providing for the spiritual comfort and well-being of all the men."

Chaplain John H. Markley, serving with the 1st Marine Aircraft Wing, was cited for "meritorious achievement in connection with the operations against the enemy . . . during operations in Japan and Korea from 11 August 1950 to 12 October 1950." The citation continues:

He met aircraft carrying the wounded and dying no matter what hour of arrival. He visited all hospitalized military personnel regardless of their branch of service. He ministered to their physical as well as spiritual needs, personally seeing that the men had what they sought for or needed. He carried out his duties regardless of personal fatigue, constantly inspiring all who observed him with the strength of his faith in God, his humility, and his love for all to whom he ministered.

Chaplain Patrick A. Killeen was awarded the Bronze Star for service from 15–21 September 1950. His citation reads in part:

A most capable and inspiring religious guide, his wise and friendly counsel was constantly sought by men of all faiths within the battalion. His untiring efforts and unswerving devotion to duty were an inspiration to all who observed him, and aided materially in the maintenance of high morale within the battalion.

The citation accompanying the Bronze Star awarded Chaplain Godfrey J. Reilly follows in part:

Serving with the forward medical company, where casualties were in greatest number, he frequently moved to battalion aid stations when he considered his services to be needed. Displaying at all times utter disregard for his personal safety and comfort, he labored long, arduous hours under extremely adverse weather conditions, and often under enemy fire. His untiring efforts contributed materially to the maintenance of

high morale in the Division, and his wise counsel and guidance were constantly sought by men of all faiths.

In addition to the Silver Star awarded Chaplain Bonner and the eight Bronze Star medals thus far mentioned, two other awards were given Navy chaplains for outstanding performance of duty. Chaplain Kevin J. Keaney received the Letter of Commendation award citing his service during the period 15 September to 2 October 1950.

Chaplain Bernard L. Hickey, who with Ingvoldstad, Tennant, and Sporrer had accompanied Marine ground units from the early days of the Korean War, received the Bronze Star for meritorious service from 15 September to 2 November, the terminal date of what the Defense Department later marked out as the First Korean Campaign. The services cited in Hickey's award now begin to run like a refrain through the commendations that would be awarded chaplains for devotion to duty during periods of intense fighting. No lesson is clearer from the experience of the Korean War than that it came to be expected that it could be said of each what was here said of a particular chaplain, that he "continuously moved among the assault units of his regiment and conducted services, administered spiritual comfort to the sick and wounded, and assisted in the treatment and evacuation of casualties." Thus exceptional performance of duty sets the pace and in time becomes the norm by which all service is measured.

Chaplains Afloat

Elements of Joint Task Force Seven, the principal striking arm of United States naval power in the Far East, commanded by Vice Adm. Arthur D. Struble, had been on station in Korean waters since late June. Serving as chaplain in the flagship, the ROCHESTER, was Fenelon D. Hewitt, Jr., Southern Baptist, aboard since April 1949. In September he was relieved by Edwin F. Carr, a Roman Catholic. Having returned to active duty on 18 August, Carr remained in the ROCHESTER until July 1952. Protestant ministrations were made available whenever possible; it has been noted that Chaplain J. E. Zoller was temporarily aboard for the month of October.

In the TOLEDO since 31 August was Chaplain Lawrence C. M. Vosseler, a Lutheran, whose tour of duty continued until July 1952. Aboard the WORCESTER since September was Chaplain Charles L. Dickey (Presbyterian), a Reserve, who remained in that ship until released to inactive duty in January 1952. Chaplain David J. Kosky,

Burial at Sea.

Chaplain L. C. M. Vosseler conducts burial at sea for Lt. (jg.) David H. Swenson, of TOLEDO, off Korea. LYMAN K. SWENSON, named for the deceased's uncle, lies in the background.

a Roman Catholic, served in the MANCHESTER from September 1950 to August 1952.

The carrier BOXER had two chaplains assigned. Joseph P. Cusack, Roman Catholic, had been aboard since July and remained until October 1951. George A. Hoglan, Presbyterian, another of the many Reserves who voluntarily returned to active duty, reported in September 1950, finishing his tour in October 1952. It will be noticed that the average shipboard tour was about 2 years.

One of the busiest ships in the area was the MOUNT McKINLEY, an AGC, or amphibious force flagship, headquarters of Rear Adm. James H. Doyle's Amphibious Group One, Pacific Fleet. Early in 1950 General MacArthur had asked for Navy and Marine units to train occupation forces in Japan in amphibious techniques. They had hardly arrived and begun work when the outbreak of hostilities turned these amphibious specialists from training to operational activities.[9] On July PhibGru One put the 1st Cavalry Division ashore at Pohang-dong. For Inchon, naturally, Admiral Doyle's amphibious force was a mainstay; most of the planning was done on board the McKINLEY, and when it was time to mount the operation MacArthur chose to proceed from Sasebo to Inchon in that ship.[10] The chaplain at the time was Edward E. Helmich, a Moravian, who was assigned additional duty as Doyle's Staff Chaplain.

The largest number of troop and attack transports were not assigned chaplains, owing to the shortage. As always the Marine Division Chaplain tried to place his chaplains in those transports which had none of their own or otherwise arrange for the widest distribution of chaplain personnel en route to the invasion. At least the following transports at Inchon carried one chaplain each.

BAYFIELD (APA)	Edgar A. Day	BAP (A)
GEN. J. C. BRECKENRIDGE (AP).	Leonard B. Dohrmann	EVAN & REF
GEN. H. W. BUTNER (AP)	Edward R. Martineau	RC
HENRICO (APA)	Carroll M. Mershon	PRESBY (U)
PRESIDENT JACKSON (AP).	Harry A. Porter	BAP (A)
THOMAS JEFFERSON (APA).	Henry F. Maxwell	CONG

---

[9] *Ibid.*, pp. 4ff.; 13ff.

[10] *Ibid.*, p. 84.

Chaplain Maxwell described in his questionnaire reply something of the duty of the THOMAS JEFFERSON during these early months of the war. During July and August they transported troops from the United States to the Far East, including Marines of the 1st Division from San Diego to Japan. In September they participated in the Inchon invasion, and brought out casualties on their return to Japan. In early November they helped put the 7th Infantry Division ashore at Iwon, as part of the X Corps drive to the Manchurian border. In December the ship returned to San Francisco. Writing of his work, Maxwell said:

As ship's chaplain and librarian, as the JEFFERSON transported wounded back to Yokosuka, Japan, I made the rounds with library books and with religious brochures, seeing each patient two or three times daily to trade books, and visit or counsel as occasion demanded. The ship's welfare fund served as a source of money for purchase of comfort items, which the chaplain and his assistants distributed daily to the wounded.

The chaplain contributed a "Thought for the Day" in the ship's daily newspaper, which was mimeographed and distributed by his office staff. I endeavored to make the brief column timely and worthwhile: spiritual encouragement to men who knew that shortly some of their number would be dead and men also who had come through the worst and lived.

Ships of Mercy

The first hospital ship to arrive in Korean waters, the CONSOLATION, docked on 12 August 1950, while the 1st Marine Provisional Brigade was assisting 8th Army efforts to stem the Red advance at the Pusan Perimeter. Since July 1949 Chaplain Charles F. Holland (Lutheran) had been serving aboard. He would be joined in November 1950 by Chaplain Victor J. W. Lustig (Roman Catholic). On 16 September, the second day of the Inchon landing, CON-

Worship on Hospital Ship.
Chaplain Leroy C. Austin conducts Sunday services on board the CONSOLATION in Pusan.

SOLATION arrived in Inchon harbor and began receiving casualties aboard.

On the same day a second of these "ships of mercy," the REPOSE, reported for duty in Korea. These great white ships, a gleaming Red Cross painted on their sides, furnished with the best equipment and staffed by doctors, nurses, and hospital corpsmen, maintained constant vigilance to provide the best possible surgical and medical care for the United Nations personnel. Chaplains in the REPOSE were Henry P. White (Methodist) and Charles F. Karnasiewicz (Roman Catholic).

"Mighty Mo"

The MISSOURI was the only battleship in operation at the outbreak of the Korean War. Its chaplains were Emil F. Redman (Protestant) and Eugene I. Van Antwerp (Roman Catholic). Both men were relieved before the ship was transferred from Norfolk to the Far East, Van Antwerp being ordered to the 1st Marine Division; and when she arrived in Korean waters, on 14 September, her chaplains were William H. Hoffman (Roman Catholic) and Charles L. Arnold (Southern Baptist).

On the deck of the MISSOURI, as everyone knows, the formal surrender of Japan took place on 2 September 1945. It was after the Japanese representatives had signed the surrender documents that General MacArthur had concluded, "Let us pray that peace be now restored to the world, and that God will preserve it always." In a time when popular sentiment was inclined to the view that "it doesn't matter what you believe as long as you live right," MacArthur had affirmed on this same occasion his opinion that the problem of war and peace is "basically theological." [11]

Chaplain Hoffman continued the custom of daily prayers over the ship's speaker which was reported in volume II of this Chaplain Corps History. Just at dusk the bo'sun's pipe would sound, followed by the announcement, "Stand by for evening prayers."

[11] From a clipping from the Los Angeles Roman Catholic newspaper *The Tidings;* clipping undated, but contents indicates a date in 1951.

Worship on MISSOURI.
Worship is conducted under the 16-inch guns of the MISSOURI by Chaplain Arnold.

The two chaplains took turns in leading the short devotion. It would be foolish, naturally, to suppose that all the ship's personnel, or even the majority of them, were actively religious; but it should not be underestimated that on this ship as on many others prayer had become an expected part of the daily routine.

Victory in the Grasp

In early October, Task Force 77 departed the Yellow Sea for Sasebo. The Marines were at Inchon, outloading. Eighth Army now had effective control of the western parts of South Korea, and the ROK I Corps was poised at the eastern end of the 38th Parallel, the enemy in rout all along the front. Victory seemed within the grasp.

The success of the September operation, one of the most unusual and hazardous ever undertaken, must be attributed to the coordinated efforts of ground, air, and sea forces.[12] After the humiliating setback of the first weeks of the Korean War, it was with both pride and immeasurable relief that after Inchon-Seoul the United Nations Command could assure the world:

A successful frontal attack and envelopment has completely changed the tide of battle in South Korea. The backbone of the North Korean army has been broken and their scattered forces are being liquidated or driven north with material losses in equipment and men captured.[13]

The Communist challenge to the free world had been countered. It was now clear that only the intervention of Communist China or Soviet Russia could save the North Korean People's Republic from complete defeat.

---

[12] For estimates of the Inchon-Seoul operation see Montross and Canzona, *op. cit.*, vol. II, pp. 292–298; Cagle and Manson, *op. cit.*, pp. 101–106.
[13] Montross and Canzona, *op. cit.*, vol. II, p. 298.

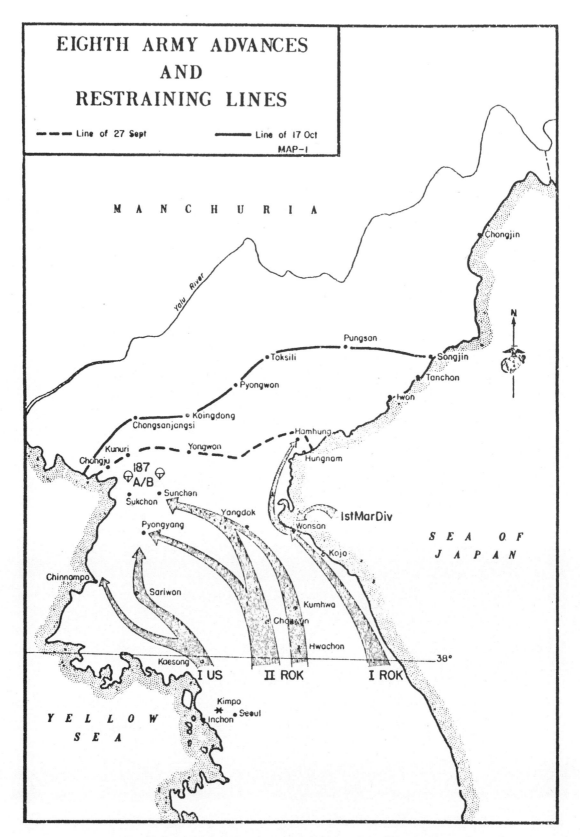

EIGHTH ARMY ADVANCES
AND
RESTRAINING LINES

— — — Line of 27 Sept   ————— Line of 17 Oct

MAP—1

MANCHURIA

Yalu River

Chongjin

Pungsan

Toksili

Songjin

Pyongwon

Tanchon

Koingdong

Iwon

Chongsanjangsi

Hamhung

Kunuri

Yongwon

Chongju

Hungnam

187
A/B

Sunchon

Sukchon

IstMarDiv

Yangdok

Wonsan

Pyongyang

SEA OF
JAPAN

Kojo

Chinnampo

Sariwon

Kumhwa

Chorwon

Hwachon

38°

Kaesong

I US   II ROK   I ROK

Kimpo

Inchon   Seoul

YELLOW
SEA

N

Reproduced by permission from *U.S. Marine Operations in Korea.*

— 28 —

CHAPTER 3

COMMUNIST CHINESE AGGRESSION

3 November 1950–24 January 1951

Within 3 months after the North Korean Army invaded South Korea, it had been decisively defeated. The tide which had carried the victorious Communists over all of South Korea except the small area behind the Pusan Perimeter had been turned. By the completion of the Inchon-Seoul operation, that part of the North Korean Army not killed or captured was broken into many small units, each trying to get back across the 38th Parallel the best way possible, or else remaining in hiding in the South Korean hills.

General MacArthur called upon the North Korean leaders to surrender; his demand was ignored. The United Nations Command then decided to send its forces across the 38th Parallel, allowing for the possibility but not expecting that this in turn would call the Chinese Communists into the struggle.[1] On 7 October 1950 the Marines in the vicinity of Seoul were relieved and ordered to Inchon, where they embarked on 12 October for Wonsan on the east coast. There they disembarked on 25 October, after delays necessitated by hazardous and prolonged minesweeping operations.

During the time at sea, the chaplains of the 1st Division were busy writing letters of condolence to the next-of-kin of deceased Marine personnel. Most of the chaplains had completed this duty by the time the transports reached Wonsan. The processing of these

[1] Montross and Canzona, *op. cit.*, vol. III, *The Chosin Reservoir Campaign* (Washington, 1957), ch. 1.
See also: Cagle and Manson, *op. cit.*, ch. 4. Karig *et al.*, *op. cit.*, chs. 22–36.

Holy Communion at Sea.
Communion is held aboard the BAYFIELD for United Nations troops enroute to the Wonsan invasion by Chaplain Edgar A. Day.

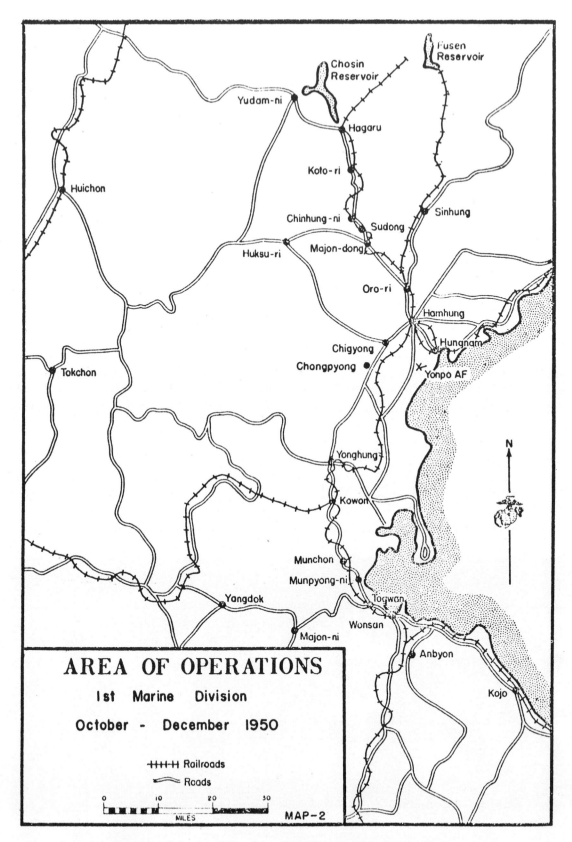

AREA OF OPERATIONS

1st Marine Division

October - December 1950

+++++H Railroads

Roads

0   10   20   30
MILES

MAP-2

Reproduced by permission from *U.S. Marine Operations in Korea.*

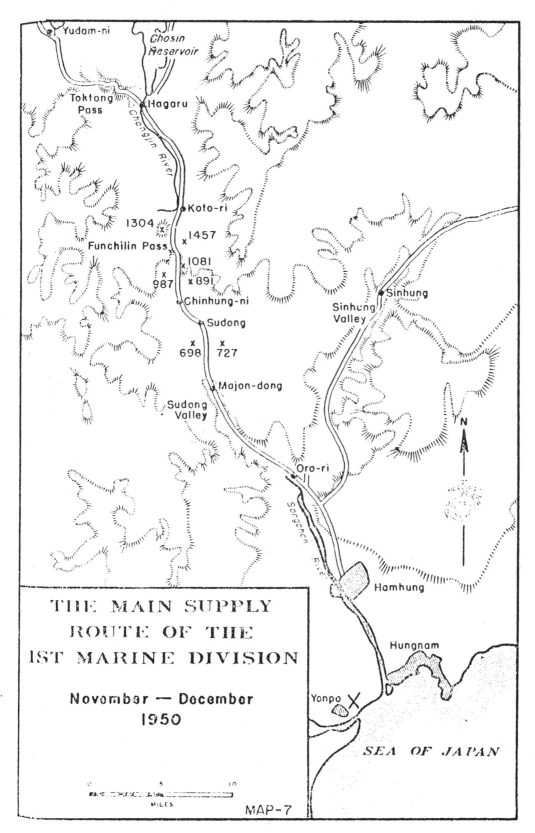

THE MAIN SUPPLY
ROUTE OF THE
1ST MARINE DIVISION

November — December
1950

MAP-7

Reproduced by permission from *U.S. Marine Operations in Korea.*

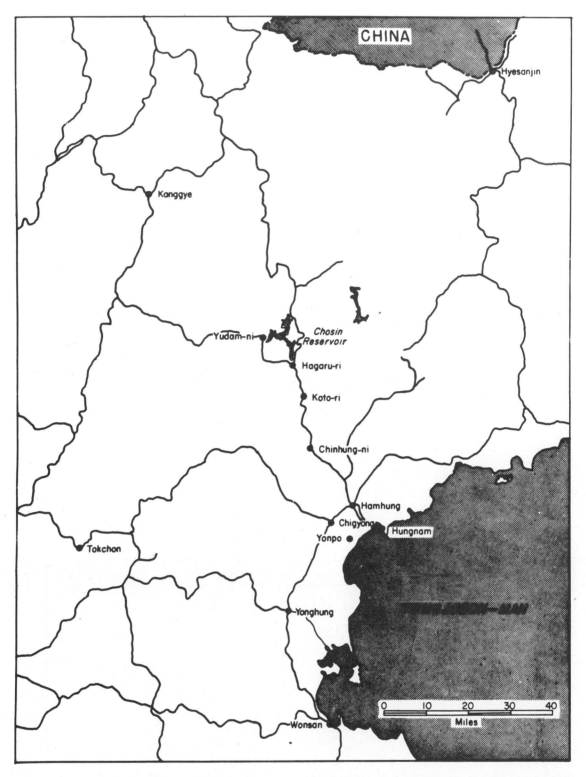

Breakout at Hungnam. Reproduced by permission from *The Sea War in Korea,* by Malcolm W. Cagle and Frank A. Manson. Copyright 1957 by the U.S. Naval Institute.

letters was the responsibility of Division Chaplain Schwyhart. That the ministry of chaplains, and particularly their ministry of consolation and encouragement to bereaved families, was appreciated by the American people may be noted from the following excerpt from a letter sent by Gen. Clifton B. Cates, Commandant of the Marine Corps, to Chaplain Ingvoldstad in October 1950.

Your diligent self-application and devotion to your sacred duties has been forcefully brought to my attention by the many letters which I have received from the grateful parents of young men who have made the supreme sacrifice on the Korean battlefields. These parents, wives, these relatives have paid glowing tribute to you in correspondence which reflects nothing but gratitude for the knowledge that their sons or husbands died in the company of one close to God Almighty.

A few changes in the complement of chaplains attached to the 1st Division took place before 31 October. Chaplain Glyn Jones was detached as Regimental Chaplain of the 1st Marines, in compliance with Bureau of Naval Personnel orders, and Chaplain William N. Lyons, already with the Division, was ordered as his relief. Chaplain Kline d'A. Engle joined the Division before it sailed from Inchon. Certain reassignments of duty were made within the Division. With the detachment of Chaplains R. L. Bonner and W. G. Tennant as casualties, the number of chaplains attached to the Division was reduced to 26.

Wonsan to the Reservoir

From the last of August United States Naval vessels had cooperated with the ROK Capital Division as it advanced up the east coast from Pohang. On 1 October the ROK 3d Division had crossed the Parallel and began an advance of some 50 miles up the east coast. In the following months, the bombardment force would continue to furnish harassing and interdiction fire against enemy positions along the eastern coast. Air operations were intensified when elements of the 1st Marine Aircraft Wing began moving in to Wonsan on 14 October.

The Division effected an administrative landing at Wonsan as part of X Corps, on 25–26 October, and at once fanned out in pursuit of North Korean forces.[2] The landing was unopposed as the ROK I Corps had already captured the city by 10 October, without a fight. Delayed by the minesweeping operations, the Marines were chagrined to find that air maintenance crews had beaten them to Wonsan by 12 days. Even

more humiliating, on the evening of the 24th Bob Hope had been featured in a USO show which was larded with "cracks" at the hapless Division going back and forth like a yo-yo outside Wonsan harbor!

The 1st Battalion, 1st Marines was dispatched south by rail about 35 miles to the supply center of Kojo, guarded by an ROK detachment. Here a two-night engagement took place as North Korean forces tried to control the main communication route through the valley. Chaplain Glyn Jones accompanied this unit; but when it became necessary for him to leave, to carry out orders returning him stateside, the area was completely surrounded by enemy forces so that he had to be flown out by helicopter to Wonsan.

General Almond now ordered his X Corps forward. The 1st Marine Division was to branch off at Hamhung and proceed north and west to the Chosin Reservoir. Certain ROK units were to follow the coastline northward; and the 7th Army Division, put ashore at Iwon, south of Wonsan, on 29 October was to move inland toward the Pujan Reservoir.

As X Corps proceeded to its mission, 8th Army had begun a parallel movement northward in the west.[3] Elements of I Corps, including British, ROK, and American troops, spearheaded by the 1st Cavalry Division, crossed the Parallel and by 21 October had secured the North Korean capital, Pyongyang, and its port, Chinnampo. With other ROK forces in the middle, it was MacArthur's plan to link X Corps and 8th Army in a concerted drive to the Yalu River and the Manchurian border.

The Marines proceeded to Hamhung, about 75 miles from Wonsan, by truck, and rail, meeting little opposition en route. Hamhung lies inland about 5 miles from Hungnam, its seaport. Prior to the departure to Hamhung, Chaplains Craven, Cornelius J. Griffin, and Kester M. Hearn of the 7th Marines spent several nights in a burnt-out Benedictine Abbey in Tokwan, about 8 miles north of Wonsan. The three chaplains settled down in the Abbey's undamaged school building, and in the chapel each conducted religious services. Chaplain Griffin, a Roman Catholic, was greeted with joy by many of the natives who said that he was the first priest they had seen for over a year.

Later Chaplain Griffin, in an interview published in the *Monitor* for 5 January 1951, commented on the enthusiastic reception given to him by the Roman Catholic Koreans at Tokwan. He said:

[2] Montross and Canzona, *op. cit.*, vol. III, chs. II–IV.

[3] *Ibid.*, pp. 34–37. See also *Korea, 1950* (Department of the Army), pp. 150–153. For the Navy at Chinnampo, see Cagle and Manson, *op. cit.*, ch. 5.

The reception by the people was unbelievable. They fell all over me when they learned I was a priest and begged me to come and celebrate Mass. Several hours afterwards I did—my first High Mass in the Navy.

In that time more than 500 villagers had assembled at the Abbey. Lt. George Balzer of San Diego and Brother Pincentius, O.S.B., a Korean, led a hastily assembled choir of more than 100 in the Gregorian music of the Mass. Nothing has ever sounded more beautiful to me. Practically everybody there received Communion.

Here the Marines were seeing at first-hand some evidences of the way the Communists were persecuting the Christians. They learned how the Communists, when they retreated from the Wonsan area the first part of October, had spread straw through the beautiful Abbey church, poured on gasoline and set it afire. Many other examples came to the attention of the Americans of the repressive measures practiced by a Communist-dominated government against Christians throughout North Korea.

Air Wing Chaplains

When elements of the 1st Marine Aircraft Wing arrived at Wonsan, Chaplain John P. Murphy soon discovered that out of a Catholic civilian population of about 3,000 in Wonsan, only 2,000 remained. Roman Catholic Christians had suffered a loss of one-third of their number under the Communist regime. The leaders had been methodically eliminated. Priests and seminarians had been killed or carried off to the North, never to be heard of again. Of the 50 Benedictine brothers and 80 nuns, only 10 brothers and 12 sisters remained. The monastery in Wonsan had been turned into a "People's Agricultural College." The cross had been sawed off the top of the church and the interior desecrated.

Chaplain Murphy took on a double load. In addition to his duties with the Marines, he tried to help the civilian Catholic population, now led by a candidate for the priesthood in deacon's orders. Beginning with a small room in a private home, he celebrated Mass for the poorly clad, hungry, but devout Koreans who crowded in for his ministrations. The room overflowed and the civilians crowded the dingy hallway and winding stairway. In addition to helping the local church, Chaplain Murphy set up the North Korean Catholic Relief Society. The local military com-

---

Food for the Needy.

Liberated grain is being passed out to all returning destitute citizens of Wonsan. Chaplain John P. Murphy (at right) arranged the distribution. He, in predawn services, resumed celebration of mass for the parish.

Wonsan Pastor.

The Reverend Han June Myung of Jesus Church, Wonsan, after preaching to Marine airmen, received the offering contributed to his work from Chaplain George W. Cummins. The Korean minister survived the masacre of 300 civilians in a cave where they were machinegunned by retreating Communists. November 1950.

---

mand had taken over a large amount of barley and beans when the city was captured. Some of these supplies were turned over to the Relief Society for distribution to the hungry people, regardless of religious affiliation.

The situation in the 1st MAW had been extremely fluid during the first months of the war. Besides its headquarters base at Itami, Japan, operational fields at Kimpo and now Wonsan had to be covered. Chaplain George W. Cummins (Southern Baptist) was attached to Marine Air Group 12, which gradually was established at Wonsan. At Kimpo, in the vicinity of Seoul, Chaplain J. H. Markley was still with Marine Air Group 33. Since Roman Catholic services were available at Itami, Murphy divided his time between the two operational groups. Protestant services were conducted by Markley or Cummins whenever they were able to get over to Japan.

Cummins earned for himself the reputation of being a regular Humphrey Bogart of a chaplain. Accompanying official photographers to an ROK command post, where they sought information about the scene of a reported massacre of hundreds of political prisoners by the retreating Communists, the chaplain attempted to explain their purpose. When words proved unsuccessful, Cummins resorted to pantomime; holding his arms as if handling a machine gun, he emitted a vocal imitation of rapid fire. It seemed to work; the ROK captain's eyes lighted up in understanding, and he turned into the command post—to emerge bearing a captured "burp" gun, which he thrust upon the astonished chaplain. Doubtless proud of himself, he stood smiling after the departing jeep, in which Cummins sat holding gingerly his unexpected and unwanted weapon.

Chaplain Charles E. Webb (Roman Catholic) arrived on 15 November; but before he could report to Marine Aircraft Group 33, his assigned duty station, the Chinese offensive had forced a withdrawal of United Nations forces, and Webb operated in Japan until January when he joined Marine Aircraft Group 12, now relocated at Pusan.

Chinese Intervention

The 7th Marines, the most recently formed regiment of the 1st Division, with the largest percentage of Reserves, spearheaded the thrust northward from Hamhung toward Chinhung-ni, about 35 miles distant. On the night of 2–3 November this advance force engaged a full Chinese Communist division in the gorge country in the Sudong area a few miles south of Chinhung-ni.[4] Thus the 7th Marines had the distinction of being the first American unit to be engaged with a Chinese Communist force in large-scale combat. A furious 5-day battle followed, during which the enemy's casualties were estimated to have run as high as 9,000 with over 660 killed. The Marine casualties included 46 dead and 264 wounded.

During the battle, two battalions of the 7th Marines were attacked from the front and on both flanks for about 24 hours. With these two battalions were Chaplains Griffin and Kester M. Hearn. Here Chaplain Griffin so distinguished himself that he was recommended for and later received the Silver Star. A part of his citation reads as follows:

During the late morning of 3 November, the same units of the 7th Marines were subjected to heavy small arms fire. Chaplain Griffin left the comparative security of the battalion sick bay where he was rendering aid to the wounded and moved back to the front lines. Here he repeatedly exposed himself without regard for his personal safety to render what aid he could to the wounded men in the attack. Chaplain Griffin served as a veritable pillar of strength for the men of the organization and served as an unforgettable inspiration to all who observed him.

---

[4] Montross and Canzona, *op. cit.,* vol. III, chs. V, VI. See also Cagle and Manson, *op. cit.,* ch. 6, pp. 165–169.

From Chinhung-ni, which lies at an elevation of 1,000 feet, the narrow, tortuous road climbs steeply for the next 10 miles over a 4,000-foot pass to Koto-ri, situated on a high plateau just "over the hump." After the decisive defeat of the Chinese Communists at Sudong, the Marines met little resistance on their march northward through Koto-ri to Hagaru-ri, another 11 miles distant. Hagaru-ri, 56 miles from Hamhung, was located at the foot of the Chosin Reservoir. The Marines reached this point on 15 November.[5]

Maj. Gen. O. P. Smith, in command of the 1st Division, felt considerable misgivings about his position and about alternate operational plans being considered by General MacArthur. He wrote to Gen. Clifton B. Cates, Commandant, as follows:

I believe a winter campaign in the mountains of North Korea is too much to ask of the American soldier or marine, and I doubt the feasibility of supplying troops in this area during the winter or providing for the evacuation of sick and wounded.

And in conclusion he expressed concern over "the prospect of stringing out a Marine division along a single mountain road for 120 air miles from Hamhung to the border."[6]

Small streams were noticed to be frozen over. Rice paddies had been glazed since October. And on 15 November when the 7th Marines occupied Hagaru, the temperature was 4° below zero. Already the Marines, though equipped with winter clothing and sleeping bags, were reporting cases of frostbite. An ominous calm had ensued following the battle with Chinese Communists at Sudong. Taking a dim view of the possibility of a successful race against time, weather, and unknown enemy, the Marines nevertheless made preparations to fulfill their mission. Reports were received from local Koreans of the presence of many Chinese troops in the vicinity; yet temporarily the enemy refrained from offering further resistance.

Thanksgiving Day, 1950

In the lull before the storm, the chaplains attached to the 1st Division were able to carry on most of their usual duties in spite of many difficulties. Writing to the Chief of Chaplains on 1 December 1950, Chaplain R. M. Schwyhart, the Division Chaplain, summarized:

During the month of November 1950 the Division took positions covering an area all the way from Wonsan to Hagaru-ri. In spite of this, communication with the chap-

lains has been relatively good; furthermore I have personally seen all but three of them during the month. All of the chaplains are doing a most commendable job. Performing their tasks as chaplains amidst the barriers of the distance and shortage of transportation, subfreezing temperatures, mountains and snow has not been easily done; nevertheless, I have not heard or seen evidences of any complaints, only that this conflict cannot be brought to an end.

Chaplain Kenneth D. Perkins, Force Chaplain, FMF Pac, arrived at Hamhung for an official visit on 18 November. Of this Schwyhart wrote in his letter to Chaplain Salisbury:

The next day, Sunday, he favored us by delivering the sermon at the Division Headquarters Protestant Divine Service. Later that day we attended, by invitation, a large meeting of local representatives of all Presbyterian churches in Hamhung. The following day we drove by jeep to Hagaru-ri to see the chaplains in the 7th Regiment. We spent Tuesday morning visiting at the Division Cemetery at Hungnam at which time there were 93 Marine burials. He departed by plane for return to Pearl Harbor at noon, 21 November 1950.

During the few days of comparative calm spent at Hagaru-ri, the chaplains gave great encouragement to the native Christians who had suffered much at the hands of the Communists. Chaplain Sporrer reported on his questionnaire:

Two little churches, one of them at the Reservoir, were reopened for the first time since the Red forces closed them. The congregations had secreted the altar furnishings in their respective homes, and candlesticks, pictures, and crucifixes appeared as by magic from all over the villages.

One of the congregations, as a collection, placed three eggs on a plate in the rear of the church for me to take as I left.

The native Christians looked upon the Marines as their heaven-sent deliverers from the Communists. Several of the Navy chaplains who penetrated into North Korea with the Marines had thrilling experiences with the Christians. Chaplain Craven reported one such incident in his questionnaire.

At Hagaru-ri we met an old Presbyterian minister and his saintly wife. They had been hiding in the caves and rocks for several months before our arrival. The church had been destroyed but their parsonage was still standing with a small cross on the highest peak. We obtained permission to use the bombed out theater building for their first church service in several months. I returned their church bell which the Communists had used for an alarm bell in the police headquarters. The tears of joy flowed freely down the old Presbyterian pastor's face. He insisted that I preach to his people through an interpreter. Next day I met in the pastor's home with 35 baptized believers for Bible study.

Chaplain Schwyhart in his letter to Chaplain Salisbury of 1 December wrote concerning some of the

[5] Montross and Canzona, *op. cit.*, vol. III, ch. VII.
[6] *Ibid.*, pp. 132–134.

Church Bell Restored.

Chaplain John H. Craven returns the church bell used by the Communists at police headquarters to its rightful owners, Christians at Hagaru-ri beside Chosin Reservoir, at the first religious service after 3 years of persecution. The recipient is Korean Pastor Lee In Soup.

Something of the damage to the church is indicated in this photograph. Military and civilian committees began work to rebuild the church founded by Canadian missionaries but soon North Korea was taken by Chinese troops.

Expressing Gratitude.

The Reverend and Mrs. Lee En Suep of the Central Presbyterian Church, Hagaru-ri, thanking Lieutenant Colonel Murray for the liberation "of our country and our church." Participating in the thanksgiving service and pictured with the group is Chaplain Ingvoldstad.

events of the preceding Thanksgiving Day: "Chaplain Ingvoldstad, Regimental Chaplain, 5th Marines, joined in a service with the local Presbyterian pastor at Hagaru-ri who gave thanks for the liberation of his Korean people from the hands of the Communists who had so long prevented their worship." Unfortunately for the Korean Christians, the later withdrawal of the forces of the United Nations left them at the mercy of the Communists who were ruthless in wreaking vengeance. This accounted in part for the waves of refugees who surged southward by every possible means to get to safety behind the anti-Communist lines.

Thanksgiving Day, 1950, was celebrated by the Marines of the 1st Division with special attention being given to the religious significance of the day. Chaplain Schwyhart sent out a memorandum to all chaplains of the Division suggesting that each hold as many services as possible. This was done. Chaplain Howard H. Groover, 1st Service Battalion, held two out-of-door services that day; Chaplain Patrick A. Killeen, 1st Signal Battalion, conducted two Catholic Masses, both largely attended; and by arrangements with the mess officer, each chaplain said a blessing at the "chow-line."

On 25 November the Marines continued their northward march toward the Yalu River by taking the road which led from Hagaru-ri in a northwesterly direction over the 4,700-foot Toktong Pass to Yudam-ni 14 miles away. Here was another twisting, narrow road that had to be traversed. Some 15,000 Marines were now at the Reservoir ready to join a part of the Army which was advancing north by a more westerly route. But the union of the Marines with the Army never occurred.

Crisis at Yudam-ni

Yudam-ni marked the most northern advance of the Marines in Korea.[7] On the night of 27–28 November bugle-blowing, screaming Communists began to attack at Yudam-ni and it was soon apparent that they were present in overwhelming numbers. Shortly afterwards enemy forces, deployed along the thin supply line which connected the advance body of Marines with its base at Hamhung, began to cut the motor supply route in several places. The temperature was dipping to subzero readings during the nights. Little wonder that many were nearing the edge of nervous exhaustion: not far enough gone in battle fatigue to

warrant hospitalization, but giving clear signs of bone-weariness: wan face, trembling hands. "Shook," they would say of such a one; "he is shook." Dietary deficiencies were beginning to appear because of the lack of hot food, and many of the Marines were suffering from diarrhea. Weapons often froze to such a degree they were rendered unserviceable.

Chaplain Craven later described some of the difficulties faced regarding the care of the wounded:

Taking care of the wounded during this period also presented problems to stagger the imagination. During the first 2 days of heavy fighting at Yudam-ni, we suffered so many casualties that we ran out of tents in which to place them. I had a working party gather hay from the scattered stacks and spread it out on the courtyard of a native house. We placed the wounded foot to foot on the straw and covered them with a large tarpaulin. . . . This arrangement helped to conserve on our tentage and also facilitated our ministry to the wounded.

During these days, under ever-increasing pressure from the enemy, the doctors and the chaplains had little or no time for sleep.[8] Chaplain Craven, for instance, who was working with the regimental surgeon, stated that he went without sleep for 3 days. Once he was sent to an empty tent to rest and had hardly stretched out when another consignment of wounded arrived who were put in the same tent. Of course there was no opportunity then for sleep when the wounded needed help so desperately.

On 30 November the order was given to the Marines at Yudam-ni to withdraw. By that time there were 600 wounded men, many of whom were ambulance cases. Transportation was a problem. The more serious cases were given priority in all available ambulances and trucks. The need for fighting men was so urgent that the walking wounded were given guns.

Just before leaving Yudam-ni, Chaplain Craven conducted a brief funeral service for about 80 Marines who had lost their lives in the fighting at that place. In his reply to the questionnaire Craven commented: "The problems involved in attempting to bury bodies during the Chosin Reservoir campaign when the frozen ground was covered with ice and snow and the temperature about 20 below zero are beyond words to describe."

The following seven chaplains were with the Marines at Yudam-ni: 5th Marines—O. Ingvoldstad, B. L. Hickey, and L. R. Phillips; 7th Marines—J. H. Craven and C. J. Griffin; and 11th Marines—O. E. Sporrer and B. C. Howland.

[7] *Ibid.*, chs. VIII–XI. For a brief sketch of activities of other UN forces during this critical period, see *Korea, 1950* (Department of the Army), ch. V, pp. 227–229.

[8] *Marine Corps Gazette* (December 1952). See Lynn Montross, "They Make Men Whole Again: The Medical Battalion and Chaplains in Korea."

Interview.

Chaplain Craven counsels with a marine at the aid station during the 7th Marines campaign in the reservoir area.

Brief Pause.

Exhausted marines take advantage of a lull in the continual fighting from Yudam-ni to Hagaru-ri to catch a moment's rest.

The Bitter Withdrawal

The withdrawal of the Marines from Yudam-ni to Hamhung, which was reached on 11 December, proved to be a most bitter experience.[9] Writing to Chaplain Salisbury on 1 December 1950, Chaplain Schwyhart referred to the precarious situation in which the Marines were then placed. "We have many wounded," he wrote, "and the road-blocking leading up to Hagaru-ri has made evacuation of the wounded nigh impossible." He closed his letter with the expression of a hope that the situation would improve. The very opposite was the case. Even as he wrote, the Marines formerly at Yudam-ni were fighting their way southward over the 4,700-foot Toktong Pass where a Marine company had been completely surrounded by the enemy for 5 days before being rescued.

Writing to Salisbury on 15 December, Schwyhart called the withdrawal of the Marines to Hamhung "the toughest and worst experience" in the whole history of the Marine Corps. He continued:

It is not possible to adequately describe or relate the events of the past 17 days: ambushed convoys leaving many men

---

[9] Montross and Canzona, *op. cit.,* vol. III, chs. XII–XV. For details of Navy and Marine air coverage of the redeployment, see Cagle and Manson, *op. cit.,* ch. V, pp. 169ff. *Korea, 1950* (Department of the Army) sketches in the withdrawal of 8th Army from the northwest; pp. 229ff.

killed, wounded, missing or POW; entrapped troops fighting their way back from Yudam-ni to Hagaru-ri, thence to Koto-ri, against overwhelming numbers of enemy troops and the elements, with temperatures going as low as 15° below zero; men with frozen feet and legs; heroism and deeds of valor which officers and men had little thought that they would be called upon to perform; the life-saving performance of the air-delivery platoon which dropped tons of supplies, including food and medical supplies, and which evacuated the wounded by air from Hagaru-ri and Koto-ri.

In a Division Memorandum dated 19 December, Gen. Oliver P. Smith declared: "This withdrawal, which was concluded when the last elements of the Division closed the Hamhung area on December 11, will become an epic in the annals of the Marine Corps." And he added: "Seldom, if ever, have Marines been forced to battle against comparable odds." The temperature dropped as low as 20° below zero and the narrow, winding road became even more hazardous covered as it was with snow and ice.

First Stage

The withdrawal from Yudam-ni to Hagaru-ri was completed on 4 December at a cost of 2,260 casualties of whom 358 were killed, 153 were missing, and 1,749 were wounded. In addition, another 1,072 had become nonbattle casualties, largely owing to frostbite. In his description of those heart-rending days, Chaplain Craven wrote:

When we left Yudam-ni we had about 600 wounded in trucks and strapped to jeeps and when we arrived at Hagaru-ri, 14 miles away, about 3 days later we had over 1,000 wounded. Chaplain Orlando Ingvoldstad, regimental chaplain of the 5th Marines, and I worked closely together in ministering to these wounded. During periods when the convoy was held up by heavy fighting, we filled the large native cooking vats which were a part of the kitchen stoves with water and heated the C-ration cans to feed the patients on stretchers. While this heating of food was going on we permitted ambulatory patients to come into the rooms of the native huts to warm on the radiantly heated floors. After 20 minutes these men would be turned out and another group admitted who had been standing outside in the cold. Occasionally the chaplain had to get a little rough with some of the men who wanted more than their share of the heat.

The most heart-breaking experience came when trucks or weapons-carriers turned over on icy roads in the middle of the night, and the already wounded men would be killed or receive further injuries. Trying to pick up these wounded men and find places for them on other vehicles previously loaded with casualties, while the bluish-green Communist machine-gun bullets were flying around, was a nightmare I shall never forget.

At Hagaru-ri I worked all one night with two British Navy hospital corpsmen attached to the British Royal Marines. The three of us had four tents and two native houses filled with stretcher cases to care for as best we could.

We were isolated from the large Field Hospital, and no doctor could be spared to stay with us. The next morning I secured a large utensil filled with hot cakes and a gallon of jam. We spread jam on the cakes, rolled them up and passed them out to our patients. I don't suppose anyone ever appreciated homemade jelly rolls as much as they did.

At Hagaru most of the men of the 5th and 7th Marines enjoyed hot food again for the first time in 8 days. Writing to Chaplain Salisbury on 5 December, Schwyhart stated: "I have checked on the chaplains of the 5th and 7th Regiments and am glad to report that they are well. They are dreadfully tired, having been without sleep for 2 and 3 days and nights."

Among the chaplains with Division troops at Hagaru-ri was Chaplain W. M. Hearn. In his reply to the questionnaire, Hearn wrote:

Those chaplains who were in the Hagaru area during the "trap" tried to cover the hospital units. I had a small Communion set and gave Communion to as many as possible as they were brought into the field hospital at Hagaru. Divine services involving large groups were dangerous; so I went from tent to tent for brief prayers during these times, or in foxholes or wherever men were together. My most memorable prayer was given on the running board of a moving truck as I prayed with the men driving, at their request. Bowed heads and closed eyes were, of course, impossible— at least for the driver.

Chaplain B. C. Howland in his reply to the questionnaire likewise referred to his ministry to the men who escaped from the Communist trap at Yudam-ni. He wrote: "At Hagaru-ri, where I was stationed, when they came down from the Reservoir there was a united expression of desire to receive Communion." Chaplain Joseph G. Power reported holding a Communion Service with the men standing in 2 feet or more of snow.

The first chaplain to be wounded in the Chosin Reservoir campaign was Chaplain Kevin J. Keaney who received three machine gun wounds in the left thigh and ankle on 29 November. At the time Chaplain Keaney was going from Koto-ri to Hagaru-ri to join the 3d Battalion, 1st Marines. The convoy in which he was riding was attacked just above Koto-ri. Chaplain Keaney's description of what happened was published in the Newport *Navalog* of 8 June 1951, from which the following has been taken:

The Communists opened up at us with machine guns. I jumped behind a tree and made myself as thin as possible. The bullets chipped off hunks of bark all around me. When the firing quieted we could see the enemy moving about on the snow-covered hillsides in the distance.

The men sought refuge in the ditch by the side of the road. There was but one machine gun in the group, in addition to side arms, so the enemy had little fear. After dark the Communists moved in closer, some setting up machine guns within 30 yards of the entrapped men. When a Marine was wounded, Chaplain Keaney moved to his side to give assistance. Seeing a jeep nearby, several decided to take a desperate chance to get the wounded man to safety. Chaplain Keaney helped to get the wounded man into the jeep. His account continues:

> We had just got him in when I felt a sting in the lower part of my left leg. I jumped into the back of the jeep and another blast hit me in the leg. The jeep started to move. However, the heavy machine gun fire forced the driver to leave the road and the jeep careened into a ditch of near frozen water. It was the cold water on my wounds that probably saved my life.

The arrival of a tank and some trucks rescued the group. Keaney was taken to Hagaru-ri, and evacuated by air to Japan on 4 December. Chaplain Patrick A. Killeen was sent by helicopter to Hagaru-ri as the relief of Chaplain Keaney.

Psalms at Hagaru

Another chaplain who had a narrow escape on this same road which connected Hagaru-ri with Koto-ri was William M. Hearn. Chaplain Schwyhart, in his letter of 15 December, wrote:

> The hand of God is very real. One chaplain, W. M. Hearn, tried to return to one of his battalion trucks after an ambush. Within about 20 feet of the truck he noted that it was being looted by Chinese troops so he fell down in a snow bank alongside the road and stayed there for 2 hours. His convoy continued on and his people felt that the chaplain was missing but he showed up the next day.

While ministering to the men at Hagaru, Hearn found that the dramatic events through which the Marines were passing provided a new background for appreciating the Psalms. Writing to Chaplain Salisbury, after the evacuation from Hungnam, Hearn explained:

> During our days at Hagaru, we found much consolation and food for thought in many parts of the Bible. This was especially true of many passages from the Psalms. Enclosed herewith is an article based on the experience of Marines matched with passages from the Psalms.

The following are some extracts from the article which Chaplain Hearn entitled "Psalms at Hagaru."

> The sun breaks through the early morning clouds. It paints the snowy hills of Hagaru with a delicate shade of pink against blue skies. Another day, another place, this would be beautiful; but today there is no time for thoughts of beauty. There are 50,000 and more reasons why one cannot dwell on beauty this morning. Hidden some place in these hills are the 50,000 and more reasons, each armed with rifle, mortar or machine gun.

> And look yet again at the hills, at the snow, at the sun. Before the mountains were formed in the fiery fury of a young earth, before the snows, yes, before the sun cast forth its first light and flame, God was.
> "Lord, thou has been our dwelling place in all generations. Before the mountains were formed, or ever thou hadst formed the earth and the world, even from everlasting to everlasting thou art God."

The 23d Psalm took on new meaning. "The Lord is my Shepherd; I shall not want." Continuing with "He leadeth me beside the still waters," Chaplain Hearn made a reference to the "frozen ice of Chosin," "still waters" over which some of the Marines crossed to safety.

> Darkness falls and fear creeps out to cover the valley. What of the night? O Lord, my God what of the night?
> "The Lord is my light and my salvation; whom shall I fear?"
> Fear stalks above and pauses in each foxhole and leaves with each a part of itself; unwelcome visitor, intangible, but more real than gun or mountain. Time creeps by despite my assurances unto my soul. Fear creeps in and sits beside my prayers.
> "The Lord is the strength of my life; of whom shall I be afraid?"
> As we wait in the darkness for the morning, we watch the shadows and listen to the stillness. They move by night, silently, so silently. Oh for the sun of the morning, the planes flying over in their dawn strike, light to send the quiet menace back beyond the hills.
> "My soul waiteth for the Lord more than they that watch for the morning: I say more than they that watch for the morning."
> In the early hours of morning they charge with bugles. Fury mounts upon fury. Hell opens its very jaws.
> "Out of the depths have I cried unto thee, O Lord, Lord, hear my voice."
> The waves of hell subside and grow still with the morning. The lines have held. Yes, we have found the deliverance for which we waited through the dark and fearful night.
> "Wait on the Lord: be of good courage, and he shall strengthen thine heart: wait, I say, on the Lord."

When the Marines were safely behind the defense perimeter at Hamhung, Chaplain Hearn opened his Bible again to the Psalter and read Psalm 124. The fearful ordeal through which he had just passed gave new meaning to old and familiar words:

> Blessed be the Lord, who hath not given us as a prey to their teeth.
> Our soul is escaped as a bird out of the snare of the fowlers; the snare is broken, and we are escaped.
> Our help is in the name of the Lord, who made heaven and earth.

Chaplain Hearn was later awarded a Letter of Commendation with Combat "V" for excellent service in the line of his profession while serving with a Marine ordnance battalion prior to and during operations in Korea from 15 August to 15 December 1950.

The march south from Hagaru-ri to Koto-ri began on 6 December, only 2 days after the final elements of the Yudam-ni forces arrived at Hagaru. At 2230 of that day Chaplain Cornelius J. Griffin was seriously wounded when the ambulance in which he was riding came under severe machine gun fire. While en route to Koto-ri, Chaplain Griffin was giving the last rites of his church to a dying young Marine. With the chaplain was his assistant, Sgt. Matthew Caruso. On a narrow mountainous road leading into Koto-ri, the convoy ran into a roadblock. Although the ambulance was clearly marked with the Red Cross, such a symbol of mercy was not respected by the Communists. A machine gun bullet tore through the chaplain's lower jaw, causing a deep wound. Another bullet hit him in the right shoulder. Sergeant Caruso flung himself over his chaplain just in time to catch another bullet which took his life. In an interview published in the *Monitor* of 5 January 1951, Griffin said:

> My clerk was killed as he lay alongside me. He was a 20-year-old grenadier and rifleman assigned to cover me, one of the finest kids I ever knew, Sgt. Matthew Caruso of Rocky Hill, Conn. He never left me, saved me I don't know how many times and even covered me with his body. He died 20 minutes after I had given him Communion.

Chaplain Griffin was knocked unconscious by the terrific blow on the jaw. Word was quickly passed to Chaplain Craven, who was then about a mile away, that Chaplain Griffin had been wounded. When Griffin regained consciousness, he was aware that some one was bending over him trying to get him to say the Act of Contrition: "O my God, I am heartily sorry for having offended thee . . . and I detest all my sins . . ." As the wounded chaplain began to repeat the words of the Roman Catholic prayer, he realized that the one bending over him was none other than his friend, John Craven, a Baptist. The story of this incident was recorded in the spring of 1951 and widely broadcast during Brotherhood Week to illustrate the meaning of brotherhood.

Several months later at a ceremony at Pearl Harbor when Chaplain Griffin was awarded the Silver Star for conspicuous gallantry while in action against the enemy on 3 November, Gen. Lemuel C. Shepherd said to Griffin as he pinned on the medal: "They don't give a damn whom they shoot, do they, Chaplain?"

Chaplain Griffin was evacuated from Koto-ri to Japan by air on 8 December. His wound in the jaw required many operations and much plastic surgery during about a year and a half spent in Navy hospitals. Chaplain Griffin was the most seriously wounded of all Navy chaplain casualties of Korea. A chapel at Camp Pendleton has been named in honor of Sergeant Caruso.

Among those who rendered notable service in the withdrawal from Hagaru-ri to Koto-ri were Chaplains Robert L. Patton and William D. Lyons. Both received the Letter of Commendation award for their tireless devotion to the men of their units, frequently exposing themselves to enemy fire in their efforts to minister to the wounded.

In the midst of such constant danger, where death might come flying with the speed of a bullet and where no one knew what a few minutes might bring forth, many Leathernecks found strength and consolation in religion. Navy chaplains were there to lead them in the worship of Almighty God. Chaplain B. C. Howland in his questionnaire commented on an experience which took place at Koto-ri.

> The most impressive service of Holy Communion in my experience as a minister occurred at Koto-ri on the way down from the Reservoir. Chaplain Preston D. Parsons, assigned to the 2d Battalion, and I conducted the service with the snow lightly falling on the heads of the men knelt in prayer. Over 100 gathered there not knowing whether we would ever get back to Hamhung but thankful that so far the Division had been able to make it down the roads. The faces of those men, as I placed the wafer on their tongues, showed that they were putting their trust in the Master of all men as they united in professing their loyalty to Him.

. . . to the Sea

South of Koto-ri, the withdrawing column of Marines ran into a new difficulty when they discovered that the enemy had destroyed a 29-foot section of a bridge on the road leading down from the 4,000-foot summit. The road at that point was on a shelf of a cliff which could not be bypassed. On 7 December a successful air-drop of the necessary 2,500 pound Treadway bridge section was made; the necessary repairs were completed on 9 December within 3 hours after the materials were made available at the site, and the march continued.

By the morning of 10 December the advance units of the 7th Marines were moving out of Chinhung-ni, and on the afternoon of that day they finally reached Hamhung, where hot food and warm shelters were awaiting them. The last elements of the Division reached Hamhung at 1300 the next day and the long ordeal which began at Yudam-ni on 30 November was over. The Marines succeeded in bringing back to the protecting lines around Hamhung all their wounded, many of their dead, much of their equip-

To the Sea.

Marines fight their way through hordes of Chinese communists in subzero weather down the mountains.

Mountain gale hinder their progress.

ment, and even some prisoners. Such items as were of necessity left behind had been destroyed.

"Shores of Tripoli"

Not only were hot food and warm shelters awaiting the battle-weary Marines at Hamhung but also mail from home. Before leaving the Mediterranean area on 15 August, Chaplain Craven had sent a roll of Kodachrome film to the processing laboratory for development. The package of finished slides was a part of the mail that the chaplain received at Hamhung on 10 December. Among the slides was one which showed the chaplain in a bathing suit on the French Riviera. Chaplain Craven held the film up to the light—the contrast was striking! Four months earlier he was in the pink of condition. He looked in the mirror and saw a gaunt, drawn face. The scales told him he had lost some 30 pounds and the ribs showing through his sides bore eloquent testimony that the scales were not lying. Chaplain Craven held the picture up to the light again and asked himself the question: "Can it be that I and this person in the picture are one and the same?" His experience was that of all the survivors of that 6th Fleet battalion. Within 3 months these men had been taken from the balmy shores of the blue Mediterranean and hurled into battle in the freezing temperatures of North Korea. And after another month they had become veterans of one of the toughest campaigns in the annals of the Marine Corps history.

Chaplain Craven was awarded the Legion of Merit for "exceptionally meritorious conduct in the performance of outstanding services" from 28 November to 10 December 1950. The citation reads, in part, as follows:

On one occasion, he participated in an evacuation operation in which more than 600 wounded Marines were loaded into trucks and transferred to rear aid stations. By his complete devotion to his fellow man in the face of extremely adverse combat conditions, Lieutenant Commander Craven served to inspire and encourage all who observed him. His fortitude, professional integrity and courageous conduct throughout were in keeping with highest traditions of the United States Naval Service.

But the stereotyped language of an official citation can hardly convey the living reality of the dedicated ministry of a chaplain. More meaningful is the following letter of Capt. Don France who, before he was killed during the Chinese offensive on the night of 5 December 1950, wrote about Chaplain Craven to his home church.[10]

[10] *Marine Corps Gazette* (December 1953), p. 18. D. D. Nicholson, Jr., "Their Faith Is Yours."

CATHEDRAL OF SAINT PHILLIP,
Atlanta, Ga.

DEAR DEAN WALTHOUR: This is the interim period when all of us are trying to catch up with our letter writing. . . . I landed at Inchon on D-day, was among the 1st Marines to cross the Han River, fought to capture Seoul, and it was my regiment that made the drive to Uijongbu. . . . In all those days one man stood out in my mind as the real leader, spirit and principle for which we are fighting. He is a mild-mannered Navy chaplain who answers to the name of John Craven. I met Chaplain Craven back at Camp Lejeune. Everyone liked him and I remember saying to myself at the time, "When things get rough, it is going to be comforting to have him around."

Since landing in Korea, I know that Chaplain Craven has spent more time in the frontlines than any other man in the regiment. Often on patrols I encountered him talking to the men—the dying, and instilling confidence in all those he met. By his very presence everything seemed better and easier and the men accomplished deeds that will live forever. To all of us, he has been a shining example of a chaplain, a father, and a man.

Chaplain Craven has the distinction of having served with the Marines through seven campaigns—four in World War II (the Marshalls, Saipan, Tinian and Iwo Jima) and three in the Korean War. It is believed that this has established a record in the history of the Chaplain Corps.

Chaplain Ingvoldstad was also awarded the Legion of Merit for "exceptionally meritorious conduct in the performance of outstanding services" from 28 November to 10 December 1950. The citation reads, in part, as follows:

Untiring in his efforts to be of service to the men in his regiment, Lieutenant-Commander Ingvoldstad frequently exposed himself to accurate enemy small-arms and machine-gun fire in the field to comfort and cheer the troops, administer first aid to the wounded, and assist in evacuating casualties. He directly contributed in saving the lives of many wounded. His constant contributions in feeding wounded, shifting wounded to motor vehicle hoods to keep the badly hit from freezing to death, patrolling the column to assist corpsmen in administering first aid all contributed immeasurably in saving some 1200 wounded. His fortitude, professional integrity and courageous conduct throughout were in keeping with the highest traditions of the United States Naval Service.

Wall of Fire

Worried by the situation in North Korea, senior naval officers had already in early November begun planning for the eventuality of a United Nations withdrawal.[11] A number of ships, including the BOXER, en route to stateside, were recalled, and all available shipping began to be collected. And fortunately so:

[11] Cagle and Manson, *op. cit.*, pp. 179–192.

for in December the Navy found itself ordered to take off 8th Army troops from the west coast, at Chinnampo and Inchon, and X Corps troops from Wonsan and Hungnam on the east. Actually, since a large part of 8th Army was finally able to withdraw overland, the naval redeployment in the west was not a major task, and outloading at Wonsan proceeded methodically and with a minimum of opposition. But it was far otherwise at Hungnam.

With three American divisions (1st Marine, 3d Army, 7th Army), a number of ROK regimental combat teams, and mountains of gear on the beaches, the Navy raised a wall of fire around the port city. As 13 ships poured shells into a perimeter surrounding the area, planes from 7 carriers provided an umbrella overhead. VALLEY FORGE, hastily recalled from the United States, and PRINCETON, newly arrived in early December, joined LEYTE and PHILIPPINE SEA, which had been providing air support for X Corps from the beginning of this operation. Also present were the escort carriers SICILY and BADOENG STRAIT, now joined by the BATAAN. In addition to rocket ships and destroyers, naval gunfire was furnished by the MISSOURI and the heavy cruisers ROCHESTER and ST. PAUL.

Serving as chaplains in the LEYTE were Clovis A. Frame (Methodist) and Charles A. Szczesny (Roman Catholic), both of whom reported on 28 August 1950. In the PRINCETON were Raymond F. McManus (Roman Catholic), from August 1950 to February 1952, and George J. Enyedi (Presbyterian), a Reserve who returned to active duty in August 1950 and was aboard until September 1951. The light carrier BATAAN had as its only chaplain a Roman Catholic, John J. Coffey, from July 1950 to July 1952. Chaplain in ST. PAUL, also from July 1950 to July 1952, was Faber H. Wickham, a Presbyterian (USA).

End of an Epic

Heavy casualties were suffered by the Marines in the withdrawal to Hamhung. Writing to Chaplain Salisbury on 5 December, Chaplain Schwyhart reported:

I have been spending the majority of time at the clearing center, Yong-po Airport, where they evacuated by air from Hagaru-ri a thousand casualties yesterday and an estimated 1,100 today. Today we begin a heavy schedule of burials at the Division Cemetery. This past week, since a week ago today, has been what Sherman said war was.

On 9 December, he wrote again: "Yesterday we buried 149 at Koto-ri; today more burials, now totaling 216, at Hungnam." And on 15 December, in an-

other letter to Chaplain Salisbury, Schwyhart stated: "At the Division Cemetery at Hungnam, there were 324 graves, mostly Marines, a few Army, 3 British Commandos, and 29 ROKS."

According to official statistics,[12] the Marine losses from 27 November to 11 December 1950 were as follows:

Killed in action	432
Died of wounds	101
Missing in action	249
Wounded	2,710
Total	3,492

In addition there were over 3,600 nonbattle casualties, largely from frostbite. Enemy losses for the same period were estimated at a total of 37,500—15,000 killed and 7,500 wounded by Marine ground forces, plus 10,000 killed and 5,000 wounded by Marine air strikes.

On 13 December a memorial service was conducted at the Division Cemetery at Hungnam in which the following chaplains took part—R. M. Schwyhart (Protestant), Garson Goodman (Jewish), and P. A. Killeen (Roman Catholic). Even as Gen. Oliver P. Smith, the Division Commander, delivered the address, preparations proceeded for the burial of the last bodies brought down from Chinhung-ni.

Chaplain Goodman, attached to Division headquarters at Hamhung, was the only Jewish chaplain with the 1st Marine Division. On 5 December he conducted two services for Hanukkah. As was to be expected, the number of men of the Jewish faith in the 1st Division was comparatively small; yet at one time Chaplain Goodman found 12 Jewish patients at the 121st Evacuation Hospital and 4 at the Division Hospital, and among markers placed over the mounds in the different military cemeteries were those bearing the Star of David.

In his letter of 15 December to Chaplain Salisbury, written aboard the BAYFIELD, as it sailed from Hungnam, Chaplain Schwyhart summarized as follows the role played by the chaplains in the Chosin Reservoir campaign:

Throughout the operation the chaplains, all of them, gave unsparingly of themselves to render assistance and to minister as chaplains wherever and whenever possible. Frankly, it is not possible to point out outstanding performances, because everyone in his own way did just that.

Four Chaplains Award, B'nai B'rith

Chaplain Schwyhart would be the first Navy recipient of the Four Chaplains Award, which was es-

---

[12] *Marine Corps Gazette* (November 1951), Lynn Montross, "Breakout From the Reservoir: Marine Epic of Fire and Ice."

Memorial Services, Hungnam.

Chaplain Robert M. Schwyhart, Division Chaplain, is shown participating in the memorial services for marines after their breakout from the Chosin Reservoir. The services are held in the Division Cemetery at Hungnam.

Memorial Services, Hungnam.

Chaplains Goodman, Killeen, and Schwyhart lead the marines of the 1st Division as they remember fallen buddies at memorial services at the Division's Cemetery at Hungnam, following the breakout from Chosin Reservoir.

tablished by the Alexander D. Goode Lodge, B'nai B'rith, of New York City. The award honors the memory of the four Army chaplains lost in the sinking of the Army troop transport DORCHESTER on 3 February 1943; of these one was a Roman Catholic, two were Protestants and the fourth, Alexander D. Goode, Jewish.

In February 1951 the Lodge presented a check for $500 to the Chiefs of Chaplains of each of the three branches of the Armed Forces for presentation to that chaplain in each Chaplain Corps who should be selected as best representing the spirit of brotherhood and cooperation displayed by the four chaplains lost in the DORCHESTER. A committee of Navy chaplains appointed by Chief of Chaplains S. W. Salisbury chose 1st Marine Division Chaplain Robert M. Schwyhart to be thus honored.

The presentation ceremony was held 31 March 1951, after Schwyhart had been relieved from duty in Korea, at the Naval Gun Factory, Washington, D.C. The citation reads:

Commander Robert M. Schwyhart, Chaplain Corps, U.S. Navy has expressed his firm faith in God by exemplifying to the men whom he served, the 1st Marine Division, Fleet Marine Force, great steadfastness in the face of adversity; notable courage when circumstances tended to promote fear and discouragement; a broad charity which manifested itself in service to all his men regardless of their creed, rank, or position; the spirit of sacrifice which caused him to give of his strength with compassion and to suffer hardship and danger with equanimity; and faithfulness in his stewardship of the things of God which was consistent with that of the four chaplains in whose memory this award is presented.

Back to the Bean Patch

The battered United Nations forces, including the 1st Marine Division, were evacuated from Hungnam during the period 12–24 December, in an "amphibious landing in reverse." The summary statistics are nearly incredible: 105,000 military personnel (Army, Navy, Air Corps, and Marine, together with ROK units), 91,000 civilian Korean refugees, 17,500 vehicles, and 350,000 measurement tons of cargo, outloaded in 193 shiploads by 109 ships.[13] Although Communists were beginning to press upon the defending perimeter, the loading proceeded systematically. By 15 December the last of the 1st Marine Division sailed for Pusan, where they were soon established in a rest camp in the former bean field near Masan.

The withdrawal from the Chinese trap was executed against overwhelming odds: 12 Chinese Communist divisions, subzero weather, and exceedingly hazardous terrain. By skillful deployment of ground forces and effectively integrated ground-air operations, the Division came through with tactical integrity, its wounded properly evacuated and its serviceable material salvaged.[14] Meanwhile the enemy had been in large part rendered militarily noneffective and the evacuation of X Corps from Hungnam rendered possible. Military historians were quick to compare the withdrawal to the famous "March of the 10,000" described by Xenophon in his *Anabasis*. Weapons and ideologies had changed; but relying on the same indomitable courage, the same base of training and discipline, and much the same infantry tactics, the

Marines like the Greeks before them successfully fought their way through Asiatic hordes to the sea.[15]

The 1st Marine Division (reinforced) was awarded a presidential unit citation for its heroic action during the Chosan Reservoir campaign, covering specifically the dates 27 November–11 December, from the Yudam-ni crisis to the completion of the withdrawal to Hamhung. This was the Division's second PUC in the Korean War, its fifth since the award was first established. The 1st Marine Aircraft Wing received the Army Distinguished Unit Citation for the period 22 November–14 December 1950.

Operation Helping Hand

Worth special notice was the Navy's magnificent job in providing transport for more than 90,000 Korean civilians to the relative safety of South Korea. When the forces of the United Nations drove northward, multitudes in the liberated areas had welcomed them with great joy. The Christians among them, many of whom had gone "underground," came out of hiding and made themselves known. But when the withdrawal began, all alike viewed with consternation and alarm the new situation which faced them. To remain behind and come again under the Red regime was tantamount to death for the Christian leaders.

As the troops of X Corps withdrew into Hungnam, they were followed by hordes of pitiful civilians who were sometimes panicked by the Chinese Communists harassing the rear guard of the Marine column. The long bitter march by foot to Hungnam was marked by miserable circumstances. Babies were born en route. People were cold and hungry. Of necessity the natives left behind most of their goods, taking with them only the barest necessities. They crowded into Hungnam expecting that the U.S. Navy would take them to South Korea—and this the Navy did. The first 50,000 were jammed into three Victory ships and two LST's. "It became standard practice to embark at least 5,000 on an LST, not counting children in arms, and one ship set a record with 12,000." [16]

Among the Navy chaplains especially active in helping collect and evacuate the North Korean refugees was 1st Marine Aircraft Wing Chaplain, John P. Murphy. Later Chaplain Murphy was awarded the Bronze Star. The citation mentions his work with the native Christians at Wonsan, to which reference has already been made, and then adds:

---

[13] Montross and Canzona, *op. cit.*, vol. III, p. 345.
[14] *Ibid.*, ch. XV.

[15] *Ibid.*, p. 357.
[16] *Marine Corps Gazette* (December 1951), p. 25, Lynn Montross, "The Hungnam Evacuation."

When the evacuation of Wonsan and Hungnam became necessary, he worked endless hours with military and civilian agencies in planning and effecting a safe evacuation of thousands of Christian North Koreans to a place of safety.

And so the United Nations Command saved not only its troops and equipment but thousands of helpless civilians as well.

In Time of Trouble

Northeast Korea had proved a peculiarly dangerous and costly area of combat. As the closing months of 1950 saw steadily mounting casualty totals, chaplains in ships were more and more engaged in ministering solace to the wounded and honor to the dead. By faithful performance as well as in word they proclaimed, "God is our refuge and strength, a very present help in time of trouble."

Even before X Corps went ashore the fleet was encountering serious difficulties—from mines, often simply let loose upstream and floated into the sea.[17] The first casualty was the destroyer BRUSH, on 26 September. Rendered instantly helpless, her bow a full fathom low, much of the ship open to the sea, her forward steering gear gone, BRUSH was taken in tow and escorted 470 miles to Sasebo, Japan. Thirteen men had been killed, 34 seriously wounded. Chaplain Charles L. Dickey, in the WORCESTER, wrote in his questionnaire reply:

We had 34 casualties aboard for the 3 days we were accompanying the BRUSH to Sasebo. I had prayers with each man every day, and two yeomen to read and write censored letters for each man.

Chaplain Edwin F. Carr, in the ROCHESTER, flagship of Vice Admiral Struble's Joint Task Force Seven, wrote concerning the minesweeping operations at Wonsan, which had been a source of desperate concern, so thickly and thoroughly had the enemy planted mines there:

I consider all the activities performed by me under these various headings [of the questionnaire] as merely routine. However, celebrating Mass in a bombed-out warehouse in Wonsan for the men who had given their lives on minesweeps sunk by mines was impressive. [Their devotion] remains to bear witness to our faith in freedom.

Without their sacrifice the landings could not have been made; as it was, 15 days had been expended and over 200 casualties sustained.

A happier story concerns the transfer of needed medical supplies from the ROCHESTER to a small Korean hospital in Wonsan. Employing Latin as a medium, Chaplain Carr was able to act as "interpreter" between the ship's doctor and a Korean priest representing the hospital. Thus a "dead" language proved effective in helping sustain life in a time of desperate trouble.

Transport chaplains had their hands full. Henry F. Maxwell in the THOMAS JEFFERSON reported serious casualties "flowing in a stream" to the transports immediately after the landings. Of the period barely a month later, Chaplain Leonard B. Dohrmann wrote:

During the November–December 1950 evacuation of wounded from the Hungnam area, the BRECKENRIDGE carried several loads to Yokohama. I assisted in loading and caring for these wounded.

Chaplain Charles W. Adams recalled that his ship, operating under MSTS, Pacific, ferried "shiploads" of wounded to Yokosuka; he called it "round-the-clock" duty.

And at Yokosuka? Charles W. Lawler, Roman Catholic chaplain at the Naval Hospital there, later wrote: "Over 3,000 casualties were admitted within 48 hours. The hospital grew from a 70-bed dispensary to a hospital of about 5,000 beds." Charles H. Shackelford, the Protestant chaplain, wrote that he spent every Sunday afternoon and evening administering Holy Communion to bed patients. "Often this would continue up to 2130 or 2200, because of the large number who wished to receive. . . ."

Chaplain J. E. Zoller was temporarily attached there during the peak of the casualty load. He reported that it was necessary in some wards to use double-deck bunks, often placed so closely together that one had to turn sideways to slide between them.

Many of the patients were not ambulatory and could not attend chapel services. Most of them were fresh from the combat zone. Many had not received the Sacrament for a long time and desired to receive it. After consecrating the elements in the chapel, I carried the chalice in my hand and went to the wards to serve individual communions. I would slide between two double-deck bunks and say to the four men (two on each side) that I was a Protestant chaplain prepared to serve communion to those who desired to receive it. The response among the Protestant patients was almost unanimous.

Afterwards I would ask the men if they had any special prayer requests . . . Many were suffering a great deal themselves, but in no case, not one, did a man ask prayer for himself. Most frequently it was requested for his buddies back in the combat zone and occasionally for his loved ones at home.

Back at Hungnam, as the last ships pulled offshore, the dock area was set ablaze and destroyers shelled anything that might be useful to the incoming Communists. One last fighter plane from the PRINCETON

---

[17] Cagle and Manson, *op. cit.*, pp. 130–146.

circled overhead. A long column of ships turned southward. Heading for home the pilot signaled the MOUNT McKINLEY and they "exchanged greetings." It was Christmas Eve.

First Korean Christmas

Writing to Chaplain Salisbury on 1 January 1951, Division Chaplain Schwyhart reported that most of the chaplains at Masan had been able to obtain squad tents to be used as chapels. "On Christmas Eve and Christmas Day," wrote Schwyhart, "a total of 71 services were conducted by chaplains in the Division with a total of 13,077 attending."

Chaplain William A. Rennie wrote of his Christmas Eve service as follows:

At Masan, Korea, during the winter of 1950–51, the neighboring Presbyterian church offered the use of its small sanctuary for the Protestant worship services of the Medical Bn. For the Christmas Eve service, one of the Catholic corpsmen volunteered to create a manger-scene tableau with about 10 of the children of the church. Everything went off fine, as by candlelight, with the Korean congregation as our guests, the choir sang "Silent Night" and the life-like tableau was posed in a corner of the church. Corpsmen and Marines placed their gifts at the foot of the cradled-babe. A very effective service of worship and dedication was the result.

Incidentally, a few days later, the pastor of the church, in order to show the appreciation of his people for the gifts given to the church, presented me with about 180 pounds of roasted peanuts for the "church men and sick patients."

Chaplain B. C. Howland, in his reply to the questionnaire, commented as follows on his memories of that first Christmas in Korea:

I believe our regiment was one of the first to raise money for a Korean church. On Christmas Sunday in our rest camp area at Masan both Chaplain Parsons and myself made an appeal to the men to help out the Presbyterian church which was doing such a good work. The results were heartening to both of us chaplains.

Christmas Mass, Masan.
Catholic marines attend mass in the 50th Marine Regiment area on Christmas Day at Masan.

Attending a Korean children's Christmas party is one of the experiences that will linger long in my memory. After we had raised the money on Christmas Sunday I took it to the Korean pastor. Through an interpreter he conveyed his message of gratitude and requested that I attend the party on Christmas day. With me went one officer and three enlisted men and never in that big Sunday School room have we ever seen such a mass of young humanity packed like sardines together. The children sang the carols that we all knew and there were recitations as well, but when we came in there was a special greeting in song from the children to us, as they seemed to sense that we were their friends who would help them as much as we could.

I found that these Christian friends of ours were ready to reciprocate in whatever manner they could. Because I felt that it would be a fine idea to have organ music at the services, and there being an organist in our regiment, I conveyed that idea to a Korean resident and member of the Presbyterian church. He immediately made arrangements through a music teacher in the city to borrow an organ.

Chaplain Howland also reported an interest in Bible study and discussion groups. "In the rest camp at Masan New Testaments were greatly in demand," he wrote. "I would go from one tent to another and always I had no trouble getting rid of the Testaments I carried. Many a religious discussion went on in those tents and I was able to take part in the discussion."

Nor were chaplains in the ships less busy. Chap-lain O. B. Salyer wrote that he organized Christmas caroling throughout the BADOENG STRAIT on Christmas Eve, with proper religious observance of the holy day. His usual routine, besides Sunday services, included daily morning prayers and Scripture reading in the ship's library, just after securing from morning quarters. Each Wednesday evening a study and discussion group met in the library.

Chaplain John R. Thomas, a Reserve returned to active duty, was assigned to Destroyer Squadron Seven, operating off Korea. In his questionnaire reply Chaplain Thomas wrote:

I served under at least 12 different destroyer captains and 4 division and squadron commanders. Attitudes of all except one destroyer commander made it possible for evening prayers underway on the ship's intercom system. The squadron commander enabled us to broadcast the Christmas Eve service to all the destroyers in the carrier screen off East Korea, Christmas, 1950.

Concerning this same Christmas Chaplain Wylie R. Bryant, Presbyterian (Cumb.), one of the many chaplains assigned to Military Sea Transport Service, North Pacific Subarea, wrote as follows:

During the days we sat offshore at Inchon there were no passengers aboard, so we invited 80 soldiers aboard the ship on Christmas 1950. The crew and military department of the ship decided to forego their Christmas dinner that these

Christmas Mass on Hospital Ship.
Chaplain C. E. Karnasiewicz conducts Christmas mass and directs the choir aboard the REPOSE.

men might enjoy a day of rest and entertainment. Christmas services were conducted, and afterward a movie was given for them.

Bryant was serving at the time in the USNS MARINE ADDER. Such were chartered ships operated by the civilian merchant marine, with a military department to supervise and look after the needs of military personnel (and in peacetime, dependents) being transported therein.

The season which for Christians commemorates God's gift of Himself in Jesus Christ seemed naturally to suggest, even to men caught in the toils of war, the wish to do something for others. A choir of crewmen from the ELDORADO, an amphibious command ship, went aboard the HAVEN to sing Christmas carols in the wards. ELDORADO, as flagship of Commander Amphibious Group Three, had participated in both the Inchon and Wonsan landings; her chaplain at the time was Richard J. Holmes, Roman Catholic.

Chaplain Zoller wrote, concerning Christmas Day in the Yokosuka hospital, as follows:

> After an afternoon of celebrations and parties throughout the hospital, I took my accordion and went to the ward for paraplegics and multiple amputees. After playing casually for a while, the men began requesting and singing Christmas carols, then folksongs, campfire favorites, spirituals, and hymns.
>
> Just after taps I stood beside the bed of a young man not yet 20 years of age. I wondered how he kept the smile on his face. Both feet had been amputated, and all the fingers on each hand. He was in constant pain. . . .
>
> "Chaplain," he said, "could you play 'The Old Rugged Cross'?"
>
> Then followed a request for "Rock of Ages."
>
> When I finished playing, he was asleep, with the trace of a smile still on his face. As I left the ward, nearly everyone was sleeping. At the office the nurse motioned me inside.
>
> "Chaplain," she said, "those quiet hymns did more to relax these men than any medicine. Thank you."

In Keeping With the Highest

The withdrawal from the Chinese trap could not have been effected without close air support furnished by Navy and Marine pilots. During the first stage of the redeployment, on 4 December, when LEYTE planes were supporting the Marines at Hagaru-ri, there occurred an awe-inspiring act of heroism.[18] Ensign Jesse L. Brown, the Navy's first Negro pilot, was forced to make an emergency landing 5 miles behind enemy lines. Circling pilots could see that Brown was alive but apparently unable to extricate himself from the plane's slowly burning wreckage.

With darkness approaching and in near-zero weather, Lt. (j.g.) Thomas J. Hudner successfully landed his plane nearby. Finding it impossible to extricate the injured pilot, he radioed for cutting instruments and a helicopter, and then using snow extinguished the flames. The rescue 'copter arrived quickly, but Brown died before he could be freed from the wreckage. For his act of selfless devotion Navy pilot Hudner was subsequently presented our nation's highest military decoration, the Congressional Medal of Honor.

Among the chaplains commended during this time, three were serving on carriers. Both the Protestant and Roman Catholic chaplains, C. A. Frame and C. A. Szczesny, in the LEYTE were awarded the Letter of Commendation with Combat "V" for meritorious service during air operations against the enemy from 8 October 1950 to 19 January 1951. For his service from 5 August 1950 to 9 January 1951 in the BADOENG STRAIT Chaplain O. B. Salyer was also honored with the Letter of Commendation award.

Chaplain George W. Cummins, of Marine Aircraft Group 12, located first at Wonsan and then at Yongpo, was cited for the period 12 October–22 December 1950. At Wonsan, volunteering his services as a member of an atrocity investigation team, Cummins had spent many hours in guerrilla-infested area helping ascertain facts concerning this dreadful aspect of man's inhumanity to man. Cummins' citation mentions, in addition, his work during the redeployment to Hungnam.

> During this period of daily air evacuation of casualties from the Koto-ri airstrip, he maintained a constant vigil at the unloading point, giving unstintedly of his time and attention to the wounded.

He was awarded the Bronze Star.

During the first 6 months of military operations in Korea, 21 Navy chaplains had won 28 awards, including 5 Purple Hearts. Fifteen of the twenty-eight chaplains attached to the 1st Marine Division were recipients of an award—a remarkably high percentage. The record is even more impressive when we remember that some of the other chaplains received awards in later actions. In addition to those serving with the 1st Division, three chaplains attached to carriers (Frame, Szczesny, and Salyer) and three chaplains with the 1st Marine Aircraft Wing (Markley, Murphy, and Cummins) were also thus honored.

An analysis of the awards granted shows that 5 chaplains received the Purple Heart; 2, the Legion of Merit; 3, the Silver Star (including 1 from the

---

[18] *Ibid.*, pp. 176f.

Army); 12, the Bronze Star (including 1 from the Army); and 7, Letters of Commendation. Seven chaplains, including of course each of the 5 who were wounded, received two awards each. Such recognition speaks eloquently of their faithfulness and devotion. Official citations become formalized in language; yet the words with which many of them close are rich in meaning . . . "in keeping with the highest traditions of the Chaplain Corps and of the Naval Service".

That those traditions are characterized by unassailable integrity is in no small part due to the ministry of those clergymen in uniform who through the years have kept faith with God and their fellows. After the deliverance from Hungnam [19] one chaplain who had seen action in World War II preached a thanksgiving sermon on the text from Psalm 116:

The sorrows of death compassed me, and the pains of hell got hold upon me: I found sorrow and trouble.

Then called I upon the name of the Lord; O Lord, I beseech thee, deliver my soul. . . .

Return unto thy rest, O my soul; for the Lord hath dealt bountifully with thee.

For thou hast delivered my soul from death, mine eyes from tears, and my feet from falling.

A ministry inspired by such a faith can but command the gratitude and respect of thoughtful men. Of it one may say, simply, "In keeping with the Highest."

At Masan the battle-weary Marines spent several weeks recuperating and integrating newly arrived reinforcements. On 31 December the Division passed from X Corps to 8th Army control and was assigned to the Pohangdong area for possible future commitment.

Enemy High Tide

Meanwhile General MacArthur had found it necessary to withdraw the 8th Army from north of the 38th Parallel in the west.[20] As 1950 drew to a close he was trying to establish a line of defense along the parallel. On 23 December Lt. Gen. Walton H. Walker was killed in a traffic accident and was replaced on 26 December by Lt. Gen. Matthew B.

Ridgway. On 30 December MacArthur warned the Joint Chiefs of Staff that the Chinese forces were capable of driving the United Nations out of Korea altogether. To General Ridgway, MacArthur gave complete authority over operations in Korea, passing on the orders of the Joint Chiefs to withdraw if necessary, while inflicting maximum damage on the enemy consistent with keeping his own units intact.

After a night of artillery bombardment the Communist forces opened an attack all along the line at daybreak on New Year's Day, 1951. The UN forces were driven back some 70 miles below the 38th Parallel. Inchon, Kimpo airfield, and Seoul fell again to the enemy. On 13 January the 1st Marine Division was ordered to protect the city of Andong, northeast of Taegu, with the two adjoining airstrips, from further southward penetration of the Communists. In the 2-week engagement that followed the Division reported 11 killed and 45 wounded, all these casualties having been suffered by the 7th Marines.

Clearly the enemy was not capable of following up his punch; he had outrun his supply lines. His pressure now diminished, and reconnaisance patrols indicated deep areas forward of the UN defensive positions in which no Chinese or North Koreans were to be found.

Below this line there were, however, constant contacts with guerrilla bands, North Koreans who had been left behind when their Army had retreated to the north in the autumn, or others who had infiltrated into the south in order to harass the United Nations forces. Units of the 1st Marine Division had been engaged in helping suppress these irregular activities shortly after the Division reached Masan.[21] During most of January and the first half of February they would be largely occupied fighting the guerrillas.

As the period here under review came to an end, the feeling became general that the situation was now less desperate. Gen. J. Lawton Collins, Army Chief of Staff, in Korea on an inspection tour, announced to correspondents the intention of the United Nations Command to stay and fight. Eighth Army, he notified Washington, could handle the new threat presented by the Chinese intervention. There was no longer any question of evacuating Korea.

---

[19] *Marine Corps Gazette* (December 1953), p. 21, D. D. Nicholson, Jr., "Their Faith Is Yours."

[20] See *Korea, 1950* (Department of the Army), ch. V, esp. pp. 229–232. Also John Miller, Jr., Owen J. Carroll, and Margaret E. Tackley, *Korea, 1951–53* (Department of the Army: Office of the Chief of Military History, 1956), ch. I.

[21] *Marine Corps Gazette* (January 1952), Lynn Montross, "The Pohang Guerrilla Hunt."

CHAPTER 4

FIRST UNITED NATIONS COUNTEROFFENSIVE

25 January–21 April 1951

The changing fortunes of the contending armies in Korea during the early months of the war have been likened to the swinging of a giant pendulum. At first the hard-smashing North Korean People's Army overran the South Koreans and then, the U.S. Army troops were hurriedly thrown into the breach. The only free territory remaining late in August 1950 was that contained within the Pusan Perimeter. With the arrival of United Nations reinforcements the pendulum began to swing in the other direction.

The North Koreans suffered a humiliating defeat in the Inchon-Seoul operation and during the succeeding weeks, as 8th Army forces pounded their way out of the Pusan Perimeter northward toward Seoul, linking up with X Corps on 26 September. When the NKPA refused to surrender, the fateful decision was taken by General MacArthur to strike above the 38th Parallel. On 1 October ROK units crossed the Parallel on the east coast. In the west a multination force drove north and secured the North Korean capital of Pyongyang. On 26 October the ROK 6th Division had the distinction of being the first UN unit to reach the Manchurian border, near Chosan, in the northwest. For a short time it looked as though all North Korea would be brought under the jurisdiction of the United Nations.

The entry of the Chinese Communists into the conflict injected a new factor which caused the pendulum to swing in reverse direction. United Nations forces suffered a disastrous setback toward the close of November and early in December. Separated by precipitous mountains when struck by the Chinese, both 8th Army and X Corps were forced to retreat. The New Year's offensive launched by the Communists forced a further withdrawal, and for a time the United Nations bid to support the Republic of Korea against unwarranted attack seemed frustrated.[1]

United Nations Counteroffensive

On 25 January the pendulum began swinging northward once again, as General Ridgway put in motion Operation Thunderbolt, a cautious and methodical advance all along the UN line, designed to clean out the enemy ridge by ridge, phase line by phase line.[2] Meanwhile, still in the south, the 1st Marine Division was ordered to the Palgong-San area on 31 January to clean up remnants of the North Korean 10th Division. Air support proved particularly effective during "Thunderbolt," and naval bombardment along the west coast included the massive firepower of the "Mighty Mo," the battleship MISSOURI. By 10 February the 25th Army Division had secured Inchon and Kimpo airfield; but so great destruction had been wrought in January by the evacuating UN forces that several months elapsed before either was fully operational again.

On 16 February the 1st Marine Division, relieved of its antiguerrilla mission, began moving into the Chunjo sector, the lower end of the vertical Wonju-Hoengsong-Hongchon axis in central Korea.[3] The Division was made part of IX Corps, commanded by Maj. Gen. Bryant E. Moore, which included besides, the 24th Infantry Division, the 1st Cavalry Division, the ROK 6th Division, and the 27th British Commonwealth Brigade.

---

[1] When Ridgway assumed command of the U.S. 8th Army, MacArthur relinquished personal supervision of 8th Army and X Corps. X Corps was now incorporated into 8th Army, so that the 8th Army commander controlled all ground forces in Korea. The largest unit was the ROK Army, under Ridgway's control but not part of 8th Army. To 8th Army were attached certain Air Force, Marine Corps, and United Nations units. Ridgway commanded at this time about 365,000 troops. So far 15 members of the UN had contributed combat forces: Australia, Belgium, Canada, France, Greece, India, the Netherlands, New Zealand, the Philippines, South Africa, Sweden, Thailand, Turkey, the United Kingdom, and the United States. See Miller *et al., op. cit.,* p. 4.

[2] *Ibid.,* ch. II, esp. pp. 13ff.

[3] *Marine Corps Gazette* (February 1952), p. 31, Lynn Montross "Buttoning up the Offensive: The Marines in Operation Killer."

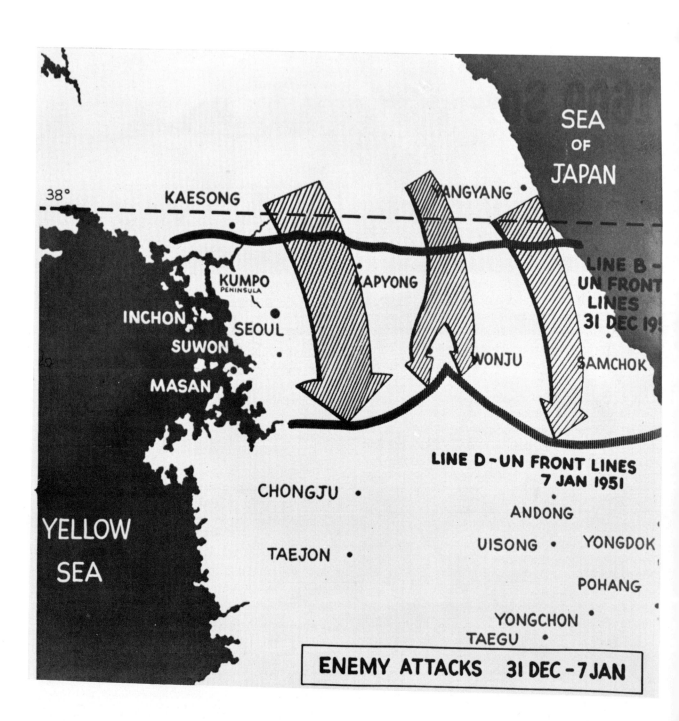

SEA
OF
JAPAN

38°   KAESONG

YANGYANG

LINE B –
UN FRONT
LINES
31 DEC 195

KUMPO
PENINSULA

KAPYONG

INCHON

SEOUL

SUWON

WONJU

SAMCHOK

MASAN

LINE D –UN FRONT LINES
7 JAN 1951

CHONGJU

ANDONG

YELLOW
SEA

TAEJON

UISONG   YONGDOK

POHANG

YONGCHON

TAEGU

ENEMY ATTACKS   31 DEC – 7 JAN

On 21 February, to deny the enemy a chance to re-organize, another general advance was initiated, dubbed Operation Killer.[4] The Marines secured their initial objective, the high ground overlooking Hoeng-song, on 24 February; but advance was slow every-where along the line. The weather was still cold, with occasional snow and extensive rain. The begin-ning of the thaw was turning ravines into raging torrents and paddies into beds of slime. Terrain and weather were as troublesome as the enemy. There were no roads worth the name. Nevertheless the UN offensive kept moving, and by March first the Com-munist breakout had been largely repulsed. "Killer" came to an end on 4 March, with the Marines solidly entrenched on phase line "Arizona," a string of five hills north of Hoengsong. The entire area south of the Han River was again in United Nations control. A stable line lying about halfway between the 37th and 38th parallels began at Inchon, moved along the Han, then ran north of Hoengsong, and so northeast-ward out to Kangnung on the east coast.

"Operation Ripper"

A new advance, Operation Ripper, began on 7 March, the purpose of which was primarily to keep the enemy under such pressure as to prevent his re-grouping for a counteroffensive.[5] Again and again General Ridgway insisted that gaining ground was secondary to the destruction of Chinese Communist personnel and equipment. With I Corps and the ROK Army holding the left and right flanks, respec-tively, IX and X Corps, the former including the 1st Marine Division, slugged slowly forward in the center against stubborn opposition, the enemy taking advan-tage of the precipitous slopes and lack of roads to hold on as long as possible before pulling back. On 14 March elements of I Corps reentered Seoul and the Republic of Korea flag was hoisted again over the National Assembly building.

The Communists now began to pull back all along the line, fighting only delaying actions. The 7th Ma-rines entered the important communication center of Hongchon without a fight. The enemy's object was to reorganize a line just north of the 38th Parallel, based on fortifications apparently constructed before the initial invasion of South Korea in 1950.[6] The

central anchor of this line, dug into rock and protected by log and concrete reinforcement, was the area bounded by Chorwon, Kumha, and Pyonggang. Here, in what became known as the "Iron Triangle," lay the hub of protection for the North Korean communica-tion and supply network.

Clearly the enemy was preparing to regroup. That he would be ready for a spring advance, with at least some air potential, was clear from intelligence reports. The UN units were by now up against the Parallel again. Thinking it better to keep his advantage, Ridgway, as the responsible field commander, ordered his forces toward the so-called Kansas line, north of the 38th. On 4 April the Marines were among the first UN troops to cross the Parallel. Phase line "Kansas" had been reached by 9 April everywhere ex-cept in the center.

On 11 April 1951 General MacArthur was relieved of his command by the Commander-in-Chief, Presi-dent Harry S. Truman, and replaced by General Ridg-way.[7] Lt. Gen. James A. Van Fleet, Ridgeway's successor as 8th Army commander, ordered the tactics already in operation to continue. The advance con-tinued toward phase line "Utah," and by 21 April UN forces were up against Chorwon, the southwestern pivot of the Iron Triangle. Van Fleet's line now began on the west coast near Kyodong, several miles above Inchon, moved sharply northward in a 45° angle to Chorwon, nearly 40 miles above the Parallel, and then eastward in an irregular line which skirted the Hwachon Reservoir and continued on to the east coast. Along this line forces of the United Nations were to meet the unleashed fury of the Communist counter-attack.

Rotation System

Beginning in December 1950 the Bureau of Naval Personnel instituted a system of rotation for chaplains serving with Marines in Korea. All who had had 6 to 8 months of duty during the extremely difficult and hazardous opening months of the war were to be or-dered back stateside. The first to be relieved under the rotation system were the chaplains who had landed at Pusan with the Provisional Brigade. The first re-placements reported for duty on 7 January 1951.

Chaplain Ingvoldstad, Regimental Chaplain of the 5th Marines, was relieved by Chaplain Verner N. Carl-sen, who reported on 7 January. Ingvoldstad was ordered to the faculty of the newly reestablished Chap-

---

[4] Miller *et al., op. cit.,* pp. 18f. Also Lynn Montross, "Buttoning up the Offensive: The Marines in Operation Killer," *Marine Corps Gazette* (February 1952).
[5] *Marine Corps Gazette* (March 1952), Lynn Montross, "Advance to the 38th Parallel: The Marines in Operation Ripper". Also Miller *et al., op. cit.,* ch. III, esp. pp. 21ff.
[6] Miller *et al., op. cit.,* pp. 24ff.

[7] See M. B. Ridgway, *Soldier: The Memoirs of Matthew B. Ridgway* (New York, 1956), p. 220 and ch. 27. For Ridg-way's account of his months as 8th Army commander, see chs. 23 and following.

lain School, located at Newport, R.I. He was the first of the chaplains who had seen duty in Korea to be assigned to the school.

Previously, in October 1950, Chaplain W. N. Lyons, already attached to the Division, had relieved Glyn Jones as Regimental Chaplain, 1st Marines, when Jones was ordered to the Personnel Distribution desk in the Chaplains Division. Chaplain Leslie L. O'Connor, reporting on 13 January, now relieved Craven as Regimental Chaplain, 7th Marines; Craven reported for duty in the Chaplains Division, in charge of the Ecclesiastical Relations desk. Chaplain Joseph C. Fitzgerald, who reported 14 January, followed Sporrer as Regimental Chaplain of the 11th Marines. Other chaplains reporting during this first major rotation were John M. Quirk (7 January), Solomon K. Johnson (14 January), George C. Bingaman and Howard E. Waters (both on 17 January).

Division Chaplain R. M. Schwyhart was having personnel problems. Chaplain Preston D. Parsons, after a jeep accident on 20 January, was evacuated to Japan. Within 9 days all three chaplains in the 11th Marines (Sporrer, Howland, and Parsons) had been changed. Chaplain Van Antwerp was hospitalized after being wounded on 26 January. On 5 February Chaplain Carlsen was evacuated to Yokosuka after a flareup of peptic ulcers. On 6 February Chaplain Killeen was flown from the 1st Marines area to Division Hospital for an emergency appendectomy. Reporting all these moves, Schwyhart added:

It does seem that we have chaplain difficulties: two in the hospital and another evacuated within a period of 12 days. I have been keeping in close communication with all other chaplains, by jeep, telephone, and radio, and am glad to report that all is well with them. On Monday, 5 February, I went by plane to Masan to check on some items at our Administrative Rear Echelon and to see Chaplains Ham, Engle, and Bingaman, whom I hadn't seen for 3 weeks, since my move north.

Chaplain Francis W. Kelly, who had served tours of duty with the 1st and 2d Marine Divisions during World War II, receiving the Legion of Merit for heroism in combat, was ordered as the relief of Schwyhart as the Division Chaplain. Chaplain Kelly had performed exceptional service with the Marines in the battles of Guadalcanal, Tarawa, and Okinawa. His courage and closeness to the fighting men was depicted in the movie *Guadalcanal Diary*, with the well-known actor Preston Foster portraying Chaplain Kelly. In *The Marines Take Tarawa*, a Marine Corps documentary movie, Chaplain Kelly himself plays one of the principal roles. Kelly had been released to inactive duty in July 1946 but returned to active duty 4 years later when the Korean hostilities began. Before going to Korea, he served with the 2d Marine Aircraft Wing at Cherry Point, N.C. Because of his distinguished service with the Marines, he was sometimes known as the "Fighting Padre." Kelly relieved Schwyhart on 20 February 1951.

Other replacements were gradually made during the spring months of 1951 so that by June a complete turnover of chaplains attached to the 1st Marine Division had been completed. After the front line became more stabilized, the tour of duty for chaplains serving with Marines in Korea would be extended to 10 months and finally to a year. Following the Korean Armistice, the duty was lengthened from 12 to 15 months.

Corps Expansion

The expansion of the Nation's Armed Forces necessitated by the continuing war naturally made great demands on the Chaplain Corps. It was Chief of Chaplains S. W. Salisbury's policy to meet the need for more personnel through a voluntary and selective recall of chaplains in the Inactive Reserve.

Chaplains desiring to offer their services submitted a request for active duty orders to the Chief of Naval Personnel. A selection board consisting of both officers of the line and members of the Chaplains Division reviewed their jackets, taking into consideration each applicant's record, as well as age, rank, and denomination. A chaplain was then either ordered to active duty or else placed in category II, the latter making him available in the event of total mobilization.

As always the needs of the service determined selection. In the nature of the case, the chaplains in the Reserve tended to fall into the higher grades, whereas the need was for younger men in the rank of lieutenant and lieutenant (junior grade). Denominational distribution also naturally entered into the picture. Each applicant was advised that the necessary ecclesiastical endorsement was the individual's responsibility; and it proved necessary to warn applicants not to give up their civilian positions or otherwise make plans for entering upon active duty until officially notified by the Bureau of having been accepted.

The *Navy Chaplains Bulletin* (spring-summer, 1951) carried a summary of the chaplain personnel distribution picture. As of 15 April the Corps had 743 allowances and 608 chaplains on active duty. Although 8 percent was allowed for contingent unavailability (chaplains in transit, on sick list, etc.), the actual figure was proving nearer 12 percent, because of casualties in combat, a high rate of sickness among chaplains, partly due to overwork, and the long travel time to and from the theater of war.

Because activities in the combat area had priority for personnel, other activities suffered correspondingly. Allowances in certain types of ships were given up altogether; the optimum in training activities was 75 percent of allowance.

The rotation of chaplains in combat of course affected rotation throughout the Corps. Normal tours of continental shore duty were shortened by as much as 3 to 6 months, that at overseas bases correspondingly lengthened. On change-of-duty orders, 10 days leave was normally granted chaplains returning from sea-and-foreign-shore duty, 5 days for all leaving continental shore duty. All chaplains were advised to take such leave as might be possible aboard a duty station.

The Chief of Chaplains commended the way in which all hands were meeting the emergency and hoped that the policies then in operation would be sufficient to expand the Corps to meet the need without further undue strain upon the personnel already involved.

New Division Chaplain

Chaplain Schwyhart wrote to the Chief of Chaplains on 16 February 1951:

On the eve of Chaplain Kelly's arrival and my detachment, I want to state that it has been a privilege to have served as Division Chaplain during this time. It has been no sinecure; rather very strenuous but at the same time rewarding. The chaplains in the Division have performed their duties in a traditionally excellent manner and it has been a privilege for me to coordinate our mutual efforts.

In the same letter he reported that Van Antwerp was about ready to return to duty, that Killeen had had to be evacuated, and that replacements were needed for Van Antwerp, William Hearn, Reilly, and Lyons, in that order.

A copy was enclosed of the Standing Operating Procedure for the Chaplains Section of a Marine Division which had been submitted through Force Chaplain Kenneth D. Perkins to Fleet Marine Force, Pacific with recommendation for adoption.[8]

---

[8] For examples of a Standing Operating Procedure see app. C (Fleet Marine Force, Pacific) and app. D (1st Marine Division).

Award.
Chaplain Robert M. Schwyhart receives Bronze Star Medal from Maj. Gen. O. P. Smith, commanding the 1st Marine Division.

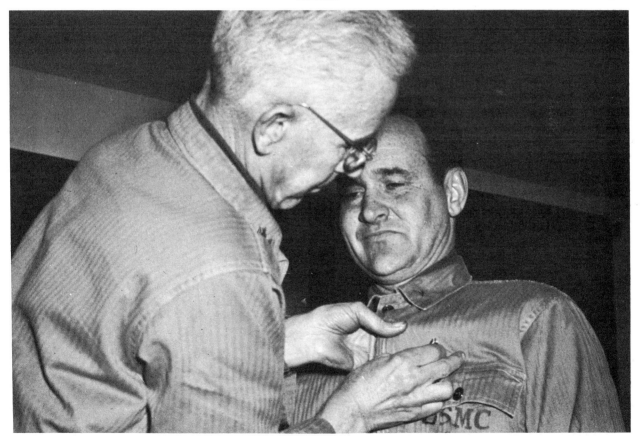

On 11 March the new Division Chaplain, F. W. Kelly, reported to the Chaplains Division the recent arrival of Chaplains Joseph D. McDonald, Henry E. Austin, and Henry H. Hayes. Chaplain O'Connor, Regimental Chaplain, 7th Marines had been evacuated because of illness. Kelly continued:

At present our 1st and 7th regiments are moving forward, with the 5th ready in reserve. [This was during Operation Ripper.] Our CP [command post] moves right along behind. Since we are in possible artillery range, we must wear helmets at all times, and black out at nights. The rest of the Division is strung back as far as Masan. I feel that it is better for me to be in this forward CP where I can be in contact with the regiments, rather than in the rear where I would be out of contact except by dispatch.

Later in March Kelly reported that Chaplain Joseph P. Trodd had reported on the 15th. Having advised some of the chaplains about due for rotation that dispatches had been received on their reliefs, he reported that one looked at him "like a fairy godfather who waved a magic wand." The rotation plan, he added, was having a "fine effect on the morale of the chaplains."

Kelly submitted the following roster on 31 March 1951.

Headquarters Bn	F. W. Kelly	CDR	RC
	Garson Goodman	LTJG	JEWISH
	H. H. Hayes	LTJG	DISC
Motor Transport Bn	J. P. Trodd	LT	RC
Ordnance Bn	Garson Goodman	(TAD from Headquarters Bn)	
Engineer Bn	K. M. Hearn	LT	METH
Shore Party Bn	K. d'A Engle	LTJG	PE
Tank Bn	W. M. Hearn	LTJG	BAP (A)
Amphibious Tractor Bn	G. C. Bingaman	LTJG	EVAN & REF
Service Bn	A. J. Juntunen	LT	LUTH
1st Marines	J. D. McDonald	LCDR	RC
	C. S. Pigott	LTJG	BAP (S)
	H. E. Austin	LT	BAP (A)
5th Marines	L. R. Phillips	LT	CONG
	J. M. Quirk	LT	RC
	S. K. Johnson	LT	PRESBY (USA)
7th Marines	J. S. Ferris	LT	METH
	E. I. Van Antwerp	LT	RC
	R. L. Patton	LTJG	METH
11th Marines	J. C. Fitzgerald	LCDR	RC
	H. H. Groover	LTJG	DISC
	H. E. Waters	LTJG	BAP (S)
Medical Bn	G. J. Reilly	LT	RC
	W. A. Rennie	LT	METH
Combat Service Group	W. N. Lyons	LCDR	BAP (A)

Chaplain Field Training

Chaplain James S. Ferris, reporting on 30 March, had informed Kelly that all chaplains ordered to the 1st Division were now being routed via Marine Barracks, Camp Pendleton, Calif., for indoctrination and training. Camp Chaplain J. Floyd Dreith later reported on this program. "'Last stop before Korea' is the phrase applied to Pendleton not only by the thousands of men sent out regularly as replacements for the 1st Marine Division but also by the chaplains going out to bring spiritual enlightenment, comfort and courage to those men."

Marine Corps organization, procedure, and nomenclature, official and slang, were studied so that the chaplain might know his way around. Refresher courses in first aid and conferences with medical officers suggested ways that chaplains could be of the greatest possible service in working with casualties. And not least, there was rigorous physical training, "lest the hills of Korea prove too much for an inadequate flesh no matter how willing the spirit."

Most important, the chaplain was trained in ways to render the most effective spiritual ministry. He was reminded that he would have a minimum theological library. Sermons, he was told, must eventually result from the hammering of actual experience with men in combat upon the anvil of one's own spiritual life. The chaplain was supplied with a compact Communion kit, told what supplies would be available to him in Korea, and advised not to burden himself with too much equipment in any case. One chaplain had written back to Dreith:

I packed my pack and set out on Saturday morning to hold services in the 2d Battalion the following day. For 8 days we climbed hills, each one a little steeper than its predecessor; I finally held my service one week later. I suggest that a chaplain take along as many hymnals as he can conveniently carry for 8 days up rugged mountains, in addition of course to a 60 pound pack.

Chaplains Wounded

Two chaplains—Eugene I. Van Antwerp and Charles S. Pigott—were wounded in action during the 4th Korean campaign. Van Antwerp received a flesh wound as the result of enemy mortar fire on 26 January. He was flown back to the Division Hospital by helicopter where he received treatment. Chaplain Schwyhart, reporting to the Chaplains Division in a letter dated 1 February 1951, stated:

The doctors advised that he would be ready for a return to duty in about 10 days. Chaplain Van Antwerp strongly desires to return to his 7th Marines. Our chaplains become extremely devoted to their units.

Chaplain Van Antwerp was awarded the Bronze Star for heroism while under fire in an engagement which began 20 January and included the period up to the time of his being wounded on the 26th. This occurred during the Division's antiguerrilla mission. His citation reads in part as follows:

On one occasion, when a rifle company on patrol in the vicinity of Chiso-dong, Korea, encountered a numerically superior enemy force and was held up by intense small arms and automatic weapons fire, with complete disregard for his own personal safety he voluntarily moved forward of the front lines, over open terrain, in order to rescue a wounded Marine. Throughout the entire action, he worked tirelessly and fearlessly in assisting in the treatment of wounded Marines until he was seriously wounded by enemy fire and had to be evacuated.

Chaplain Charles S. Pigott received a slight wound in the hand on 7 March. He was not incapacitated for duty. Chaplain Pigott later received a Letter of Commendation "for excellent service in the line of his profession while serving as Chaplain with a Marine infantry battalion during operations against the enemy in Korea from 2 January to 10 May 1951."

Chaplains Cited

Three other chaplains were awarded citations dur-

ing this campaign. Chaplain Henry E. Austin was honored with the Bronze Star and Chaplains Paul J. Knapp and Abner C. Cook with Letters of Commendation.

Chaplain Austin served with the 2d Battalion, 1st Marines at the front line in the central sector of Korea north of Wonju from 3 March to 4 April, when the Division was engaged in Operations Killer and Ripper. In his report to the Regimental Chaplain following this duty Chaplain Austin described in some detail the nature of his work. This account may be taken as typical of the activities of all Navy chaplains who lived up to the ideals and traditions of the Chaplain Corps while serving in Korea under combat conditions. Austin wrote:

The chaplain's zone of action was the battalion aid station, and at times our battalion aid station was as close as 20 yards from the fighting, and occasionally under fire. Since joining this battalion, I can sincerely say that none of our wounded has left the front without being seen by a chaplain. Throughout this portion of time, the 2d Bn had 102 men wounded in action, three of whom died as a result of wounds. In addition five men were killed in action. In four out of the eight deaths, I was able to hold a closing prayer before the men died (two Catholic and two Protestant prayers).

On 11 March, the 2d Bn "kicked off" on a forward push which was to take the men in various rifle companies on a ridge-hopping maneuver of anywhere from 50 to 65 miles up and down the steepest and most rugged terrain I have ever walked, much less carried a full pack. At night we were all so tired that we were just able to dig our "foxholes" before "hitting the rack." Suffice it is to say, the terrain was "terrific"!

On the afternoon and evening of 15 March, the battalion was under heavy fire. Chaplain Austin assisted the doctors and corpsmen in the evacuation and care of the wounded. "On that night," he reported, "it was impossible to evacuate two men . . . who were seriously wounded in the leg and groin by mortar fire. In both cases I helped Dr. Dow administer serum albumen, in addition to trying to give spiritual comfort to men who were obviously dying." He also helped in the evacuation of 47 wounded men that day by helicopters, "which acted as 'Angels of Mercy' ".

Carrying his violin with him to provide music, Austin managed during a month of most adverse conditions to hold 20 services, with an attendance of 1,710, and 290 receiving communion. In addition the chaplain reported 33 "decisions for Christ" and 14 baptisms.

Men travel many avenues to God; in the extremities of human experience some draw near to Him through fear. In the face of imminent death, the

Special Music.

A quintet of marines add to the worship service which is conducted by Chaplain Henry E. Austin out of doors.

values of life may stand out in clearer perspective. Some men, indifferent to other evangelical appeal, respond under circumstances when even the bravest are not ashamed to admit they are afraid. In any case men are likely to be more responsive to the ministry of a man of God who is sharing their own experiences. Whatever may be the final truth concerning "combat conversion," there can be little doubt that the combat chaplain is in a position to influence many who would hardly otherwise come within reach of a religious ministry.

Chaplain Austin was awarded the Bronze Star "for meritorious achievement in connection with operations against the enemy while serving with a Marine infantry battalion in Korea from 19 March 1951 to 4 April 1951." The citation continues in part:

Serving as battalion chaplain, Lieutenant Austin consistently displayed outstanding courage and devotion to duty

in ministering to the spiritual needs of the officers and men of the battalion. Frequently exposing himself without regard for his personal safety to intense enemy mortar, artillery, automatic weapons and small arms fire, he moved fearlessly with forward elements of the battalion in order to better perform his duties.

The two chaplains serving aboard the VALLEY FORGE received the Letter of Commendation for combat service in Korean waters for the period 25 June 1950 to 22 March 1951. Paul J. Knapp, the Roman Catholic chaplain, received a citation which states in part:

By his determination to make divine services and instructions available at all times of the day or night to the Catholic personnel, he rendered invaluable support to the high morale of that ship. The crew of his ship and its air group were inspired to accomplish greater achievements by his untiring devotion to the objectives of uplifting men's spirits and morale; thus, he contributed immeasurably to the successful conclusion of the ship's mission.

Baptism.

A Marine is baptized by Chaplain Solomon K. Johnson during a lull in the Korean fighting.

Abner R. Cook, senior chaplain aboard the VALLEY FORGE and a Protestant, was likewise commended for meritorious service. His citation reads in part:

Devoting himself with energy and tenacity to all phases of the mental health and welfare of the officers and men during the period of prolonged combat operations, he performed immeasurable service in maintaining high morale. His broad knowledge of spiritual needs in times of stress contributed greatly to the success of the operation.

Chaplains at Work

Not all chaplains serving with the Marines in Korea were in the combat zone nor were those attached to combat units on the front line all the time. As far as the exigencies of the situation allowed, combat battalions were rotated from the front lines to reserve. The ordinary duties of a Navy chaplain continued meanwhile. Divine Services were conducted, the sacraments administered, the sick and wounded visited, and countless numbers of consultations held. The difficulties attendant upon fighting a war became part of the normal routine. The unusual became the usual. Some of the chaplains reporting as replacements arrived without having had field training, but for the most part quickly adapted themselves to the difficult conditions.

The questionnaire sent out by the Chaplains Division in the spring of 1954 asked for an account of experiences which would illustrate unusual activities or initiative on the part of chaplains. In reply to this, Chaplain James S. Ferris, who is entitled to wear three battle stars for service in Korea, wrote: "Whatever initiative I have shown or taken is typical of all chaplains." Chaplain Leslie L. O'Connor commented:

I cannot claim any unusual activity or initiative out of the ordinary. I was there as a chaplain, pastor, friend, and comrade-without-arms during the guerrilla fighting between Andong and Pohang-Dong and during the first phase of "Operation Killer."

He told of visiting isolated companies of Marines in the guerrilla country with the armed chow truck carrying hot food and noted how appreciative the men were to see a chaplain. "Their smiles and conversation," wrote O'Connor, "was like the winsome gratefulness of a tired puppy."

Chaplains belonging to denominations practicing baptism by immersion often made use of clear running streams for that purpose. On one occasion Chaplain Austin baptized six Marines in the Pukhan River, while a congregation of native Koreans and military personnel gathered on the makeshift bridge over the swiftly flowing river.

An interesting and potentially dangerous episode in the UN advance concerns this same river. Rising in the mountains of North Korea the Pukhan flows into the Hwachon Reservoir and thence southeastward to its confluence with the Han River near Seoul. On 9 April the enemy opened several sluice gates of the Hwachon dam, thus destroying bridges on the lower river and providing a serious obstacle to the UN advance as the waters of the lower Pukhan rose swiftly.[9] A task force dispatched to wrest control of the dam failed; but the opening of the sluices actually affected UN operations less than had been feared and the mission was abandoned.

Chaplain George C. Bingaman described an unforgettable Communion service which he conducted as follows:

The service near Yangu in a rice paddy located near one of our Marine artillery battalions was interrupted by sniper fire directed at the chaplain preaching the communion sermon. It was the only time in my ministry where the congregation told the chaplain what the next act of the service was to be. I "hit the deck" like every other worshipping Marine, especially after they shouted to me to do so.

The coincidence was most unusual. I had been developing the point in my sermon on "faith" that this attitude was an everyday feeling of confidence in God. At this point came the sniper interlude. This served excellently to illus-

[9] Miller *et al., op. cit.,* pp. 25f.

trate the second point which I was to make—that faith is also common sense. One should not ask God to do what you can do for yourself. In this case it was divine expediency to "duck" rather than to depend completely upon God to influence the sniper to miss his aim in your direction. This unusual incident has always been a lesson to me illustrating the fact that God expects us to do as much as we can for ourselves, including the protection and safeguarding of men, women, and children from aggression and attack.

Chaplain Garson Goodman was the Jewish chaplain with the 1st Marine Division from 6 July 1950 to 22 May 1951. While his peculiar responsibility was a ministry to men of the Jewish faith in the Division, he found many opportunities to serve men of other faiths and to assist in the work for civilian refugees and orphans. Commenting on his work, Chaplain Goodman wrote:

Not only did I carry out my duties as the only Jewish Chaplain for the entire Division, but I also served men of all faiths in my battalion. On one occasion while assigned to the medical battalion, I went without sleep for a 48-hour period serving the wounded and assisting the corpsmen as necessary. While attached to the Ordnance Battalion, I saw to it that a chapel was built for the specific purpose of worship. I set up a smoothly running library, and for the first time all the men were well supplied with writing paper, pens, and all toilet articles which I had "procured" from stateside organizations and other sources. In addition to being the chaplain, I was the special services officer and librarian. The greatest satisfaction derived was that the men found a true friend in their chaplain under all circumstances.

Easter 1951

Nor were other Navy chaplains any less busy. Easter Day was on 25 March in 1951, and was everywhere celebrated with appropriate religious observances. Chaplain E. R. Barnes reported a Sunrise Service on the flight deck of the PHILIPPINE SEA for not only his ship's personnel but all forces afloat in Yokosuka harbor. Chaplain Arthur J. Wartes, on board the repair ship JASON since October 1950, also reported a sunrise service on the top deck. Doubtless there were many others.

The following account by Chaplain Charles H. Swift, Jr., was sent in as part of his questionnaire reply.

On Easter Day, 1951, services were conducted at Naval Air Facility, Oppama, outdoors, as the chapel space was too small. An LST which had been converted to an ARVE [aircraft repair ship (engine)], the USS AVENTINUS, was moored bow first at the seaplane ramp. With the bow doors open and the ramp down, this formed a setting for the altar. The ship's company had made a large white cross which hung in the opening against a background of blue curtains. Greenery and flowers decorated the opening and formed a frame around it. The altar and pulpit were set up on the ramp. This beautiful setting, with the sun coming up in

the East, recalled to mind that beautiful song, "Let Us Break Bread Together on Our Knees."

Oppama is fairly close to the great port city of Yokosuka. The Naval Air Facility was mainly concerned with the maintenance and repair of carriers and aircraft.

Chaplain James D. Hester, aboard the THOMAS JEFFERSON, a transport operating under MSTS, Pacific, out of San Francisco, from January to July 1951, wrote in his questionnaire of Easter celebrations as the ship carried personnel replacements toward the Far East.

The chaplain had made provision before leaving stateside to provide as fully as possible for all the familiar decorations. These were used in both the Protestant and Catholic services. This particular group of replacements was landed at Pusan, airlifted to the perimeter of the forward battle line, and three days after leaving the ship committed to battle. On the next trip out it was learned that this group had suffered heavy casualties—about thirty per cent. It was comforting to the chaplain to remember that only 10 days previously they had knelt on the deck at the Communion Table and received the Sacrament of the Lord's Supper.

In the 1st Marine Division, as far as operations allowed, special services were planned for Holy Week and Easter. During Holy Week weather had been pleasant but it rained all day on Easter. Travel was difficult as the chaplains "rode the circuit" of their several separated units. Chaplain G. C. Bingaman, stationed with the Amphibious Tractor Battalion, held a service which he later described in the following fashion.

Easter—1951.

Chaplain R. E. Jenkins holds an Easter sunrise service for the 5th Marines.

Mass is said by Chaplain Joseph Fitzgerald.

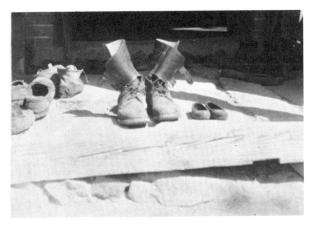

Shoes.

In deference to Korean custom, marines attending worship at Poon-suwon Church leave their dusty field shoes at the entrance, alongside the sandals worn by Korean worshippers.

In Masan, Korea, 1951, there was a most unusual Easter Day. Seven Korean Protestant congregations had committed themselves and their choirs to worship with us in a beautiful mountain spot overlooking the local harbor. Their combined choirs had rehearsed frequently. The Marines erected a huge cross constructed from the native pine trees. The service was anticipated with a great deal of interest.

On Easter morning a steady downpour of rain ruled out any thought of an outdoor service. Many Marines assumed the chaplain would cancel the service. However, we had an emergency plan—to set up indoor services in our Motor Transport area. Fifty Marines braved the elements to attend the indoor service. Most of us began to feel, like many who had stayed in their sleeping bags, that the Koreans would not come because of the storm.

A few minutes before the service time our trucks arrived in camp with almost 100 Koreans, dressed in their finest, soaked to the skin because they had no protection from the rain. They sang the great hymns of Christendom while they approached our area. Never before in so dismal a situation had I celebrated a more triumphant Day of Resurrection.

Korean Christians

Contacts with Korean Christians became a normal part of the experience of all the chaplains serving there. On many occasions Koreans attended Divine Services conducted by the chaplains. Joseph D. McDonald described one such experience.

While offering Mass in a valley, about 75 Korean civilians were in attendance. Where they came from was doubtful. The area was under attack not infrequently. Their manifestation of faith and gratitude was indeed a source of edification even to the troops.

The chaplain was called to baptize a 2-year-old infant. No missionary had been in that area for over 2 years.

Often chaplains were able to conduct services for the Koreans. Chaplain Thomas B. Uber II reported holding weekly services for "120 South Koreans attached to a labor battalion assigned to my unit," speaking through an interpreter. At the request of the United Nations Command, the Republic of Korea had organized a Civil Transport Corps, largely members of the ROK National Guard who lacked sufficient training for military service. Willing native laborers were plentiful, for they received not only food and clothing but also pay. Formed into companies, they were especially useful during the spring of 1951; working their way forward on foot, carrying tremendous loads on the traditional "A-frame" supported on their backs, these native laborers furnished logistical support for the northward drive when military vehicles were often bogged to the hubs in heavy mud.

When Chaplain Joseph C. Fitzgerald heard confessions, said Mass and gave Communion to a congregation of about 100 Koreans and 40 Marine artillerymen in the bullet-pocked church in Poon-suwon, those Koreans had the ministry of their church for the first time since invading Communists had murdered their native priest the summer before. As reported by combat correspondent Sergeant Ted Sell, USMCR, there were among the women with their immaculately white linen headpieces only five men, four grandfathers and one cripple; the rest were off fighting. During the service American bombers droned overhead; outside a bulldozer pulled off the road to allow an ambulance to pass on its way to the rear. Once more a chaplain of the Navy had fulfilled his duty as a servant of man and God; scenes vary and circumstances change, but the Word of God standeth ever sure.

Special Services

Chaplains have long been concerned with morale activities as well as their more distinctively religious ministry. Indeed, on occasion some commands have seemed to treat their Chaplain Section as a glorified recreation department. Sometimes individual chaplains have gone along with such an interpretation of their duties; under some circumstances chaplains have become involved in serious difficulties because of disagreements with their commands over the extent and character of their collateral duties. Since moral character, spiritual vitality, and high morale are likely to be intimately related, written directives are not usually sufficient to define precisely the chaplain's duties within the command responsibility for the total welfare of its personnel.

Cooperation with Navy Relief and American Red Cross activities, the administration of libraries, the organization and execution of athletic and recreational programs—these and many more collateral duties have fallen to the lot of chaplains. In general those serving with Marines have had fewer such assignments than those serving other naval activities, especially, of course, in ships. A Marine Division has a Special Services Section, operated on every echelon from division throughout battalion; its duties, like those of the Chaplain Section, are spelled out by official regulations but their implementation naturally varies with circumstances.

On 31 March Division Chaplain Kelly wrote to the Chief:

I had quite a discussion with our Division special services officer, Lieutenant Colonel Batham, about where there might be confusion or overlapping of our [respective duties.] I had in mind particularly the recommendation of your meeting of District and Force Chaplains concerning collateral duties. We both are of the opinion that most commanding officers have no idea of the large scope of special services. They believe that a special services officer merely arranges ball games, shows and movies.

So we decided to draw up a resume of special services duties and chaplain duties, [then] visit the various commanding officers and discuss the entire problem. [We hoped] to give the CO's a clearer view of the importance of special services with the hope that better fitted officers be assigned to that post, who will not have to depend on the chaplain.

When asked if the special services officer could be a chaplain, I agreed with qualifications. And they were, that I would first discuss the situation with the individual chaplains in the smaller units and if they feel that they could first do a 100 percent job as a chaplain [and then] have reasonable time to devote to special services, it would be agreeable. However,

with the larger units, such as regiments, I felt that being a chaplain was a full time job.

So when we have threshed this out completely, armed with the Special Services Manual, Chaplain's Manual, Marine Corps Manual, and the recommendations of your conference, we will approach the Chief of Staff. If he agrees, we will approach the unit CO's. The two of us appearing together will remove any thought of conflict between departments, or that I am trying to get the chaplains out of something reasonably in their department. Colonel Batham is wholeheartedly in favor of this solution and feels that it will benefit his department.

Relief Work

One of the notable aspects of the work of Navy chaplains in Korea during and especially after hostilities was the extensive relief work carried on under their direction for thousands of Korean refugees.

Reference was made in his answer to the questionnaire by Chaplain Lawrence R. Phillips, a Protestant, to what was doubtless the first work of Marines with Korean orphans. He wrote:

Upon entry of Inchon I found the Catholic church with some 40 orphans. Through cooperation with Marine authorities food, medicine, and clothes were gathered for the immediate relief of the situation.

Soon such charitable endeavor became a normal part of the work of chaplains and Marines. Chaplain Schwyhart wrote to Chief of Chaplains S. W. Salisbury on 16 February 1951:

A great portion of this week has been devoted to the distribution of 800 boxes of Marine Corps League gifts of clothing, shoes, and toys given by the children of American Marines to the children of Korea. In cooperation with the civil affairs officer, we made distribution in 5 cities and villages to an estimated 15,000 children. It was an experience I shall not soon forget.

In his reply to the questionnaire Schwyhart enlarged on that particular effort. He wrote:

During the first week in February 1951, at which time the 1st Marine Division was in the area of Pohang-dong on the east coast of central Korea, a large shipment of clothing, shoes, and toys arrived by LST from Pusan. This shipment, totaling about 800 boxes, had been collected in east coast cities of the United States by the Marine Corps League and shipped to the 1st Marine Division for distribution to children in Korea. The commanding general of the 1st Marine Division appointed me to organize the distribution. A staff of several officers and many enlisted Marines aided in the distribution at three local points in the area of Pohang-dong. It was estimated that approximately 25,000 children received some item of clothing, shoes, or a toy on the date of distribution, which was 12 February 1951. The mayor of the city of Pohang-dong and all school principals aided in organizing the civilian community in the distribution of clothing.

If the number of distribution centers had been reduced from 5 to 3, the estimated number of children had risen from 15,000 to 25,000. Perhaps the chaplain had received further information! Still, nothing can dim the luster of what was in fact a notable example of American philanthropy and Christian brotherhood.

After the front lines became more established, the chaplains were later able to organize their relief work on a more permanent basis. Individual units of the fighting forces often accepted the responsibility of supporting a Korean orphanage in whole or in part. The pitiable condition of the homeless waifs of Korea gripped the hearts of the American service men. Chaplain W. M. Hearn described how the men of his unit sometimes "adopted" orphans. Hearn wrote:

> One time when we moved out we had three little girls who had lost their parents. We took them back to a MG [military government] unit to be sent to a home, but the whole company were like a bunch of bereaved parents. The fathers in the HQ company who had little girls at home helped to take care of them. When we gave them a bath we found that they each wore five to seven dresses, all of their worldly goods.

> At another time we left a boy at an orphanage and found him back in 2 days—a walk of several miles. Many times we had Koreans in our church services. One boy was quite disturbed by the undignified slouch of our men during services. As he demonstrated, they should sit erect with folded hands or bow their heads and hold their hands together during prayer.

Guide.

Chaplain R. L. Patton leads two small children to safety somewhere near the front.

Many of the chaplains wrote letters to churches, service clubs, relief organizations, and individuals in the States urging them to send clothing, toys, and other needed items to be given to the needy and destitute children of Korea, innocent pawns of war.

Particularly impressive was the initiative shown by the Marines in contributing money, materials, and labor for the rebuilding of churches, schools, and orphanages. The generosity of the Marines confronted by the needs of civilian Korean refugees proved to be a constantly recurrent theme throughout the story of UN operations there.

Marine Air Wing

After the evacuation at Hungnam the 1st Marine Aircraft Wing had found itself involved in the relocation problems of the 5th Air Force. Only a limited number of usable fields were available; and with the fall of Kimpo in the January Communist offensive Far East Air Forces, the senior air command, had pulled many of its units back to Itazuke, Japan, including the jet aircraft which could not operate from any of the available Korean fields. Headquarters of the 5th Air Force, as well as that of 8th Army, were installed at Taegu.

Maj. Gen. Field Harris, Commanding General of the 1st Marine Aircraft Wing, settled both his Wing headquarters and those of both Marine Aircraft Group 12 and Marine Aircraft Group 33 at Itami, the Air Force base near Osaka, Japan which had been assigned the Wing in August 1950 by agreement between Commanding General, Far East Air Forces and the Commander, Naval Forces Far East.[10] Itami had been all along the Wing's center for personnel reassignment, supply, and repair. On 10 January 1951 there began a giant airlift of personnel replacements from the West Coast, and eventually Itami became the air terminal for Marines en route to the Division in Korea.

After helping cover 8th Army's withdrawal in western Korea, operating off the carriers SICILY, BADOENG STRAIT, and BATAAN, the tactical squadrons were at Itami for repairs and training. When in February they returned to combat the

[10] Brief notices in Lynn Montross, "Buttoning up the Offensive: The Marines in Operation Killer," *Marine Corps Gazette* (February 1952), pp. 35f; Montross, "Advance to the 38th Parallel: The Marines in Operation Ripper," *Marine Corps Gazette* (March 1952), p. 21.

The author was kindly permitted by Mr. Montross, of the Historical Branch, G–3, Marine Corps Headquarters, to read the first draft of vol. IV, the official Marine Corps history of operations during the period here under consideration. Ch. I (Addendum: Redeployment of the 1st Marine Aircraft Wing) and ch. II are concerned with the Air Wing.

various squadrons came under direct Air Force control, and were no longer immediately at the call of Marine ground units in accordance with Navy-Marine Corps close air support doctrine. By March first six squadrons were in combat, four operating from Pusan, one from Pohang, and one carrier-based. During the UN counteroffensive they supported other 8th Army units as well as the 1st Marine Division.

The 1st Marine Aircraft Wing was awarded a Republic of Korea Presidential Unit Citation for its support of the United Nations effort, from 3 August 1950 to 26 February 1951. The earlier date marks the 1st Marine air strike over Korea, by eight Corsairs of VMF–214, operating from the SICILY.

Air Wing Chaplains

Concerning the chaplains Wing Chaplain John P. Murphy wrote to the Chief of Chaplains on 18 April as follows:

Since the middle of February MAG 33 has occupied a field near Pohang and Chaplains [John H.] Markley and [Charles E.] Webb are stationed there. The Wing and MAG 12 have been together near Pusan and Chaplain [George W.] Cummins and I have been there.

While we have provided fair coverage we have not done as good a job as we should and would if we were up to T/O strength. There has been a great increase in the number of personnel attached to Marine Tactical Air Control Squadron and their T/O calls for a chaplain. They are scattered all over and it is tough not to be able to care for their small groups.

This has left the Marine Wing Service Squadron at Itami with Marine and Naval personnel numbering one thousand to be cared for by Catholic civilian clergy and an Air Force Protestant chaplain.

Now a couple of squadrons of MAG 12 have been sent to Seoul and I have not yet decided how best to cover them. It was because of this pressure that the Commanding General on 22 March sent the following dispatch to BuPers.

From: C. G. 1st MAW
To: BuPers
Infor: CMC

Table organization 1st Marine Air Wing presently understrength two chaplains X Wide dispersion units this command necessitates complement X one Catholic one Protestant needed to accomplish mission.

Far be it from me to attempt to say what is going to happen in Korea and what future disposition the Air Force is going to make of the 1st MAW, but with the present setup there should be, as the T/O provides, two chaplains with each MAG, one with MTACS, and one with the Wing. Further there should be one more chaplain to take care of MWSS1, the Wing's service squadron at Itami . . . There are several Army hospitals in the Osaka-Kobe area and a number of Marine and Navy casualties are sent there. Liaison work as well as taking care of our own will keep a chaplain as busy as a cat on a tin roof.

At Pohang the chaplains of Marine Aircraft Group 33 secured from their Commanding Officer two Quonset huts to be erected into a chapel. There was one hitch: assembling a Quonset hut requires the use of no less than 5,500 screws! Two Quonset huts, 11,000 screws! Chaplain Webb wrote in his questionnaire:

About 20 Marines cooperated without hesitation or complaint in this thankless task during their off duty hours. [Both Catholics and Protestants], they had been subjected to the very poor acoustics of a large and "holey" hospital tent and realized its deficiencies in contrast to the relative solidity of the Quonset hut for Divine Services.

Noting that these Marines sacrificed their time and energy ungrudgingly, he added:

While this kind of spirit endures, we chaplains know that there will always be a definite, concerted core of strength on the side of God.

He concluded: "I did not remain long enough in Korea to witness the finished product but have heard that Chaplain Cleaves carried the project to a successful completion."

Seaborne Artillery

While UN ground and air forces continued their assault against the Chinese Communists, naval forces prosecuted their assigned missions with vigor and success. According to the authors of *The Sea War in Korea*[11] there were five ways in which the Navy kept the Communists on the run after UN forces resumed the offensive following the forced withdrawals of December and early January 1951. Amphibious demonstrations were made again and again; mindful of the decisive nature of the Inchon landing, the Reds were sensitive to the danger of surprise attack and of course never knew, until the critical moment had passed, whether such movements were feints (as they were) or the "real McCoy."

Further contributing to keeping the enemy off-balance were frequent commando raids put ashore and covered by naval gunfire. Heavy bombardment was utilized to lay siege to important Communist ports, notably Wonsan; there round-the-clock interdiction began on 16 February and continued to the beginning of the armistice, on 27 July 1953, the longest such operation in modern American naval history.[12] Besides Wonsan two other east coast ports, Hungnam and Songjin, in the far north, were besieged.

A fourth technique was naval gunfire against the

---

[11] Cagle and Manson, *op. cit.*, pp. 305f.
[12] *Ibid.*, ch. 12.

coastal flanks of the enemy frontline, directed by forward reconnaissance upon enemy troop, armament, and supply concentrations. And finally, along the enemy's exposed coastline, bombardment was maintained unremittingly against all major military targets, inflicting both physical and psychological damage.

Seaborne Padres

Illustrative of the difficulties under which chaplains carried on their ministry during this period are several paragraphs from the questionnaire reply of Chaplain Oscar J. Harris, who was attached to Destroyer Squadron 16 from August 1950 to September 1951. He wrote, in part, as follows:

On a destroyer in the combat area Divine Services were not conducted according to schedule. A time might be set, but chances were the schedule would be interrupted. In many instances the chaplain would have to wait until after the evening meal. . . .

Attendance was good considering the difficult routine the men had to endure. Their rest periods were interrupted by constant general quarters and watch-standing. Every opportunity they had to "sack in" they took full advantage of.

In one instance the chaplain was conducting a service when general quarters sounded. The sonarmen thought a submarine was lurking in nearby waters. After a 2-hour chase and discharging several depth charges, it was discovered that a few whales had been playing havoc on the sonar gear. Result: no Divine Service.

Duty of a different sort is illustrated by the following excerpts from a letter to Chaplain Salisbury on 15 February 1951, in which Chaplain Edward E. Helmich told of his work in the amphibious flagship MOUNT McKINLEY.

We have just completed a very successful campaign for the March of Dimes and the Ship's Company and Staff responded with a total of $1,422 collected and sent via channels to the national foundation. The average came to $1.74 per person.

Attendance at Divine Service has showed a marked increase, and what pleases me especially is the large percentage of officers attending. . . . There has also been a definite upswing in attendance at the Sacrament of Holy Communion. Then too, a Sunday Bible Class, recently organized with an average attendance of 27 thus far, indicates a definite interest and appreciation for such a class.

Several weeks ago I was able to secure the Korean Navy Information and Education Music Group—a 45-piece symphony orchestra and 60-voice choral group—for a series of 3 concerts. All of us were more than pleased with the renditions.

The Bridge of Toko-ri

Diverted from their attack upon Yalu River bridges, carrier planes of Task Force 77 were employed from the end of January 1951 in attempting to disrupt the railway network in eastern Korea over which reinforcements and supplies were moving to the front.[13] Three main lines running south from Manchuria provided plenty of targets: 956 bridges and 231 tunnels, an average of 1 bridge every 1.2 miles of track, 1 tunnel every 5.

On 2 March a PRINCETON pilot spotted the nearly perfect target: a six-span bridge 600 feet long and sixty feet above the floor of what the flyers came to call "Carlson's Canyon," a tunnel at each end, and paralleled by a partially completed second bridge. It was this which became James Michener's *Bridge of Toko-ri*. Exactly a month was spent bombing it; again and again the Reds desperately repaired it, until finally they took the only alternative and built a bypass through the canyon on low ground.

Involved in this "struggle to strangle" were the carriers VALLEY FORGE, PRINCETON, and PHILIPPINE SEA. On 27 March "Old Faithful," the VALLEY FORGE, was relieved by the BOXER, aboard which was the first carrier air group composed of organized Naval Air Reserve Squadrons to see duty in Korea. The LEYTE had left the Korean theater on 19 January. Concerning her skipper Chaplain C. A. Frame later recalled:

The captain of our ship was (and is) a fine man. If he had a problem troubling him, he would call the chaplain in and ask for spiritual guidance. We usually ended by having prayer together. I felt that those talks and prayers helped in some way to clarify his mind and make it easier for him to carry on his difficult mission. Needless to say, it always made the chaplain feel very humble and inadequate.

PatRons

The necessary but largely routine activities of support groups tend to get lost in the backwash of the "shootin' war." Everyone recalls the poignantly humorous efforts of "Mister Roberts" to get a transfer from his rusty supply ship to the firing lines of World War II. In the Korean War, as always, various units devoted themselves to the faithful performance of duties almost guaranteed never to make a stateside headline.

Among such were the Navy patrol squadrons (PatRons) whose vigilance added greatly to the effectiveness of 7th Fleet operations in the Far East.[14] Surveillance of merchant shipping, antisubmarine patrol, weather reconnaissance, aerial mine spotting and destruction, occasional flaredrops for Marine night-fighting planes and naval gunfire target spotting, and even logistical transport—such were the

[13] *Ibid.*, pp. 229–236.
[14] *Ibid.*, ch. 10 and app. V.

duties of men rarely in the limelight except when rare encounters with Chinese aircraft or surface vessels momentarily emphasized their continuing contribution.

Under overall control of Fleet Air Japan, the PatRons, both land and seaplanes, were grouped in two headquarters. Fleet Air Wing Six at Itwakuni, Japan, with three to five squadrons plus seaplane tenders, was responsible for operations in the vicinity of Japan and Korea, from Siberia south to Okinawa. Fleet Air Wing one, consisting of one land-based squadron (at Naha, Okinawa) and one seaplane squadron aboard a tender, exercised surveillance of the international sea lanes south through the East China Sea and the Straits of Formosa to the Philippines. Its tender anchored off the Pescadores Islands except when typhoons forced them to sea.

Based in the Pescadores were some 40,000 Chinese Nationalist troops. No Americans had been seen there since World War II. There were nothing but squalid villages ashore and consequently no liberty for naval personnel. Chaplain William W. Parkinson served in the seaplane tender PINE ISLAND, first at Iwakuni and after June 1951 off the Pescadores. In an interview with the author Parkinson recalled the situation. Swimming was prohibited, though occasionally the men were allowed ashore long enough to play baseball. It was naturally difficult to maintain *esprit*. The men were bored, their work was monotonous, and like many others they wondered why they were there at all. As the only Navy chaplain in the Formosan area, Parkinson ministered to the ship's company and the flyers who were running daily patrol missions, trying to meet some of their needs with daily religious services and by regular, sustained contact with all personnel.—

Parkinson was followed in the PINE ISLAND by Robert L. McCachran in May 1952. The SALISBURY SOUND had as its first chaplain Daniel M. Jordan, after October 1950, and then Richard P. Chase, after August 1952.

MSTS

At the outbreak of Korean hostilities George W. Thompson was Staff Chaplain, Deputy Commander, Military Sea Transport Service, Pacific, in San Francisco. In assigning Thompson to this new billet Chief of Chaplains S. W. Salisbury had written on 30 September 1949:

We will keep you informed of developments but you can know that it will be your responsibility to insure perfect integration of Navy chaplains into this new type work as we take over from the Army between 1 October 1949 and 1 April 1950.

The Military Sea Transport Service had been organized in 1949 as part of the unification program, to handle all ocean transportation of both personnel and materiel for all the Armed Forces. The responsibilities of the Chaplain Corps in this development were set forth by Chaplain Salisbury in a Memorandum of 3 October 1949 to all Fleet, Force, and District Chaplains, from which the following extracts are taken.

In accordance with this policy, present plans call for a chaplain to be attached to the Staff of Deputy Commander, MSTS, Atlantic Area (New York City), Deputy Commander, MSTS, Pacific Area (San Francisco, Calif.), and Deputy Commander, MSTS, North Pacific Area (Seattle, Wash.). Chaplains being nominated for these billets are: Chaplain George W. Thompson for San Francisco, Chaplain Daniel S. Rankin for New York, and Chaplain Seth E. Anderson for Seattle. It is planned to cover the Gulf Area (New Orleans) by giving additional duty to the District Chaplain, 8th Naval District. A chaplain from the Chaplains Division, BuPers, will have additional duty on the Staff of Headquarters, MSTS, in the Navy Department. All other chaplains assigned to the MSTS will serve aboard the vessels of this service.

At least one-tenth of our Corps will be in this given field at all times. The whole rotation schedule may have to be revamped with a return to the old days when there was more Sea Duty than Shore Duty. All chaplains assigned to MSTS will have the responsibility of not only doing their immediate job, but also of setting a pattern that will continue the high standard of service for which the Navy is noted and in which our Corps takes pride.

The transfer of ships and embarkation facilities from Army to MSTS took place during the following months with less difficulty than might have been the case; and fortunately so, for midsummer 1950 brought skyrocketing demands upon sea transport. Of Chaplain Seth E. Anderson, Staff Chaplain, MSTS, North Pacific, the Army Port of Embarkation chaplain had written to the Chief:

This transfer . . . could prove to be a difficult project should understanding and cooperation be lacking by any parties concerned. Chaplain Anderson's fairness, sincerity, and enthusiastic willingness to cooperate makes a difficult problem easier to solve.

If all Navy chaplains assigned to MSTS measure up to the high standard which Chaplain Anderson has already established [here], there will be no occasion for the least concern on your part about the success of chaplains who are undertaking this new project under your supervision.

Chaplain Anderson was relieved by Chaplain Edgar C. Andrews, who reported 14 September 1950. Chaplain Thompson served in San Francisco from October 1949 to October 1952. By 1 March 1950, when the Navy assumed full command responsibility for MSTS, he had completed the indoctrination of all the chaplains assigned duty in ships of MSTS, Pacific, written a syllabus for their guidance in program planning, and taken responsibility for supplying audiovisual equipment and religious supplies to all ships of the command. Later he took on the further job of procuring and shipping, in the custody of MSTS ships' chaplains, religious supplies for the use of chaplains in the war theater.

Chaplains assigned MSTS duty were attached to the headquarters command and under the direction of the supervisory chaplains rotated among the various ships to meet the greatest need. While aboard, chaplains were temporarily attached to the Military Department of the vessel.

Itinerating

The plan may be illustrated by reference to the questionnaire replies of several of the chaplains. John W. Myrose, for instance, wrote:

[I was] attached to Military Sea Transportation Service, North Pacific Sub Area, Seattle, Wash., for duty afloat aboard USNS transports operating between Seattle and the Far East. This duty was from 25 August 1950 to 25 August 1952. Because of a shortage of chaplains there was a rotation from one ship to another. I was aboard the following ships at various times in both Japanese and Korean waters: USNS JAMES O'HARA, USNS GEN. LEROY ELTINGE, USNS PVT. SADAO S. MUNEMORI, USNS MARINE PHOENIX, and USNS GEN. R. L. HOWZE.

He reported a high percentage of attendance at Divine Services, daily and Sunday, on both east and west crossings. "Over 8,600 men attended services during one round trip during which a total of 12,000 were aboard, 3,000 at a time."

Chaplain Cecil V. Marley had served in two different transports under MSTS, North Pacific, before the Korean War began. From August 1950 to November 1951 he was in the SITKOH BAY, an aircraft carrier operating under MSTS to ferry planes from the United States to the theater of war. (SITKOH BAY was employed, for instance, in moving two squadrons of Marine fighters when the 1st Marine Aircraft Wing was deployed to Japan in late August 1950.)

Chaplain Paul R. Elliott reported the following tour of duty:

USNS GEN. M. C. MEIGS_ December 1950–January 1951
USNS PVT. SADAO S. January 1951–May 1951
    MUNEMORI.
USNS GEN. S. B. BUCK- May 1951–July 1951
    NER.

Chaplain Prescott B. Wintersteen served in the MARINE PHOENIX from August 1950 to March 1951, and in the GEN. HUGH J. GAFFEY from March to November 1951. Chaplain Franklin C. Black reported duty in the C. C. BALLOU during August and September 1950, and then in the FRED C. AINSWORTH from October 1950 to March 1951.

Services

Chaplain Ernest L. Carter, whose exact itinerary was not furnished, wrote concerning his work:

Aboard ship we had daily noon hour devotional services for all faiths, using recorded hymns and prayers from the prayer books of the different faiths. Protestants, Catholics, Jews, Christian Scientists, Seventh Day Adventists, Latter Day Saints, and Greek Orthodox personnel attended these services.

Carter also edited the ship's paper, supervised the library, and had responsibility for recreation and entertainment on various ships. Following the Hungnam evacuation he wrote:

With the last ones from the bridge on our ship, and traveling in blackout, after the noise of battlefire from shore and ships for 11 days and nights, at the Christmas Eve service we sang "Silent Night" in three languages: Americans in English, Puerto Ricans in Spanish, and Koreans in Korean, singing both separately and together. This was a very impressive occasion for everyone and they were glad to be alive.

Chaplain Beryl L. Burr reported over 75 percent of the men aboard in attendance at Divine Service after the departure from Hungnam. Services were held hourly from 0800 through 1300.

"Over 400 attended daily services at both Protestant and Catholic services aboard MSTS ships going to Korea," reported Chaplain Edwin W. Andrews, who served with MSTS, North Pacific, from August 1951 to August 1953. And Chaplain Allen L. Irwin wrote: "Daily services on transport with men en route to battle areas during Korean conflict were especially well attended and their response was excellent. About 50 such services were held, with a total attendance of over 8,000."

Chaplain Charles W. Adams held services every day on transports carrying troops to Korea. "As many as 11 services a Sunday were held on the way to Pusan," he wrote. "Chaplains worked night and day on the many personnel problems that came to the office." He distributed "thousands of New Testaments" and some 2,500 copies of the whole Bible, very few of which were left aboard when troops debarked.

Chaplain William R. Petre wrote in his questionnaire reply:

A group of men requested the establishment of a weekly meeting of prayer, worship, and spiritual refreshment in addition to the regularly scheduled services. This was done, and largely run by the men themselves. It was an excellent means of religious growth. On the troopship the religious quest of the men was of a high order. Men going into combat eagerly sought a personal relation with God.

Chaplain John E. Watts was accustomed to hold three Sunday morning services and a late afternoon vesper service, on deck, weather permitting. Chaplain Elliott noted, in addition to religious duties, establishment of classes for the study of Japanese and Korean, taught by personnel aboard familiar with those languages.

Chaplain James R. Marks submitted the following account along with his questionnaire.

A large number of Marines came aboard the GENERAL GREELY at a Japanese port for the trip to Korea. Shortly after the ship got underway I announced that religious services would be held in the designated compartment, three decks below the main deck. Two Protestant services were scheduled that afternoon. A Roman Catholic rosary service was scheduled for an early hour next day.

All preparations were made and the word was passed that Holy Communion would be observed at 1500. Before the organist had completed his prelude, the room was filled. All chairs were occupied. Other Marines were sitting in every available spot on the deck. A few stood against the bulkhead. The majority of those present received Communion. It was nearly 1600 when the service was completed. Several minutes were required to empty the compartment, but during that time two Marines approached me to say there were some who came to the service but could not get into the compartment. I told them another service was just about to begin. I was surprised to see the compartment almost full the second time.

Chaplain Marks also reported many baptisms on his several trips. Always he required the candidate to come to his stateroom for an interview and instruction "in order that each person would have an understanding of its religious import." On each occasion, usually in the evening, the candidate came to the chaplain's room accompanied by two witnesses and there "accepted Jesus Christ as his personal Saviour and Lord."

In attempting to assess the ministry of all the chaplains it must not be forgotten, however, that there *are* atheists in foxholes and that often piety evaporates in direct proportion as the pressure lets up. Men in uniform are hardly different in this regard from any others. One chaplain wrote after he had returned from a tour of duty with Marines, "The sacraments became less important in the lives of the men [back home] than had been the case [in Korea]." And one MSTS chaplain observed: "Going to Korea attendance at Holy Communion was very high; but on coming home, troops returning had again relapsed into the normal tendencies of home life."

"Operation Welcome"

Service of a different sort was inaugurated in 1951 by MSTS Chaplain Edwin W. Andrews. Noticing how shy and obviously nervous were the Japanese brides traveling in the USNS M. M. PATRICK with their servicemen husbands to life in the States, he began a series of informal lectures, suggested by the orientation program chaplains have long given troops bound overseas. He told them something of our customs, government, religions, and life in our cities and on our farms, and followed with a question period. Later he added education films, such as "This Is America," an account of small-town life, and "Our Nation's Capital," a documentary about the Federal Government. Sometimes an interpreter was needed but one was always found. On one trip there were 31 "war brides" and their husbands. "I like to think my lectures and movies help some of the girls adjust to life in the United States," the chaplain was quoted in a Navy press release. "The girls enjoy it and perhaps it helps them a little. That makes it all worth while."

Annual Report

The following data, from Chaplain Allen L. Irwin's annual report to the Secretary of the Navy for calendar year 1950, may illustrate the work of MSTS chaplains. Recalled to active duty in August 1950, he was assigned to MSTS and spent 2 weeks aboard the GEN. M. M. PATRICK undergoing indoctrination. Next he served aboard GEN. M. B. STEWART on a crossing to the Far East. Detached in October he flew back from Tokyo to Seattle, where he served as Assistant to the Staff Chaplain, MSTS, North Pacific. In December he was assigned to the M. M. PATRICK.

Aboard ship basic duties were performed as follows:

1. Conduct of Protestant Divine Services and administration of the sacraments.

2. Supervision of daily Protestant devotional service conducted by myself and/or passenger chaplains.

3. Provision for Roman Catholic Mass, Sundays and daily, when a passenger chaplain was available; assistance to the Roman Catholic chaplain as needed and desired for confessions, choir practice, supplies and equipment; provisions for Roman Catholic Rosary Service when no Roman Catholic chaplain was aboard.

4. Provision for Jewish Divine Service when a sufficient number of interested personnel was on board.

5. Facilitation of meetings for other distinctive religious groups as desired.

6. Arranging church parties as needed.

7. Parish visitations: sick bay, brig, in dayrooms, about decks and living quarters.

8. Personal counseling.

9. Christian instruction.

10. Procurement and distribution of New Testaments, devotional materials, and religious supplies.

11. Orientation of passenger chaplains.

12. Participation in orientation periods for voyage staff and passengers.

13. Presentations of chaplain's lectures on "Citizenship and Morale" in the Troop Information and Education Program.

14. Extension of aid to advanced base chaplains through provision of supplies, extension of ship hospitality, and Christian Fellowship.

Chaplain Irwin's duties in Seattle indicate what the Staff Chaplain's office was doing to aid chaplains in the ships. He supervised a supply warehouse, procuring, and distributing gear aboard ship. He assisted the Staff Chaplain in "unofficial" inspection of the ships' chaplains' work, in maintaining liaison with the Army Port Chaplain, and in counseling MSTS personnel and their dependents. Further, he maintained liaison with civilian religious groups and service clubs, occasionally "supplied" for chaplains, and participated in civilian religious services.

A composite typical work day aboard ship might go as follows:

0730 Breakfast.

0800 Check in office; plan work of the day; arrange for daily services.

0945 Brief conferences with passenger chaplains; check on newspaper.

1000 Instruction classes; personal counseling; study; preparation of services or administrative work.

1130 Lunch and free period.

1300 Check on libraries, special services, movie program, newspaper; administrative work.

1400 Visitation, about decks, in recreation rooms, and living quarters.

1500 Instruction classes, personal counseling; study or administrative work.

1630 Supper.

1715 Visits to sick bay and brig.

1800 Check on movies; free time for attending movies, social visitation or study.

2000 "Coffee hour" and social visitation; conferences with chaplains, or free time.

2230 Personal devotions and lights out.

But, he added, "this is a highly theoretical day, as the program was adapted to the various needs according to the stage of the voyage. Many special occasions such as hymn sings, shows, embarkation, debarkation, or special problems made each day in the voyage a separate entity, to be dealt with as creatively as possible."

Sundays were much the same as any other day, except for Divine Services. At that time Protestant service was held in the Troop Theater at 0900, with Mass in the lounge; at 1030 another Mass was said in the Troop Theater and a second Protestant service held in the lounge.

Besides all this, the chaplain was charged with the ship's paper, library, and entertainment programs, including movies and assisting the special services program, and also assistance with the Troop Information and Education program.

MSTS Pac Roster

The roster submitted by Chaplain Thompson in March 1951 showed the following disposition of MSTS, Pacific chaplains.

Adams, Charles W.	PE	GEN H. J. GAFFEY
Beck, Max G.	LUTH (MoSy)	GEN. S. B. BUCKNER
Bost, Warren L.	PRESBY (USA)	GEN. W. WEIGEL
Burr, Beryl L.	BAP (A)	GEN. S. HEINTZELMAN
Erickson, Paul F.	EVAN MISS CONV	GENERAL R. L. HOWZE
Hawkins, Elmo M. T.	METH	GEN. D. E. AULTMAN
Holmes, Norman B.	CHRI SCIENCE	SGT. C. E. MOWER
Howard, Edwin R.	CONG	GEN. C. G. MORTON
Lloyd, Paul A.	RC	GEN. E. D. PATRICK
Metzger, Ernest W.	METH	GEN. D. I. SULTAN
NONE AT PRESENT		GEN. WILLIAM BLACK
Nicholas, Philip	PRESBY (USA)	GEN. W. O. DARBY
Norwood, Herman R.	BAP (A)	GEN. W. F. HASE
Somers, Lester I.	EVAN & REF	GEN. N. M. WALKER
Stowater, Seattle A.	UNIT	SGT. HOWARD E. WOODFORD
Terhune, Cornelius A.	PRESBY (USA)	GEN. A. W. BREWSTER
Vitz, Robert H.	EVAN & REF	GEN. JOHN POPE
Wheeler, Wendell C.	CONG	AIKEN VICTORY
Watts, John E., Jr	PRESBY (USA)	GEN. E. T. COLLINS
White, Leonard F.	RC	LT. R. O. BEAUDOIN
Below, Ralph W.	BAP (S)	GEN. A. E. ANDERSON

Dohrmann, Leonard B.	EVAN & REF	GEN. J. C. BRECKENRIDGE
Hester, James D.	BAP (A)	THOMAS JEFFERSON
Jenkins, Robert E.	BAP (A)	GEN. WM. MITCHELL
Karnasiewicz, Charles F.	RC	REPOSE
Kuolt, Milton G	LUTH (MoSy)	GEN. W. A. MANN
Marley, Cecil V.	PRESBY (USA)	SITKOH BAY
Martineau, Edward R.	RC	GEN. H. W. BUTNER
McCarthy, Eugene W	RC	WINDHAM BAY
Meier, Kermit I.	METH	GEN. G. M. RANDALL
Morton, Frank R	LUTH	CAPE ESPERANCE
Porter, Harry A	BAP (A)	PRESIDENT JACKSON
Potter, Paul K.	METH	HAVEN
Reardon, John J	RC	HAVEN
White, Henry P.	METH	REPOSE

Eve of Fury

By 1 April 1951 ominous reports had reached the United Nations command of the influx of some 700,000 fresh Chinese Communist troops via Manchuria. Division Chaplain Kelly had written to Chaplain Salisbury on 31 March: "There is no spectacular fighting going on at present. There is always the ominous feeling that the Reds might unleash something." And on 21 April, he wrote:

Nobody knows what to expect from the enemy. We know they have a terrific concentration of manpower somewhere above us. They have concentrated supplies. Prisoners have given all kinds of dates for their big push. So we are just moving along wondering where and when they are going to hit. Everybody expects that when it comes, it will be all out. However, the general feeling is, "Why don't they start it? Then we will find out how tough they are."

During the months of the First United Nations Counteroffensive (late January through the middle of April), UN forces were constantly striking at the enemy and gradually forcing him farther and farther northward, until they were well forward of approximately the eastern two-thirds of the 38th Parallel. Even as elements of the 1st Marine Division captured the Hwachon Reservoir on 22 April, thus securing the southeastern approaches of the Iron Triangle, enemy activity erupted all along the front. Chinese and North Koreans poured forth and boldly counterattacked; the long-awaited spring offensive had begun.

CHAPTER 5

CHINESE COMMUNIST SPRING OFFENSIVE

22 April–8 July 1951

Two reservoirs figure prominently in the history of Marine operations in Korea, the Chosin and the Hwachon. In the latter area the Division was now to have some of its hardest fighting, in little-known actions which Lynn Montross has called worthy of comparison with the battles of Inchon-Seoul and the Chosin Reservoir.[1] It was apparent that the enemy, with an army estimated at 700,000 Chinese and North Korean troops, was prepared to fight for a decision. His goal was nothing less than the expulsion of United Nations forces from the peninsula and the extension of Communist rule over the whole of Korea.

The long-expected strike began at 2215 on 22 April. By midnight the ROK 6th Division, in the center of IX Corps, with the 24th Army Division on the left and the 1st Marine Division on the right, had given way. To protect its exposed left flank the Division ordered the 1st Marines from reserve. On the right flank the 1st Korean Marine Regiment, attached to the Division, repelled a succession of attacks designed to isolate the Division from X Corps on its right. The Division warded off threatened envelopment; but the enemy was attacking in such overwhelming numbers and with such utter disregard for human life [2] that, commencing on 25 April, Gen. Van Fleet ordered 8th Army to begin moving back to prepared defensive positions.

The attack against IX Corps proved to be a secondary, though the initial, thrust. Some 36 enemy divisions were committed in the sector between Hwachon and the west coast. It was now clear that his real objective was Seoul, perhaps not so much for its strategic value as for its symbolic significance. To be able to celebrate May Day in the Korean capital would be to announce to the world, and more particularly to the uncommitted smaller nations, the futility of resistance to Communist imperialism.

Gen. Van Fleet, by falling back deliberately through a series of planned defensive positions, while at the same time inflicting overwhelmingly heavy losses upon the aggressor, was able to implement a policy which has been described as "trading real estate for destruction of the enemy." By the end of April a line had been stabilized in front of Seoul and the Han River, and there was a momentary lull. Van Fleet now reorganized his forces and planned a counter attack.

Second Punch

The agile Chinese command beat him to the draw; a second major attack was launched on 16 May.[3] The 1st Marine Division, commanded by Maj. Gen. Gerald C. Thomas, who had relieved Maj. Gen. Oliver P. Smith on 25 April, was now again part of X Corps, commanded by (now) Lt. Gen. E. M. Almond. Making its main bid this time in the eastern sector, the Communist force pierced the UN line and poured through the gap left by the fall-back of two ROK divisions for a gain of some 30 miles, thus exposing the Marines' right flank.

Tactical shifts made in Marine positions enabled them to contain and finally repulse the enemy's penetration. By 19 May it became evident that the second Chinese attack would fail of its objective. All along the front UN troops had brought the enemy's offensive to a standstill, and by the end of May a counter-attack was under way. So suicidal had been the massed Red assaults that his casualties for the month of May were estimated at 105,000, including 17,000 dead and 10,000 prisoners.[4]

---

[1] *Marine Corps Gazette* (July 1953), p. 17, Lynn Montross, "Red China on the Offensive."

For summary information on this period see also Miller *et al., op. cit.,* ch. IV, "The Enemy Strikes Back." Also helpful are the sections in vol. IV of the official Marine Corps history of operations in Korea dealing with this period, at the time of this writing not yet published.

[2] Montross says that the enemy suffered an estimated loss of 70,000 during the first week of their spring offensive ("Red China on the Offensive," p. 23).

[3] *Ibid.,* p. 24.

[4] *Marine Corps Gazette* (August 1953), p. 17. Lynn Montross, "Advance to the Punchbowl."

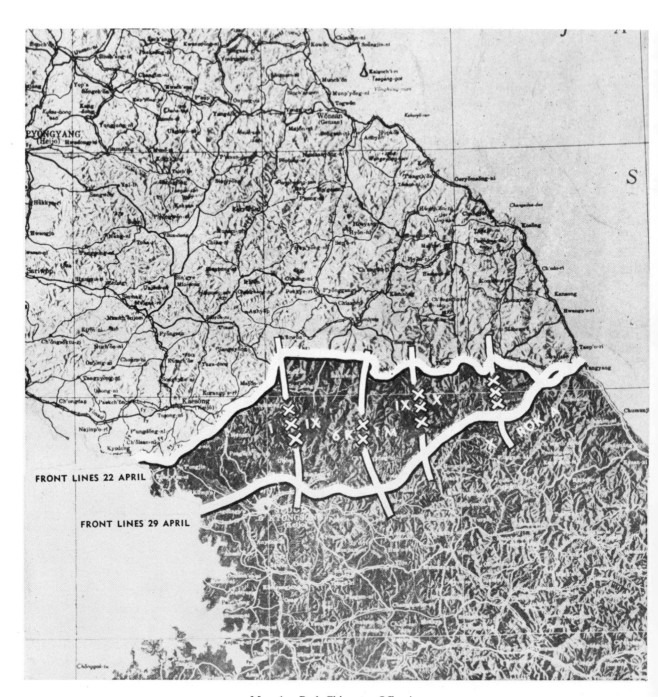

MAP 1.—Red China on Offensive.
Reproduced by permission from the *Marine Corps Gazette*.

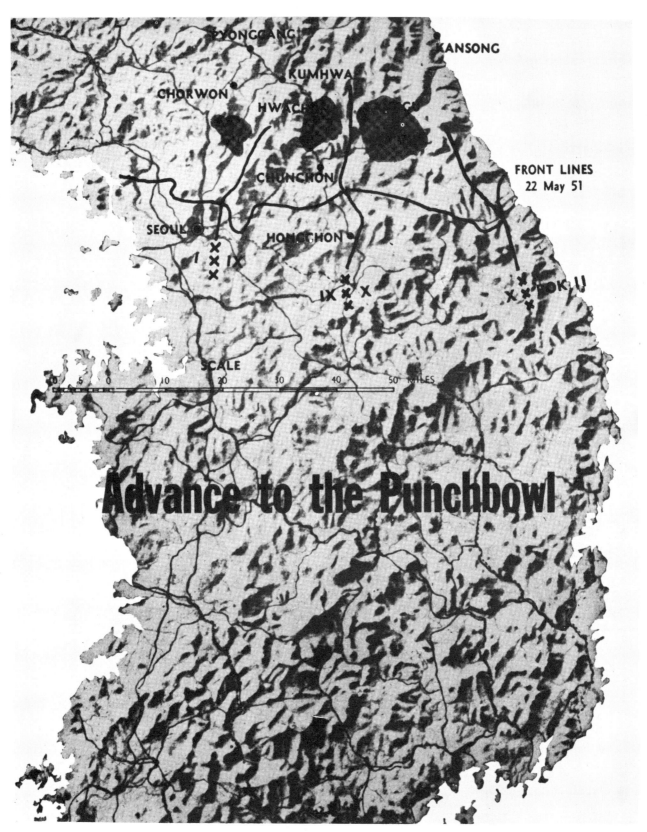

MAP 2.—Advance to the Punchbowl.
Reproduced by permission from the *Marine Corps Gazette* (August 1953).

The UN counterstroke got underway on 22 May. By 27 May the Marines were fighting in a sector east and south of the Hwachon Reservoir, advancing toward Yangu on its eastern tip.[5] During the first part of June the Division was moving through mountainous country with peaks rising to 3,000 feet. The terrain was cut by deep ravines with precipitous sides; roads were practically nonexistent. The enemy had dug in along the ridges behind well-protected log bunkers. The sides of the valleys were so steep that artillery was frequently ineffective, though tanks paralleling the infantry advance poured flat-trajectory shells upon the entrenched bunkers. Nests of resistance had to be cleaned out by hand-to-hand combat, much of it at night. Yet the advance continued toward an objective north and east of Yangu, a circular mountain-rimmed valley which became known as the Punchbowl.

Losses were heavy, especially among the Korean Marine regiment, whose personnel could expect no mercy from their Red compatriots.

During the first 10 days of June, in fact, 1st Mar Div personnel losses were higher than during any full month of the year so far. The 1st KMC Regt suffered more than 500 casualties from all causes during this period, and the 1st Marines had 67 KIA [killed in action] and 1,044 WIA [wounded in action] from 1 to 30 June, most of them incurred during the first 2 weeks. This was a higher total of battle casualties than that reported by the regiment in the Chosin Reservoir operation.[6]

In the west meanwhile I and IX Corps had exerted continuous pressure toward the Iron Triangle. By 11 June, Operation Pile driver had brought a force consisting of the U.S. 3d Division, the ROK 9th Division, and the Philippine Battalion into Chorwon and another consisting of the U.S. 25th Division and the Turkish Brigade into Kumhw.[7] Soon the apex of the Triangle, Pyongyang, was secured also; but since the whole area was so completely dominated by surrounding heights, neither side attempted to hold it thereafter.

First Anniversary

The end of June 1951 found the United Nations occupying the most favorable line they had held since the Chinese intervention. Beginning at the mouth of the Imjin River on the west, it ran through the middle of the Triangle, over the mountains and along the southern rim of the Punchbowl, and northeast to the coast at Chodo-ri. The Communists held 2,100 square miles less than when they had begun their aggression a year before. Lynn Montross has written: [8]

By the most conservative estimate considerably more than a million Chinese and North Koreans had been killed, wounded, or captured, and losses of enemy equipment included 391 aircraft, 1,000 pieces of artillery, and thousands of automatic weapons, machine guns, and mortars. North Korea, which had been the industrial region of the peninsula, lay in ruins everywhere, its cities and factories and power plants pounded into rubble by UN bombs and shells.

In fact, the aggressors in Korea were defeated.[9] The best proof of this lies in the hints of a desire for truce talks which now began to be given out by the enemy.

Summarizing the contribution of the Marines to the first year of the Korean War, Montross states that of a total of nearly 50,000 who had served so far in the combat theater 1,385 casualties had been returned stateside for hospitalization, 80 reserves sent home for release, and 7,352 men rotated to stateside duty.[10]

On 21 April, on the eve of the Chinese Communist push, Kelly submitted the following roster of the 29 chaplains then attached to the 1st Marine Division. Recent arrivals had been Keene H. Capers, John E. Hollingsworth III, Arthur M. Kulinski, William B. Leonard, Jr., and Thomas B. Uber II.

---

[5] *Ibid.*, pp. 15ff. Also Miller *et al.*, *op. cit.*, ch. V.
[6] Montross, "Advance to the Punchbowl," p. 21.
[7] Miller *et al.*, *op. cit.*, p. 111.

[8] Montross, "Advance to the Punchbowl," p. 22.
[9] Montross says the enemy was not yet beaten in June 1951, though he had good military as well as political reasons for wishing to have a breathing spell (*ibid.*, p. 23). Cagle and Manson both give it as their opinion and quote Gen. Van Fleet to the effect that the Reds were definitely whipped; but since the UN forces were not to be allowed to prosecute the war to a successful conclusion, the inevitable result was stalemate (*op. cit.*, pp. 308–310).
[10] Montross, "Advance to the Punchbowl," p. 22.

ROSTER OF CHAPLAINS

Headquarters Battalion	F. W. Kelly	CDR	RC
	H. H. Hayes	LTJG	DISC
1st Engineer Battalion	K. M. Hearn [1]	LT	METH
	W. B. Leonard	LT	PRESBY (BIBLE)
1st Tank Battalion	W. M. Hearn [2]	LTJG	BAP (A)
1st Medical Battalion	G. J. Reilly	LT	RC
	W. A. Rennie	LT	METH
	G. Goodman [2]	LTJG	JEWISH

See footnotes at end of table

Ordnance Battalion	T. B. Uber	LT	LUTH
1st Amphib. Tractor Bn	G. C. Bingaman	LTJG	EVAN & REF
1st Shore Party Bn	K. d'A. Engle	LTJG	PE
1st Motor Transport Bn	J. P. Trodd	LT	RC
1st Service Battalion	A. J. Juntunen	LT	LUTH
1st Combat Service Group	W. N. Lyons [2]	LCDR	BAP (A)
	A. M. Kulinski	LCDR	RC
1st Marines	J. D. McDonald	LCDR	RC
	H. E. Austin	LT	BAP (A)
	C. S. Pigott	LTJG	BAP (S)
	K. H. Capers	LTJG	PRESBY (USA)
5th Marines	J. E. Hollingsworth	LCDR	BAP (S)
	L. R. Phillips [2]	LT	CONG
	S. K. Johnson	LT	PRESBY (USA)
	J. M. Quirk	LT	RC
7th Marines	J. S. Ferris	LT	METH
	E. I. Van Antwerp [2]	LT	RC
	R. L. Patton [2]	LTJG	METH
11th Marines	J. C. Fitzgerald	LCDR	RC
	H. H. Groover	LTJG	DISC
	H. E. Waters	LTJG	BAP (S)

[1] Awaiting orders.
[2] Awaiting relief.

Kelly Reporting

A vivid picture of both the military situations and the chaplains' activities during this period may be gained from the regular letters written by Division Chaplain Francis W. Kelly to the Chief of Chaplains. Chaplain Kelly's letter of 27 April reflects the situation which developed after the Chinese Communist forces launched their big drive. He wrote:

We have come through a tough time, and we don't know what next. So far we have had no casualties amongst our chaplains although they have been exposed to terrific pressure. Everything was going along smoothly. We were advancing steadily when suddenly the Reds cut loose.

We had two regiments on the front and one well back in reserve. The 7th had been on the lines with the 1st Cavalry Division. When we reached the Kansas line, the 1st Cavalry was replaced with our 5th Regiment. It was planned that the 1st Regiment would replace the 7th, so that they would get a rest. Our CP [command post] had moved up to about four miles behind the lines because such progress was being made. Our 1st Regiment was about 5 miles behind the CP. On Sunday everything was moving up. I started out to find an Army Battalion of the 17th Field Artillery but they were on the move. In looking for them I ran across Van Antwerp moving up with the 7th and Fitzgerald with the 11th. I also ran into the 5th moving up. Fortunately for me I didn't stay overnight in that area because . . . things really broke loose in that spot. All of China seemed to descend on us on that Sunday night.

In a desperate effort to contain the Chinese Communist forces penetration of the front lines, the 1st Battalion, 1st Marines bore the brunt of some heavy fighting. Kelly, describing this situation, wrote:

The 1st Marines were rushed up Sunday night and two battalions really ran into a terrific condition. The Chinese tried to smash through the area held by the 1st Battalion of the 1st Marines, but were unsuccessful. It looked for a while another Hagaru. We had no idea how many enemy had poured through on our left or how far they had gone. The ROK [6th] Division left a complete sector unguarded.

Another view of that night of fury is furnished by the Bronze Star citation of Joseph D. McDonald, Regimental Chaplain, 1st Marines.

Serving as regimental chaplain, Lieutenant Commander McDonald displayed outstanding courage and initiative when the battalion to which he was attached was subjected to violent attack during hours of darkness by a numerically superior enemy force. Having relinquished his foxhole to a wounded man, he fearlessly and with complete disregard for his own safety moved in and about the sick bay area, which was subjected to almost constant enemy mortar and automatic weapons fire, to render aid and spiritual assistance to the wounded.

He repeatedly gathered urgently needed men to assist as stretcher bearers, and on at least two occasions, when adequate bearers were not available, moved courageously to the line through withering enemy fire to help carry casualties to the aid station. During the attack the following morning to break out of an enemy encirclement, he was continually found at the side of a wounded man, although this required that he move back through the column toward enemy-held ridge lines and through increasing enemy fire. When offered vehicular transportation, he refused it, and was among the last to leave the area where the enemy was closing in, leading wounded

Marines through heavy fire to a position from which they could be evacuated. His great personal bravery and constant material and spiritual assistance throughout the battle were an inspiration to all members of the command.

Chaplain Kelly's account continues:

Nobody knew when a horde of Chinese would overrun us. No one got much sleep with artillery and machine guns going all night. Tuesday morning the CP was moved back 5½ miles. . . . That night we were in a CP with an artillery perimeter. About 200 yards away from us 8-inch field guns fired all night in three directions, and a battery of Marine artillery were facing southwest. An ambulance evacuation point was set up. Reilly, Capers, and Hayes covered that. Trodd from Motor Transport covered the hospital. The next day Reilly went back to the hospital and Trodd and Capers covered the casualties coming through. Casualties are moderate considering the situation.

As we have seen, the Chinese Communist forces breakthrough obliged the UN forces to fall back in orderly retreat. Chaplain Kelly concluded his report to the Chief:

Even though we are still dropping back, the morale is high. The [men] are dead-tired, but still fighting. We expect the CP to move back tomorrow. I am proud of the work of the chaplains in this tough operation.

Chaplain Kelly's next letter to Chaplain Salisbury was dated 7 May. By that time Chaplains Van Antwerp and William Hearn had been relieved. Chaplains Harold H. Cummings (Presbyterian), Ross H. Trower (Lutheran), Richard T. Peeters (Roman Catholic), Jesse L. Swinson (Methodist), and George R. Brosius (Lutheran) had reported for duty.

Regarding the military situation Kelly wrote:

Things have settled down considerably. Our Command Post has stopped moving. For the past week we have been settled in one spot. The week before that we moved four times. We are getting to be like a bunch of gypsies. Our front is moving north again. Contact with the enemy has been very light. Our patrols are fanning out without much contact. These Chinese are odd people. They must crawl into the ground. One day they are running all over the place. The next day you can't find them. From our intelligence we know that they have tremendous numbers in North Korea. Most of the outfits are identified and their strength estimated. All we have to do is to guess when and where they will hit. The only thing we can be fairly certain is that it will be at night.

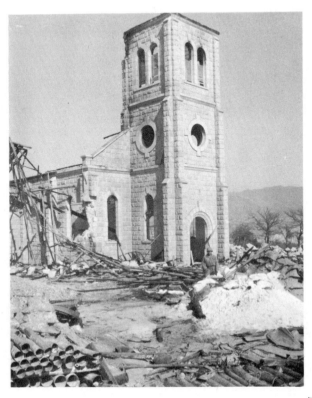

Damaged Church.

Marines examine a church atop a hill in Chunchon area which was shelled when the war passed through the area.

Memorial Services at the Front.

The 1st Marines hold a brief service in memory of their fallen comrades. Participants are (from left to right) Pfc. Marvin Blankfield (Jewish), Chaplain Henry E. Austin (Protestant), Chaplain Joseph D. McDonald (Catholic) and Chaplain Keene H. Capers (Protestant).

Chinese Strike

They had not long to wait. Kelly's letter of 25 May reported on events of the previous week.

Operation Yo-yo still goes on. Last week conditions looked very dismal. The Chinese ran wild again. All the damage done has not been definitely clarified. It certainly looked as though they were playing for keeps. I will attempt to give you the picture. We were straightening out from the debacle at the end of April by holding a defense line and sending patrols up in the area of Chunchon. Just before dark on the evening of May 15, the 3d Battalion of the 7th Marines moved into a new position along the Chunchon-Wonju road. About 4 o'clock in the morning the Chinese tried to break through in force. The 7th really clobbered them. It was estimated that they suffered over 400 casualties. When they tried to drop back they were caught in a curtain of artillery. Over 60 prisoners were taken by the 7th. If they had successfully broken through, they were going to fan out and attack our lines from the rear. They did not break through.

The South Korean soldiers, who often distinguished themselves by their bravery, sometimes lacked the tenacity to dig in and fight which was displayed by the U.S. Marines. Some of the most difficult conditions faced by the United Nations forces in this 5th Korean campaign resulted from the failure of ROK troops to hold the line. Chaplain Kelly wrote: "Somebody said, 'The Chinese yell *Banzai,* the Koreans yell *Pusan,* and both take off.'"

Referring to another bad situation which had developed because of a Communist breakthrough, Kelly wrote:

Again we were endangered on our flank. It looked for a while that we were going to fall back to Wonju. Elements of the 3d Army Division came in on the right. Now we are on the move again. If it works it will be very good. If it doesn't it will be curtains. There is a chance that we can cut off the Chinese who broke through. I hope it won't be another Hagaru-ri.

I saw some of the results of the Chinese break through the other day. Our 5th Regiment jumped off Wednesday morning, right through the territory where the 38th Army had been clobbered. Word came back that in their advance they found a lot of wounded and dead Army personnel, so I took off to lend a hand with the wounded. We didn't locate many wounded, but we found plenty of dead.

Meanwhile Chaplains Groover, Reilly, Rennie, and Goodman had left for home. Goodman, the Division's Jewish chaplain, was replaced by Chaplain Elihu H. Rickel. Chaplain William A. Taylor (American Baptist) had also reported for duty with the 1st Marine Division.

Chaplain Howard J. Groover, was awarded the Bronze Star for "meritorious achievement . . . while serving with a Marine artillery regiment in Korea from 15 September 1950 to 15 May 1951." The citation reads in part as follows:

Although operating under the most severe weather and field conditions, he, without regard for his own personal safety, continually ministered to the needs of the wounded. His presence in the front lines added immeasurably to the morale and spiritual well-being of the men. His outstanding conduct under fire in treating and giving spiritual consolation to the wounded served as a source of encouragement to those around him.

Chaplain Kelly reported that 8th Army was holding a memorial service at the UN cemetery. All units of UN forces were to be represented. Kelly was asked to give the invocation. Unit chaplains were asked to hold memorial services in their own areas as military conditions permitted. Again and again, as far as the exigencies of continuing combat allowed, the Marines would pause to pay their respects to their comrades-in-arms who had fallen.

Beginning of Advance

Kelly's letter of 25 May was written just after the beginning of Van Fleet's forward advance. During the heavy fighting that followed, two more chaplains were cited for the Bronze Star. The first was Henry H. Hayes, for distinguished service on 31 May. His citation reads in part as follows:

Serving as battalion chaplain, Lieutenant (jg.) Hayes displayed outstanding courage and initiative when an adjacent battalion was subjected to a devastating enemy artillery barrage while preparing to move forward. Hearing the cries for aid, he . . . ran through the heavy enemy fire to reach the stricken men. Despite sporadic artillery fire, he courageously moved from casualty to casualty, dressing wounds, organizing stretcher parties, and comforting the wounded. His great personal bravery and unswerving devotion to duty were an inspiration to all who observed him, and aided materially in saving many lives.

The second chaplain cited was John M. Quirk who, hearing that a rifle company of his regiment had sustained heavy casualties, assembled a party of Korean laborers to act as litter bearers and after all were loaded in a truck started out on the errand of mercy. The truck struck an antitank land mine. Chaplain Quirk was hurled some 50 feet through the air and landed in a rock-strewn field. He was painfully bruised and cut but not too seriously wounded. Reporting on the incident to Chaplain Salisbury on 5 June, Chaplain Kelly wrote:

Chaplain John M. Quirk, Catholic Chaplain with the 5th Marines, was wounded yesterday. His condition is not too serious, but he will not be available for duty in less than 2 months. He was a victim of a land mine. He received fragmentation wounds in the legs and right arm, a large wound in his left arm, and a contusion which caused quite a bit of swelling on the right side of his face. However, his eye was not injured and they don't think any facial nerves were affected. He also suffered shock. I tried to get to him, but they flew him by 'copter to a rear medical company.

Chaplain Quirk's citation for the Bronze Star contains the following further account of what happened:

Despite his serious injuries, he attempted to crawl back to the burning truck in order to render aid to the injured laborers. His bravery and complete disregard for his personal safety were an inspiration to all who observed him.

Two days after Chaplain Joseph P. Trodd replaced Quirk in the 5th Marines, a shell landed outside his tent. The chaplain's clerk and a brother officer were wounded by the explosion but, although Trodd was knocked to the ground and badly shaken, he was not seriously hurt.

In this same letter of 5 June, Chaplain Kelly commented as follows on the military situation as it then existed:

In my last letter I told you that we were pushing forward again. Well, we have really pushed forward. We are almost up to where we were when things broke back in April. However, we are on the right side of the Hwachon Reservoir, whereas the first time we were on the left. The 5th and 1st Regiments are moving up with the 7th ready to swing in on the right. Resistance has stiffened very much recently. The regiments have been taking a pounding. The enemy have been using a lot of mortars and some artillery. In a few days with some good breaks we may reach the line where we will defend for a while. That is good, because our men are getting awfully tired. Just climbing these hills day after day is enough to wear them out.

The Marines suffered severe losses during the first 2 weeks of June 1951. Writing to Chaplain Salisbury, Kelly reported that in one 36-hour period, some 500 patients had been received at "A" Medical Company. The work there for the chaplains became so heavy that four attached to other units of the Division assisted the three chaplains who were serving with the Medical Battalion. By the middle of the month, however, the daily number of Marines listed as casualties began to decline.

Regarding the tactical situation Kelly wrote to Chaplain Salisbury in this same letter of 15 June:

The resistance in our area has been very stiff. The enemy have thrown a terrific amount of mortar and artillery. Since they have held high ground with good observation, the mortar and artillery has been very accurate; hence the terrific damage to our men. They must have our locations zeroed in. Up till Wednesday the weather was bad and made air support impossible. They also have the quaint practice of rolling hand grenades down the hills on top of our men coming up. They have heavily mined the area through which we are moving. We have lost 10 tanks to land mines in a very short time.

One other award, and an unusual one, was given a chaplain at this time. Chaplain Joseph C. Fitz-gerald, serving with the 11th Marines, the Division's artillery regiment, had utilized every available means of transportation to reach his separated units. He was now cited for the Air Medal for "making 21 flights over enemy territory, where the plane could have received fire from unfriendly forces." The period covered was 22 December 1950–9 June 1951.

Comic Relief

A lighter note in the story of the chaplains' activities during these days of fighting is found in an experience of Chaplain Richard T. Peeters, serving in the 7th Marines. One day a group of Marines were resting a short distance behind the front lines. Suddenly they were alerted by a shout from Chaplain Peeters: "Hey, look what I've got!"

To the amazement of the Leathernecks, there strode their chaplain up the dusty Korean road with four ragged enemy soldiers following him! In answer to the incredulous queries as to how an unarmed chaplain happened to be taking prisoners, Chaplain Peeters explained. He was just looking through some empty Korean houses when the four Chinese soldiers ran out with their hands in the air and surrendered. Noticing the cross on his uniform, one of the Chinese kept shouting: "You ding hao. You ding hao." In the Mandarin dialect "ding hao" means "very good." The Chinese may or may not have known of the existence of chaplains with the Marine units. However, the very fact that they noticed the cross on the Chaplain's uniform is evidence that they knew he was a Christian and would undoubtedly exercise mercy in receiving them.

After hearing Peeters' account of what must go down in the history of the Chaplain Corps of the U.S. Navy as an unprecedented experience, one of the listening Marines deflated any pride the chaplain may have felt in his exploit by saying: "Everyone's takin' 'em today." Chaplain Kelly, reporting this incident to the Chief in his letter of 15 June, added: "These 1st Division chaplains are a rugged people."

Chaplain Peeters, for devoted service from 10 May to 29 June, was awarded the Letter of Commendation. Part of his citation follows:

During that period, in which the battalion was constantly in contact with the enemy, Chaplain Peeters' untiring efforts on behalf of the front line personnel were a source of marked pride to the entire command. Time and again on every critical operation, under the most adverse physical conditions and under fire from the enemy, which included heavy enemy mortar and artillery fire of the most intense variety, he worked feverishly at the forward aid stations to help the wounded and minister to the dying.

Emergency Call.

When communications failed at a forward aid station during the fighting, Chaplain Joseph P. Trodd made a hurried trip over treacherous roads to call for a helicopter to evacuate two wounded men.

Immersion.

Chaplain John E. Hollingsworth conducts a baptismal service at a Marine command post.

Operation Polaroid.

Chaplain Rickel takes a picture of Chaplain Trower talking with a marine wounded the day the picture was taken. The camera develops the print in just a few minutes and the print is given to the man.

It will have been noticed that one of the most frequently occurring references to chaplains' work concerns their ministry to casualties. Recalling the advance to the Punchbowl, Chaplain G. A. Bingaman wrote: "During June 1951 nearly 1,500 Marines passed through an emergency aid station we had set up in a 3-day period of crisis. Two doctors, two corpsmen, and three chaplains met a tremendous need in a situation described later as 'light action on the east-central front.'" Chaplain J. D. McDonald commented that, besides administering the last rites of his church to Catholic personnel, he prayed with men of all denominations when wounded or dying. Chaplain Henry H. Hayes recalled that it was "standard procedure in his battalion aid station to refer all men admitted with 'combat fatigue' to the chaplain before being evacuated or else returned to duty."

Services

Letters and reports from combat chaplains frequently referred to the Marines' appreciation for their presence. Many a brief religious service was held for a small group in a bunker or improvised shelter, when the chaplain would simply read a passage of Scripture and lead in prayer. Sometimes even in advanced situations Protestant chaplains would administer the Lord's Supper, while Roman Catholic chaplains would hear confessions and say Mass. Chaplains reported numerous instances where the men themselves took the initiative in conducting devotional services. Many Testaments, prayer books, and items of devotional literature were distributed.

Chaplain Jesse L. Swinson (a one time outfielder for the Boston Red Sox) reported: "As Chaplain to the Tank Battalion I was invited by my men to accompany them on patrols in enemy territory, which I did, and I felt it was appreciated by them. I always encouraged them to pray, and Holy Communion was available to them before and during each engagement."

Chaplain Keene H. Capers, who was with the 1st Marines during some bitter fighting, wrote:

The mere presence of a chaplain can have a tremendous influence on the fighting spirit of a battalion or a ship. For a man who has been on the line for some time the sight of the chaplain walking the lines specifically to talk to him, if he wants to talk, can affect that man's staying power. Acting as a mailman, carrying fruit juice, or any practical demonstration of the chaplain's abiding interests in the welfare of the men can give truth to the words he speaks to them in his sermons. A chaplain must be where he is needed regardless of personal inconvenience or danger.

During the advance to the Punchbowl, the 1st Marines had its fiercest struggle assaulting the ridges overlooking the Hwachon Reservoir from the northeast. The battle raged most of June 9–10. A firsthand account may be found in the following letter which Chaplain Henry E. Austin wrote several days later to some of his friends. (Hills in this mountainous area were most frequently razor-sharp peaks; they received their names from their height, given in meters.) Austin's letter is so vivid in its description and so revealing in its account of the work of combat chaplains that it is given in its entirety.

OFFICE OF THE CHAPLAIN

2D BATTALION 1ST MARINES

F.P.O. SAN FRANCISCO, CALIF.,
13 June 1951.

DEAR FRIENDS: Many thanks for your prayers and interest in my work. I received a backlog of 14 letters today—up on the top of bloody Hill No. 676—elevation: 2,000 feet straight up! Some time ago, I said that I honestly thought we had the best battalion in the 1st Marine Regiment and in the entire 1st Division for that matter. Yesterday we met the test and our men covered themselves with glory—via the time-honored "Blood, sweat, and tears" route.

At the moment, I have my foxhole dug right on the top of 676 which we paid for with 261 men wounded and 16 men killed. Last night was our roughest night, since I joined the 2d Battalion, so I stayed up all night and helped the doctors. It was 4 a.m. before we could evacuate the first wounded, because we had to carry them over 2½ miles along a mountain ridge under enemy fire in the drizzly-dark. I helped as stretcher bearer, prayed with the seriously wounded and dying, gave out cigarettes [and] water, and tried to give some comfort to the men.

Some of the wounded who walked in got lost in the dark. We had to observe strict blackout regulations, but all were eventually accounted for. Everyone cooperated and did a magnificent job. Col. "Big Foot" Brown personally came by the evacuation point and thanked both the doctor, the corpsmen, and the "padre" for seeing all the wounded. Four artillery shells "hit the area" at that moment, so both he, the "Doc," and I "hit the deck" at the same time.

One thing that made Hill 676 tougher than any mountain I've seen since Suribachi on Iwo Jima was the fact that we had no air-support due to bad weather. Then, since the slope was very steep, the artillery could only continue to a certain point. The Chinese and North Koreans were really dug in and poured murderous concussion grenades, machine gun and burp-gun fire, plus mortars down our throats (literally), so in the Marine tradition our battalion took the objective on blood and guts alone. In the face of what looked like annihilation, our men stormed up 676 and secured the same at 2115 (9:15 p.m.) Sunday, June 10.

I never prayed more sincerely in my life and God blessed us, because most of the wounds of our men were clean, and

I think the majority of our wounded will live. The view from my foxhole is beautiful, and one thing is sure—I'll never forget this mountain.

We expect to hold a special thanksgiving service tomorrow. You'd be interested to note "The Secret Place" reading for June 10 was entitled "A Mountain to Climb"—coincidence, isn't it: Keep praying—God is blessing, over 200 men have accepted Christ out here, and to date I have baptized 97 of our fighting Marines.

    Sincerely,

                          (S) H. E. Austin.
                              H. E. AUSTIN.

Writing again to his friends on 8 July, Austin reported that his unit had been sent back to a rest area and that he was about to be detached to another unit. He wrote:

I have just finished holding my final service with the 2d Battalion. Our Regimental Commander and Battalion Commander, along with 240 men, were present. Our Marine choir sang and it was a very touching service. We have a beautiful outdoor chapel here in the regimental rest area.

Seven more men made a profession of faith in Christ today and I am baptizing them this afternoon in the clear waters of the Hwachon Reservoir. (My 110th since February 28.) The Lord has been at work in our midst, and I am very thankful for the prayers of my friends.

Chaplain Austin was relieved in the 1st Marines by Chaplain George R. Brosius and assigned to the 1st Combat Service Group at Masan.

"Such a Man as I"

A splendid illustration of how one chaplain—in this case Keene H. Capers—dealt with a Marine facing the stark face of fear in his life and helped him to an answer founded upon religious faith is revealed in the following story.[11]

A Marine captain of my acquaintance, fighting in Korea when I was there recently, was well beloved of his men. One day he and two other officers undertook a reconnaissance patrol into enemy territory. One of the three tripped a concealed wire which detonated an antipersonnel mine. The popular captain was killed, the other two officers seriously wounded.

I held memorial services for the captain whose courage and devotion to duty had won the admiration and respect of all. For my text I chose a sentence from the 6th chapter of Nehemiah, the 11th verse: *Should such a man as I flee?*

As the service broke up I came across a young rifleman whose presence there surprised me. We'll call him Sam. I knew that Sam had been offered an opportunity to return to the rear, so as I greeted him I asked, curiously, "What are you doing here, Sam"? For reply he tossed back at me the

[11] As told by K. H. Capers to Ken Jones. First published in the magazine *Brief* (December 1952) under the title "I Was With Your Boy in Battle." Republished as ch. III of Ken Jones' book of Korean stories, *I Was There* (New York, 1953). Used by permission. The wording here follows that of a typescript on file in the Chaplains Division, which is not exactly reproduced in either of the published versions.

words of Nehemiah which I had just quoted: *Should such a man as I flee?*

Without knowing the facts you might think that Sam was being cocky. He wasn't. In that instant a 19-year-old boy reached a magnificent pinnacle of inspired, determined, resourceful, and responsible manhood. Let me tell you Sam's story, which is typical of what many American boys are experiencing in Korea today.

When I first met Sam he was "shook." That isn't good grammar but it's mighty meaningful military slang, and as the boys come home in greater and greater numbers from the fighting fronts you're going to hear the word more and more. The American fighting man in Korea who is "shook" has reached the razor edge of emotional endurance. He's had all he can take of mud, blood, and death. He may have some resources of physical stamina left, but his nerves are playing him false. His hands shake; his speech may be halting and almost unintelligible; an uncontrollable fear, which he can't name, burns deep in his wide hollow eyes. It's an easy condition to recognize. Among fighting men it reflects no stigma of cowardice. Put under enough pressure any man will be "shook." These boys are under pressure.

Our troops were seesawing back and forth over the 38th Parallel at the time. It was early afternoon of a fine, clear day. My tent had just been put up at the foot of a bluff on the edge of a rice paddy. I sat at my portable desk; the Coleman lantern hung ready on the tentpole, and I was sharing a desultory bull session with my tentmates, two medical officers, and two TAC people—Tactical Air Control.

Sam walked up to the tent flap and just stood there. He didn't say anything; he didn't have to say anything. I had eyes to see, and what I saw made me rise quickly, although I was careful to seem casual. "Suppose we take a walk, son," I suggested as I stepped out of the tent and left the others behind. This wasn't their kind of show.

We headed toward a shallow ravine at the edge of the rice paddy, maybe 20 or 30 yards from the tent. Neither of us said anything more at the moment. When we reached the ravine Sam unslung his M–1 from his shoulder and placed it carefully on the ground. We squatted facing each other on a small hummock which may, for all I know, have been a Korean grave.

"Smoke . . .?" I held a pack of cigarettes toward the boy, but he shook his head. I took the brief opportunity while lighting my own cigarette to study Sam. He was young—19, as I learned later. His beard was scraggly, and probably had been growing for weeks. He stood about 5 feet, 9; I guessed his weight at 140 pounds; and where I could see his cheeks they were ruddy, although he was incredibly dirty.

Sam tried to speak after a moment, but emotional tension had him in an iron grip. His jaws worked, but no sound issued from his lips. Then without further ado, he burst into a tempest of tears. I didn't move, but I spoke to him softly, urging him to cry all he wanted to and pay no attention to me. I knew, of course, that the release he would find through tears eventually would make it possible for him to gain some measure of control. Deep sobs racked him but after some minutes a quieter key crept in and finally, in a flat, desperate, hopeless voice he told me: "Chaplain, I don't know what's wrong, but I just can't go back on the hill!"

Sam wasn't the first boy I'd seen and talked with who

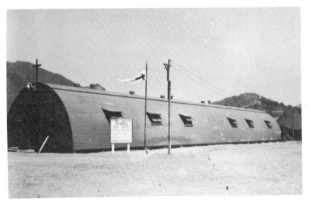

First Permanent Chapel.

Many services were held in Korea out in the open or in temporary shelters. This permanent building with a seating capacity of 200 served U.S. fighting men and Korean Christians.

Chapel Dedication.

Chaplain Ross H. Trower talks with members of his congregation after the dedication. The chapel was built in two weeks.

"didn't know what was wrong" but who "couldn't go back on the hill." And I knew at once that Sam wasn't afraid of any rendezvous with death which might be waiting him "on the hill." His problem was more subtle than physical fear. Sam was afraid he would be afraid. If that seems an anomaly, any man back from the fighting in Korea can explain it to you. I'll try to explain it myself a little further along, because it lies at the root of what's happening to your man in this war. (I say "your man" advisedly.) You may have sent away a boy, but a man will return in his place, and of that you may be sure!

I got Sam talking about himself. He was an only child, and he and his mother had been very close to each other in the little midwestern town where they lived. As he talked the boy pulled out a badly cracked snapshot and a much-folded and grimy leaflet.

"That's my mom," he said simply, offering the snapshot for my inspection. I studied the portrait of a rather pretty woman who appeared on the youngish side—a typical, wholesome, small-town mother.

"And here's my church bulletin," he added, unfolding the grimy leaflet. "See—here's my name, right here!" The church bulletin, I noted, was dated sometime ago, and announced that Sam was slated for service in Korea. He'd been carrying it with him as a pitiful link with a safe past amid the confusion and death of battle. But, as he said, there was his name, right there.

The rest of my conversation with Sam need not be detailed here.

I reminded him that we were not alone—that there was Another present—and that if he really wanted to, we three could lick any situation. I also pointed out to him—and this is terribly, terribly true—that it's easier for us to be courageous as we get older and experience more things. Sam was pretty new to combat. I knew that if I could help him overcome his fear of fear itself—get him to want to go back up there on the hill some way—half of his battle would be won. He was at the low point through which every man must pass on the road to becoming a battle-seasoned veteran. Things couldn't possibly get any worse for Sam; they could get a lot better if he rose to the challenge.

Eventually, we got to talking about the prospects of hot chow—always an absorbing speculation at the front. Then I sent Sam to the nearby river with instructions to jump in, dunk himself in the shallow water, relax, soak up as much sunshine as possible, and pick me up at my tent later in the afternoon. Before the sun set I walked with Sam back up the hill to his unit, and I left him with the reminder, "Son, don't forget you're never alone. There's always One other with you!"

It was a month after this little episode that Sam appeared at the memorial service for the captain. I taxed him with the query, "I hear you turned down a chance to go down the hill?" And he gave me the ringing answer: *Should such a man as I flee?* An American man had been born.

First Permanent Chapel

The 1st Combat Service Group, located in the vicinity of Masan, achieved the distinction of having the first "permanent" chapel of any Marine group in Korea. ("Permanent" meant anything not a tent.) Consisting of a double Arctic Quonset hut, erected on the initiative of the command, the chapel was dedicated on 20 May 1951.[12] At a military ceremony at 0930 the chapel was presented by the commanding officer, Col. John H. Cook, Jr., USMC, and accepted by the senior chaplain, Arthur M. Kulinski. Regularly scheduled Divine Services followed. In the afternoon Chaplain Ross H. Trower presided at a Protestant Service of Dedication, at which the choir of the Chung Ang Methodist Church sang. At the Roman Catholic Dedicatory Mass music was furnished by the choir of the Masan Catholic Church. Besides military personnel from neighboring Army activities and the destroyer escort WISEMAN, guests included other chaplains in the area and local Korean Christian clergy.

[12] Information from material on file in the jacket of Chaplain Ross H. Trower in the Chaplains Division.

In presenting the chapel Colonel Cook began by saying:

One of the finest traditions of American military life is the desire of men to build a House of God wherever duty may take them. In addition to providing a place of worship, it gives beauty to things sometimes drab, its skyward-pointing cross inspiring men to finer living.

Recalling how so many activities had built chapels during World War II, "taking the materials at hand to fashion some kind of suitable place of prayer," the Colonel continued: "Today we dedicate a new and beautiful chapel in this command. Its doors are being opened while we are continuing projects to build quarters, shops, offices, and recreational facilities." He concluded:

It is my pleasure to present this chapel to the officers and men of the 1st Combat Service Group [that it may be dedicated] to the worship of Almighty God. May the prayers that are said here be for the comfort of our comrades in arms, for the realization of freedom through the world, for the binding together in love of our families, and for the hope of peace among men.

Marine Air

During the intense fighting incurred in the drive toward the Punchbowl the Division had, fortunately, the close air support of elements of the 1st Marine Aircraft Wing. The Wing was still under operational control of 5th Air Force, with a joint operational center at Seoul; but after two squadrons had been installed on an airstrip at Hoengsong (K–4b), by informal arrangement 5th Air Force designated them to provide support for the hard-pressed Division.[13] That arrangement continued until 13 July; by then the truce talks had begun and the Hoengsong field was closed for repairs.

As the period under review in this chapter opened, the 1st Marine Aircraft Wing was disposed as follows: Wing Headquarters and Marine Aircraft Group 12, with three squadrons, were at Pusan; Marine Aircraft Group 33 was at Pohang with two squadrons; and VMF–312 was operating from the light carrier BATAAN. Late in May the forward air strip was opened at Hoengsong with the arrival of VMF–214, followed in June by VMF–312, while VMF–323 went aboard the SICILY.

New Wing Chaplain

On 16 May Ernest R. Barnes reported to relieve John P. Murphy as 1st Marine Aircraft Wing Chaplain. Barnes had come from the PHILIPPINE SEA and Murphy reported there on 2 June. In his first letter to the Chaplains Division, Barnes wrote that he had spent a day at Marine Aircraft Group 33 with Chaplains J. H. Markley and C. E. Webb.

Among other things John [Markley] and I visited MGCIS–3 unit out on a coastal point about 22 miles away. There are roughly 200 people attached. Following their morning services at MAG 33 John and Charlie [Webb] go out to the point for services, returning in time for afternoon Mass and evening vespers at MAG 33. I would say that chaplain coverage up there has been excellent. The field is known as K–3 and is located on the east coast near Pohang.

[13] Montross, "Advance to the Punchbowl," pp. 21f.

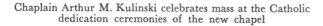

Chaplain Arthur M. Kulinski celebrates mass at the Catholic dedication ceremonies of the new chapel

Colonel Cook presenting the chapel. Chaplain Kulinski is at his immediate right and Chaplain Trower is on the right of Chaplain Kulinski.

Things were pretty quiet by then in the vicinity of Pohang—or so it seemed. "By May of 1951 [Chaplain Markley and I]," wrote Chaplain Webb in his questionnaire reply, "had become so confident that we no longer felt that we needed the help of our assistant who had been accustomed to 'ride shotgun' with us on our trips to a radar station some 20 miles from K–3."

Emboldened by the show of friendship of the natives along the way, I decided there would be no danger in making the trip alone on Monday nights [for a study class], and forthwith dispensed with the company of PFC Choyce Hoy, our genial assistant from Dallas, Tex. On 21 May 1951, while making this trip in a jeep that could not be moved out of second gear because of a mechanical defect and which required, as a result, to be stopped several times along the way to allow it to cool off, an untoward incident occurred.

About 2200, while returning from the radar station, I had stopped the jeep for about the third time to allow the cooling-off process to set in. Walking down the road a short distance for a bit of exercise, I heard a noise behind me and turned to find a Korean native about 5 yards away coming stealthily in my direction with what looked like the largest knife I had ever seen gleaming in his hand. His intentions were obviously evil, and in the ensuing struggle I was fortunate enough to take away from his knife and throw him over a steep embankment; after which I ran back to the jeep and drove to the base at high speed with no more delays. . . . Needless to say, the remaining Monday evenings on which I went to the radar station were in the welcome company of PFC Hoy.

At least one had been overlooked in the Division's famed "Pohang guerrilla hunt."

Chaplain Markley, who had been in Korea with Marine Aircraft Group 33 since the early days of the war, was relieved on 19 May by Chaplain Richard D. Cleaves. Cleaves and Webb continued work on the Quonset chapel, the start of which has earlier been noted. Barnes in his first letter to the Chaplains Division referred to it as "probably the first permanent Marine chapel in Korea," but as we have seen, Combat Service Group, not having to depend on volunteer labor to insert 11,000 screws, built their chapel in 4 days, and dedicated it 2 days before Barnes wrote.

Further Activities

Barnes' letter to the Chief of Chaplains continued:

The airfield here is K–1 [Pusan]. We have the Wing Headquarters and MAG 12 on this side of the field and on the other side MACG–2 (Marine Air Control Group 2) and an Army antiaircraft battery of about 200 men. The Marine Ground Control Interceptor Squadron and the Marine Tactical Air Control Squadron came out piecemeal but now a command unit has arrived, namely MACG–2, with a full colonel in charge to coordinate the whole activity. They have a T/O for a chaplain as well as a doctor; the latter is

already here. The CO was asking me yesterday and again today how soon he could expect his chaplain to arrive. They have 800 people. . . .

The Wing coordinates its air support and movements to the need of the Division. As the situation changes they move their closeup fields. . . . In order to give proper coverage for the fluid and widely scattered aspects of this organization, it seems important that we obtain enough chaplains to fill our T/O. Presently we are understrength by two. One Catholic and one Protestant would seem a minimum.

He wrote that the Marine Aircraft Wing units at Itami, Japan continued to be covered by civilian priests and Air Force Protestant chaplains. Later, on 26 June, he would write that he had visited Japan and hoped to borrow a chaplain, if only for a few months, from Chaplain Walter A. Mahler, Staff Chaplain, Commander Naval Forces, Far East. "Counting transients and R&R [rest and rehabilitation] personnel, Itami usually has about 1,700 there."

Speaking of chapels, Barnes' survey report continued:

The chapel here is just a bare Japanese prefab building used for lectures, movies, and Divine Services. It is closely flanked on one side with a new Quonset NCO Club and on the other by the enlisted beer hall. My request for a Quonset Chapel has been turned down by the Chief of Staff. He has agreed to designate the present building as chapel only and make some improvements. However I don't see how he will be able to avoid using it for lectures and when cold weather comes, for movies. Also the location is undesirable.

I wish a high level decision would be reached that at all Marine and naval establishments, when transition from field tents to permanent buildings is initiated, chapels be assigned at least as high a priority as beer halls, NCO clubs, and officer clubs. I have a feeling the American taxpayer would want it that way.

Whether the latter opinion be true or not, many another chaplain has echoed the underlying sentiment here expressed.

Barnes had another constructive criticism to register.

At the present time there are only two enlisted men in the Wing with spec. number [military occupational specialty; MOS] as chaplain's assistant. I have recommended to G–1 that appropriate request be initiated for four more. The struggle for clerks is so keen that the chaplain hardly has a chance. My contention is that if BuPers fills the T/O with six clergymen, the least the Marines can do is make every effort to supply six assistants.

This too would elicit a hearty Amen from many a chaplain.

On Barnes' second Sunday in the Wing, 27 May, an offering was taken at the Protestant service for the Chosin Presbyterian Seminary, formerly located in Seoul but now established in tents in Pusan. Among the entries for that date in the official Wing

Diary is that of the Chaplain Section, where Barnes notes that the offering amounted to $72.[14] In the afternoon he visited the seminary and presented the Marines' gift to the 5 teachers and 108 students.

Some of the chaplains' work was reminiscent of stateside duty.

We are operating our Navy Relief drive about a month later than stateside. I think it will go off well. I have not done much with it except to set it up and run off some dodgers for distribution. El Toro Navy Relief has been very good to our people. It is hoped that their appreciation will be shown by their contributions.

Barnes would later report that $1,694.80 was contributed and remitted by the command to the Navy Relief Auxiliary, Marine Corps Air Station, El Toro, Calif.

Supplies were of course a continuing problem. Barnes noted that the Army had set up a warehouse for chaplain supplies at Pusan to serve all chaplains in Korea, including the Marine Division and Air Wing.

Shortly after John Murphy departed, Kelly was here from the Division. We worked out plans whereby I will ship air freight to him the expendable supplies he needs for his chaplains.

Noting that the Army Chaplains' Warehouse would also share books, magazines, and comfort kits, Barnes reported that he had already shipped Chaplain Kelly 27 boxes of such items.

On 29 June Chaplain James A. Sullivan reported as relief for Chaplain Webb, who departed 2 July. The Chaplain Section of the Wing was still understaffed; because of the particular dispersal of the Wing's various units, the Itami contingent had no chaplain at all and needed one pressingly. Barnes wrote that as soon as his complement should be filled, he would detach one chaplain there. Chaplain Salisbury wrote in reply:

Up to this moment we have not been able to improve your situation. Our shortage of chaplains is proving very embarrassing, and we are frequently forced to do things which we would not prefer to do. Let us hope matters improve in the near future, once our involuntary recall program has swung into high gear.

ComNavFE

The expansion of Admiral Joy's command during the early months of the war led to the establishment of a Staff Chaplain billet for ComNavFE. The first to be assigned was Chaplain Walter A. Mahler. Ordered from supervision of the Reserve program in the Chaplains Division, Mahler reported on 20 November 1950. Arriving in Yokohama the chaplain was con-

fronted with taking a bus which was carrying all naval personnel to Yokosuka. Writing to Chaplain Salisbury, he described his adventures in characteristic vein:

Three of us were assigned to Tokyo and we tried to talk our way there. No luck; and since our luggage was all headed for Yokosuka we decided to trail along. We arrived there tired, hungry, and dirty. I was determined to get to Tokyo that day or bust. A LCDR aviator and a pay clerk decided to string along with me. So, followed by my little army of Two, I started out to find a way.

Going around the corner who do I bump into but [a mutual friend]. Boy, I was never so glad to see anyone in my life. Tears as big as baseballs welled up in my eyes. Wiping the tears from his own, he officially welcomed me to Japan, asking about the [Chaplains] Division and his old friends SWS [Chaplain Salisbury] and DFM [Chaplain Meehan]. I explained my situation. "Follow me," he says. That I did, that I did, and in a short while we were on our way to Tokyo with all our gear, in a truck.

Arrived in Tokyo the chaplain was billeted at the Dai Iti hotel.

Last night I had quite an experience—I took a bath in a Japanese tub. "Experience" is the only word for it. I had been invited to Admiral Morehouse's [ComNavFE Chief of Staff] home for dinner . . . so thought I should scrub up a bit. You won't believe it, but the tub was so crowded there wasn't room for the soap! You get in with the aid of a shoe horn. I managed finally to get myself out of the thing, leaving bits of the tub hanging to me, and presented myself at the Admiral's quarters right on time. Right now my problem is this: Should I just be content with being the dirtiest chaplain here or get another tub? Your advice will be appreciated.

ComNavFE Chaplain Roster

On 6 July 1951 Chaplain Edward B. Harp, Jr., Pacific Fleet Chaplain, issued a roster of chaplains in the Fleet and Pacific Ocean Area. The following slate was then current in ComNavFE.

Force Chaplain....	W. A. Mahler.....	CDR	RC
ComNavFE.......	D. R. Kabele.....	LCDR	LUTH
Commander Service, Squadron 3.	S. E. Anderson....	LCDR	BAP (S)
Commander Service, Division 31.	T. J. Burke.......	LCDR	RC
Fleet Activities, Yokosuka.	J. E. Reaves......	LCDR	METH
	E. D Bennett.....	LT	METH
	J. J. O'Neill......	LT	RC
	J. L. Remias......	LTJG	RC
	C. H. Swift, Jr....	LTJG	DISC
	H. E. Tillberg....	LTJG	PE
Feet Activities, Sasebo	E. M. Turner.....	LTJG	PE
Naval Air Station, Atsugi	C. L. Sullenberger.	LT	CONG
Naval Hospital, Yokosuka	C. W. Lawler.....	LCDR	RC
	C. H. Shackelford..	LCDR	PRESBY (USA)

[14] Filed in the Library, Historical Section, G–3, Headquarters, Marine Corps, Washington, D.C.

Yokosuka

Chaplain Swift served in ComNavFE from February 1951 to July 1952. As Ships and Docks Chaplain, Yokosuka, one of his main duties was visiting ships in the harbor. He reported some 355 separate visits to ships ranging from landing ships to fast carriers. Most had no chaplain; even on the largest there might be only one, and if he were Roman Catholic Swift would offer to conduct Protestant worship. In his questionnaire he recalled the following incident:

On one particular Sunday a service was scheduled for a Destroyer Mine Sweep, to be held on the weather deck. However, it was raining, and no other space was available. Across the pier from this DMS was an LSD [Landing Ship, Dock]. I contacted the officer of the deck and asked if the LSD would be willing to act as host for the service. Arrangements were made and the service transferred to the LSD, with personnel from both ships in attendance.

The chaplain had additional duty at the Naval Air Facility at nearby Oppama. Frequently "I would conduct an early service with Holy Communion aboard a ship, then conduct my regular service at Oppama, and then take a third service aboard another ship."

Representative as it must be thought to be of the work of other ComNavFE chaplains, that of Swift was different in at least one respect. Belonging to the Disciples denomination, he practiced baptism by immersion. Several persons were baptized in the swimming pool in the early morning. "It was very peaceful," he wrote, "and I feel that God's Presence hallowed the setting."

Swift also served as supply chaplain for the Far East, setting up a supply center at Yokosuka and shipping religious gear to chaplains in Korea and in ships at their request. His supplies came out aboard MSTS ships, under an arrangement with the Staff Chaplain, MSTS, Pacific. Upon being transferred to Sasebo, where there was no swimming pool, he asked the maintenance officer to rig for him a portable baptistery.

Instead, he selected a spot between the chapel and the waterfront which was semisecluded and constructed a concrete baptistery. Not only did I use it, but it was made available and used by ship's chaplains who practiced immersion.

NEW JERSEY

The second battleship committed to action in the Korean War was the NEW JERSEY, which received its "baptism by fire" on 20 May 1951 at Kangsong.[15]

---

[15] Cagle and Manson, *op. cit.*, p. 306.

Moving on to participate in the siege of Wonsan, she was hit on the 22d; one man was killed and three wounded. Chester L. Hults, Episcopalian, was chaplain from October 1950 to January 1952. In his reply to the Chaplains Division questionnaire, he noted that the ship raised approximately $6,500 as a memorial to that man. Upon returning to the United States the gift was presented to the Damon Runyon Cancer Fund, this organization having been chosen by vote of the crew. Chaplain Peter H. Brewerton served as the NEW JERSEY's Roman Catholic "padre" from January 1951 to January 1953.

Other Ships

Chaplains prosecuted their duties of many kinds. Faber H. Wickham, in the ST. PAUL from July 1950 to August 1952, reported that during their first Korean tour they lost 8 shipmates, and during the second, 30. Many came to the chaplain for assistance in those dark hours, he reported. "The sobering effect of these events cannot be underestimated."

Chaplain Charles B. Robinson, assigned to the escort carrier SITKOH BAY in July 1951, encouraged small groups of men to arrange services of their own. He reported that the Latter Day Saints personnel frequently did so.

Charles W. Ackley reported a group of six men in the submarine tender SPERRY planning to study for the Christian ministry after discharge from military service. He organized them into a "Pastors Class," meeting regularly on Friday noon, for study and discussion of their intended profession. Ackley also wrote that he inherited and further developed "one of the best hobby shops in the Pacific Fleet." He also gave much attention to developing an excellent ship's library, a resource for study and recreation that chaplains have long considered it a privilege to encourage.

Collateral duties occupy a good deal of the chaplain's effort, especially on shipboard, where every officer is likely to wear several hats. If sometimes a chaplain has thought his commanding officer rather trespassed on his primary responsibility of being a clergyman, another has often thought that his collateral ministry not only offered an avenue of service to men not directly interested in his spiritual functions but sometimes established relationships which paved the way for future religious ministries.

Chaplain Merlin A. Ditmer, Jr., serving in the BRYCE CANYON, a destroyer tender, from November 1950 to October 1952, wrote that he had organized volunteer variety shows which entertained casualties in the Naval Hospital in Yokosuka, Japan. Chaplain

L. C. M. Vosseler organized sightseeing tours in Japan for his men in the TOLEDO whenever the ship's schedule made it possible.

The following are excerpts from a letter written by Chaplain Vosseler to the Chaplains Division, 4 August 1951.

Since reporting to the ship we have been in the Far East much of the time. Is it anticipated that I'll be spending 2 years aboard? [He had been aboard then for 1 year.]

Recent months find Divine Services averaging over 100 per Sunday. Catholic Mass is arranged whenever possible. In the past 4 months six Catholic chaplains, some of them more than once, have come aboard for Confessions and Mass.

I have conducted services aboard HELENA, MANCHESTER, and ELDORADO.

Other duties include editing the daily press-news [serving as] adviser to the ship's paper [membership on the] Recreation Council, and attending Enlisted Recreation Committee meetings.

Bible studies are conducted Wednesday evenings. A daily radio program from the library is originated each day. The chaplain reads the daily news, asks the crew a sports question, and says an evening prayer. . . .

Commendation.

Chaplain Harold E. Meade, who served aboard the PHILIPPINE SEA from August 1950 to May 1951, received a letter of commendation award. His citation reads in part: "He devoted himself tirelessly to daily contacts with the officers and men, being especially attentive to the embarked air group, and removed many of their personnel problems in order to allow their full attention to the operations."

Among the activities Chaplain Meade had described in letters to the Chaplains Division was a March of Dimes collection in the astounding amount of $9,281. Upon hearing this Chaplain Mahler [Meade wrote] "went off into grand, dramatic gestures."

From the practical standpoint, I wish to suggest that the materials for ships afloat outside the continental limits for drives such as March of Dimes, Red Cross, and Navy Relief be sent as far as possible in advance. Our material arrived on board on 23 January.

Meade had begun his letter, "As Little Boy Blue said as he reached for his trumpet, 'I think I'll blow my own horn.'" To which the Chief replied, "I trust you remember a famous sermon on the Sadducees."

ComCruDesPac

Circuit-riding destroyer chaplains are an innovation in the Chaplain Corps.[16] After preliminary discussion initiated by the then Chief of Chaplains William N. Thomas, and (then) Atlantic Fleet Chaplain S. W.

Salisbury, a "trial run" was organized in 1949. The years 1950 and 1951 saw the new program "shaken down" and put on a working basis.

On 24 July 1950 billets were established for one chaplain on the staff of each destroyer squadron commander in the Atlantic and Pacific Fleets, except for destroyer escort squadrons. One chaplain was assigned to each Destroyer Force as staff chaplain, with the rank (after February 1951) of commander.

The first chaplain to serve on the staff of Commander Cruiser Destroyer Force, Pacific (both types were incorporated into one Force in the Pacific Fleet) was Richard P. Heyl, a Roman Catholic, who was relieved in September 1950 by Raymond C. Hohenstein, Lutheran. Hohenstein served with ComCruDesPac until February 1953, when he was relieved by Chaplain F. D. Hewitt, Jr. The Force headquarters were in San Diego.

Chaplain Hohenstein was the first to hold the Force Chaplain billet. He wrote in his questionnaire reply:

What made this duty somewhat other than ordinary was the fact that the specific work at hand was to establish the newly authorized program of placing chaplains in destroyers on the staffs of DESRON [destroyer squadron] commanders [and] of initiating activity in character guidance and lay leadership in the DD [destroyer] and DE [destroyer escort] type ships.

This involved public relations work with the squadron commanders and commanding officers in connection with all three of these fields; training the chaplains themselves (the first ones reporting direct from civilian life to which they had returned after World War II); and publicizing these activities to the personnel of the command.

To accomplish the above, I personally conducted two Divine Services each Sunday aboard various type ships, and made periodic cruises in DDs, ADs destroyer tenders, and CAs cruisers—to Mare Island, Calif.; Seattle, Wash.; Pearl Harbor, T.H.; and Sasebo-Yokosuka, Japan.

It is of course impossible to mention (or, indeed, at the date of this writing to discover) every chaplain who served with destroyers in the war theater. The roster of chaplains issued by the Pacific Fleet Chaplain in July 1951 listed the following under Commander Cruiser Destroyer Force, Pacific.

Force Chaplain....	Hohenstein, R. C..	CDR	LUTH (MoSy)
BRYCE CANYON	Ditmer, M. A.....	LT	PRESBY (USA)
ComDesRon 8....	Fay, J. P.........	LTJG	RC
ComDesRon 16....	Harris, O. J.......	LTJG	BAPT (S)
HAMUL.........	Hunter, W. M....	LTJG	REF
ComDesRon 3....	Jeffers, H. W......	LTJG	METH
PIEDMONT.....	Keefe, J. M	LT	RC

[16] *Navy Chaplains Bulletin* (Fall, 1953), pp. 7–8, W. S. Peck, "The Destroyer Chaplaincy."

Worship at Sea.
Chaplain Robert A. Vaughan conducts services aboard the DIXIE.

ComDesRon 11	La Duca, P. J[1]	LTJG	RC
ComDesRon 16	Lee, E. J[1]	LTJG	BAPT (S)
ComDesRon 13	Moran, J. L[1]	LTJG	BAPT (S)
ComDesRon 1	Powell, W. D	LTJG	BAPT (S)
ComDesRon 5	Smith, L. C	LT	LUTH
ComDesRon 7	Thomas, J. R	LT	PRESBY (USA)
DIXIE	Vaughan, R. A	LCDR	METH
PIEDMONT	Wolf, A. J[2]	LT	RC
PRAIRIE	Wren, L. J	LCDR	RC

[1] Ordered to report.
[2] Ordered detached.

The ships listed were destroyer tenders.

Some notice has been taken already of the work of chaplains assigned to destroyers operating in Korean waters. Chaplain John R. Thomas reported amazement on the part of "tincan sailors" when he first came aboard that the Navy was interested in *them* and that chaplains were willing to serve aboard destroyers! In 15 months of such duty he had made 23 transfers among the ships of DesRon 7. Chaplain Willie D. Powell reported extending his destroyer ministry to three British ships, finding excellent attendance at Divine Service. (He also reported holding services on a British hospital ship.) Powell served in ComCruDesPac from February 1951 to January 1952.

Many chaplains reported that they organized re-ligious schedules in each of the ships of their squadron so that, during the chaplain's presence in one of them, the personnel of the others would be prepared to carry on weekly Bible classes, Rosary services, and even Sunday Protestant worship. This was of course part of an expanded emphasis upon lay leadership which was everywhere receiving attention during this period.

Destroyers are often referred to as the "work horses" of the fleet. Certainly their chaplains worked as hard as the other "tincan sailors," and by their efforts successfully pioneered one further area in which the Chaplain Corps was learning to carry on its mission.

Why We Fought

Over and over again chaplains wrote to the Chief that an important part of their work was trying to give their men satisfactory answers to the frequently asked question, "Why must I be here?" Though it bore more urgently upon the men in the war zone and upon their families, it was a question on the lips of many others, especially Reserves whose peacetime lives had been interrupted by sudden recalls to active duty. And indeed it was a question the nation asked itself repeatedly.

One answer, which may commend itself to some, was given in a memorandum by Col. W. S. Brown, Regimental Commander, 1st Marines, issued on 14

June 1951, summing up the regiment's operations during the preceding 2 weeks. Colonel Brown wrote:

> A lot of comrades, officers and men, have died or been injured in this "police action." I fear that more, very probably, will be before it is over. But you are making traditions of valor and professional skill that will rank alongside of, or outrank, the achievements of Marines of the First World War, the Second World War, and all our minor campaigns. And I urge you all to believe, whether or not you are, or have been, religiously inclined, that in this struggle for decency among men, we are fighting on the side of the Lord. The Communists who oppose us are fighting to deny His existence.

One thing at least is plain: The Communist invasion of the Republic of Korea had shown itself a serious menace to the spirit of freedom; this was no minor "police action," but full-scale war, and in the balance lay the future of, at the least, common decency among mankind. Just as plainly the balance had been tipped by the United Nations forces in the direction of victory.

Truce Talks

At this juncture the Communists made a new move. On 23 June 1951 Jacob A. Malik, Russian delegate to the United Nations, in a radio address in New York suggested the possibility of truce talks in Korea.[17]

---

[17] For brief introduction, see Cagle and Manson, *op. cit.*, pp. 310ff.; includes extended quotation from (then) Rear Adm. Arleigh Burke, Deputy Chief of Staff, ComNavFE, the second Navy member of the UN delegation. Admiral Joy was, of course, head of the delegation.

Two days later the Chinese Communist regime unofficially endorsed the proposal. The United Nations Command immediately signified its willingness to discuss preliminary terms, and on 8 July truce negotiations began at Kaesong, a site near the Parallel and just inside the Communist lines. This date marks the end of the 5th Korean Campaign.

The first meeting of the main delegations was scheduled for 10 July. Although the talks had begun, actual fighting did not stop, though limited to minor skirmishing and patrol actions. Writing to Chaplain Salisbury on the 10th, Division Chaplain Kelly said:

> The best news that our Division received was the word that we are to go into Corps Reserve of the X Army Corps. The plan is that we are to pull out of the line and move down near Hongchon for rest and training. The boys really need the rest. It has been a long hard grind, and our casualties have been heavy. We have been attacking and being attacked since February. And during that time we stopped two major offensives.

The move to the rest area was scheduled to begin 15 July. A little more than a year had passed since North Korean forces had crossed the 38th Parallel, the year of the heaviest fighting during the whole conflict. Five of the ten campaigns which would be recognized by the Defense Department had taken place within this period. It remained to be seen whether a military truce might be arranged which would allow representatives of the contending powers to work out a settlement for the political future of Korea.

CHAPTER 6

UNITED NATIONS SUMMER-FALL OFFENSIVE

9 July–27 November 1951

The last 2 years of the Korean War included few outstanding military campaigns. The peace talks which began in July 1951 dragged on through interminable delays and exasperating double-talk until the armistice was finally signed on 27 July 1953.[1] There were of course combat operations during these 2 years; the Department of Defense has recognized five distinct campaigns, each of which entitles personnel who participated in it a battle star on the Korean Service ribbon. For the most part limited to actions seesawing back and forth from one hill to another, for the men who fought in them these operations were nevertheless often as perilous and always more monotonous than had been the more renowned battles of the first year of the war—and mostly without the glory. War has a way of becoming commonplace to those on the "home front."

Breathing Spell

The 1st Marine Division had enjoyed a brief respite during the winter of 1950–51 at Masan. On 15 July 1951 it went into 8th Army reserve in the Hongchon area, its second and last relief from the line until May 1953. Division Chaplain Kelly suggested to the Chaplains Division that the truce talks might provide a good time for rotation; but it was felt that until the cease-fire negotiations should have taken effect, it was best to leave the current rotation system in operation. On 20 July Kelly held a meeting of the Division chaplains, which was addressed by Colonel Platt, G–1 (Division Personnel Officer) and Colonel Hager, G–4 (Division Logistics Officer). Both stressed the important work being done by chaplains and expressed command appreciation for it. Chaplain Kelly emphasized the primacy of the chaplain's spiritual ministry and the importance of his own attitude toward his work. "The job ahead of us," he told them, "is tough, but we are dedicated to God and therefore we

should be ready to make sacrifices. Certainly we all want to go home when our time is due, but we must not build up arguments with men for getting out of here. We must help them to realize what personal sacrifices may be required."

In the rest area, although the Marines were engaged in training, there was time for athletics and amateur entertainment; the chaplains had a hand in arranging these. Kelly felt that they were also showing "great ingenuity in constructing chapels."

From this period of relative quiet Chaplain Keene H. Capers recalled the following delightful incident.

We had built a beautiful little chapel in a grove of trees. The chapel area was surrounded by a rail fence made of rough logs and painted white. The altar was made of stone. Probably more than any other chapel, this one was *mine*. I had cut the logs, carried the stones, built the fence.

We were having our regular Sunday morning service. I had asked our Jewish chaplain, Elihu Rickel, to preach the sermon. My organist, a Korean, was playing the prelude. For some reason the music was not having its usual quieting effect. There was more talking than usual, even laughter; and then I realized what it was. The organist was playing the old hymn "O Happy Day, That Fixed My Choice on Thee My Saviour and My God." But to the Marines he was playing "Nobody Knows How Dry I Am!"

Work Goes On

During these days Kelly was visited by Chaplain Ivan L. Bennett, Staff Chaplain, Far East Command (General Ridgway's command), Chaplain Tobey (8th Army Staff Chaplain) and Chaplain Jones (X Corps Staff Chaplain). At the request of Chaplain W. A. Mahler, ComNavFE Staff Chaplain, Kelly lent him Chaplain Austin on Temporary Additional Duty, with the proviso that in case of emergency he would have to be immediately recalled. Several chaplains had been ill, usually with dysentery; Chaplains Uber and Wissing both contracted hepatitis, and although Uber was returned to duty after hospitalization aboard the HAVEN in Pusan, Wissing had to be evacuated to Japan and did not return to the Division.

---

[1] See C. Turner Joy, *How Communists Negotiate* (New York, 1955). Foreword by Matthew B. Ridgway, and Vatcher, Wm. Jr., *Panmunjon* (N.Y., 1958).

Memorial Service, Hongchon.

Chaplain Francis W. Kelley gives the invocation at services held 3 August for marines who died in Korea. Behind him, left to right, are: Maj. Gen. Gerald C. Thomas, Commanding General of the Division, Brig. Gen. William J. Whaling, Assistant Division Commander, and Chaplain Rickel. Chaplain Hollingsworth also participated but is not pictured here.

On 3 August a memorial service was held in memory of those Marines who had given their lives since 29 December 1950. Chaplain Kelly gave the invocation, prayer was offered by Chaplain John E. Hollingsworth, and the benediction given by Chaplain Elihu Rickel. The address was given by Maj. Gen. Gerald C. Thomas, Commanding General, 1st Marine Division. A letter sent from General Thomas to bereaved families included the following:

The ceremony . . . was held on a hillside in the valley of the Hongchon River, in an area where a considerable number of the heroes whom we gathered to honor had fallen. Several thousand men of the Division attended, and I know that I express the heartfelt sentiment of each one present when I say that we share fully in your sorrow and bereavement.

Chaplain Joseph C. Fitzgerald, 11th Marines Regi-mental Chaplain, was cited for "meritorious service . . . during operations against enemy aggressor forces in Korea from 14 January to 15 July 1951," a period stretching from the Pohang guerrilla hunt until the Division went into reserve. The citation accompanying the Bronze Star reads in part:

An able and resourceful officer, Lieutenant Commander Fitzgerald displayed exceptional understanding and confidence in ministering to the spiritual and physical needs of the men in the regiment. Exposing himself to intense enemy fire on many occasions, he unfailingly gave immediate consolation to the wounded, lending comfort to them in their distress.

Chaplain Joseph D. McDonald, Regimental Chaplain of the 1st Marines, was awarded a Gold Star in lieu of a second Bronze Star. His citation, covering the period 25 January to 17 July, includes the following:

Working under extremely trying conditions which included 1 period of 43 consecutive days in the attack, he frequently was busy day and night, evacuating and cheering the many wounded, and often administering last rites on the front lines, with no regard for the danger involved nor his own fatigue.

The roster of chaplains submitted on 1 August showed that the Chaplains Division had on the whole been successful in its rotation policy. Seventeen of those included in the roster of 21 April had been returned stateside, and 15 chaplains had reported since to the 1st Marine Division. Recent arrivals had been assigned as follows:

Service Bn........	Stanley I. Ray....	LT	PRESBY (USA)
Shore Party Bn....	Bashford S. Power.	LTJG	METH
Motor Transport..	John L. Wissing...	LT	RC
5th Marines.......	Donald W. Jolly...	LTJG	PRESBY (U)
Medical Bn.......	Robert J. Schneck.	LT	LUTH

A feeling of tense expectancy enveloped the Marines in their rest area as rumors reached them in August that the Communists were massing large reinforcements of troops and supplies in the North. Writing to Chaplain Salisbury on 11 August, Chaplain Kelly said: "There are over 650,000 Chinese and North Koreans in North Korea. Including the troops in Manchuria, they can muster a million men." Allied aviators returning from reconnaissance over enemy territory reported a tremendous number of trucks heading south with supplies. The Marines remembered how such signs were observed on previous occasions before an enemy offensive. Kelly continued:

On August 15 we shall have been in reserve for a month. That is about the length of time that a Division can expect to remain in reserve. So it is generally expected that any time after that may find us committed to the lines. It is generally felt that should the peace negotiations break down, our Division will be called upon to make an amphibious landing behind the enemy lines.

Kaesong Truce Talks

The cease-fire negotiations had begun when the chief delegates met for the first time on 10 July, Vice Adm. C. Turner Joy, Far East Naval Commander, acting for the United Nations Command. Lieutenant General Nam Il was the spokesman for the enemy. After settling on an agenda, they had become stalled during August over the first item, the demarcation of a buffer zone between the opposing forces.

The United Nations delegation held out for a demilitarized strip 20 miles deep in front of the current UN line; the Communists insisted on a zone extending 10 kilometers on either side of the 38th Parallel.[2]

[2] *Britannica Book of the Year,* 1952; article, "Korean War."

Baptism.
The waters of the Hwachon Reservoir are used for baptism by Chaplain Austin on 11 July 1951.

Besides requiring a serious withdrawal of UN forces, the Communist proposal would have given the UN a line 210 miles long as compared to the 125 miles they then had to defend. The Parallel was an arbitrary line with no military value and was, besides, objectionable to the Republic of Korea as emphasizing the artificial nature of the original division of Korea at the end of World War II. On 23 August the principal talks were broken off; for two months negotiations were conducted by subordinates, largely over alleged violations by one side or the other of the neutrality of the Kaesong area.

During the early days of the talks it became evident that the Communists were trying to accomplish by devious wrangling what their armies had failed to achieve by fighting. Any equivocation, any delay that promised to serve their purposes was considered justified.[3] The UN Command became convinced that they were using the lull to build up their defense in depth; captured equipment proved that China was supplying reinforcements. At the same time hope for peace was stirring Americans to expressed resentment of what had proved an unpopular war. Increasingly Van Fleet would find his activities restricted by the Far East Command, presumably acting on instructions from Washington,[4] which doubtless reflected widespread unwillingness on the part of the people to support the war to a successful conclusion.

UN Offensive

The breakoff of the principal negotiations occasioned by a walkout of the Red delegates on 22 August may have signalled their readiness to resume large-scale combat. In any event, the United Nations forces seized the initiative and during the last week in August began attacking in eastern Korea.[5]

Movement of Marine units was begun on the night of 26 August, to relieve elements of the 2d Army Division and the ROK 8th Division, deployed along the Kansas Line on the southern fringe of the Punchbowl. A successful thrust in this area would provide further security for the Hwachon Reservoir, the source of both water and electricity for Seoul, and for the Chorwon-Seoul rail line. One objective of this offense was the Punchbowl itself, and on 31 August the 1st Marine Division with ROK Marine Units attached opened a drive northward.

Writing to Chaplain Salisbury the next day, Chaplain Kelly commented on the difficult conditions under which they were living:

> Our Command Post has moved up pretty far. We are approximately 4 to 5 miles behind the front line. Some of the big artillery is firing from behind us. It practically knocks us out of our beds when they open up. Physically this has been one of our toughest moves. We ran into a rough, rainy period. When we arrived in our new C.P. we found it a sea of muck. It rained for about 3 days steady. We arrived on Monday and finally late Friday afternoon we were able to move into our area and set up our tents. We spent all day Saturday just trying to get set up and dried out.

11–18 September

September saw the Division engaged in heavy fighting as they captured the Punchbowl and moved on to secure the northwesterly leg of the Soyang River above it. The worst of the fighting occurred between 11 and 18 September. On 11 September, as the 1st Battalion, 7th Marines was committed against a strongly defended enemy position, Chaplain Richard T. Peeters, Roman Catholic, and James S. Ferris, Methodist, made their way to the forward aid station.

More details are supplied in the citations accompanying the Bronze Star awards subsequently given these chaplains. That of Peeters read:

> For 24 hours he gave spiritual and physical aid to the many casualties arriving at his command post. Learning on the following morning that the unit of which he was originally a member was about to be committed, he passed through a valley subject to enemy artillery fire to rejoin it. He again stationed himself at the forward aid station and began to give assistance. In addition to his regular duties he dressed wounds, organized stretcher parties, prepared hot food for the wounded and assisted in numerous other ways. Three times during the night he led native stretcher bearers through mined areas and enemy fire to the rear aid station, and on his return trips brought much needed supplies. When all casualties had been evacuated, he volunteered to maintain a security watch in order that the doctor and corpsman might obtain some rest, and remained awake throughout the night guarding the aid station. Only when the battalion was relieved was his vigil ended.

The citation for Chaplain Ferris states in part:

> When the battalion was engaged in the attack of a strongly fortified enemy position, he voluntarily stationed himself at the forward aid station where he could provide religious rites for, and succor to, the maximum number of Marines. In addition, he rendered distinct service to the battalion medical officer by organizing stretcher parties and performing the duties of a corpsman when large numbers of casualties were present. On one occasion, when a critically wounded Marine was reported lying in an exposed area under heavy

---

[3] Cf. Joy, *op. cit., passim.* See also C. Berger, *The Korea Knot* (Philadelphia, 1957), pp. 141ff.; Cagle and Manson, *op. cit.,* pp. 310–321. Also helpful is ch. VIII of vol. IV of the official history of U.S. Marine operations in Korea, unpublished at the time of this writing.

[4] *Life* (May 11, 1953), J. A. Van Fleet, "The Truth About Korea," p. 133.

[5] Montross, unpublished vol. IV of the history of Marine operations in Korea. Also Miller *et al., op. cit.,* ch. VI.

enemy artillery fire, he unhesitatingly proceeded to the spot where the wounded man lay and assisted in his evacuation. He continued to give assistance for a period in excess of 48 hours without rest.

A third chaplain was decorated for devoted action on that same 11 September. Henry H. Hayes, who had previously received the Bronze Star, was given the Letter of Commendation award. His citation reads in part:

> While under continuous fire from enemy artillery and mortars, he fearlessly stationed himself at the forward aid station, and with utter disregard for his own personal safety, went about ministering to the wounded and providing them the utmost in comfort and safety. When not performing these duties, he voluntarily organized and dispatched stretcher parties and medical supply trains to the infantry companies. Through his determined efforts and unselfish actions, the lives of many of the critically wounded were saved.

Two Chaplains Wounded

Two chaplains received light wounds during this period. Chaplain Ferris was wounded on 14 September. Hearing that the Marine artillery unit supporting his regiment had received direct hits, Ferris hurried to the place and en route was knocked down by a shell which exploded about 10 feet from where he was walking. A lad accompanying the chaplain was killed. In a letter to Chaplain C. L. Drury (then Chaplain Corps historian), dated 20 August 1956, Chaplain Ferris described the event:

> All I can say is that the good Lord was with me. It wasn't until later that evening when I had returned to my own outfit and was changing my clothes that I discovered my clothes were covered with blood, not necessarily my own blood. My clerk noticed I had a number of cuts on my back. Thinking that there might be some small splinters of shrapnel, I reported to sick bay and found everything to be O.K.

An examination showed the wounds to be slight. However, Ferris was reported as a casualty and his wife received a telegram to that effect before he could write and let her know that he was not seriously injured.

The second chaplain wounded was J. E. Hollingsworth. Somehow a report was circulated which reached his wife at home that the chaplain had died of his wounds; actually the wound was not serious enough to require hospitalization. He would later receive the Letter of Commendation award for "excellent service . . . during operations against the enemy . . . 20 April to 15 October 1951." His citation includes the following:

> Despite the threat of enemy action, he often held Divine Services for the infantry companies within easy range of the

enemy positions. On one such occasion, he was wounded while holding services. He refused to be evacuated until he had reassured the Marines in their faith.

The "Medics"

If chaplains sometimes received decorations, and often both silent and expressed respect and appreciation from their fellows, they in turn were warm in their regard for the sacrificial spirit evidenced around them.

The Division's Jewish chaplain, E. H. Rickel, wrote of one 30-hour period in which "A" Medical Company cared for some 675 wounded Marines. Every man, he wrote, from highly trained specialist to truck driver, sweated and worked at furious pace according to his skill. And he quoted with obvious approval the remark of a surgeon, washing up after an extremely delicate operation, "I'm damned proud to be a member of this outfit. I've never seen anything like it."

About 8 o'clock on Sunday evening 80 men were brought in from the enemy line; 78 turned out to be ROK Marines, 2 were North Koreans. Accompanied by interpreter and chaplain, a doctor began routine admissions work. The Korean equivalent of "Where do you hurt?" was repeatedly called out, as doctors and corpsmen ascertained the extent and nature of wounds and prepared initial charts.

> The chaplain bent down to hold a canteen of water to the mouth of one of the wounded enemy. A gleam of life flashed into the half-closed almond-shaped eyes; he lifted his head up, bowed in thanks, and drank deeply. A South Korean Marine looked on with amazement and shouted, "He is the enemy." The chaplain asked Yu to explain that here and now there were no enemies, only wounded.

Chaplain Rickel's account continued:

> The devotion to duty of the medical personnel was reinforced, was only equalled by the conduct of the wounded. Faces showed pain, involuntary anguished moans escaped, but at no time did anyone hear loud outbursts. The wounded waited patiently, with closed eyes, tight lips, and gratitude that they were still alive.
>
> And when they did talk, this is what one heard. "I'm okay, Doc, take care of him." "Do you think I'll make it, chaplain? Gee, my poor wife, she'll be so hurt." "Pray for me, padre, I promised my little boy that I'd take him on a camping trip when I got back."

As one warrant officer said, if that number ever hit a hospital in the States, they'd have to declare a city-wide emergency. But men can and do rise above themselves, above what they commonly think is expected of them and indeed expect of themselves. Perhaps, as Rickel said, "You have to see it to believe it"; but when it happens, one can only pause in humble gratitude.

Chaplain Harold H. Cummings also worked with a medical company during these harrowing days. Almost overwhelmed with casualties, the "medics" worked around the clock, and the chaplain along with them. Later he was cited for the period 15–21 September, being awarded the Letter of Commendation, which speaks of his spending "approximately 18 hours a day administering spiritual aid to wounded and dying Marines."

Vignettes

Two incidents from the heavy fighting in September, 1951 may serve to document the experience of chaplains in combat. The 3d Battalion, 1st Marines was on the east coast north of the 38th Parallel. Moving up with the forward aid station, Chaplain K. H. Capers would set up what came to be known as the "Chaplain's Galley." There "honest-to-goodness" coffee and even steak, bacon, and eggs were offered casualties and battle-weary Marines who chanced by. The helicopter pilots evacuating the wounded would replenish the larder on their return trips.

On one occasion, when the aid station had just moved forward, it became impossible for bearers to evacuate litter cases over the mountainous terrain to the rear aid station. Until helicopters should arrive, there was a long wait. Capers rigged for church, 65 stretchers providing "pews" for that many seriously wounded, with less serious casualties sitting around. The chaplain's organist, Pak, interpreted for the enemy casualties, among whom was a North Korean officer, seriously wounded, who had refused coffee and cigarettes and had sneered at the chaplain's efforts to be comforting. During the service, however, he appeared to be listening and afterward asked to talk to Capers. Pak interpreted: "The prisoner says that he knows the imperialists are butchers and show mercy only to gain their own ends. But he says he likes that Man you were talking about and would like to save your life. He says you'd better get out of here because the North Koreans are going to attack tonight in great strength to rescue him, and if you don't escape you will be killed with the rest of the Americans." In fact, the Communists did not attack, though they were well able to do so. But that Communist prisoner had been provided every ministry our own troops received and was evacuated by helicopter with our own wounded.

Chaplain Capers was given the Letter of Commendation award for service during the period 27 April–9 October. His citation reads in part: "He moved with the battalion under all conditions and remained with the forward aid station where his work could best be performed. His faith and sincere interest in all gave strength to the wounded and the weary."

Further Awards

By the third week in September fighting in the 1st Marine Division sector of X Corps front began to show results. There was much more to come, however, both in the 2d Infantry Division's sector, and further west, along the IX Corps front.

A fifth chaplain, Joseph P. Trodd, would be awarded the Bronze Star for outstanding service during this period, specifically for 16 September–8 October. While his battalion was engaged with enemy forces in the vicinity of E-dong, Trodd remained at the forward aid station, assisting with the casualties. Taking no thought for his own danger or fatigue, tirelessly he ministered to the men who passed through the aid station, offering solace and reassurance and spiritual strength.

Three others received the Letter of Commendation: Chaplain Donald W. Jolly for excellent service during the period 8 July–18 October; Arthur M. Kulinski for 25 August–27 October; and William A. Taylor for the period 9 May–19 November 1951.

Jolly was in the 5th Marines. His citation especially mentions an occasion when the command post was subjected to artillery barrages; the chaplain "moved about the area fearlessly, giving comfort and spiritual aid to the wounded men, and through the night maintaining a cheerful conversation. . . ."

Chaplain Kulinski was serving in the Medical Battalion. He followed an exhausting schedule to provide Roman Catholic ministrations for adjacent units lacking a chaplain of that faith. "He voluntarily spent many hours at the medical companies, ministering spiritual reassurance and comfort to the wounded. When an artillery unit was subjected to the counter-battery fire, he proceeded to that unit to make himself available for those wounded who sought comfort in his encouragement and confidence."

Taylor's award covers a long stretch, but his citation centers upon a particular incident when his regiment (11th Marines) occupied positions in the area of Yanggu.

He learned that an adjacent infantry regiment was suffering heavy casualties and was endeavoring to evacuate its casualties under serious handicaps and lack of facilities. He promptly went to the regiment's aid and established communications, arranged transportation, and assisted in securing additional medical aid for the wounded. When it began to rain, he sought out blankets, ponchos, and shelter halves to

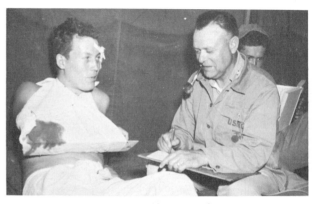

A Letter Home.
Chaplain Elihu Rickel takes dictation at an aid station for a wounded marine.

Care for the Wounded.
Chaplain J. P. Trodd administers rites to a wounded marine as the corpsman gives him plasma.

Makeshift Altar.
It is said "necessity is the mother of invention." Pictured here is a demonstration of one of the methods used to set up an altar near the front.

protect the wounded men. With complete disregard for personal comfort and fatigue, he spent long hours, day and night, at the evacuation relay point, giving comfort to the casualties and writing letters home for them. During another period, when two battalions of the regiment were being subjected to daily counterbattery fire, he continued to make frequent visits to the two units, comforting and inspiring the wounded, as well as those who had to continue their work under fire.

Chaplains serving in the Division during this Sixth Korean Campaign received five Bronze Star awards, seven Letter of Commendation awards, and two Purple Heart awards. Approximately 50 percent of the Chaplain Section were decorated, not considering those who had earlier received citations or would later do so. Never before in the history of the Navy Chaplain Corps had so many from such a relatively small group won such recognition in so short a time.

Chaplain Peck Comes Aboard

From 1 August until Chaplain Kelly was relieved, the following new chaplains had arrived: Edmund W. Pipho (Lutheran), James F. Follard (Roman Catholic), Walter J. Vierling (Lutheran), Robert N. Ruleman (Methodist), and John J. O'Neill (Roman Catholic). On 10 September Kelly wrote to the Chief:

Colonel Krulak asked me again the other day when an Episcopal chaplain was coming. General Shepherd, FMF Pacific, was here for a visit and commented that there is no Episcopal chaplain in any part of FMF Pacific. I know Krulak is Episcopal, so I guess General Shepherd must be also.

Chaplain Kelly had been suffering from dysentery. He wrote on 17 September that the doctors had ordered him to the hospital ship CONSOLATION; the next day, upon his evacuation, Chaplain J. C. Fitzgerald was assigned duty as Division Chaplain until Chaplain W. S. Peck, Jr., on his way as Kelly's relief, should report in. Peck reported to the Division CP on 8 October 1951 and Fitzgerald was detached to return to the States.

The Chief, replying to Peck's first letter from Korea, requested that as Division Chaplain he continue certain practices which his predecessors had evolved

Seminary Gift.

Chaplain Richard E. Barnes looks on as Sergeant Powers hands Dr. Kim Cha Choon, Acting President of Chosen Presbyterian Seminary a monetary gift for his institution.

for keeping the Chaplains Division cognizant of the situation there.

I would appreciate, for example, a weekly letter from you, no matter how brief, which will enable me to keep abreast with the status of our chaplains in the Division. Any letters of length which you have time to prepare will also be much appreciated, since we peruse every line with an eagle eye. We shall expect you to make recommendations with regard to your chaplains, particularly if any are not well or should, in your opinion, be rotated for other reasons in advance of the normal date.

We would also like to receive from you a monthly roster of your chaplains, indicating especially their current assignment and their date of reporting to the Division. . . . For your information, I send the word that we will no longer order chaplains to Korea to relieve others by name. We have found in several cases that the system resulted in some chaplains serving over the required time and others being returned to the States short of their normal period. We shall instead detach chaplains on or about the seventh month after reporting regardless of the arrival of reliefs and will depend on you to keep us current at all times as to the number of chaplains aboard, desirable denominational distribution, and any other matters of that sort on which you have an opinion.

We want you to feel that you have top priority of all commands in the field, and that you will get what you want if you let us know what it is, within the limitations under which this office works.

On October 13–16 Pacific Fleet Chaplain George A. Rosso and FMF Pacific Chaplain Martell H.

Twitchell made a visit of inspection, and were afforded opportunity to see many of the chaplains in the field.

On 29 October Peck issued his first Memorandum as Division Chaplain, establishing an SOP for the requisition of chaplain supplies and appointing the Combat Service Group chaplain as Supply Chaplain. Apparently the problem of supplies was a continuing one, for on 4 December Chaplain J. P. Mannion, Assistant Director, Chaplains Division, wrote to Peck as follows:

We are constantly receiving complaints regarding the availability of chaplains supplies and equipment for the Division. The truth of the matter is that we have never received a request from the Division since it has been in Korea for either supplies or equipment. We know that some supplies have been furnished by the Staff Chaplain, Commander, MSTS, Pacific.

It is proper to rely, in so far as necessary, upon the Army for equipment and supplies. However, there are certain items . . . which we normally supply which the Army does not have available.

Would it be possible to discuss the following with your G–4? We are quite willing to make available, without reimbursement, all portable equipment needed by our chaplains. We anticipate that under the conditions under which you operate you need both equipment for immediate use and equipment in reserve. If you will give us your requirements by letter or by requisition, we will act on it immediately.

Our greatest need is for adequate shipping instructions. . . . Please let us have your G–4's reaction to this.

Air Wing

From the Punchbowl area and the Division's front ground lines our attention must be turned now to the air-support units and their headquarters far to the south. On 12 August Wing Chaplain Barnes wrote to Chaplain Salisbury:

As for the "truce" talks, no appreciable progress seems to have been made. The troops at the front have had a lull, but not so the aviators. This command is carrying as heavy a load as ever or more so. We are regularly losing planes and pilots. The ground fire has seriously increased in volume and accuracy.

With the arrival of Chaplain Stephen G. Horvath the 1st Marine Aircraft Wing was able to provide Roman Catholic ministrations for its personnel at Pusan. Brig. Gen. Thomas J. Cushman, commanding the Wing, wrote to the Reverend Brian Geraghty, Superior of the St. Columban Missionary Society:

During the absence of a Catholic chaplain . . . you and other priests of the Columban Order have graciously extended to us the deeply appreciated ministry of your services at Mass, Confessions and personal counseling. Please accept my gratitude and that of my officers and men.

Some of the more interesting of Wing Chaplain Barnes' reports concern the work of Marines in aiding the often destitute and homeless Korean civilians. On 12 August he wrote:

My work here has thrown me into contact with missionaries and refugee church groups, as it did John Murphy. Among others is a Presbyterian Seminary, which, formerly in Seoul, is now in Pusan. Out of a student body of 300 they have assembled from the far corners 170 students and 5 professors. Their Christian faith and courage is astounding. We and other commands have helped them with offerings, surveyed tenting, and scrap wood. They are living and holding classes in two squad tents and a few nondescript shacks they have built. . . . Their chow consists of two bowls of rice per day. It was my privilege to give one of the commencement addresses via interpreter, who by the way was the dean of the seminary and holds a Ph D. degree from Toronto University.

The whole of South Korea is filled with amazing stories, stories which should thrill the church at home with the heroic Christian courage of this infant church to absorb punishment, adapt itself to disruptive and chaotic conditions, gather together in the most unexpected places, and hold church, Sunday School, and study classes. One group of refugee pastors on Chejudo Island of all things asked me to get them 20 Greek New Testaments! Believe it or not, they were organized into a Greek New Testament class, meeting every day.

The singing of these church people is inspiring. I have invited two Korean church choirs and the Korean Navy Symphonic Orchestra and Chorus to K–1 [Pusan] for concerts. The officers and men could hardly believe their ears when these people rendered portions of the *Messiah,* "Open the Gates of the Temple," Stephen Foster folk songs and other numbers, and all in English. (The Korean Navy organization was acquired by simply taking the whole Seoul symphonic organization, men and women, into the Korean Navy.)

The Wing continued short of its complement of chaplains. On occasion Chaplain Cummins of MAG 12 went for a week to the Itami (Japan) units, and Barnes had himself gone over twice for counseling on some critical cases. The Wing's new commander, Maj. Gen. C. F. Schilt, on his own initiative pressed the matter of chaplain shortage, especially at Itami. Barnes wrote to Salisbury: "I gave him the picture and told him I had been in correspondence with you and that you were aware of the problem and were doing everything possible to bring us up to T/O."

Moral Welfare Program

Barnes wrote that General Schilt was greatly concerned about the moral problems confronting the command. During June Chaplain Cummins was given T.A.D. (temporary additional duty) at Itami to cooperate in a venereal disease control program directed by the Medical Department. On four afternoons the chaplain and a doctor gave lectures, and the new film produced by the Chaplains Division *To Be Held in Honor* was shown. During July and August the film, borrowed from ComNavFE Chaplain Mahler, was shown in all units of the Wing except a few isolated radar groups. Writing to Chaplain Edward J. Hemphill, Assistant to the Chief of Chaplains for Material and Special Projects, Barnes reported agreement among doctors and chaplains that the film was well done. The response of the men had been favorable, although "some wiseguys always find opportunity to make cracks."

Hemphill in his reply emphasized the importance of audience preparation. "It was not intended that this film would be shown . . . without first preparing them for the subject it treats." He suggested the following as a useful procedure:

1. A lecture by the chaplain on the moral factors of incontinence.
2. The screening of the film.
3. A discussion by the group of the meaning for them of the points included in lecture and film.
4. Second screening of the film.

Barnes and Mahler were agreed that Far Eastern commands deserved a high priority on distribution lists for moral guidance materials. Hemphill replied:

We are quite conscious of the fact that you are located in

an area which justifies the use of a great amount of program resources in the field of morality training. As you know, there are no established Training Aids Sections nearer than Guam. We are quite willing to furnish the program resources if you or Chaplain Mahler will indicate from where they can be circulated. From here, we are not certain where the program resources should be sent that they may be available to a large number of chaplains.

I am sure I speak for the Chief when I say we want our chaplains in the forward area to receive everything they think they need. We are willing to reduce supplies for other chaplains in order to meet this top priority need. Therefore, feel perfectly free to come directly to us with your requirements, making sure that the shipment instructions are adequate to insure delivery, and we will get the material to you. We can worry about going through channels when you are out of an emergency situation.

In August Barnes flew to Japan to confer with Mahler and others about the marriage of Marine personnel to Japanese nationals. More than once the chaplains pointed out that their approach to problems of morals and morale aimed to be positive, not simply prohibitory. Strenuous efforts were made to acquaint service personnel with the better aspects of Japanese and Korean culture and life, and to remind them of the values of their own. On one occasion, 3,000 paper bound books were received by air shipment and distributed through the Wing. Early in June Chaplain Barnes had taken steps to secure books through the Library Services Branch, Bureau of Naval Personnel.

Venereal disease was of course a continuing problem in units more or less permanently located. While the chaplains willingly cooperated with their commands and Medical Departments, their primary concern was never either disciplinary or therapeutic measures, but moral and spiritual health as a positive factor in a happy, wholesome life. The chaplain's ministry is first and always a concern for the well-being of total personality.

Barnes subsequently wrote that an active moral guidance program was under way and indicated that the 1st Marine Aircraft Wing Chaplain was in an excellent position to act as custodian and distribution source for chaplains' films. Therefore in December 1951 Chaplain Mannion, Assistant Director of the Chaplains Division, made arrangements for certain films to be forwarded to the Wing Chaplain. He wrote: "As other films become available, we shall forward them directly to you for use with the Wing and the rear echelon units of the 1st Marine Division."

Late in April 1952, after Chaplain J. F. Parker, S. Baptist, had become Wing Chaplain, the Chaplains Division would send to the Wing two of the recently developed "Black Magic" boards with accompanying cardboard symbols to be used in moral guidance lectures. This expensive visual aid equipment was intended to be circulated from the Wing Chaplain's office for use in individual commands.

Chaplain Barnes' Diary

The following notes have been taken from Chaplain Barnes' monthly contribution to the 1st Marine Aircraft Wing Historical Diary.[6] They are here paraphrased.

13 July 1951. Visited Dr. Appenzeller, Executive Head, Church World Service in Korea, at Pusan. Delivered to him eight cartons of refugee supplies shipped from churches in the States and Kobe, Japan.

17 July. Accompanied Wing Surgeon to visit Danish hospital ship JUTLANDIA and refugee children's hospital, Pusan.

18 July. Attended commencement exercises of Chosan Seminary; addressed them through an interpreter. Marines of Air Wing and Protestant congregation at Pusan contributed $280 and scrap lumber for rebuilding.

29 July. Offering of $68 for a graduate of Chosan Seminary going to Japan for further study.

30 July. Address through interpreter at commencement exercises of Methodist Seminary of Seoul, now in Pusan.

Needless to say, such contacts between Navy chaplains and the leading institutions of the Korean Christian community were helpful in building good relations between United States military forces and Korean nationals.

2 September 1951. Visited Chosan Seminary with Sergeant Powers to present donation of 600,000 *won* [$100], a gift from Powers' mother's church in Texas. PIO pictures and story prepared for release in San Antonio papers.

12 September. Concert by the All-Korean Pilgrim Choir, 30 trained voices, all in English. Reception at General Schilt's quarters for distinguished missionaries and Korean guests before concert.

22 September. Chapel at K-3 Pohang finished and furnished except for seating. Chapel chairs on order.

24–28 September. Attended Protestant Chaplains annual retreat at GHQ Chapel Center, Tokyo. Speakers were George Buttrick, Edmund D. Soper, and Laton Holmgren. Arranged by Army chaplains in Tokyo.

Barnes' letters to the Chief from the middle of September on indicated the 1st Marine Aircraft Wing in process of moving most of its units, thus requiring new plans for chaplain coverage. Chaplain Edwin R. Weidler, Evan. & Ref., had reported on 21 August, relieving George W. Cummins in MAG 12, who left for home. On 17 September Chaplain Howard A. Seymour, Methodist, arrived, and was assigned at

---

[6] Filed in the Historical Section, G-3, Marine Corps Headquarters, Washington, D.C.

Itami. A Marine antiaircraft artillery battalion was being established at Pusan; their commanding officer had requested a chaplain's billet but it was disallowed. Barnes wrote that once the MAW had left Pusan, he would try to get Army or Air Force chaplains to cover that unit.

On 12 October Chaplain Horvath was injured when a weapons carrier in which he was riding went off the road. A plane had gone down about 15 miles short of the base and Horvath was in the searching party. He suffered a broken hip and was evacuated to Yokosuka Hospital.

Barnes' last letter from the period of the 6th Korean Campaign reported further moves by the Marine air units. "The Wing continues to fly heavy schedules and we continue to lose planes and pilots. The new HMR–161 boys have been making the news with their helicopter lifts up at the front." Once again it was necessary to rely on missionary priests for Roman Catholic coverage and Barnes was hard put to distribute the services of his chaplains to best advantage.

Helicopter Troop Lifts

Barnes' reference to the "HMR–161 boys" deserves comment. During the 1st Division's rugged fight at the northern rim of the Punchbowl, 11–18 September, in terrain of appalling difficulties, helicopter squadron HMR–161 began ferrying in supplies and evacuating casualties. On 21 September they completed the first troop lift in combat, a move dubbed "Operation Summit." During the weeks that followed they moved company-sized units, and in October a whole battalion. These maneuvers have been hailed as opening a new phase of Marine Corps amphibious doctrine.[7] The evacuation of casualties by helicopter also initiated a new technique of medical care and has been credited with saving countless lives of seriously wounded personnel.

"Track Busting"

September saw the interdiction effort of the carrier task force enter a third phase.[8] (The first had been breaking the Yalu bridges and those of the rail net in the northeast. The second, dubbed "Operation Strangle," was the effort during the summer of 1951 to cut the highways.) Now relieved of their missions in support of the September ground advance, by mid-October the BON HOMME RICHARD, the ESSEX, and the ANTIETAM were concentrating on pinpoint

---

[7] See Lynn Montross, *Cavalry of the Sky* (New York, 1954), ch. IX.
[8] Cagle and Manson, *op. cit.*, pp. 241–260.

bombing of rail lines. Though no night carrier was in service, the carriers worked "round the clock," for it was soon obvious that the Communists worked at night to repair the damage.

BON HOMME RICHARD

From February 1951 to January 1953 the senior chaplain in BON HOMME RICHARD was Howard M. Day, a Southern Baptist. The following excerpts from his questionnaire reply present a vivid picture.

The executive officer asked me if I would say grace before each meal in the wardroom. This was quite an unusual procedure at that time, though I understand it is now becoming commonplace. The Catholic chaplain said grace at the first sitting and I at the second, at lunch and dinner. No blessing was said at breakfast since it was served over a period of time. The reaction was universally favorable . . . and several expressed regret that it was not feasible to have a similar arrangement for the general mess.

(In the general mess there are no "sittings," but continuous serving by means of a cafeteria line. Grace at meals has, of course, had a long, if sporadic, history in the Navy.) Chaplain Day's account continued:

When operating off Korea it was not possible to use either the mess decks or the hangar deck for Sunday services. We therefore held services in the wardroom, utilizing the lounge and main section. About 400 could be accommodated by using folding chairs and having many stand.

This resulted in considerable inconvenience for our officers, who had to eat breakfast in the small after-section of the wardroom on a "hot seat" basis. My executive officer was somewhat dubious as to the reaction . . . to this arrangement, but there were no complaints at all.

In fact several officers started attending as a result of hearing our services on the public address system while eating their breakfasts. As one jokingly expressed it, "Efficiency is a good thing, but trying to feed the body and the spirit at the same time is carrying efficiency too far. I'm going to do my eating between services and start attending as I should."

As on many ships, there were evening prayers just before Taps over the P.A. system. Chaplain Day alternated this duty with John A. Keeley, Roman Catholic chaplain from May 1951 to January 1952.

At first we thought to have such prayers only while at sea. When we stopped the practice, upon first entering port, a large number of men wanted to know why we had stopped. Thereafter prayers were said both at sea and in port. . . . There were a great many favorable comments from both Christian and non-Christian men.

Chaplain Day made use of laymen in holding two Bible classes each week, one for elementary, another for more advanced study. He thought discussion was better when laymen were in charge. "It did not reduce my workload, however," he wrote, "since I still had to prepare each lesson, assist the teacher in his preparation, and be ready at the class to answer questions that were raised."

Assigned additional duty as special services officer, the chaplain supervised the library, which was kept open at least 8 hours a day while at sea; published the daily press news and the weekly ship's paper; supervised the athletic officer's work and the hobby shop; edited the ship's cruise book; supervised the daily 4-hour broadcast of transcriptions and "disc jockey" programs; and provided "live entertainment" in the form of "Happy Hours" at sea and professional acts in port. Added to all this he arranged sightseeing tours in various ports. "At sea, reading was perhaps the major form of recreation. Approximately 18,000 pocket books (of considerably higher quality than found on the average newstand) were secured and distributed during the 23 months I was aboard."

Day worked alone until joined by Chaplain Keeley in May. Upon reporting, Keeley wrote to the Chief:

> This ship is still in the process of breaking in, though the worst is over. The men have been driven hard but have maintained their spirits admirably. Church attendance has been exceptionally good for both of us and cooperation from the command had been from good to excellent. We are short on space and the workload demands more men than we have at our call, but we shall get along all right.

Near the main gate of the U.S. Naval Base, Yokosuka, men on liberty from BON HOMME RICHARD passed a small, faded sign reading "Mikasi Chapel." Investigation led Chaplain Keeley to the Japanese pastor, Father Hatada, and from him was learned the need of a new building. Back at sea the men began making contributions at Sunday masses, and only one month later, when the ship was again in Yokosuka, $200 was contributed to the building fund. To express their gratitude, Father Hatada and a choir of 40 Japanese children came aboard to sing in Latin the traditional chants of the Mass.

ESSEX

Among the missions of the carrier ESSEX was a raid, long desired by the Far East Command and finally approved, subject to careful precautions, by the Joint Chiefs of Staff, on the port of Rashin in the far northeast of Korea, 17 miles from the Soviet frontier and less than 110 miles from Vladivostock.[9] The immunity afforded Rashin by Washington's care not to violate the Russian border had allowed it to become a most important supply center for the Communist war effort. Finally in August 1951 the strike was accomplished by B–29's, escorted by jets from ESSEX.

Her chaplains at the time were Joseph J. Buzek and Paul C. Morton. Recalled to active duty in September 1950, Chaplain Buzek reported aboard ESSEX in June 1951. His activities may be taken as typical. Arising before dawn he would administer Holy Communion to pilots preparing for an early morning strike. After breakfast, he checked incoming messages to see whether any of them might call for the chaplain's help in breaking news to a crewmember. Next followed the daily visit to the sick bay, and then a tour of the ship, dropping in on the men in their working compartments.

Afternoons were spent in prayer and study, interspersed with conferences with those seeking advice and help. Daily mass was said at 1630, in a classroom. Evenings were devoted to choir practice, religious instructions, and devotions. When the ship was not engaged in actual operations, Sunday services were held on the hangar deck, with a Hammond organ to aid the "church atmosphere." At other times services were held in the crew's messing compartment, which made necessary several services to accommodate all who wished to attend.

In December 1951 Chaplain Buzek arranged for Archbishop Maximilien de Furstenburg, Apostolic Delegate to Japan, to administer Confirmation to a group of 19 sailors whom he had prepared for that sacrament. The rite took place in the Archbishop's private chapel in Tokyo.

Chaplain Morton had been in ESSEX since January 1951. The following story, taken from his questionnaire, reply, gives its own quiet but eloquent testimony.

> On the night of 26 September 1951, after a crash, explosion, and fire on the flight deck, I was in the sick bay with the injured. One young man was so badly burned he was not expected to live. He was not what one would call religious. In his pain he would say, "Chaplain, just stay where I can see you." Six weeks later he died, but not until he had accepted Christ.

ANTIETAM

Senior chaplain in the carrier ANTIETAM was Paul C. Pieri, from June 1951 until his release to inactive duty in July 1952. Pieri had been a member of an Organized Reserve unit and was recalled to active duty in August 1950, being first assigned to Marine Barracks, Camp Pendleton, Calif.

His cohort, Protestant Chaplain Don M. Michael, was just out of Chaplains School (class 2–51), reporting also in June 1951. Michael served until September, when he was transferred to the IOWA where he

---

[9] Ibid., pp. 245–7.

remained until November 1952. His 2-year sea tour was completed by duty in the repair ship BRIAREUS, to July 1953.

Seaborne Artillery

Other ships meanwhile were lending their support in engagements of various kinds. Destroyers sought out coastline bridges and railroads to shell.[10] Heavier ships added their fire to frontline targets. In late July, to counteract the Communist claim at the Kaesong talks that the Reds controlled a large area south of the Parallel and to keep the approaches to Seoul open, a naval force entered the Han estuary and lobbed shells into the frontlines, guided by plane spotters.

The leading ship in this demonstration was the LOS ANGELES, whose chaplain was William J. Organ, a Presbyterian. In September her fire power would be used against enemy troops and gun positions in the Kojo area, and again in November, when shelling from LOS ANGELES was instrumental in saving the ROK I Corps, low in ammunition and in danger of being overrun by a Communist breakthrough. The NEW JERSEY was similarly engaged in support of the 1st Marine Division during September and early October.

PhibPac

From the beginning ships of the Amphibious Force, Pacific had been engaged in the Korean conflict. Besides Force Chaplain William J. Kuhn and two others stationed at the Amphibious Base, Coronado, Calif., the following chaplains were on duty with PhibPac in July 1951.

Day, Edgar A.....	LT	BAP (A)	BAYFIELD
Helmich, Edward C.	LCDR	MORAVIAN	MT McKIN-LEY
Holmes, Richard J.	LT	RC	ELDORADO
Kokoszka, William J.	LT	RC	GEORGE CLYMER
Ruder, Frederick A.	LT	METH	CALVERT

Of these ships BAYFIELD, GEORGE CLYMER, and CALVERT were attack transports; MT McKINLEY and ELDORADO, amphibious command ships. Chaplain Robert T. Noland, Southern Baptist, served with Naval Beach Group ONE from September 1950 to January 1952.

Hospital Ships

Brief mention was made in chapter 2 of the arrival of the hospital ships CONSOLATION and REPOSE in the war zone. Serving in CONSOLATION was Protestant Chaplain C. F. Holland. After a month at Pusan, the ship moved to Inchon to receive casualties from the Inchon-Seoul operation, and later, following in the wake of attacking UN forces, to Wonsan and thence to Hungnam.[11]

In November Roman Catholic Chaplain V. J. W. Lustig reported aboard, having traveled to Korea in the tanker CIMMARRON. He wrote later that the crew had told him he was the first chaplain ever to have ridden in CIMMARRON, and that to the best of their knowledge his was the first Mass celebrated aboard. He mentioned also holding a "general service," a type of worship held for Protestants by Roman Catholic chaplains in the absence of a Protestant chaplain. The Catholic men had been holding Rosary services on their own, he reported, and the Protestants informal gatherings for worship. Lustig was aboard on Thanksgiving Day and was invited to say a blessing at dinner.

Serving aboard the CONSOLATION, Chaplain Lustig had a special cabinet built in his stateroom for the reservation of the Blessed Sacrament. "Thus I could give daily Communion to those who desired [it]. Some days as many as 38 patients received in their wards. Holy Viaticum was thus always available for the dying, even though we had no chapel aboard the ship."

Chaplain Holland was relieved by Leroy C. Austin in the summer of 1951. Lustig served until April 1952, being replaced by Chaplain Martin J. Hoar. Austin was relieved by Chaplain Franklin C. Black in July 1952. Arthur M. Kulinski, who had earlier seen duty with the 1st Marine Division, would later relieve Chaplain Hoar in July 1953. There were thus (after the initial buildup) two chaplains aboard at all times, their tours staggered so that continuity was provided by one experienced chaplain as the other was in turn relieved.

The second AH (hospital ship) to report for duty in the war theater was REPOSE, arriving 16 September 1950. Aboard were Chaplains Henry P. White (Methodist) and Charles F. Karnasiewicz (Roman Catholic), both of whom had reported in August. Others subsequently assigned to REPOSE were:

Allen L. Irwin......	CONG	August 1951–October 1952
Leonard F. White....	RC	June 1951–October 1952
Luther E. Olmon....	LUTH	September 1952–July 1954
Earl W. Smith......	RC	August 1952–March 1954

---

[10] *Ibid.,* pp. 323–30, for this and following paragraph.

[11] Montross and Canzona, *op. cit.,* vol. III, p. 139.

On 13 October 1950 a third hospital ship arrived for Korean service. In the HAVEN were Chaplains John J. Reardon, Roman Catholic, and Paul K. Potter, Methodist, both of whom had reported in September. Reardon was relieved in October 1951 by Francis J. Klass, and Potter in December by Edwin R. Howard. Howard in turn was relieved in October 1952 by Chaplain John R. Tufft, and in December of the same year Klass was replaced by Chaplain John D. O'Leary.

It will be noticed that the average tour was approximately 1 year during the earlier part of the war; after 1952 the time began to be extended to from 18 months to 2 years.

In chapter 3 has been mentioned the hazardous minesweeping of Wonsan harbor by the U.S. Navy. At the same time General Walker's 8th Army had captured the North Korean capital, Pyongyang, and the need for opening Chinnampo, its port, was imperative; it too was heavily mined. The Navy took on a second simultaneous minesweeping job. Finally, on 20 November 1950, a deep channel was opened; the first deep draft vessel to be piloted in was the hospital ship REPOSE, with less than 1 foot of water to spare. The officer in charge of minesweeping radioed his congratulations to the pilot, an Australian naval officer named Gladstone, regretting however that he must stay aboard overnight. Gladstone replied that he could doubtless stand the company of 50 nurses for 1 night! [12]

"Talking Letters"

The summer of 1952 saw introduced a novel service for badly wounded patients, unable to write letters home. Free disc recording was instituted by the ship's welfare departments. It came about when REPOSE, returning stateside after a 16-month tour in Korean waters, was being resupplied. Professional type recorders were purchased from welfare funds, one for each of the three hospital ships. It is believed that this is the first time such facilities were made available in forward areas.

The chaplains were alerted to watch for an incapacitated patient, who was asked if he would like to make a recording and have it sent home without charge to himself or his family. After clearance with the commanding officer, the man was given time to plan what he wished to say and a time set for the actual recording.

Ten minutes was required to fill a disc on both

sides. Often the chaplain would begin, and sometimes the ward nurse would add a few words of encouragement for the "folks back home." The man himself then used the remaining time, the microphone being set up by his bunk. Enclosed with a letter from the commanding officer, the disc was then mailed in a special envelope first class to any desired address in the United States.

The superiority of "talking letters" over those which otherwise would have been written by the chaplain or someone else, is obvious. Nothing could more personally convey to a man's family a sense of his individuality than his own voice, even on a record.

Services

Services of worship were held daily in the hospital ships by both Protestant and Roman Catholic chaplains. It was possible for men in their bunks to listen in over the head-sets which also carried news, music, and diversionary fare. Usually morning and evening prayers were also carried to the patients in this fashion.

The following examples of work by chaplains serving later on may be taken as representative. Chaplain J. D. O'Leary noted in his questionnaire reply that his duty in the HAVEN was particularly satisfying, administering Extreme Unction, Confessions, and Holy Communion daily. At the request of the commanding officer of the Danish hospital ship JUTLANDIA, he cared for Roman Catholic personnel and patients aboard. Twice a week opportunity for Confessions and Communion was offered confined patients, and each Sunday, ambulatory patients. This schedule was followed from February to June 1953, when the JUTLANDIA returned to Denmark.

Aboard both that ship and his own, O'Leary found it necessary to hear the confession of non-English-speaking personnel. To meet this need questionnaires were prepared in Danish, Greek, Italian, and Korean, "keyed to our own English questionnaire."

The chaplains found opportunities to minister to other than their own particular "parishioners." Chaplain L. E. Olmon reported holding services aboard APA's (attack transports) and CVE's (escort carriers) without a Protestant chaplain. "Special attention was also given to small ships anchored with us and to Fleet Activities and MSTS, Inchon."

As the story of the Korean War unfolds, it becomes increasingly clear that laymen were being encouraged to, and were taking responsibility for religious services in the absence of chaplains. Olmon wrote: "Reports

[12] Cagle and Manson, op. cit., p. 162. The whole of ch. 5 concerns the Chinnampo minesweeping operation.

International Conversation.

Chaplain Walter S. Peck talks with Wong Dong Lee of the Korean Navy who is studying methods used by American Chaplains in serving United Nations Forces.

from patients that prayer groups and Bible study groups were held in frontline bunkers by lay personnel. Ships without a chaplain reported that enlisted men and officers were conducting worship services, hymn sings, and Bible study." Anchored at Inchon, Olmon was frequently consulted for advice concerning such lay work, and made available supplies of religious literature.

"Well Done"

Two of the hospital ships were honored with the Republic of Korea Presidential Unit Citation for service terminating during the period here under review. CONSOLATION was cited for the period 11 August 1950 through 31 August 1951. REPOSE was awarded the KPUC for service from 16 September 1950 through 31 July 1951. HAVEN would later receive the same award for service from 18 October 1950 through 25 June 1952.

Korean Navy Chaplaincy

Chaplain H. P. White, in the REPOSE, was early in contact with the Korean Navy Chaplain Corps in its formative stage. He wrote to Chaplain Salisbury:

I have tried to assist the ROK Navy in every possible way, and in turn the ROK Navy has been very helpful to us in the

REPOSE. For sometime, Admiral Sohn [Soh Won Il (?)] of the ROK Navy was a patient aboard this ship, and we were fortunate in having his Navy band, more than 50 pieces, aboard for a concert. . . .

The first Chief of Chaplains of the Republic of Korea Navy was Lt. Comdr. Dall Bin Chung, originally commissioned a line officer in 1948. Graduate of the Kwang Sung Methodist mission school, he later received a divinity degree from the Kwan Sei University in Japan. Pastor and teacher before entering the Navy, Chaplain Chung had headed the educational department of Methodist headquarters in Seoul and served as chaplain to the well-known Ewha Girls School there. In the Navy he rose to the position of Chief of Education and Information, and on 24 May 1951 was appointed to head the newly organized Chaplain Corps.

Chaplain White's letter continued:

When Chaplain Chung was made Chief of Chaplains, I did everything possible to help him get started. Words of gratitude and appreciation arrived from Admiral Sohn for this service. Chaplain Chung's office is not too far from the REPOSE, and I go over there as often as I can to assist him in getting his organization set up. He makes frequent visits to my office, and I'm sure this splendid relationship will prove enriching and rewarding.

At the time of White's writing, there were nine ROK Navy chaplains on active duty, seven with ROK Marine units, two at naval bases.

Further information was supplied by Chaplain A. M. Oliver, obtained from Korean Chaplain Won Dong Lee, serving the 1st ROK Marine regiment. Converted to Christianity by Presbyterian missionaries, Chaplain Lee was graduated from the Chosen Presbyterian Theological College and had served one pastorate before entering the Navy.

He reported a gratifying response to his military ministry, saying that the non-Christians usually respected his effort and many listened to his preaching of the Gospel. "I believe that one day Christianity will be the dominant religion throughout Korea," he added. "It is the one cause in which both my people and the North Koreans can always find a common devotion."

According to Lee, it was the remarkable impression made upon high ranking Korean military officials observing U.S. Marines attending Divine Service at the time of the Inchon landing that led some of them to ask American officers to explain the place and function of the chaplaincy in the United States military establishment. Although only a small percent of Koreans were Christian, it was decided to organize a Korean chaplaincy.

Chaplain Chung

Actually it appears that Chaplain Chung had had some such idea all along, even when he entered the Navy as a line "jg." and spent 3 years doing "PIO" work.[13] The actual beginnings of the chaplaincy predate its official commissioning. Admiral Soh Won Il, then ROK Chief of Naval Operations, allowed Chung time to carry on his religious ministry, including both counselling and holding services. The latter were held in private homes in Seoul, and after the retreat began, wherever Chung found himself.

With the formal establishment of the Corps, Chung's first task was to recruit and send chaplains to the newly organized ROK Marine Corps, placing in direct charge Chaplain C. S. Park. Much time was spent expanding and consolidating the embryonic Corps. Lent a copy of the U.S. Navy *Chaplains Manual* by Chaplain White, together with copies of the *Navy Chaplains Bulletin,* Chung drew up a leadership manual for his own chaplains, compiled a bilingual hymnbook, a catechism, and a character guidance manual,

and began publishing a monthly bulletin. After a while he was able to put chaplains aboard Korean vessels.

Chaplain Frederick W. Brink, when serving at Fleet Activities, Sasebo, wrote the Chaplains Division that he had assisted ROK Chaplain S. F. Shin in the baptism of 21 officers and men from the crew of ROK ship TAEDONG, all previously Buddhists. The sacrament was administered in the Fleet Activities Chapel.

Supplies had been begged, borrowed, or "scrounged" from the beginning. Chaplain White helped when he could, and later, in 1952, Chaplain Harry F. Fenstermacher, 1st 90-mm Gun Battalion, FMF Pacific, aided Chung[14] in regularizing the receipt of supplies through the Korean Base Section (Army). He managed to submit to the U.S. Naval Korean Military Advisory Liaison Group what one of their officers estimated as "one of every three requests for supplies we received!"

One of Chaplain Chung's most ambitious projects was the operation of a Navy-Marine Wounded Soldiers Vocational Training School, near the naval base at Chin Hai. "The closest Korea comes to the Veterans Administration," one chaplain described it. Under the direction of Chaplain Park Bun, 200 disabled veterans every 6 months were being given vocational therapy and training in such fields as auto mechanics, farming, watchmaking, and even photography.

On Solid Ground

In 1954 Chaplain Chung, by then promoted to the rank of commander, visited the Chaplains Division in Washington. His dream was becoming an impressive reality. By then his Corps numbered 30 and he had established some 40 Navy and Marine chapels. In 1953 the first Roman Catholic chaplain was commissioned and by 1954 there were four. (Korean Protestants are reported to outnumber Roman Catholics by more than 10 to 1.) There was even a "chaplains school," meeting in Chung's office—which will remind old hands of the beginnings of our own training program. The conduct of common worship held priority with Chung's "padres," and counseling next; but there was no charitable cause or work of mercy in which they had not found a way to involve themselves.

Described by his friends as a forceful man, Chaplain Chung was not to be satisfied until his work of building was set on a firm foundation. Publicly honored by the ROK Chief of Naval Operations and by the Minister

---

[13] *Navy Chaplains Bulletin* (Fall, 1954), D. J. Silver, "Chaplain Chung's Corps," p. 13. Also A. M. Oliver, "Of One Blood All Nations," *ibid.* (Spring-Summer, 1952), p. 12.

[14] Cp. p. 192.

of Defense, his solidest monument is, as Chaplain Daniel J. Silver wrote, "the thriving existence of a Chaplain Corps which bears his signature and imprint."

Nationalist Chinese Chaplaincy

Brief notice may be taken of the emergence of another Chaplain Corps in the Far East, serving the Nationalist Chinese armed forces on Taiwan (Formosa). Although sanctioned by the government, it had no official military status, being recruited and supported by ladies meeting in a Prayer Group with Madame Chiang Kai-shek. Concerned for the morale and welfare of Nationalist troops concentrated in the already overcrowded city of Taipeh, these ladies looked for evangelists and pastors to work among the troops.

Supervising the program was the Reverend Wei-ping Chen, retired clergyman from the mainland and personal pastor of the Generalissimo and Madame Chiang. Begun in May 1950, by 1952 this "Corps" had 14 "chaplains" serving, one in a recruit training center, another in the Navy base, most of them in military hospitals.

Chaplain W. W. Parkinson, on duty with the Patrol Squadrons of 7th Fleet, occasionally made contact with the Nationalist Chinese chaplaincy and helped in whatever ways were possible.

Writing to Chaplain Salisbury in October 1951, the Reverend Wei-ping Chen stated: "Our work in these hospitals (21) is very successful. Some superintendents of these hospitals are Christians. They welcomed us from the beginning while others hesitated. Today, however, they all appreciate our service." He reported that some of the worst troublemakers among the military patients had responded to the Gospel ministry; some even had become "chaplain's assistants," doing valuable work in teaching the Bible and hymns to other patients.

Unit Citations

The 1st Marine Division was awarded its third Presidential Unit Citation during the Korean hostilities (the Division's sixth) for its gallantry in action during three periods of intense combat: 21–26 April, 16 May–30 June, and 11–25 September, all in 1951. The first two periods fell within the 5th Korean Campaign, the initial one covering the Chinese Communist offensive in April, the latter covering the counter-offensive which brought the Marines to the southern rim of the Punchbowl. The third period was the September drive which for the Marines constituted the heart of the United Nations fall offensive.

The 1st Marine Aircraft Wing also received a Presidential Unit Citation covering the dates 8 March–30 April, 18 May–30 June, and 3 August–29 September, 1951. These dates reflect missions flown largely in support of Division operations during approximately the same periods.

The Navy Unit Commendation was awarded a number of ships and smaller commands for varying periods of service. BADOENG STRAIT and SICILY each was cited for the period 3 August 1950—1 August 1951. VALLEY FORGE received the unit decoration for the period 3 July–18 November 1951. LEYTE had already been cited for her service from 9 October 1950 to 19 January 1951; and PHILIPPINE SEA had received two awards, the first covering the period 4 August 1950 to 30 March 1951, the second, 31 March–31 May 1951. PRINCETON's unit commendation covered the period 5 December 1950 to 10 August 1951.

Winterizing

While acting Division Chaplain, Fitzgerald had reported the arrival of John L. Curtis (Southern Baptist), who was assigned to the 11th Marines. On 8 October Joseph P. F. Gallagher (Roman Catholic) reported in and was assigned to Motor Transport. Commenting on the activities of the Division Chaplain for the period 15–23 October, Peck noted the arrival of four more new chaplains, assigned as follows:

Shore Party Bn..	William E. Brooks..	LCDR	BAPT (A)
Medical Bn.....	Vincent J. Lonergan	LCDR	RC
Ordnance Bn...	Barney L. Jones....	LT	METH
7th Marines.....	Alan R. Gibbons...	LTJG	RC

The United Nations drive during the summer and fall of 1951 was the last big offensive of the Korean War. By the end of October the frontlines were fairly well stabilized and hostilities were largely restricted to outpost warfare and patrol activities. Peck wrote to Salisbury on 25 October:

We seem to be digging in for winter, and it is none too soon. The nights are getting bitter cold, although the days when the sun is out are fairly comfortable. The lines are becoming more fixed. Continual raids and patrol actions by both sides cause daily casualties although not as many as on a push. I am encouraging the chaplains to prepare themselves for a program to combat the loneliness and depression which will come to their men through the winter if the front remains stable.

He added: "I wish to say that the main impression I have gained is to be deeply impressed with the work of the chaplains out here; from all sides, officer and enlisted, comes nothing but high praise." On 31

October Peck again commented on conditions in the frontlines:

> The approach of winter is the main concern here. The men and officers, including the chaplains, in the infantry regiments are having an increasingly difficult time. The stable lines mean less moving around and in cold weather that means long cold hours in the night and dreary days in the unheated bunkers. Keeping warm is difficult and positions must be kept. The 1st and 7th Regiments are on the line now.

A week later, he wrote: "Chaplain Brooks is in a forward battalion whose position requires his living in an earthen bunker and since it is high in the hills, he has had an uncomfortable time of it, but is in good spirits, has no complaints and says he is getting along fine." On 10 November two more chaplains reported in: Melvin E. Torstrick and Arnold P. Spohn, making a total of 30; but orders were expected for 6 then on board, 5 of whom were detached by 21 November.

On 14 November the 5th Marines relieved the 1st Marines in the front line and Chaplain Ruleman found himself occupying the earthen bunker formerly used by Chaplain Brooks. Back at the Headquarters Battalion, Chaplain Peck succeeded in "winterizing" the chapel by securing two stoves. Squad tents were secured to use as chapels in each of the three battalions in the reserve area with ordinary planking for pews. As usual, the chaplains were adjusting their lives and ministry to render the best possible service under whatever conditions might prevail.

Following the Punchbowl engagements the chaplains were busy, as they and their units prepared for the coming winter, writing letters to the next of kin of service personnel who had become casualties. It has been mentioned earlier that an SOP was established whereby no unit chaplain would write such letters until he had received from the Division Chaplain's Office (Rear) amplifying information on each casualty, which was secured from the Division Casualty Office. In practice, while hopefully the unit chaplain's work was thus simplified, the results were not satisfactory. Peck issued a Memorandum to the Division chaplains on 24 November 1951, pointing out that in many cases letters had been received in units from next of kin in reply to the commanding officer's casualty letter before the unit chaplain had been able to secure the necessary information to write his own letter of condolence. Therefore, Peck directed the chaplains to obtain the needed information directly from the Amplifying Reports furnished his unit command. Where letters of inquiry should be received from next of kin before amplifying information was obtainable, chaplains were to reply, stating simply that the situation (not the death) was being investigated and another letter would follow when further information became available.

Talks Resumed

While X Corps, including the Marine division, had been moving forward in the east, elements of IX Corps had secured the eastern point of the Iron Triangle.[15] Farther west elements of I Corps had established the Jamestown Line along a 40-mile front from the vicinity of Kaesong eastward to Chorwon, the western pivot of the Triangle. Successful offensives during August to October had thus given the UN forces a firm hold on commanding positions all along their front.

Perhaps because of this pressure the Communist indicated a willingness to resume negotiations. After preliminary sparring by liaison officers, finally, on 25 October 1951 the chief negotiators resumed their talks, but now in a tiny village, Panmunjom, on the Seoul highway north of the Imjin River.

For the fighting man the war went on, though the military picture remained essentially unchanged through the following months. Patrol activity was stepped up on both sides, and occasionally the Communists threw a battalion, and once a regiment, at the United Nations line. Guerilla harassment continued, and occasionally Marine units were ambushed; but nearly as serious as the enemy's opposition was the hardship entailed by the onset of winter.

---

[15] Miller *et al., op. cit.*, p. 117.

CHAPTER 7

SECOND KOREAN WINTER

28 November 1951–30 April 1952

The closing months of 1951 witnessed a return to the stalemate that had settled over the Korean conflict in July and early August, when the "peace talks" had first begun at Kaesong. Now that they were resumed, at Panmunjom, both sides adopted a largely defensive posture, content for the most part to reinforce established positions or capture others for the purpose of straightening or strengthening a front line.[1]

General Ridgway ordered the UN front stabilized and an outpost line established three to five thousand yards forward of the main positions. The main line of resistance (MLR) stretched for 155 miles, from the Yellow Sea to the Sea of Japan, manned by the following (in west to east order): U.S. I Corps, from the confluence of the Imjin and Han Rivers to a point between Khorwon and Kumhwa, along the base of the Iron Triangle; IX Corps, northward to Kumsong and thence east to the Pukhan River; X Corps, including the 1st Marine Division, eastward up and over the mountainous backbone of the Korean peninsula down to the Nam River; and, as eastern anchor, the ROK I Corps, whose line extended northward from the Nam to Kosong on the east coast.[2]

DivChap Slant

The situation at the beginning of this period, as it affected the work of the chaplains, may be highlighted by the following extracts from weekly letters from Division Chaplain Peck to the Chief of Chaplains.

28 November 1951.

Winter is here and is complicating living and supply problems. The front ahead of us is stable, with military activity confined to aggressive patrols and mortar and artillery exchanges. This results in daily casualties but not great numbers of casualties. The chaplains still have the lines to walk,

the hills to climb to reach their men, and the cold when on their rounds.

The chaplains are in high spirits and they are a continuing inspiration and source of pride to me. I have a helicopter trip scheduled for next Thursday to visit Chaplain Ruleman up in his isolated area. It is 3 hours by trail from the farthest jeep point and, due to infiltrators, one is allowed to go up and back only with a large convoy, so to visit by foot is a case of up one day and back the next.

5 December 1951.

This week I covered all the infantry battalions on the line, and in regimental reserve behind the line, plus the regimental CPs on the line. To get to Chaplain Ruleman's position on top of a mountain, I took my first 'copter ride. . . . It was quite an experience. The officers and men to whom I talked praised their chaplains without exception.

The chaplains are especially busy with the Christmas season here. Some things which seem simple enough normally, like obtaining decorations, getting out special bulletins, getting a Christmas music program together, all become major projects under conditions out here. The chaplains are not easily discouraged and keep plugging until they get them.

13 December 1951.

This is not an easy time, however, from a morale standpoint—standing by, as it were, for these Cease Fire Talks is proving a strain. I think everyone's nerves would be more relaxed if the talks would go one way or the other. Strangely enough the nearness of Christmas seems to aggravate the situation in many ways—the men have time to think, and the Christmas season with its rich memories of home only adds to the burden. Some of the chaplains are restless themselves; I counsel them to dig into the Christmas season and give the men the spiritual gems from the season to counteract the men's nervousness—and their own.

Christmas, 1951

This second Christmas in Korea was considerably different from that of 1950, when the last elements of the Division were still being brought into rest areas following the terrible withdrawal from the Chosin Reservoir. True, Marines were on the front lines, but combat was limited and the situation was relatively quiet. Special Services had distributed decorations and each unit has lighted Christmas trees. Those

---

[1] Miller *et al., op. cit.,* p. 206.
[2] *Ibid.*

desiring them had been furnished Christmas greeting cards to mail home. Incoming mail brought not only greetings and gifts from families, but from individuals and groups who had voluntarily provided gifts for Korean troops, among them the Armed Forces Wives Club of Boston, the Women's Division of the Jewish Welfare Board, and employees of the Kiplinger News Agency in Washington. A USO troupe provided entertainment, in addition to movies. President Truman's Christmas message was screened. Tons of hot turkey with trimmings were flown by helicopter to forward positions where men relieved one another from the line long enough to eat Christmas dinner.

Cardinal Spellman was in Korea for a Yuletide visit to the U.S. forces in the Far East. He celebrated Mass at the Division Command Post on Christmas Day, with an estimated 3,000 in attendance.

Division Chaplain Peck wrote to Chaplain Salisbury:

The Christmas coverage was tops. Things were quiet enough, militarily speaking, that a full religious observance could be made. The chaplains really put out; I am proud of them. For men in bunkers on the line, the infantry chaplains walked the hills to take the message of Christmas to them. One chaplain had 8 services, another 11. Chaplains Felder of the Engineers and Stamper of the 11th Marines had laymen, officers and enlisted, conducting Christmas Eve services throughout their units—19 such lay-directed services were held.

Felder had prepared a mimeographed Order of Service which was used in each of four simultaneous services in outlying companies of the 1st Engineer Battalion, with laymen reading a sermon prepared by the chaplain. Felder took his own congregation, augmented by Korean personnel, out on a mountainside where, as they sang Christmas carols in both English and Korean, two loudspeakers were directed out over a valley holding several thousand troops. Truly the "welkin rang" as the valley echoed "Glory to the new-born King."

At the suggestion of his commanding officer, Chaplain R. C. Fenning of 1st Signal Battalion conducted a 10-minute service nightly during the week preceding Christmas. Consisting of carols sung by a 12-man choir and a brief talk, each service was broadcast throughout the entire battalion area, reaching about 1,000 men.

On Christmas Eve a songfest followed by coffee and cake was held in the mess tent of each of the 23 batteries of the 11th Marines. Regimental Chaplain R. L. Stamper had arranged with line officers to organize

Christmas Decorations From the States.

Chaplain Henry C. Duncan assisted by Sergeant Beeson opens a shipment of Christmas decorations sent to the chaplain by Beeson's mother, who belonged to the Navy Mother's Club the chaplain had contacted for such items.

carol-singing and to read the Nativity story. Protestant services were held in two battalions and midnight Mass celebrated in two, with further services on Christmas Day.

Christmas in *VALLEY FORGE*

The VALLEY FORGE spent its second consecutive Christmas "on the line." Many of her personnel had been aboard both those holidays, away from home and all it means at that season. Chaplain Abner R. Cook, one of those, was determined to make it as cheerful as possible, and his captain heartily concurred.

With the good help of a sailor named Wheeler, who had been a choir director in a Presbyterian church in Los Angeles, a small choir had been trained. Instead of the usual bugle for reveille, on Christmas morning the crew was awakened with appropriate music by this group. During the day, when they were not singing in one of the several Divine Services, they went to many sections of the ship, from the Admiral's cabin to sick bay, and sang. Usually the officers and men joined in.

By night everyone wanted to sing so all hands, except those on watch, crowded on the hangar deck and in total darkness.

for no light was permitted, sang Christmas carols far into the night. Presently the sound of the singing carried to other ships. While we were too far apart to sing together, they caught the spirit and we could hear them singing.

It had been a good Christmas.

1st MAW

Chaplain E. R. Barnes was detached before the arrival of his relief and on 27 November 1951 Chaplain Howard A. Seymour, who had been at Itami since his arrival in September, was ordered to duty as Acting Wing Chaplain by the Wing Chief of Staff. Writing to Chaplain Salisbury on 14 December, Seymour indicated progress along several lines: a new jeep for the chaplain, a much better qualified chaplain's assistant, a chapel in the Wing's new location, including office space for the chaplain, and living quarters in a building rather than a tent. Seymour had, in addition to taking Protestant services at Wing headquarters, arranged for missionary priests to afford Roman Catholic coverage where needed. He noted preaching in a nearby Presbyterian Church through an interpreter, keeping in touch with the chaplains of the Wing, and attending the Command Staff meeting on Monday mornings. Concerning relief work he wrote:

In line with the policy of the command, clothing sent to the Wing from the States for the refugees and all excess food has been distributed from this office through proper organizations. We have concentrated our efforts on the Presbyterian Seminary in Pusan and the Korean Blind School. However, because of the extremely cold weather here we have handed out many coats directly to Korean refugees who live near by.

Christmas in the Air Wing

The Wing headquarters had before Christmas nearly completed its move from Pusan to Pohang, farther up the east coast. (See ch. 6.) The new chapel was unfinished; Seymour described it as "an adequate structure seating 160 personnel," adding that through his contacts at Itami he had "scrounged" white paint for the interior. "The General insists upon a dedication service before the arrival of the Wing Chaplain; so Chaplain La Duca and I are aiding him

Chaplain Stephen Horvath reads the epistle at Christmas Eve mass at the First MAW chapel.

Chapel for MAG 12.

This is a chapel located on the east coast at K–18 above Pohang.   The group was later moved to K–1.

A New Dress.

Chaplain Weidler and Sergeant Pearson admire a little Korean girl's new dress which has arrived from America.

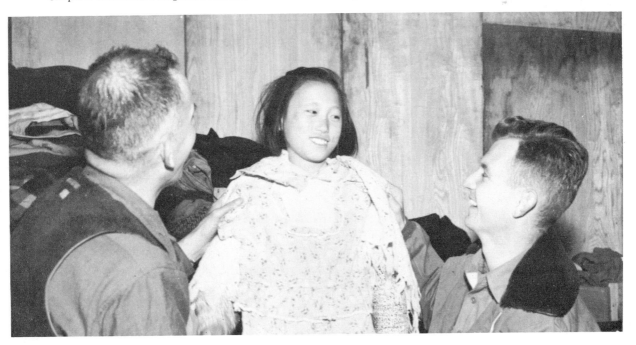

in that service on Sunday afternoon, 13 January." Roman Catholic Chaplain Paul J. La Duca reported the first week in January.

Concerning Christmas activities Seymour wrote on 6 January:

> Our Christmas activities at the Wing were not as complete as we would have desired due to the fact that the camp was in process of moving. However, we had a Mass and a Protestant Divine Service in the unfinished Chapel on Sunday, 23 December. On Christmas Eve we had a Protestant Communion service at 2330 and a Catholic Mass at 2400. We were able to find a French priest who was very willing to aid us, even though he could not speak English. A newly formed choir from the band aided in both services. We had a watch night service on New Year's Eve.

Chaplains Horvath (who had returned to duty) and Weidler were building a chapel at Marine Aircraft Group 12, which was far enough along to be used for Christmas services. MAG 12 was now located at Kangnung, just south of the 38th Parallel on the east coast.

> On 24 December at 1900 Chaplain Weidler led the Christmas carolers to Kangnung where carols were sung at the two orphanages; later the party returned to the base and sang at the enlisted men's club. At 2200 he offered Christmas Eve Communion in the group chapel. The choir of Central Church, Kangnung, sang at this service.
>
> At 2400 Chaplain Horvath offered High Mass and the orphans of the Kangnung Catholic Orphanage sang the Mass. On 25 December Sunday schedule was maintained.

On Christmas Day orphans from the four Kangnung homes (one Roman Catholic, the others administered by the UN Civil Assistance Commission, Korea) were guests of MAG 12. They were treated to dinner, movies, and a complete outfit of clothing.

Chaplains Sullivan and Cleaves were doing outstanding work in Marine Aircraft Group 33, at Pohang. According to Seymour's report to the Chaplains Division, Cleaves was especially active in refugee work, having aided in building a church and establishing an orphanage.

> Their Christmas activities consisted of the regular services with a Christmas emphasis on Sunday, 23 December, a Christmas Eve Protestant Communion Service at 2100 and a Catholic High Mass at 2400. Chaplain Cleaves supervised a caroling party which sang at all commands in the area. Both chaplains attended Christmas parties at orphanages.

Chaplain Charlie R. Harrison had reported in November and had been left with the units remaining behind at Pusan. He acted also as Supply Chaplain for the Wing, being the only one left near the Army Chaplains Supply Depot. Conducting Protestant worship, he had secured the services of a civilian priest for Christmas masses. The Wing units at Itami had been covered by Air Force chaplains.

Cardinal Spellman arrived in the Wing on 29 December. Seymour wrote:

> We had a schedule arranged for him and he followed it to the letter. Chaplains Sullivan, Horvath, Cleaves, and I accompanied the generals and the Cardinal in the tour of our activities. Arrangements were made for him to meet the troops, which he did very graciously. The commanding general, Maj. Gen. C. F. Schilt, is very kindly disposed toward the Chaplain's Department and took the entire day attending . . . the Cardinal.

Wisconsin

During the winter months from November 1951 onward, the Division faced an enemy securely dug in on the reverse of the heights, manning the forward slopes with mere sentry forces.[3] It was the opinion of Maj. Gen. J. T. Selden, 1st Marine Division commander, that only naval gunfire could effectively destroy such positions, some of them regimental command posts, often connected by long tunnels with the exposed forward positions.

Consequently, for 2½ months, guns of the WISCONSIN and the cruisers ST. PAUL, ROCHESTER, and MANCHESTER supported the Division by deep naval gunfire, at a range of from 10 to 16 miles. Not only were enemy bunkers and artillery emplacements reduced, but enemy morale was notably shaken. One prisoner revealed that his battalion's political "commissar" had thought the American Navy was using atomic artillery, so huge were the craters resulting from the explosion of 16-inch shells.

The WISCONSIN was the third battleship recommissioned and ordered to duty in Korea. (MISSOURI had been relieved in March 1951, and would return in October 1952. NEW JERSEY was relieved in November 1951, returning to the war in April 1953.) In December she participated in a heavy bombardment of the east coast port of Wonsan, as part of the siege which had been going on since February.[4]

The Roman Catholic chaplain in WISCONSIN was Eugene J. Kapalczynski, who had reported to the ship in Norfolk on 21 October 1951. Attached to the 2d Marine Division, Kapalczynski had received his orders "in the field," for the Division was engaged in maneuvers on the island of Vieques, P.R. After flights via Roosevelt Roads and San Juan, P.R., Miami, and Marine Air Station, Cherry Point, N.C.,

---

[3] Cagle and Manson, *op. cit.,* pp. 332–4.
[4] *Ibid.,* p. 414.

Cardinal in Korea—1951.

Francis Cardinal Spellman thanks men of MAG 33 for "the wonderful job you're doing for America here in Korea."

Mass Aboard Ship.

Chaplain Eugene J. Kapalczynski holds Mass aboard the WISCONSIN of the U.S. 7th Fleet.

The Morning Scripture Lesson.

Personnel of the WISCONSIN hear the reading of Scripture by their chaplain, H. W. Buckingham.

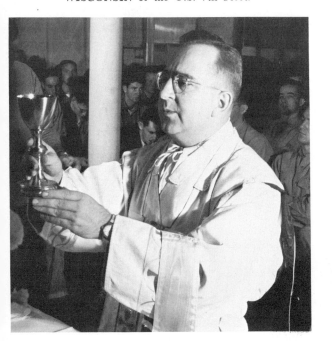

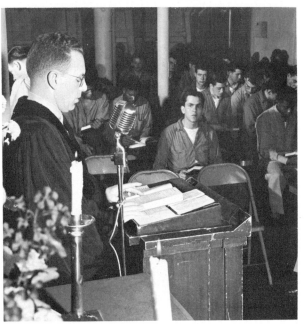

the chaplain was detached by Commanding Officer (Rear Echelon), at Camp Lejeune, and proceeded to join his ship. He was, he wrote the Chief of Chaplains, received most cordially by Chaplain Herbert W. Buckingham, Bapt. (A), who had been aboard already since January.

During service in the war theater the chaplains kept busy. Kapalczynski reported that during General Quarters he took his battle station on the bridge. It was his practice to pronounce a General Absolution and the Lord's Prayer over the "I.M.C." (an internal communication system operating directly from the bridge). Like so many others, he offered his services to ships without a chaplain. "Even during operations, on and off the Korean bombline, Sunday Divine Services were conducted for destroyers. Transportation was by helicopter or highline."

Cardinal Spellman came aboard during Christmas-tide, arriving by helicopter, and was greeted by Vice Adm. H. M. Martin, Commander 7th Fleet, whose flag had been transferred to WISCONSIN. During a day of touring the ship he chatted with officers and men, delivered a Christmas message over the ship's radio station, WHIZ, and offered to send a personal message, when he returned home, to next-of-kin of any personnel desiring it. (More than 600 took him up on the offer.) Next day, following an early Mass, the Cardinal returned ashore.

Chaplain Buckingham reported that occasionally members of ship's company were wounded by enemy fire and sometimes others brought aboard for treatment. In December an unidentified North Korean prisoner of war, severely wounded, was transferred to WISCONSIN. A hospitalman, Harold Berger, donated blood for use during an operation but strenuous efforts to save his life failed. The next day, in a

Casualty Coming Aboard.
Helicopter approaches the landing platform of the CONSOLATION with a casualty.

Absent Rabbi.

In the absence of a Jewish chaplain, Lt. (jg.) William Jasper leads the services on the ANTIETAM.

surely unusual ceremony, that former enemy was buried at sea. Eight sailors acted as pallbearers, and the ship's Marine detachment and band provided military honors. Both chaplains read prayers.

Hanukkah

There are usually only a limited number of Jewish chaplains on active duty, assigned to large bases. The T/O also allowed a Marine division one Jewish chaplain. Those who served in the 1st Division in Korea had been Garson Goodman, Elihu Rickel, and, in the period here under review, Reuben Siegel. In November 1951 Arnold J. Wolf was ordered to Fleet Activities, Yokosuka to minister to Jewish personnel in units under Commander Naval Forces, Far East.

Often other chaplains encourage Jewish men to conduct their own services and sometimes they do so on their own initiative. One such group was to be found in the ANTIETAM. Composed of 25 officers and men, the congregation was organized in September 1951 shortly after the ship sailed for Korea. Jewish religious affairs tend to be democratically organized and the presence of a rabbi is not necessary for

the conduct of worship. It is, however, customary to have a "president"—in this case Lt. (j.g.) William Jasper, a dental officer.

Some of the men were from Conservative background, others Reform, and still others Orthodox. The problem of what type service to hold was settled by encouraging a different person to conduct worship each week, so that from week to week the service would reflect first one tradition and then another.

Probably the Jewish congregation in the "Flying A" was the first to celebrate Rosh Hashanah, 5712 (1951). The ship had just crossed the date line, and thus its service really began the New Year for the Jewish world. Only 14 hours later would the hour of ushering in the New Year have arrived in New York, and 21, in Hawaii.

On Yom Kippur the ship was docked at Yokosuka, and arrangements were made for the men to attend Day of Atonement services in the Army chapel at Yokohama. Sukkoth (Feast of Booths) found the ship in the Sea of Japan, so the congregation held their own service.

Hanukkah came while the ship was again at sea. Air operations made it impossible for the Menorah (the traditional eight-branched candelabrum) to be lighted on each of the eight nights, but on the first night the first one was lighted and a discussion of the meaning of the festival followed.

A strong feature of ANTIETAM's Jewish religious program was a weekly discussion held after the Sabbath eve service. Topics included differences in the three American Jewish communities, as well as such as the following: the American Jew and the State of Israel, religion by television (based on an article in the New York *Times*), and Jewish post-Biblical literature.

Division Roster

On 1 January 1952 Chaplain Peck sent to the Chief of Chaplains the roster of chaplains then serving with the 1st Marine Division in Korea. With the exceptions of Chaplains Power, Jolly, and Schneck there had been a complete change from that given for 1 August 1951.

Peck, W. S., Jr......	CDR	Div Chaplain..	PRESBY (USA)
Brooks, W. E........	LCDR	1st Marines....	BAP (A)
Ecker, J. L.........	LCDR	Hdq Bn........	RC
Stamper, R. L......	LCDR	11th Marines...	PRESBY (US)
Felder, G., Jr......	LCDR	1st Eng Bn.....	LUTH
Schneck, R. J......	LCDR	7th Marines....	LUTH
Pipho, E. W........	LCDR	1st Marines....	LUTH
Ruleman, R. N.....	LCDR	5th Marines....	METH
Oliver, A. M.......	LCDR	Hdq Bn........	METH
Vierling, W. J......	LCDR	1st AmTrac Bn.	LUTH
Lonergan, V. J......	LCDR	11th Marines...	RC
Gallagher, J. P. F....	LCDR	1st MoTr Bn...	RC
Follard, J. F........	LT	Med Bn.......	RC
Curtis, J. L........	LT	Serv Bn.......	BAP (S)
Jones, B. L.........	LT	1st Ord Bn....	METH
O'Neill, J. J........	LT	5th Marines....	RC
Fenning, R. C......	LT	1st Sig Bn.....	LUTH (MoSy)
Power, B. S........	LT	5th Marines....	METH
Spohn, A. P........	LT	7th Marines....	LUTH
Jolly, E. W........	LT	1st CmbSerGp.	PRESBY (US)
Forney, J. F........	LT	11th Marines...	DISC
Torstrick, M. E.....	LTJG	1st ShParBn...	BAP (S)
Gibbons, A. R......	LTJG	7th Marines....	RC
Siegel, R...........	LTJG	Hdq Bn.......	JEWISH
Duncan, H. C......	LTJG	1st Tank Bn...	METH
Hoar, M. J.........	LTJG	1st Marines....	RC
Wolfe, B. N........	LTJG	11th Marines..	BAP (S)

Korean Winter

There was no significant change in the pattern of ground hostilities during the first 4 months of 1952. Peck wrote to Chaplain Salisbury on 4 January:

There is no change in the military situation, except the knowledge that the enemy can now bomb us if they desire. Therefore our foxholes have been dug a bit deeper than before, and many rear area chaplains (including me!) who formerly hadn't bothered have now what might be called an alternate residence, in case of necessity.

Since November, in fact, the Chinese had begun to show unusual activity in the air. Intelligence reports indicated their possession of 1,400 planes, about half of them Russian MIG jets.[5] For the first time the enemy began seriously to challenge United Nations air supremacy in Korea. As the front lines dug in and became more and more stable, there was less need of close air support. Air Force B–29's continued their smashing of supply and communications lines behind the enemy front, but more and more F–86 Sabre jets were needed to escort them. The area from the Yalu River south to the North Korean capital at Pyongyang in northwest Korea was dubbed "MIG Alley" by UN aviators. In February more than 3,500 sight-contacts of MIG's were made and at least 51 were shot down or damaged in aerial combat.[6] At sea naval units of nine nations maintained a coastal blockade, and naval bombardment joined artillery and air bombing to reduce enemy logistic support.[7]

Enemy guerillas continued to harass the UN forces back of the front lines; larger patrols were sent out into "no-man's land"; the weather during January and February remained cold, sometimes going to ten or twelve degrees below zero; artillery duels continued. Writing on 25 January Peck told Chaplain Salisbury: "One company area received over 600 incoming rounds in one day alone.... So far none of the chaplains has been hit, but it is becoming routine for them to get pinned down a part of each day."

In January Peck issued another memorandum concerning chaplain supplies. The Combat Service Group chaplain was continued as Division Supply Chaplain. It was noted that an order had been placed with the Chaplains Division, Bureau of Naval Personnel, for certain items of field equipment. The Supply Chaplain was to secure supplies from Navy channels (Chaplains Division, as well as Pacific Fleet Chaplain, FMF Pac Chaplain, or COMNAVFE Chaplain) as possible, and from the Army Chaplains Warehouse, 2d Logistical Command, at Pusan. Further, each chaplain was furnished a list of all items available to him through his unit S–4 (supply) sec-

[5] *Britannica Book of the Year,* 1952; article, "Korean War."
[6] *Ibid.,* 1953; article, "Korean War."
[7] Cagle and Manson, *op. cit.,* pp. 330ff. (on "seaborne artillery"); pp. 254ff. (naval air missions).

tion. Chaplain Peck noted in a letter to the Chief of Chaplains on 11 January 1952 that the "supply picture seems to be clarified."

Comment on Training

It seemed to Peck that much of the training time at Camp Pendleton for chaplains ordered to Korea was not really justified. He wrote to the Chief of Chaplains on 29 December 1951:

The type of operation the Division is presently engaged in makes the necessity of a long training period open to question. Of course the situation of a year ago could repeat itself but that is unlikely. It appears *from here* that the Pendleton training for chaplains without prior Marine experience would be sufficient with a maximum of 20 days. Further, a period of 7–10 days should be sufficient for chaplains with prior Marine experience.

I am convinced that the medical phase of the Pendleton training is of little value. . . . At the present time there are Hospital Corpsmen stumbling over each other throughout the Division. That is to say, the medical people have their own program well-organized. Even if the Division should become engaged in full-scale combat, there would be no necessity for a chaplain to perform Corpsman's duties, as was the case in the early days of the Korean conflict.

On 17 January 1952 he wrote again:

At the risk of stepping out of the area of my responsibility, may I state that it is my conviction, based on my own observations and the opinions expressed by many of the chaplains serving here who have gone through the training at Pendleton, that much of the training which is designed either for medical personnel, or for enlisted and line personnel, is no longer greatly applicable to the work of chaplains in Korea at the present time. . . . A longer time than the 20 days he had recommended earlier might be indicated for men fresh out of Chaplains School. But I think that for more experienced hands, even the 20 days could be cut in half without any serious loss of effectiveness in their ministry in Korea.

The Chaplains Division was of course desirous of giving its men whatever training would render them most effective; at the same time, being short-handed, it could not afford needless delay of chaplains from actual duty. Chaplain Mannion wrote on 6 February from the Chief of Chaplains' office, "We appreciate your suggestion to send chaplains . . . without too much delay at Camp Pendleton and are in hearty agreement with you on this score."

Composite Picture

In order to obtain definite information on the religious coverage within the Division, Chaplain Peck assembled data from which a statistical analysis was made, listing the actual coverage throughout the Division by denominational services held, by chaplains conducting the services, and by units where services

were held. One section of this report is included as appendix E to this volume. While obviously some of the information would be out of date by the time it appeared in print, inasmuch as services were frequently shifted because of work schedule or tactical situation, the report gives a dramatic sampling of the work actually being done at a particular time.

During the period 1–15 February, Chaplain Peck's semimonthly report to the Assistant Chief of Staff, G–1, detailed the following chaplains' activities.

A. Number of Sunday services conducted—134.
   Attendance—6,655.
   Number of week-day services conducted—207.
   Attendance—4,583.
B. Adequate Protestant, Roman Catholic, and Jewish coverage was afforded all Medical Companies of the 1st Medical Battalion. Regimental and battalion aid stations were afforded continued Protestant and Catholic coverage.
   (a) Number of visits to hospitals and aid stations— 157.
   (b) Number of patients visited—952.
C. In addition to the above, the chaplains attached to the 1st Marine Division, FMF, held 1,327 counselling interviews, wrote 157 letters with reference to personnel problems, and conducted 91 special services or Bible class sessions.

Typical of other reports for similar periods, the figures cited here indicated that a higher percentage of the 1st Marine Division personnel were attending Divine Service than was probably the case in the average civilian community in the States.

Individual Aspects

With no decisive battles being fought, the winter and early spring of 1952 were nonetheless grim enough. Taking a religious ministry to the men of the 1st Division was always difficult and often hazardous. Algernon M. Oliver, Regimental Chaplain, 1st Marines, writing for himself and his associates, Chaplain Melvin E. Torstrick and Martin J. Hoar, reported:

A large number of services are necessary if all the men are to be given the opportunity to attend. In some cases services are held for units as small as a platoon, since men on the lines often cannot leave their positions to attend services as a company CP. Recently I conducted eight services in one day, on the move from early morning until late afternoon. In a short time you learn every hill in your sector and know just how long it will take you to go from one place to another.

Perched high atop Korean mountains, many of the men could be reached only after an exhausting climb up icy, treacherous trails. Word that the "padre" was about to have Divine Service would be passed from bunker to bunker. The small portable altar

A Spiritual Haven.

As the Korean war rages with fury a short distance away, marines able to attend divine services are calmed by the words delivered by Chaplain A. M. Oliver.

---

would be set up, using ammunition boxes, C-ration cases, or the top of a bunker. Usually the men stood, though when Communion was served some of them would kneel in ice and mud. Under such conditions baptisms would sometimes be administered. On one occasion, within a short distance of entrenched Chinese and North Korean positions, with friendly artillery beating a deafening accompaniment, Oliver baptized Marine Pfc. M. P. Longon, using the "all-purpose" helmet as a baptismal font.

From a news release written by M. Sgt. J. P. Sheehan, Marine combat correspondent, comes the following account of a Memorial Service held by the 5th Marines during the bleak mid-winter.

As the strains of the National Anthem echoed away through the snow-covered valley, the Regimental Commander, Col. Frank P. Hager, introduced the 1st Marine Division Commanding General, Maj. Gen. John T. Selden. He reminded the Marines that "we are gathered here today to pay homage to our comrades who are no longer with us. They died with the spirit that is so well known in your unit, the 5th Marines, from Belleau Woods of World War I, to the Pacific islands of World War II, and now here in Korea. This spirit has been handed down to all those who have ever served the 5th. May God rest their souls and may you live up to the spirit for which they died."

Prayers were offered by Chaplains Bashford S. Power (Protestant), James F. Follard (Roman Catholic), and Reuben Siegel (Jewish). The roll of the dead was read by Chaplain J. P. F. Gallagher.

With the reading of the last name, a Marine firing squad fired three volleys and a bugler sounded Taps. The Marines marched off the parade ground. There were tear-stained faces but they all were faces of men who shared a particular pride and a rededicated resolution.

On a typical day Chaplain Henry C. Duncan would leave his battalion CP in the early morning, following the trail used by the "Chigger Bearers," as the civilian Korean laborers were called who carted supplies to the front lines on their backs. Accompanied by his assistant, Marine Corporal Keith Bacus, he would climb the trail straight up from a river valley some 2,300 feet to the skyline. Once on the jagged ridgeline he would go from bunker to bunker, holding brief services with small groups of men, as incoming mortar and artillery shells crashed around.

After the service the chaplain (a former Marine line officer, with combat service at Peleliu and Okinawa) would give the men a briefing on the news of the day, including the tactical situation—for front line troops never know much of the "big picture," but only what transpires in their own small sector. He went loaded down with stationery, corncob pipes, and other "luxury" items procured from friends and volunteer groups stateside, and undertook commissions from the men for money orders to be sent home, radio batteries, and the precious mantles for the gasoline lanterns which provided their light. Each day's "ridge-running" complete, the chaplain would slip and slide down the precipitous trail to finish his duties at the CP, ending the day by attending the staff briefings and working into the night to write his day's report and prepare his messages for the following day.

The other chaplains were similarly engaged. Chaplain Hoar reported: "I conducted five services on Ash Wednesday with an attendance of 207. Holy Communion was taken to the men on the frontlines." Chaplain William E. Brooks reported making approximately 650 contacts while visiting Marines in frontline dug-in positions, and Chaplain Edmund W. Pipho spent the first twelve days of March visiting men on frontline outposts and holding Divine Services there.

Chaplain Fredric J. Forney, 11th Marines, organized a chapel choir, reporting that it helped increase attendance at Divine Service. Chaplain Billy N. Wolfe wrote that services were frequently interrupted by artillery fire but "always completed." As a Southern Baptist Wolfe was accustomed to use grape juice for Communion. "However, in the Korean winter the grape juice froze solid and I was faced with a hard decision: either deny my men the Communion service they wanted, or use wine contrary to my church's

Chaplain Distributes Religious Literature.

Chaplain Arnold P. Spohn distributes religious literature to newly arrived Marine replacements.

practice and custom. I served my men and asked God's pardon under the circumstances."

Chaplain Arnold P. Spohn, while in the 7th Marines, at the front, administered Holy Communion at each service, including "at least three services on Sunday at the Command Post and larger mortar groups, and also approximately three to five services 4 days each week in the platoons along the line."

Chaplain Robert J. Schneck one Sunday afternoon "rigged for church" on the hood of a jeep in a dry stream bed. Enemy action had been relatively light and the banks appeared to afford cover. Some 20 men attended and received Communion. Schneck's own account continues:

All went well until the chaplain was facing the altar for postcommunion prayers. The enemy took that opportunity to lob a few rounds of artillery into the valley. When the chaplain turned, his congregation had all but disappeared. The chaplain again faced the altar, and as he turned a second time to pray the benediction, his congregation had somehow returned. The benediction pronounced, the chaplain again faced the altar. As he turned the third time, to say a few parting words, he discovered his congregation already departed.

With a sigh of thanks that nothing had happened, he turned to the altar preparatory to packing up. He was surprised to see everything secured and the chaplain's assistant already stepping on the jeep's starter. With a fine grin and an impatient wave the assistant declared, "Come on, Boss, let's get out of here before the blessing wears off."

"God Fixed That One"

A young Marine, perhaps 19 years old, had been brought into "A" Company, 1st Medical Battalion, in mild shock and losing blood from a missile wound through the main artery of the upper leg. The surgeon, himself young, perhaps 27 or so, was faced with a difficult decision. To amputate would be relatively safe but would condemn the young man to a life of handicap. To attempt to repair the artery was a delicate operation requiring great skill; the surgeon had seen it done but had never performed it himself. It might save the leg, but the chances of success were slighter. Chaplain Schneck was standing by. He later wrote:

The surgeon closed his eyes and so did the chaplain. And then the operation to repair the artery began. It was long and tedious.

Two days "post-op" I happened to be in the surgical ward tent at the same time our surgeon friend was making his rounds. I was behind him when he reached the cot of our young Marine. . . . He began to talk to the patient and, while talking, almost hesitatingly touched the foot of the shattered leg. A smile appeared. Turning around, the surgeon saw me. "It's warm," he said. Those two words meant that the arterial repair had been successful since blood was reaching the foot. I congratulated the surgeon with great warmth and respect. He looked at me momentarily and then remarked, "Thanks for the prayers, padre. God fixed that one."

Chaplain Felder made a practice of following up through weekly visitations the men from his unit evacuated to rear area hospitals. He would carry greetings from the officers and men of the man's unit, and wrote letters of appreciation to those men for their service, for the signature of the battalion commander.

Lay Leadership

Numerous instances were reported of laymen assisting in the conduct of religious activities. A Marine major in his artillery battalion assisted Chaplain Forney by taking services when the chaplain was fulfilling commitments elsewhere. Felder reported that officers and men conducted their own services or held prayer groups between the chaplain's visits, often utilizing literature which he brought to them. In Marine Observation Squadron VMO–6, its leading chief, M. Sgt. C. W. Horton, USMC, conducted semiweekly Bible classes at his unit's small air strip within sound of enemy fire.

11th Marines Memorial

Of all the ties of respect and friendship developed within small fighting units, perhaps none was closer than that frequently found in the "gun sections" of the artillery. Precision and skill were essential to combat effectiveness, but no more so than the cooperation of the gun section members working as a team. Such comradeship received overt recognition when the 2d Battalion, 11th Marines dedicated a memorial hall in honor of men from their unit who had given their lives in line of duty.

To save material the large tent served a triple purpose: it was mess hall, theater, and chapel in one. An altar was constructed of precious plywood, with a background made from cargo parachutes, and ammunition boxes fastened together provided seats. As the battalion gathered for the dedication ceremony, under the leadership of the battalion commander, men of all faiths listened in respectful silence as the names were read of those artillerymen, their "buddies," whose lives had become a sacrifice in the cause of justice and world order. Both Protestant and Roman Catholic chaplains took part.

Rotation

The tour of duty for chaplains in Korea had thus far averaged around 6 months. Chaplain J. P. Mannion, Assistant Director of the Chaplains Division, wrote to Chaplain Peck on 6 February 1952:

On the recommendation of the Fleet and Force Chaplains and responsible line officers, it has been determined to lengthen the tour of duty in Korea to about 10 months. This change in policy will not affect chaplains presently on duty, but only those who will be ordered after 1 February. We shall do everything in our power to relieve the chaplains presently on duty with the 1st Marine Division at the end of the sixth month or during the seventh month. However, as you know, there are so many due for rotation in April that we may find difficulty in getting them all out on schedule.

Beginning in February orders were written so that a chaplain might be detached, not when a named relief reported in, but within a 1- to 2-month period. Giving the Division Chaplain a measure of latitude regarding the detachment of chaplains serving with him was thought by Peck to have several advantages. He wrote on 14 February.

We have received the dispatch containing orders for detachment of Chaplains Ruleman, Vierling, and Fenning in March or April, and Chaplain Curtis in April or May. That is the best way of writing orders, as far as coverage is concerned out here. I believe that method of naming 1 or 2 months will keep a situation from developing where we are overstrength or under on our coverage.

On 29 February, he wrote further:

The information [in a recent letter from the Chaplains Division], from which I can figure ETA [estimated time of arrival] in Korea is a tremendous help. That information coupled with the way the orders are now being written . . . will make it possible not to have so many switches of assignment right after a man gets here, as happened when I first came and there were the same large numbers of chaplains being replaced. It will also prohibit an overlay of chaplains by having us at no time over our complement (except over Easter, perhaps, when you said to retain the chaplains in order to be amply strengthened at that time).

This is a really perfect system from our standpoint. To know in advance who is coming and when, and who is to go and when, makes it possible for whoever has my job to do a far better job, and by not being faced with necessity of changing the chaplains around too much, they can do a better job.

Later Peck reported, "The command here waits for word from this office before executing orders on chaplains."

Chaplain T/O

With units of the Division increasingly deployed over widespread areas, it was difficult with seven Roman Catholic chaplains to effect adequate coverage. Peck frequently noted in his weekly letters to the Chief of Chaplains the need for an additional one, especially since rear echelon units had of necessity been receiving Catholic ministrations from Army chaplains and non-English speaking Korean priests. Notified that an eighth Roman Catholic chaplain was on his way, Peck wrote on 29 February:

We are especially glad for the eighth Catholic chaplain; he is more needed now than before. To give you some idea of our geographical problem, these two new concentrations of our men [1,000 in 1 new place and 1,500 in another] are approximately 55 miles apart, 1 of them 8 miles over rugged hills from the Division CP, the other 47 miles the other way.

In the same letter Peck wrote concerning the Table of Organization for chaplains serving with a Marine Division.

If this Division is committed to action it needs all of the chaplains listed on the complement given at the top of my roster; of these eight (8) should be Catholic. If a cease-fire and armistice is reached, and the Division becomes a part of occupation troops, I am convinced adequate coverage could be given . . . with four (4) fewer Protestants. With a different geographical and terrain setup, which would be the case if we were pulled out of Korea, that could be increased to read five (5) fewer Protestants and one (1) less Catholic. However, that is only in the case of a so-called peacetime setup and not committed to action.

Someone did a splendid piece of work when the complement for a Marine Division was set up. It is perfect for times when committed to action. It is a bit heavy otherwise.

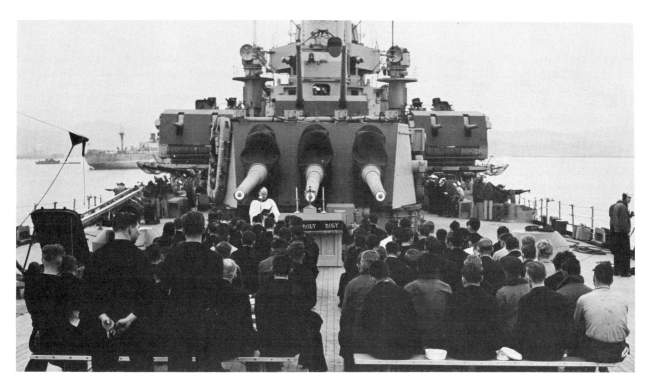

Worship at Pusan.
Chaplain Edwin F. Carr conducts services on board the ROCHESTER in Pusan Harbor.

Air-Gun Strikes

In April Admiral Joy ordered a series of coordinated air and surface ship gun strikes, the first against Chongjin.[8] Carrier plans from the BOXER and PHILIPPINE SEA joined ST. PAUL and U.S. and British destroyers in the effort. Two weeks later IOWA, joined by three destroyers and planes from Task Force 77, again pounded that target. Such combined operations were to be continued to the end of the war.

IOWA was the fourth and last battleship returned to active duty, serving in the war zone from late March to mid-October 1952. Senior chaplain was Jerome J. Sullivan who, after some 14 months in the HELENA, was ordered to the IOWA, where he served for a year. Junior chaplain was Don M. Michael, who was transferred from ANTIETAM.

The chaplains tried to serve the destroyers operating with them, usually crossing by helicopter. Chaplain Michael reported visiting the destroyer MACKENZIE on Easter Day to celebrate Holy Communion. On his own ship the service was held below decks while her guns were firing support missions for troops on the front. Of this he later commented:

[8] *Ibid.*, pp. 347–9.

"The contrast was evident to the men in attendance between the tenets of Christian faith and the conflicts of men." Experience taught him the need for a state of constant readiness; because of frequent changes in the daily operating schedule of IOWA, arrangements for Divine Service often had to be altered and services held on "as little as 15 minutes notice."

When Chaplain Sullivan was transferred to the IOWA, C. W. Ackley had become chaplain in HELENA. (HELENA was then out of the war zone, but would return in June 1952.) George R. Brosius had succeeded Ackley as chaplain in SPERRY.

JUNEAU, after participating in the first, second, and fourth Korean campaigns, returned in April 1952. Her chaplain from May 1951 to May 1953 was Arthur L. Dominy, following B. J. Davis.

E. F. Carr was still chaplain in the ROCHESTER, D. J. Kosky in MANCHESTER, and F. H. Wickham in ST. PAUL. Chaplain W. J. Organ was still serving in LOS ANGELES and L. C. M. Vosseler in TOLEDO. In May 1952 the BREMERTON would take up station in Korean waters; her chaplain was Louis C. Smith.

Destroyers

Chaplain H. W. Jeffers, previously attached to Destroyer Squadron 3, reported aboard the tender

DIXIE in January 1952, relieving R. A. Vaughan. "Tin can" chaplains were evidently still working out patterns for their ministry. Of his work Jeffers wrote:

> The Commodore, not knowing exactly how to govern my work, gave me permission to move at will from ship to ship on the condition that I keep him informed of my location. While in the forward area I tried to move at least once a week to another ship in my division to better cover the division and encourage the lay leadership program. Commanding officers were very cooperative in passing the chaplain when another ship in the division came alongside with the mail or during refueling or replenishing operations.

Other changes were made. W. S. Powell was transferred from ComDesRon 1 to the tender FRONTIER. Charles E. Hailstone had reported to DesRon 5, Harold F. Symons to DesRon 7, Raymond W. Moore to DesRon 9, and George B. Riley to DesRon 13. Edward O. Riley was assigned to Commander Destroyer Division 32.

When it is noted that all these chaplains except Edward Riley were Protestants, it would appear that the need for equitable coverage demanded that the Roman Catholic chaplain be assigned to a larger command, in order to be able to move more freely and extend his ministry more widely.

Carrier Chaplains

The carriers continued interdiction campaigns during this period. J. P. Murphy was still in the PHILIPPINE SEA. He wrote to Chaplain Salisbury of the arrival on 16 March of Gordon B. Galaty, an Episcopalian. The "Phil Sea" had been short a chaplain; for when Barnes and Murphy had, in effect, exchanged assignments in the carrier and 1st MAW, the former Roman Catholic chaplain, H. E. Meade, was also transferred. Since then nearly a year had elapsed. Murphy expressed delight that the Chaplains Division had decided to "have two chaplains aboard the CV's."

There was one hitch, however. Galaty had returned to active duty in August 1950 and it appeared that, according to current regulations, he would be eligible for return to inactive duty in late November. There was clearly still a shortage of chaplains, and the release of Reserves who had fulfilled their obligated service would in the future add further pressures.

In the PRINCETON Chaplain R. F. McManus was relieved by Thomas F. McNeill, a Reserve who, having returned to active duty in September 1950, would serve 27 months before being released to inactive duty in January 1953.

Chaplain Cook was relieved in VALLEY FORGE, after nearly 2 years, by Prescott B. Wintersteen. In its third combat tour, the ship had long since come to appreciate the nightly "lights out" prayer given by the chaplains over the "inter-com." One prayer of Chaplain Cook's may be thought worth recording.

> Almighty God, our Father, our thoughts turn tonight to our comrades-in-arms in Korea. Be pleased, we pray Thee, to grant them Thy most gracious protection against the enemy and the weather and from every peril. Let Thy fatherly hand be over them, and grant them sure trust in Thee.
>
> In these critical hours of negotiation for a cease-fire agreement, guide our leaders that they make no decision that will compromise truth, and no error in judgment of righteousness and justice: for we fight for truth and justice for all men.
>
> If peace means the sacrifice of these, for us or those who shall live after us, grant us the courage and fortitude to continue, in war if necessary, by peaceful means if possible, until, if it be Thy holy will, a lasting peace of freedom from tyranny, freedom from fear, freedom from want shall come to all the nations of earth. We pray in the name of Jesus our Savior, our friend, and our companion of the way. Amen.

Paul J. Knapp had served with Chaplain Cook during the first year of the war. Because of serious family illness he was detached without relief and VALLEY FORGE was without a Roman Catholic chaplain until Pius F. Keating reported in March 1952. Keating was a "jg." with less than a year's active duty, having served at Naval Hospital, Camp Pendleton, after graduation from Chaplains School in Class 1–51.

Chaplains in the BOXER, now in its fourth Korean tour, were G. A. Hoglan (who had been aboard since his recall in September 1950) and J. A. Keeley. Keeley had previously served in BON HOMME RICHARD but when that ship returned stateside in December 1951, the chaplain was transferred in Alameda, Calif., to the BOXER, before she started to the Far East once again. It thus appears that the Chaplains Division was forced to transfer chaplains, even after only a few months, from ships leaving Korea in order to keep the complement filled on those slated for active war service. Even so it was not always possible to have two chaplains in the large carriers.

Escort Carriers

Chaplain O. B. Salyer was relieved in BADOENG STRAIT in June 1951 by Warren L. Wolf, who would remain until May 1953. Chaplain C. O. Sullivan was relieved in SICILY in December 1951 by George A. Jacobs, who served until his release to inactive duty in December 1952. Both followed the practice of their predecessors in trying to get around to as many small ships as possible, administering Com-

Seder.

Chaplain Reuben Siegel is shown with Lt. Col. Sidney J. Altman, division provost marshal, Chaplain Slattery, Mr. Peterson, Red Cross representative of the division, and Chaplain Ernest Wolfram as they partake of the Seder meal in celebration of Passover.

Marines Sing Hymns.

Voices of marines break the cold crisp night air in Korea as they sing adoration to God during a mission conducted in preparation for the coming lenten season.

munion and encouraging whoever might be carrying on religious activities.

Chaplain J. J. Coffey was still aboard the BATAAN. Chaplain R. W. Moore, serving in DesRon 9, replied in his questionnaire:

During Holy Week 1952 it was arranged with the chaplain in USS BATAAN to have him visit my destroyers for Roman Catholic masses, while I conducted Good Friday services in his ship and other Holy Week services in the remaining destroyers. We were operating off the coast of Korea. These transfers were accomplished by helicopter.

Two other escort carriers were operating in the war theater during this period. The BAIROKO had been in Korean waters from November 1950 to September 1951; returning in December 1951, she was present until June 1952. Her chaplain was David M. Humphreys, from August 1950 to August 1952. The RENDOVA served in Korean waters only from August to December 1951. Chaplain Hugh T. McManus had been aboard since March.

Easter 1952

Chaplain Salisbury had planned to visit Korea for Easter, 1952. Maj. Gen. John T. Selden, commanding the 1st Division, wrote to Salisbury expressing his hope that the visit could be accomplished. Invitations were extended to the Chief of Chaplains to preach at an all-Division Sunrise Service and elsewhere in the Division. But it was not to be possible. Salisbury wrote on 8 March, "There are a number of matters which keep me here and my superiors feel that it would be best for me to remain within calling distance."

During March the picture began to change. The following are excerpts from Peck's letters to the Chief of Chaplains:

11 MARCH 1952.

It looks as if the worst of the winter is over. Our nights are cold, but the days are brisk, sunny springtime days—and it certainly lifts the spirits.

On the military front it has been a week of a great deal of incoming mortar and artillery rounds. The men in our sector have taken a pounding and the chaplains of the 5th and 7th Marines have had a rough go of it making the ridge-lines on their rounds. . . . The order has gone out prohibiting any walking of the ridge-line during the daylight not dictated by absolute military necessity. Therefore the chaplains are experimenting with covering the lines during the evening hours, talking to men in bunkers.

17 MARCH 1952.

There is considerable activity here right now. I cannot say more except to advise you that some of my next letters may have to be handwritten, although I will do my best to type them, since I always send copies to the CINCPAC Fleet Chaplain and the FMF Chaplain.

Peck was referring to a major move then underway. Until 12 March 1952 the Division had been located on the east flank of the X Corps sector, with the ROK I Corps between it and the Sea of Japan. In the middle of March it began moving to the westernmost end of the UN line. The excerpts from Peck's letters to Chaplain Salisbury continue:

26 MARCH 1952.

We are moved and back in business. The situation is entirely new and in a great state of flux from a religious coverage standpoint . . . I'm glad that Chaplain Slattery [Peck's relief] is here for he can learn this picture from the start and be in on whatever decisions have to be made. . . . There is even a larger geographical area we have to cover than we had before, but we are out of the mountains.

There will be a VD problem here for we have many civilians around. That will get the chaplains into a phase of activity which we haven't needed to have during the winter.

We are also located where we will get many church VIP's. I wrote once before they didn't get up into the mountains where we wintered but they are sure to come here.

As it turns out, with conditions as they are here now, I'm sure you'll find your visit later in the year will be more satisfactory. In this turmoil we couldn't have done your visit justice. I am still going to have an Easter Sunrise Service but it will not be the all-Division affair I'd planned in the other area. We will have to have a number of them.

3 APRIL 1952.

We have the problem of coverage pretty well in hand now. Palm Sunday, Holy Week, Easter, and Jewish Passover Services will all be held now, and everyone will have an opportunity to participate. They moved units and then moved them again, until it was quite a race to keep our plans for total coverage up to date. . . . Field conditions create a need for flexibility that no other place demands.

During Lent four Roman Catholic chaplains (Joseph P. F. Gallagher, John J. O'Neill, Vincent J. Lonergan, and James F. Follard) were able to conduct a 3-day mission in a rear area. Each evening as approximately 500 personnel of the 5th Marines gathered in a makeshift chapel, the chaplains preached words of guidance and comfort; and through the cold, crisp air could be heard the sound of prayers for the repose of the souls of fallen comrades, for world peace, and for protection amidst the perils and sin of the world.

On Easter Day Chaplain John L. Curtis, 1st Supply Battalion, conducted a Sunrise Service at Headquarters, 8th Army (Advance), at Munsan-ni, the camp of the UN delegates, preached the sermon. (General Harrison was well-known for his personal interest in Christian faith, and active in the promotion of the Officers' Christian Union, an interservice association of Protestant churchmen.)

I Believe.

Father James Follard, CP, teaches the beliefs of the Catholic faith during a mission conducted in Korea. Chaplains (left to right) lending their support are John O'Neill, Joseph Gallagher, and Vincent Lonergan.

Front Line Easter Services.

Chaplain Melvin E. Torstrick conducts Easter morning services for the 3d Battalion, 1st Marines, near the front lines.

Chaplain Edward A. Slattery, having reported to the Division earlier, relieved Peck on 17 April. In his first letter as Division Chaplain to the Chief of Chaplains, he reported: "On Easter we had over 80 Divine Services. In order to conduct them the boys hit the road for a total of well over 500 miles and that mileage is not on any straight smooth highway."

Just before Peck was relieved he had been visited by his opposite number, the Reverend W. W. P. Rhys, senior chaplain to the Forces of the 1st Commonwealth Division, an Anglican priest, veteran of campaigns with the Royal Army in North Africa, East Africa, and Palestine. Slattery was present at the meeting.

Toward the end of his duty Chaplain Peck wrote to Chaplain Salisbury:

I can honestly say this tour of duty has taught me a great deal as a senior chaplain, and it has been a constant inspiration and challenge to see the way the chaplains give of themselves to stomp these hills in the cold to visit their men. I feel like Bob Schwyhart [Division Chaplain from September 1950 to 20 February 1951] who wrote me when I was coming out—he said he wouldn't want to go through it again, but he wouldn't take anything for the experience. I believe some of our most trying times are our most rewarding experiences.

Citations

Chaplain Peck was subsequently awarded the Legion of Merit with Combat "V" for "exceptionally

Relief.

Chaplain Walter S. Peck, Jr., is relieved as division chaplain by Chaplain E. A. Slattery (left) 17 April 1952.

Field Mass.

Chaplain John J. O'Neill celebrates mass in the field for marines at a forward position.

---

meritorious conduct . . . as Division Chaplain for a Marine division during operations against the enemy in Korea from 8 October 1951 to 16 April 1952." The citation continues:

Commander Peck displayed exceptional ability and foresight in caring for the spiritual welfare of all the Marines coming under his jurisdiction. An understanding and capable leader, wise and persevering, he organized his section in such an outstanding manner that spiritual services and guidance were always available to those who were in the greatest need. Frequently making journeys throughout the entire division in the most adverse conditions of weather and terrain, he worked long and arduous hours with little concern for his personal health, in order to insure that all Marines received the opportunity to attend services in their own particular faith.

Chaplain John J. O'Neill was awarded the Air Medal for the period 19 November 1951 to 8 January 1952. His citation reads in part:

Utilizing air transportation to reach the front line units, Lieutenant (jg.) O'Neill repeatedly flew over action combat areas in a slow, unarmed aircraft to conduct religious services for friendly troops at the front.

Chaplain O'Neill also received the Letter of Commendation award for action on 8 January 1952.

When well-entrenched enemy forces gained fire superiority over a Marine patrol, inflicting heavy casualties, Lieutenant O'Neill left his battalion command post immediately and proceeded to the scene of the battle in order to give spiritual aid to members of the patrol. Alone and unarmed, with no thought for his own personal safety, he fearlessly worked his way through intense enemy fire to reach the patrol and for 45 minutes exposed himself while adminis-

tering last rites to the wounded and dying. To the other members of the patrol, his shouted words of encouragement served as a constant source of inspiration.

Ridge-Runners Rewarded

Five other chaplains received the Letter of Commendation with Combat "V" for periods of service terminating within the 7th Campaign. It is instructive to read their citations, noting how frequently is mentioned their ministry to small Marine units dug in on the mountainous slopes of northeastern Korea.

The citation of Chaplain Robert N. Ruleman, for the period 14 September 1951 to 17 January 1952, reads in part:

On numerous occasions he refused opportunities to retire to safer areas in the rear. His creed lay in serving with the "Fighting Man," and regardless of the situation he remained with the front line troops. Whether it was to solace the weary, comfort the wounded, or dispense the Word of God, he discharged his responsibilities in a manner which provided a reverent inspiration to all who observed him.

Chaplain William E. Brooks, Jr., was cited for the period from 29 October 1951 to 29 January 1952.

While the regiment was committed in defensive action against the enemy, he personally visited every man on the front lines many times. He conducted divine services in the forward-most areas when it was impossible for men to attend services elsewhere.

Chaplain Vincent J. Lonergan's citation, covering the period from 28 October 1951 to 4 February 1952, indicates how widespread a chaplain's ministry might be.

Lieutenant Commander Lonergan, serving as the regiment's Catholic chaplain, worked tirelessly with complete disregard for his health and personal safety, to give spiritual aid not only to the men in the regiment but to two medical companies, Army engineers, Marine engineers, and Marine service troops. On one occasion he fearlessly exposed himself to intense enemy fire to give spiritual consolation to the wounded Marines of an artillery battery and to members of an infantry regiment's command post.

Chaplain Joseph P. F. Gallagher was commended for service as a regimental chaplain from 16 January to 4 April 1952.

Working for the most part under the most adverse terrain and climate conditions, and often in areas that were exposed to enemy mortar and small arms fire, he faithfully held services for and administered to the men and officers of the regiment.

The citation accompanying Chaplain Robert G. Fenning's award, covering the period 26 January–30 April 1952, states the case very explicitly.

He constantly ministered to the spiritual needs of the men in the battalion by going from bunker to bunker in order not to assemble a group of men where they could be targets for enemy artillery or mortar fire. Traveling through extreme cold, stormy weather over rugged mountainous terrain, he continually stayed with the men, giving instructions and conducting religious services without regard for his personal safety.

MAW Chaplain Personnel

Acting Wing Chaplain Seymour's report to the Chief of Chaplains dated 12 February 1952 detailed the following personnel picture. Chaplain R. D. Cleaves had departed on 1 February, and Seymour was giving Protestant coverage to Marine Aircraft Group 33 in addition to his own duties. Chaplain Horvath, transferred to headquarters, was replaced at Marine Aircraft Group 12 by Chaplain La Duca. E. R. Weidler remained as Protestant chaplain in MAG 12. J. A. Sullivan continued as Roman Catholic chaplain in MAG 33. Chaplain Harrison was still in Pusan, attached to the Marine antiaircraft artillery battalion. There was no Navy chaplain with the units at Itami.

The Chaplains Division had run into unexpected difficulties in detailing a replacement for Chaplain Barnes as Wing Chaplain. Barnes had received orders in October 1951 detaching him on the arrival of his relief, Chaplain E. R. Brewster. Because of serious illness in his family, Barnes was detached in November without relief. On 5 December Chaplain Brewster's orders were modified, granting him 20 days delay because of the illness of his father; and on 19 December his orders to the 1st Marine Aircraft Wing were canceled because of further illness in his family. On 26 December Chaplain Joseph F. Parker was or-

dered to the Wing but his orders were canceled because his wife was critically ill. On 29 December Chaplain William J. Kuhn was ordered but upon physical examination was hospitalized in San Francisco.

After this series of setbacks the Air Wing Commanding General, C. F. Schilt, wrote directly to Chaplain Salisbury:

The 1st Marine Air Wing is one of the few organizations of the Naval Service engaged in land combat and has personnel at five main locations in Korea and one in Japan. As you know an adequate number of competent chaplains is essential to good morale in an organization committed as we are. Under the circumstances I believe you will agree with me that the Wing has not received proper treatment, having been without a Wing Chaplain since November.

After commending Seymour's work as Acting Wing Chaplain and suggesting a couple of chaplains he would like to have if available, the General concluded, "If a more senior chaplain is not readily available, Chaplain Seymour is entirely acceptable as Wing Chaplain." A postscript, handwritten, extended an invitation to the Chief of Chaplains to come to Korea himself for a tour of inspection.

Chaplain Salisbury's reply, after explaining the situation described just above, noted that Chaplain Parker's orders had been reinstated, and added, "I only wish that I could get out to see you but there are certain pressures here which require my presence for sometime to come." Parker reported on 18 April 1952 and the 1st Marine Aircraft Wing once again had a Wing Chaplain.

Divine Services

Most chaplains would regard their religious ministry as encompassing more than services of divine worship, but nothing they do, they would say, is more fundamentally important. The following statistics, included in the quarterly report ending 31 March 1952 submitted by Force Chaplain Martell H. Twitchell, covering all activities of Fleet Marine Force, Pacific, indicate the zeal of "clergymen in uniform" in providing a ministry of worship. During March 14 chaplains reported conducting from 32 to 96 separate services each. The five who conducted the greatest number were the following:

Worship for Replacements.

A large group of Marine replacements on their way to front-line duty with the 1st Division attend services conducted by Chaplain Robert C. Fenning.

		Serv-ices	Attend-ance	Com-muni-cants
J. H. Sullivan.....	MAG 33.......	96	2,163	1,132
H. A. Seymour....	1st MAW.......	53	1,663	360
R. C. Fenning....	5th Marines.....	45	984	136
E. R. Weidler....	MAG 12.......	43	1,570	190
Geo. Felder, Jr....	7th Marines.....	40	647	364

Relief Work

Chaplain Weidler wrote that during January and February 1952 numerous North Korean children were airlifted from advance airstrips to the Kangnung field, in need of food, clothing, and a place to live.

The local orphanages are the first places the youngsters receive assistance on their way south. This section of Korea has been overrun four times by war in less than a year. The buildings where the children were placed required a lot of repair work. Our men have donated many hours of labor and have written home describing the plight of the children.

From our Protestant chapel offering we have spent $585 for clothing to meet the immediate needs of the youngsters. We have been joined by the Marines at El Toro. . . . We are receiving on the average of 10 large boxes of clothing each day from people at home, in response to the letters written by the men out here.

There are 3 UNCACK [UN Civil Assistance Commission, Korea] and 1 Catholic orphanage with a total of over 250 children depending on us for fuel, clothing, and food. The chaplains serve as liaison between the Air Group and the UNCACK and civil relief personnel in making assistance available where most needed.

Commander William Lederer of CINCPAC spent a week with us, obtaining material for a story on our Air Group and its work with these children. You should be able to read his own account of our work here in Korea, in an early issue of "This Week," if his plans materialize.

According to Chaplain Twitchell's report, cited just above, Weidler had reported that Marines of Marine Aircraft Group 12 had provided clothing for 350 children in the 4 Kangnung orphanages and that $1,200 from the Chapel fund had been donated to them during March.

MAW Chaplains Cited

Chaplain Richard D. Cleaves was awarded the Bronze Star for his service with Marine Aircraft Group 33 from 23 May 1951 to 1 February 1952.

Constantly concerned with the welfare of the men of the group, he frequently spent long hours in helping to seek a solution for individual tribulations. Always ready to assist in the struggle to aid an impoverished country, he guided and directed the Marines in founding and maintaining orphanages in the vicinity of the airfield where he was serving and elected to remain at his post rather than avail himself of the rest and recreation facilities in Japan.

Two of the Air Wing chaplains received the Letter of Commendation award for outstanding performance of their duties during periods ending before the terminal date of the 7th Korean Campaign. For meritorious service as Acting Wing Chaplain from 27 November 1951 to 7 April 1952 Chaplain Seymour was cited for his "thorough understanding of the various complexities confronting the fighting man."

His work in aiding civilian refugees was singled out for comment.

Sparing no efforts in assisting the United Nations struggle to help an impoverished country, he supervised the generous efforts of Marine personnel in their desire to establish and maintain orphanages in the vicinity of Pohang Airfield.

Chaplain James A. Sullivan was commended for service with Marine Aircraft Group 33 from 30 June 1951 to 10 April 1952. "His concern for the spiritual, mental, and physical welfare of the men prompted him to assist them in their difficulties and troubles at any hour." His citation continues:

Not confining his Christian work to his unit alone, Lieutenant Commander Sullivan assisted the United Nations efforts to help an impoverished country by aiding in the rehabilitation and maintenance of churches and orphanages in the vicinity of the airfield where he was serving.

COMNAVFE Chaplains Cited

As the first chaplain to serve on the staff of Commander U.S. Naval Forces, Far East, Walter A. Mahler had successfully and with constant good humor planned and supervised the many activities necessary to meet the greatly increased scope of requirements for the chaplains' ministry throughout the command. In addition he carried duties as Headquarters chaplain. He was given the Letter of Commendation award covering service from 20 November 1950 to 11 January 1952. Part of his citation reads as follows:

His ability to achieve and maintain the proper and delicate balance between the religious and naval aspects of personnel relations and problems was outstanding. His integrity and his staunch, unswerving faith and piety set an inspiring example for all who knew him.

Chaplain James E. Reaves, Senior Chaplain, Fleet Activities, Yokosuka, also received the Letter of Commendation with ribbon for faithfulness to duty during the period 25 June 1950 to 15 November 1951.

Chaplain Mahler was relieved by Daniel F. Meehan. Other changes in the command since the roster given in chapter 5 were as follows. Chaplains E. D. Bennett, J. J. O'Neill, J. E. Reaves, and E. M. Turner had been relieved. Raymond A. Beaulieu had been assigned to Naval Air Station, Atsugi. Gerard J. Clark had reported to Naval Hospital to relieve C. W. Lawler, awaiting orders. Benoit R. Galland had reported to Fleet Activities, Yokosuka. Charles J. Horejs was ordered to the repair ship HECTOR and Bob G. Rochelle to the DELTA. Edward G. Swain was assigned to Camp Otsu, which functioned largely as a Marine casual company. In addition, A. J. Wolf, as noted earlier, had been assigned as Jewish chaplain for COMNAVFE, attached to Fleet Activities, Yokosuka.

Atsugi Chapel

On the air station, which the Navy had taken over from the Air Force in 1951, stood a large building, formerly a Japanese gymnasium and then used by the Air Force partly for storage, partly for religious purposes. During World War II Japanese pilots had used it for practicing Kendo, an ancient game of tilting involving the use of heavy staves. Included in the building were a banquet hall and a small Shinto shrine. Before Kamikaze pilots would leave on a mission, they were feasted and decorated and then participated in a Shinto ritual before the shrine. Chaplain C. L. Sullenberger, when assigned to the Naval Air Station, had been instrumental in securing the use of the entire building for religious purposes. In the years following, during the tours of Chaplains Orlando Ingvoldstad and D. M. Humphrey, this Japanese building would become the nucleus of a well-planned, expanded religious center for American personnel.

PhibPac

In the Amphibious Force, Pacific, Chaplain Earl R.

Brewster had replaced W. J. Kuhn as Force Chaplain. A roster dated March 1952 shows that Alvin O. Collins had reported to the staff of Transport Division 15. Chaplains E. A. Day, W. J. Kokoszka, and F. A. Ruder were now listed on the staffs of TransDiv 14, TransDiv 12, and TransDiv 13, respectively, rather than as attached to individual ships as formerly. Chaplain Jacob R. Thomas was ordered to relieve R. T. Noland at Naval Beach Group ONE, after nearly a year of duty with ComServPac as the Fleet's free-wheeling circuit rider.

The amphibious command ship ELDORADO had returned stateside in September 1951, her place taken by the ESTES, whose chaplain was William R. Petre. MT. McKINLEY, which had been relieved in June 1951, returned to Korean service in March 1952 as flagship of Rear Adm. F. X. McInerney, Commander Navy Amphibious Forces in the Far East. Her chaplain was Thomas M. Gibson.

MSTS

Chaplain George W. Thompson, Staff Chaplain, Military Sea Transportation Service, Pacific Area, submitted on 15 April 1952 the following list of chaplains serving in MSTS ships.

Bol, Peter	REF	GEN G. M. RANDALL
Bruns, Bruno	REF	THOMAS JEFFERSON
Childress, Elmer H., Jr	BAP (S)	GEN. N. M. WALKER
Dohrmann, Leonard B	EVAN & REF	GEN. J. C. BRECKENRIDGE
Erickson, Paul F	EVAN MISS CONV	GEN. E. D. PATRICK
Handran, Ralph E	RC	GEN. A. E. ANDERSON
Hemphill, Edward J., Jr	METH	GEN. H. W. BUTNER
Holmes, Norman B	CHRI SCIENCE	GEN. WM. WEIGEL
Irwin, Paul I	METH	GEN. JOHN J. POPE
Karnasiewicz, Charles F	RC	GEN. WM. BLACK
Kennedy, Deane W	METH	GEN. W. A. MANN
McCarthy, Eugene W	RC	WINDHAM BAY
Moran, John L., Jr	BAP (S)	GEN. E. T. COLLINS
Morton, Frank R	LUTH	CAPE ESPERANCE
Nolan, William F	RC	GEN. A. W. BREWSTER
Potter, Paul K	METH	GEN. W. H. GORDON
Robinson, Charles B	PRESBY (USA)	SITKOH BAY
Singer, Wilson H	METH	GEN. M. C. MEIGS
Stowater, Seattle A	UNIT	DAVID C. SHANKS
Sydnor, Charles E	BAP (A)	GEN. WM. MITCHELL
Terhune, Cornelius A	PRESBY (USA)	GEN. D. I. SULTAN
Tulley, Edward M	RC	GEN. W. F. HASE
Wartes, Arthur J	PRESBY (USA)	PRESIDENT JACKSON
Watts, John E., Jr	PRESBY (US)	FRED C. AINSWORTH
Wheeler, Wendell C	CONG	GEN. C. G. MORTON

Chaplains Thomas P. Dunleavy and George J. Enyedi had been recently detached. Five ships had at the time no chaplain. The WINDHAM BAY,

CAPE ESPERANCE, and SITKOH BAY were escort carriers used to ferry planes and personnel to the war theater. Aboard SITKOH BAY Chaplain

Robinson held services in the hangar deck or forward elevator when troops were embarked and in the ready room or compartment formerly housing catapult machinery when traveling without troops.

Chaplain Handran found an "amazing response to daily services on transports." In addition to daily Mass, he arranged a service for Protestants composed of Bible reading, prayers, and hymns, "usually conducted by a lay leader." All were well attended, though, he added, "It may be they had no place else to go." Chaplain Holmes reported a daily weekday attendance at Protestant services between 250 and 300 men. "On a single voyage into Korean waters, as many at 600 copies of the complete Bible would be distributed to men requesting it."

Chaplain Sydnor reported that in addition to their contribution to the March of Dimes, sailors in the GENERAL WILLIAM MITCHELL pledged $900 to help a young lady, Miss Bunting, in California attend commercial art school. Miss Bunting who was stricken 5 years before with polio was a guest of the ship in port, and was presented to the captain and taken for a tour of the vessel.

MSTS chaplains, under the leadership of Staff Chaplain Thompson, cooperated with the annual American Red Cross campaign. The first ship making its contribution in 1952 was the GENERAL E. D. PATRICK, where Paul F. Erickson was chaplain. Chaplain Thompson reported to the Chaplains Division that in 1951 MSTS ships in the Pacific area had contributed $47,671 to various charities.

Panmunjom Talks

Meanwhile, during the entire 5 months of the 7th Korean Campaign, full-scale talks had continued at Panmunjom. Resumed on 25 October 1951, a month had been consumed in debate over the position of a buffer zone and the related question whether the cease-fire should be put into operation immediately after agreement on that, or only after agreement had been reached on all other items of the agenda. The United Nations delegations insisted on the latter course lest a premature truce allow a Communist buildup while the talks continued.

Finally on 27 November (the date later designated as the end of the 6th Korean Campaign) agreement was reached on the establishment of the demilitarized zone: each side should withdraw 2 kilometers from the present point of contact if an armistice should be signed within 30 days, or from whatever lines should be held at the time an armistice should be agreed upon. The 27 November line started along the

Sachon River on the west and ran north and east through the Iron Triangle, thence to a point about as far north as the apex of the Triangle; from there the line dipped southward, though still above the Punchbowl, and afterwards turned north and ran out to the sea at Kosong. The United Nations thus held positions north of the Parallel everywhere except in the extreme west, where the truce line dipped slightly below it.

On 30 November the delegates began discussion of the composition and functions of a Supervisory Commission and matters pertaining to military stance after an armistice should be reached: troop rotations, replacement of equipment, and rehabilitation of airfields. With no agreement having been reached on these matters, on 11 December the negotiators began concurrent discussions of the prisoner of war issue. On the 18th POW lists were exchanged. UN proposals for Red Cross teams to investigate POW camps were spurned by the Communists. Talk ranged over such questions as whether the prisoners should be exchanged "one for one" or "all for all." It was agreed to screen the prisoners in order to separate bonafide civilians from combatants. The most serious stumbling-block concerned the disposition of prisoners who did not want to be repatriated.

In April 1952 the UN Command began a screening of the North Korean and Chinese prisoners it held to determine their wishes; of the approximately 121,000 in UN camps, approximately 38,000 indicated their desire not to return.[9] On 28 April the UN delegation offered the Communists a "package deal" on the three main disputed issues: They would not be party to forcible repatriation; they would concede the buildup of damaged airfields; and they would accept Poland and Czechoslovakia as members of a Neutral Nations Supervisory Commission, but not Russia, and asked the Communists to accept Sweden and Switzerland. Thus far had the talks come when the period here under review came to an end.

Change of Scene

The 7th Korean Campaign drew to a close with the end of April 1952. The battleground had become a narrow band across the peninsula, bounded by the main defensive lines of the UN forces on the south and of the Communist forces on the north. Both opposing armies were capable of offensive operations but remained for the most part in static defense

---

[9] *Britannica Book of the Year*, 1953, article, "Korean War."

positions.[10] Actual fighting occurred more often than not between combat outposts and opposing probing patrols.

In the east the lines lay well north of the 38th Parallel, slanting up and down steep hills divided by valleys wide enough only for a little stream or sometimes a narrow, twisting road connecting one tiny inhabited area with the next, usually a considerable distance away. This area, which would always be associated in their minds with the craterlike Punchbowl, Marines of the 1st Division had now left behind, doubtless without regret. After 600 trucks had shuttled back and forth transferring some 6,000 loads of gear a distance of 180 miles, the Division dug in as the western anchor of the 8th Army front.[11] Now under operational control of I Army Corps, its mission was to block the way to Seoul should the Communists attempt a new invasion of the South. Both the Division and the 1st Marine Aircraft Wing were now in new locations, their individual units often widely scattered. From the latter part of March 1952 the scene of the operations with which our account is chiefly concerned shifted to the western side of the Korean peninsula. Division Chaplain Slattery wrote to the Chief of Chaplains on 21 April: "Spring is upon us, thanks be to God the Commies are not. Blossoms are on the hillsides. Dust is thick on our hides but our hearts are high."

[10] R. A. Gugeler (ed.), *Combat Operations in Korea* (Washington, 1954), pp. 243f. Miller, *op. cit.*, p. 210.

[11] Lynn Montross, *Cavalry of the Sky*, p. 180.

CHAPTER 8

KOREAN DEFENSE—SUMMER–FALL 1952

1 May–30 November 1952

With the truce talks still continuing there were few major engagements during the summer and fall of 1952.[1] The lines were relatively stable, the United Nations troops often facing the enemy across no more than 50 yards, though sometimes separated from them by as much as 10 miles. The importance of hills and mountains for observation purposes made the battles for peaks particularly tense, especially when such an elevation protruded forward of one's own sector into the enemy's lines. Then there ensued stubborn fighting and peaks would change hands several times in seesaw actions. In such engagements artillery and close air support were often of decisive importance. Wherever the opposing units remained dug-in and contact limited, there was less need for air support. Navy and Marine fighters then concentrated on supporting Air Force missions aimed at the destruction of railroads and highways, rolling stock and trucks, marshalling yards, and supply depots. The B–29's were systematically engaged in neutralizing Communist airfields in the North.

The enemy had at no time during the Korean War posed a serious threat at sea. United Nations naval forces were engaged largely in siege and interdiction operations. Wonsan, on the east coast, which had fallen to the enemy with the withdrawal of UN forces from north of the 38th Parallel in December 1950, was denied access to the sea by continuous siege. By the end of October 1952 4 battleships, 8 cruisers, 16 aircraft carriers and approximately 80 destroyers had been at one time or other deployed in Korean waters.[2] Of the carriers 13 were United States vessels, 2 British and 1 Australian.

Perhaps the most spectacular event of early summer was the rioting of Communist prisoners-of-war on the island of Koje-do, off the southern coast.[3] A hard core of Communists had kept the compound there in turmoil for months, fomenting serious riots in February and March. Finally, on 7 May, the prisoners succeeded in seizing control of the camp and held Brig. Gen. F. T. Dodd, UN commander, hostage until his deputy signed a statement which practically conceded charges of maladministration which the Communist negotiators at Panmunjom had been urging against the United Nations Command. On 12 May Gen. Mark W. Clark succeeded General Ridgway as commander-in-chief of United Nations forces in Korea and promptly repudiated the so-called "confessions," making clear to the world that it had been secured by violence and repeating the proposal already frequently made at Panmunjom to open the POW camps of both sides to international inspection.

May Day

May first is of course a "holy day" for international Communism and UN forces were on the alert as the day approached. On 29 April Bishop Harry S. Kennedy, Episcopal bishop of Honolulu with responsibility as that church's Military Ordinary for the Pacific and Far Eastern area, arrived at the Division Command post at the invitation of Lt. Gen. Franklin A. Hart, FMF Pac Commanding General. Division Chaplain Slattery had written on 21 April to Chief of Chaplains S. W. Salisbury:

Chaplain Boyer plans a Division Episcopal service at 1830 on 30 April and I have written a memorandum to the Chief of Staff requesting that unit commanders be authorized to release the officers and men who may wish to attend the service. It will depend, of course, on the tactical situation and with 1 May looming up I am under the impression that the Commanding General will hesitate to issue such authorization.

Although his arrival was unexpectedly a day early, and both the Bishop and his military escort were ill from food poisoning (they had first visited an Army

---

[1] *Britannica Book of the Year,* 1953; article, "Korean War."
[2] *Ibid.*
[3] *Ibid.*

Visitor.

The Episcopal Bishop of Honolulu, the Right Reverend Harry S. Kennedy (right) speaks to men after his service at the 1st Division. He is greeted by the Senior Chaplain of Her Majesty's Forces, Wynn Rhys. At left is Chaplain Alexander W. Boyer of the Motor Transport Battalion. Bishop Kennedy was Episcopal Representative for the Armed Forces in the Far East.

---

installation, Slattery reported gleefully!), nevertheless a dispatch to the lines brought a few representatives from each unit and a service was held on the evening of the 29th, with General Hart and Maj. Gen. John A. Selden, 1st Marine Division commander, present. Accompanying the Bishop was Episcopal chaplain A. W. Boyer of the Division and on hand to greet him was the Reverend Wynn Rhys, senior chaplain of the British Commonwealth Division.

On 5 May Slattery wrote:

Due to Fenning's orders we had to detach him on 30 April; no relief being in sight Chaplain Brooks volunteered to plug the gap at Chaplain Fenning's battalion. That was on 30 April and 1 May. Needless to say, he slept little and then fitfully, due to a certain amount of "incoming" plus a volume (for the occasion of May Day) of "outgoing."

On 17 May the chapel which had been erected at the Division Command Post following the Division's move to the western front was dedicated. General Selden gave the address, and Chaplains Slattery (Ro-

Chapel—1st Marine Division.

The new 1st Marine Division Chapel leaves its doors open to members of all faiths.

Chaplains at Dedication.

The 1st Marine Division's Command Post Chapel was formally dedicated on Armed Forces Day. In attendance were 24 of the Division's 28 chaplains. They are shown here in front of the new chapel. First row, from left are: E. S. Jones; R. H. Willets; B. N. Wolfe; E. A. Wolfram; J. T. Callahan; A. W. Boyer. Seated: O. Weber; A. D. Prickett; E. A. Slattery, Division Chaplain; Maj. Gen. J. T. Selden; A. M. Oliver; W. P. Lane; W. D. McCabe. Standing: N. A. McDowell; H. C. Duncan; V. J. Lustig; C. W. Herrick; C. T. Duggan; A. F. Mendosa; A. W. Robertson; M. E. Torstrick; R. Siegel; R. F. Barlik; B. J. Nowakowski. Missing from the picture are H. C. Bowling; C. H. Elliot; L. A. Guillaume; and J. H. Muller.

Dedication.

Maj. Gen. John T. Selden, Commanding General of the 1st Marine Division, delivers the dedicatory address at the opening of the Division Command Post Chapel on Armed Forces Day. Seated from left to right are Chaplains Reubin Siegel, Edward A. Slattery and (obscured by the rostrum) Algernon M. Oliver.

man Catholic), Siegel (Jewish), and Oliver (Protestant) took part. Twenty-five of the chaplains assigned to the Division were present.

Regarding the military picture Slattery wrote:

Action remains sporadic. Chaplain Robertson who is with Tanks had a narrow squeak recently. He was with one of his companies when a considerable amount of "incoming" arrived. His jeep was damaged but, thanks be to God, Chaplain Robertson was not in it at the time.

I worry about these lads so much and keep urging them to be extremely cautious. They are prudent but even that is not a safeguard against the dangers which surround them. Chaplains Duncan and Mendonsa displayed courage and

their spirit of dedication a week ago in remaining at a forward aid station through a mortar barrage.

Rotation of Chaplains

On 19 May Slattery submitted a periodic roster to the Chaplains Division. He noted:

We now have 17 Protestant chaplains, 9 Catholic and 1 Jewish chaplain. With Torstrick detached we will be one Protestant under the minimum need. I understand that Chaplain Pat Adams is due here, which will bring the number of Catholics up to 10. Do you intend it to be so or have you plans to detach one of the Catholics sooner than expected? Naturally we can use everyone you send and more, but I do not want to be "piggish" about it.

ROSTER OF CHAPLAINS, 19 MAY 1952

Name	Rank	Assignment	Church affiliation
SLATTERY, E. A.	CDR	Div Chaplain	RC
BOWLING, H. C., JR.	LT	1st Cmb Ser Group	METH
OLIVER, A. M.[1]	LCDR	Headquarters Bn	METH
PRICKETT, A.D.	LCDR	Headquarters Bn	BAP (S)
LUSTIG, V. J.	LCDR	1st Medical Bn	RC
WEBER, O.	LT	1st Medical Bn	LUTH
MULLER, J. H.	LTJG	1st Shore Party Bn	REF
WOLFRAM, E. A., JR.	LT	1st Engineer Bn	LUTH (MoSy)
NOWAKOWSKI, B. J.	LT	1st Amphibian Trac Bn	RC
SIEGEL, R.	LTJG	Headquarters Bn	JEWISH
BARLIK, R. F.	LTJG	1st Medical Bn	RC
ROBERTSON, A. W.	LTJG	1st Tank Bn	BAP (S)
BOYER, A. W.	LTJG	1st Motor Tr Bn	PE
WOLFE, B. N.[1]	LTJG	1st Service Bn	BAP (S)
JONES, E. S.	LTJG	1st Armored Amp Bn	METH
FIRST MARINES			
MC CABE, W. D.[2]	LCDR	2d Battalion	PRESBY (USA)
CALLAHAN, J. T.	LT	3d Battalion	RC
TORSTRICK, M. E.[1]	LTJG	1st Battalion	BAP (S)
FIFTH MARINES			
MENDONSA, A. F.[2]	LT	2d Battalion	RC
ELLIOTT, C. H., JR.	LT	3d Battalion	PE
DUNCAN, H. C.[1]	LTJG	1st Battalion	METH
SEVENTH MARINES			
WILLETS, R. H.[2]	LT	1st Battalion	BAP (S)
HERRICK, C. W.	LT	2d Battalion	PRESBY (USA)
GUILLAUME, L. A.	LTJG	3d Battalion	RC
ELEVENTH MARINES			
LANE, W. P.[2]	LCDR	Headquarters	RC
FORNEY, F. J.[1]	LT	1st Battalion	DISC
MC DOWELL, N. L.	LT	4th Battalion	BAP (S)
DUGGAN, C. T.	LTJG	3d Battalion	RC

[1] Indicates chaplains ordered detached.
[2] Indicates regimental chaplain.

Of the 27 chaplains shown on Division Chaplain Peck's roster of 1 January 1952, only Chaplains Duncan, Torstrick, Oliver, Siegel, Wolfe, and Forney remained. Since that date 22 new chaplains had arrived, making a total of 28 on the 19 May roster.

Chaplains Prickett and Duggan had reported just prior to this roster, thus making possible within a few days the detachment of two of the five designated as awaiting detachment.

According to rotation policy then in effect, a chap-

Outdoor Worship.

Chaplain A. W. Robertson mounts his portable altar on a T46 tank at a forward outpost in Korea and conducts services.

lain serving with the Division was ordered detached after 6 or 7 months; the actual date of detachment, within the terms of the Bureau of Naval Personnel orders sent to Division Headquarters, was left to the discretion of the Division Chaplain. Normally detachment was effected in order of priority of reporting, though the overriding consideration always was the most economical distribution of chaplains throughout the Division's units. Siegel, of course, had to await the arrival of a Jewish relief, being the only chaplain of that faith in the Division. Chaplains E. A. Wolfram, Jr., and Ward D. McCabe completed the list (including the six above) of eight chaplains who had reported before 31 January, who could expect rotation in accordance with the earlier policy. Chaplains reporting on or after 1 February would be expected to serve 10 months in Korea.

Chaplain Distribution

The administrative processing of chaplains attached to the 1st Marine Division was a G–1 (Division Personnel) function, acting for the Chief of Staff and with the advice of the Division Chaplain. The chaplains had no direct command link with the Division

Chaplain; once assigned they were under the military jurisdiction of their respective commanding officers. The Division Chaplain served, however, as an effective liaison between the various unit chaplains and the Division subordinate commands.

Chaplains were reassigned within the Division from time to time, so much so during certain periods that trying to follow them resembles unscrambling a maze. There is clearly much in favor of keeping a chaplain with the same unit for an extended period, and in peacetime, at least, as long as both unit commander and chaplain are satisfied, "long pastorates" are more likely the rule. Under field conditions, however, itinerancy provided the only adequate and economical distribution of the services of a limited number of chaplain personnel (frontier churches had of course had the same experience in the early days of the westward expansion of our country).

It was the function of the Division Chaplain to see that the available chaplains were so assigned that their ministry might be utilized to the benefit of the largest number of personnel. According to the Division T/O the Division Chaplain and all others not assigned to regimental organizations were carried by

Headquarters Battalion, to form a "pool" upon which the Division Chaplain could draw for assignments to the separate battalions. The first roster given in this account, that of Division Chaplain Schwyhart on the eve of the Inchon landing, indicated such a distribution.[4] Under field conditions, however, it usually proved more satisfactory to attach a chaplain directly to the Headquarters Company of the separate battalions. In most rosters such distribution will be seen.

Each regiment was entitled to three chaplains, normally all attached to the regimental headquarters, the senior being regimental chaplain and a member of the regimental staff. He was responsible for the placement of himself and the other two chaplains within the regiment. An infantry regiment had, besides its Headquarters and Service Company and 4.2 Mortar Company, three infantry battalions. Under combat conditions it was customary for one chaplain to be with each battalion, the regimental chaplain also maintaining contact with the regimental CP and providing a ministry there. Usually the Headquarters would be located near enough one or other of the battalions to make this feasible. Since there were normally two Protestants and one Roman Catholic per regiment, a certain amount of rotation within the regiment was usually thought necessary for religious coverage. In addition exigencies arising under field conditions dictated rather frequent shifts, so that a chaplain would be found now in the first battalion, later in the third or again in the second.

Regimental chaplains were not always in agreement with one another on the best policy regarding this point; some of the differences stemmed from the nature of the varied operational assignments. One would keep himself in Regiment and assume responsibility for one of the battalions, and then assign, semiofficially and temporarily, one chaplain to each of the other two battalions. Another regimental chaplain, feeling that all three chaplains should be sensitive of their responsibility to the entire regiment, would keep himself and both the others attached to Regiment, but working in more or less orderly rotation throughout the subordinate units. While the Division chaplain would be advised on these shifts, the actual placement of chaplains within a regiment, once assigned there, was the prerogative of the regimental commander with the regimental chaplain as his adviser.

As a member of the Commanding General's staff the Division chaplain found many of his duties to be administrative, though he furnished a ministry representing his particular faith at the Division CP and Headquarters Battalion. Also at Headquarters would be a chaplain of the Christian faith different from that of the senior chaplain; for instance, through most of the period here under review, Chaplain A. D. Prickett, Southern Baptist, worked with Chaplain Slattery. In addition, the single Jewish chaplain was always assigned to Headquarters Battalion, though his duties carried him through the entire Division and on occasion he would be given temporary additional duty orders to one or other of the separate battalions. Sometimes this was necessary to provide a chaplain in a given battalion; besides, it gave the chaplain an opportunity to gain experience as chaplain in an independent unit. One or both of these chaplains were sometimes referred to as assistant division chaplain.

In filling the regimental chaplain billet seniority naturally was an important factor. Usually a lieutenant commander was assigned, though on many occasions a lieutenant filled the billet. For instance, on Slattery's 19 May roster only the 1st and 11th Marines had a lieutenant commander (McCabe and Lane), while the 5th and 7th Marines each had a lieutenant (Mendonsa and Willets). As far as possible these billets were rotated among Protestants and Roman Catholics. All other factors having been weighed, it sometimes happened that all three regimental chaplains would be of the same faith; but with new arrivals shifts would be made to bring that aspect of the distribution picture into normal alinement.

Other reassignments were made, as chaplains attached to separate battalions became senior to more recent arrivals and were shifted to regimental chaplain billets and relieved in the separate battalions by their less experienced colleagues. Sometimes chaplains were shifted from separate battalions to regimental billets, because of their own request for infantry duty, or because they seemed to the Division chaplain especially suited for such duty or because denominational and rank requirements dictated such changes. Chaplains serving with regiments would sometimes be reassigned to rear-area battalions; on occasion it was felt a chaplain had had all the front-line duty he could take for a while, or again he would have displayed particular abilities that recommended him to the Division chaplain as the right man for a particular assignment. One such situation can be inferred from the following paragraph in Chaplain Slattery's letter of 5 May to the Chief of Chaplains.

Chaplain Stamper took over in Combat Service Group when conditions there were, to say the least, unsavory. The

---

[4] See ch. 1.

officers were rather, shall we say, flamboyant in their conduct and attitude. Others followed suit. Bob Stamper who has been one of the top men here handled the situation with firm diplomacy and he reports that things are in hand now. He urged me to fill the billet with a "field grade" [in Marine terms, a major; hence, lieutenant commander] chaplain.

Another illustration may be seen in the exchange of Chaplain T. A. Newman, Service Battalion, with Chaplain C. W. Herrick, 2d Battalion, 7th Marines, and Prickett of Headquarters Battalion with Willets, regimental chaplain, 7th Marines. Concerning these shifts Slattery wrote on 15 September: "The moves were made in order to give Chaplains Willets and Herrick a rest from the pressure they have been under in 'enemy engaged' units. Both are pleased to move to rear units and Chaplains Newman and Prickett are the 'gung-ho' guys who wanted to get a taste of the fighting front." He added: "I intend shortly to make a similar switch of Adams [7th Motor Transport] and Callahan [3d Battalion, 1st Marines]."

Concerning a plan for more stable assignments which he was trying to effect, Slattery wrote on 9 June, after a meeting of the chaplains, "All agree that the present plan to keep each chaplain with his originally assigned battalion is the one most beneficial to the men and the individual chaplain."

Apparently Slattery and his regimental chaplains were assigning chaplains within a regiment at battalion level. For instance, the 19 May roster showed W. D. McCabe as regimental chaplain, 1st Marines, with duty in the 2d Battalion; J. T. Callahan was assigned to the 3d Battalion and M. E. Torstrick to the first. The 1 September roster showed K. D. Killin (ordered but not yet reported) as McCabe's relief, both as regimental chaplain and in the 2d Battalion. Callahan was still in the 3d Battalion. Oscar Weber, who had been in the Medical Battalion on the May roster, was now in the 1st Battalion. But the latter assignment had not been uncomplicated. E. S. Jones had relieved Torstrick when his time was up, coming from the Armored Amphibian Battalion. Jones was accidentally injured and sent to the HAVEN in Pusan. Weber had then been drawn from the Medical Battalion to replace Jones.

A comparison of the 19 May and 1 September rosters in the case of the 5th Marines shows A. F. Mendonsa as regimental chaplain, with duty in the 2d Battalion, on both dates; Calvin H. Elliott in the 3d Battalion on both dates; and H. C. Duncan, who had returned stateside, relieved in the 1st Battalion by Chaplain J. C. Brown, who had reported to the Division on 30 May after duty with the Air Wing's unit at Itami since 20 March.

In the 7th Marines the slate was unchanged: R. H. Willets was regimental chaplain, with duty in the 1st Battalion, on both rosters; C. W. Herrick, 2d Battalion, and L. A. Guillaume, 3d Battalion.

In the 11th Marines, with a normal complement of four battalions, W. P. Lane appears on both rosters as regimental chaplain carried at Headquarters, F. J. Forney, detached, had been relieved in the 1st Battalion by H. C. Bowling, who had previously been in Combat Service Group. N. L. McDowell continued in the 4th Battalion and C. T. Duggan in the 3d. Whether Lane covered the 2d battalion does not appear from Slattery's rosters. In any case the 11th Regiment was well served, with four aboard on a T/O calling for three.

When Forney had been due to be relieved the newest replacement was M. J. Strumski, a Roman Catholic without previous Marine duty. Lane and Duggan were also Catholic. So Bowling was brought up from Combat Service Group to the 11th Marines.

Otherwise [as Slattery wrote to the Chief] the 11th Marines would be without adequate Protestant coverage. There are four battalions, the 11th CP and three batteries of reinforcements from the Army scattered over many miles of front. I made an analysis of the possibility of coverage for Protestant services from one of the other units but find it is beyond the capabilities of the chaplains, due to heavy schedules of their own and the tactical location of the artillery.

After a short period of indoctrination at Headquarters Battalion Strumski was assigned to Combat Service Group, a rear unit not likely to be involved in combat. As things turned out, it was a happy move. On 29 July Slattery wrote:

The arrival of Chaplain Strumski was fortunate as Combat Service, which had depended on an Air Force chaplain for Catholic services, was suddenly bereft of his services due to a move by the Air Force. By coincidence the Army ordered a Protestant chaplain to a camp just 100 yards away from our Combat Service Group. So I was able to parlay the moves to our advantage.

At Division Headquarters a comparison of the May and September rosters shows the same slate, except that Siegel had been relieved on 10 July by Chaplain Samuel Sobel. (But as we have seen, within 2 weeks of the latter roster, Prickett and Willets would be exchanged.) In some of the separate battalions, the picture was unchanged: A. W. Boyer was still with Motor Transport, R. F. Barlik with the Medical Battalion, B. J. Nowakowski with the AmTracs, A. W. Robertson with Tanks, and J. H. Muller with Shore Party.

But there had also been changes. V. J. W. Lustig had been assigned to the Armored Amphibian Battalion when Jones had replaced Torstrick at 1st Battalion, 1st Marines. Weber had replaced Jones there when the latter was injured. Both Lustig and Weber had been drawn from the Medical Battalion; one would infer the need for chaplains there was not pressing at the time. Upon Jones' return to duty he was assigned there, giving the Medical Battalion once more its normal complement, one Protestant and one Roman Catholic.

E. A. Wolfram had been detached and replaced by G. E. Kuhn (ordered but not yet reported) in the Engineers. Wolfe had likewise been transfered stateside and replaced in the Service Battalion by T. A. Newman, who reported on 5 July. Bowling had been replaced at Combat Service by Strumski. The Ordnance Battalion, which had no chaplain at the time of the May roster, was now to be covered by R. C. McMillan, ordered but not yet reported. The Signal Battalion had no chaplain attached at either date but was covered for services; probably it would have been near enough Headquarters Battalion to make that feasible. Chaplain Patrick Adams, who reported 23 May, had been assigned to 7th Motor Transport, a unit not formerly allowed a chaplain. The 1 September roster showed a total of 28 chaplains, including the 3 ordered but not yet reported, with none at that time awaiting detachment.

This somewhat cursory and perhaps confusing survey at least indicates the nature of the Division Chaplain's job in trying to make sure that the complement of chaplains was distributed in such manner as to provide the most adequate ministry to the most men in any given set of circumstances. Not least of the changing conditions was the mobility of the Division's units, often necessitating this month a reshuffling of what had only last month seemed a workable distribution. Despite Slattery's "new plan" of keeping chaplains with their originally assigned battalions, it could be implemented only in part. The chaplain himself wrote to Salisbury on 22 September:

I am sure that you agree we should not indiscriminately assign a 'body' to a battalion, but should try to fit the man to the type work involved. At least, we have tried to do so, as some jobs here are more challenging than others and demand more forceful chaplains.

A survey extended through 30 November, the end of the 8th Korean Campaign, would doubtless show still further reassignments; but all the "chess playing" was, hopefully, in the interest of a more effective ministry.

Chaplains' Information Booklet

In May the Division Chaplain issued a mimeographed Chaplains' Information Booklet. Purely informational and advisory, and in no sense an official directive, it consolidated within one cover a good deal of pertinent information based upon the Marine Corps Manual, the Chaplains Manual, the FMF Pac General Order setting forth the SOP for chaplains serving with a Marine division and current Division orders.

A section on casualty letters attempted once more to clarify the procedures to be followed in writing letters to the next of kin of deceased personnel. It is quoted here in its entirety.

ENCLOSURE (2)

CHAPLAIN'S CASUALTY LETTERS TO NEXT OF KIN

Ref: (a) Chaplain's Manual, NavPers 15664, Sec. 5102.
 (b) Par 4c(1), FMF Pac General Order 19.
 (c) Par 3b(7), Annex K, 1stMarDiv General Order 50.

1. In compliance with references (a), (b), and (c), a chaplain's casualty letter will be sent to the next of kin of all deceased personnel of the battalion to which the chaplain is attached, regardless of status of death.

2. It is recommended that the following procedure be followed in compiling necessary data, writing and submission of the casualty letter:

a. Upon receipt of the casualty report, information such as rank, name, service number, component, organization, next of kin, and address of next of kin should be procured from personnel records as soon as possible. The religion of the individual should be ascertained by contacting the administrative rear, or the administrative section of the organization prior to the time the service records are mailed to Headquarters, U.S. Marine Corps. This information should be held pending receipt of the Casualty Amplifying Report, which will be forthcoming in approximately two (2) to three (3) weeks after the individual becomes a casualty.

b. Upon receipt of the Casualty Amplifying Report, the information contained thereon, such as rank, name, service number, etc., should be checked against the information you have been holding. A check should then be made to determine that the designation and address of the next of kin you have obtained from examination of records compares with the addressee of the Company Commander's condolence letter. This will insure that the same person will receive both letters. All information should be checked thoroughly before a letter is written. It is suggested that no letter be written until the amplifying report has been received, as that report will contain information relative to the disposition of the remains and will therefore be conclusive. In the event letters are received from the next of kin or relatives, they should be acknowledged, with a statement that the situation (not death) is being investigated and that information will be forthcoming as it becomes available.

c. After all data has been compiled and thoroughly checked, a chaplain's casualty letter to the next of kin will be drawn up, for the signature of the chaplain, along with an envelope addressed to the next of kin. Chaplain's casualty letters will be transmitted through official channels to the Commandant of the Marine Corps (Code DGU) for forwarding to the next of kin. Copies of this correspondence and of the casualty letter should be retained in the chaplain's files for reference and information. A copy should be made for each via in the chain of command, and an extra copy for the Commandant of the Marine Corps for insertion in the jacket of the individual at Headquarters U.S. Marine Corps.

Another section of the Information Booklet dealt with publicity concerning chaplains' activities in Korea. It quoted excerpts from several letters received from the Chief of Chaplains.

We are still concerned about receiving pictures and stories on chaplains' activities with the Marines in Korea. There are two fields which have not been publicized, but which we feel contain excellent possibilities for public relations. First, our Office and the Marine Corps Public Information Office would like very much to publicize the work of the Marines who are serving as chaplains' assistants.

Secondly, we are interested in securing the reactions of men in combat to religion. Would you please request the chaplains of the Division to secure some statements from the men in their units, who felt that religion had helped them when they were involved in fighting at the front. We are especially interested in learning of men who have had only a superficial relation with religion before. A great deal has been said and written concerning the help and strength of religion to men in combat. But we actually have very little from the men themselves as to just how they were helped and how much they feel this would affect their future life when they return home.

We continue to receive requests for pictures of men in combat engaged in religious activities. Recently we received an excellent picture of a Marine saying the rosary. It is this type of picture that we need for illustrations in religious periodicals.

We have recently learned of several awards for Navy chaplains who have served with Marines in Korea. We are embarrassed when we send out publicity concerning their awards because many times we would not have pictures of them made with the Marines in Korea. Chaplain Craven [now in the Chaplain's Division] would appreciate it if you could speak to the Public Information Officer about getting a picture of every chaplain serving with the Division while he is engaged in conducting Divine Service, interviewing a Marine, assisting with the wounded, or similar scenes of chaplains' activities.

Other sections dealt with supplies, the semimonthly report of chaplain activities required by a Division memorandum and the monthly report required to be submitted to the FMF Pac Chaplain for inclusion in his quarterly report to the Chaplains Division.

Concerning assistance to the work of the Red Cross, the booklet advised:

1. On occasion the American Red Cross field director will request a chaplain to deliver a notification of death in the family.

2. It is expected that such requests will be expedited and that American Red Cross will be notified of "mission accomplished."

3. When an American Red Cross field director requests a chaplain to accompany him for notification, the chaplain will do so for the purpose of giving spiritual comfort.

Because on "rare occasions" (as Slattery put it), commanding officers had assigned chaplains collateral duties which were a handicap to their basic work, especially in the field, the chaplains were reminded of paragraph 6, Annex K to Division General Order No. 50, here quoted:

The primary work of the chaplain is spiritual and moral leadership. He will therefore not be required to undertake duties of any other nature that would absorb the major portion of his time, and thus cause him to neglect his chaplain duties.

The booklet included a list of the chaplains then on duty in order of their reporting to the Division, with the dates of reporting, and the probable or anticipated date of detachment. Finally there was a list of all the chaplains who had served or were currently serving in the 1st Marine Division in Korea, compiled from such records as were available in the Division Chaplain's Office.

"Marine Padres, Inc."

The chaplains were dependent on their units for transportation and only rarely were actually assigned a vehicle. Often the chaplain's personal relationship with his unit CO or transportation officer had much to do with the availability of "wheels." Early in June the Division chaplain held a conference at which all 27 chaplains aboard were present. After being addressed by the Commanding General and the G–1 (personnel officer), there was a roundtable discussion, during which "the same old subject of transportation came up. However, it is clear that all CO's are furnishing wheels when a chaplain has a scheduled Divine Service." Slattery's conclusion on this matter would be echoed by every chaplain in the Corps: "Maybe someday Congress will make an appropriation for jeeps to be specially allotted to chaplains!"

The British chaplains were at least better off on that point, though from the American point of view they suffered some disabilities in turn.

One of our pleasant associations here has been with the Padres of the British Commonwealth Division. I visited their senior chaplain last Wednesday. You know their system, of course. They are envious of the fine integration of our Protestant and Catholic chaplains and of the consideration the Chaplains Division gives to the men in the field. Their tour is almost 3 years in comparison to our Marine tour. Of course they are on an Army plan. I guess the

Marine Padres, Inc.

The corporation is composed of the following chaplains (left to right) Albert D. Prickett, Samuel Sobel, and Edward A. Slattery.

only field in which they outdo us is in their mobility, due to the jeep situation.

But at least one office had its own vehicle. Over the jolting roads of Korea there used to roll a battered jeep carrying across its windshield base in bold letters MARINE PADRES, INC. On one side of this legend was a cross, on the other a Star of David. Used in turn by the three chaplains at Division Headquarters, the jeep was "kept in operation with repairs from at least a half dozen units," as it kept breaking down on the road.

That jeep was more than simply a means of transportation; it became a symbol of interfaith cooperation and of the concern of American Marines for the work of God. Concerning it Slattery wrote: "Marine Padres, Inc., declares regular dividends, spiritual in nature, but more real than gilt-edged bonds. Out of the treasury of the Bible and of religious tradition is drawn a currency which the Communists across the hills cannot counterfeit. Marines facing the fire of the enemy hear the sound of the *shofar*, the melody of a field organ, the tinkle of a Sanctus bell, and each in his own faith finds strength."

Reserve Chaplains

With the outbreak of the Korean War the Chaplains Division, traditionally opposed to using any but volunteers, was not at first willing to recall any chaplains to active duty without their consent. (As has been earlier noted, chaplains in pay billets with Organized Marine Reserve units had been mobilized with their respective units.) When the procurement of USN chaplains and the voluntary return of USNR chaplains proved insufficient to meet the needs of the service, the Chief of Chaplains reluctantly decided on a program of involuntary recall. The first thus recalled to duty were given a refresher course in the reactivated chaplains school in October 1951. A chaplain involuntarily recalled who had had a year's active duty between December 1941 and September 1945 was obligated to serve 17 months. Involuntary recallees without such prior active duty had to serve 24 months, as did chaplains who had volunteered to return to duty and those who had been mobilized with Marine Reserve units.

Now for the first time some chaplains serving in Korea were beginning to anticipate the end of their obligated service. On 26 May Chaplain Slattery wrote the Chief:

If I am not mistaken, three of the chaplains here are due for release from active duty in January 1953. I mention it at this time to assist your detail desk in their long range plans.

To this Salisbury replied:

I want to assure you that we will release Reserve chaplains when they come due. There is no intention of holding anyone beyond his obligated term of service. Of course you realize that the world situation could change this policy, but short of all-out mobilization no change is anticipated.

Since chaplains arriving on or after 1 February 1952 were expected to serve a 10-month tour in Korea, the question arose of how this would apply to Reserve chaplains whose obligated service would expire before their 10 months were up. Slattery wanted to know whether they would be returned stateside in time to be released at the termination of their required duty or whether they would be expected to remain in Korea at least until suitable reliefs should arrive. He felt that both he and the chaplains concerned should have a firm commitment from the Chaplains Division. Chaplain Mannion replied on 22 July:

We will not hold chaplains beyond the period of their obligated service or the date that they request inactive duty, whichever is later. Chaplains in Korea scheduled to be released from active duty will be returned to the United States in time to be released on schedule.

Chaplains in Action

Excerpts from Chaplain Slattery's frequent letters to Chaplain Salisbury reveal a man devoted to his work and keenly appreciative of the work of his colleagues.

16 JUNE 1952.

This past week we have had the pleasure of a visit from [FMF Pac] Chaplain [M. H.] Twitchell who has seen all the chaplains of the 1st Marine Division. . . .

On 11 June Chaplain Willets received a slight wound on the chin. He was about to conduct a service at Company level when a round came in. After his wound was dressed he returned to conduct the service.

5 JULY 1952.

The chaplains' reports for the month of June indicate how completely devoted most of them are to their religious duties. A total of 1,298 Divine Services were held during June: 392 Sunday, 495 daily, and 411 special services.

The chaplains here celebrated July Fourth by having a softball game. Due to our "advanced years" we only played five innings but found that sufficient to discover a few unused muscles. . . . After the game we all went for a swim in the Imjin River. The Southern Baptists were intent on ducking the rest of us, on the grounds that our baptisms needed some amplification. The Rabbi must have suspected that we would all try to baptize him as he stayed on the river bank to heckle us.

15 JULY 1952.

Our Catholic chaplains have sent over $1,300 to the Chaplain's Aid Association. General Selden gave his approval to the collection, which was requested by Bishop Griffiths of the Military Ordinariate Office.

On 29 July Slattery wrote further about the situation in the 1st Combat Service Group.

In order to pin down the picture . . . I asked for TAD for 5 days and went by train from Seoul to Pusan. There I conferred with the Second Logistical Command which handles our supplies. . . . By convoy I went to Masan. Convoy is required due to guerilla activities. The situation there is now well in hand. You may refer to my letter of 5 May for Chaplain Stamper's estimate of the situation there. A reformation has been accomplished, however, by a very alert CO.

The chaplain flew from Masan to Pohang for a conference with the Air Wing chaplains, finding it "a treat to sleep between sheets for a change." From there he flew to Taegu, to visit at 8th Army Headquarters.

We are not accountable to 8th Army, but since we take care of some Army units and they in turn service some of our Marines, I thought it advantageous to visit them. . . . Eighth Army is very pleased with Marine chaplains' cooperation and our high standards of personnel and "production."

These letters often contained pleasant comment as well as businesslike assessment of the work of his chaplains and the needs of the Division. For instance, earlier in the summer:

The weather is fine, dry, and warm. The nights cool off to the point where a sleeping bag is a most welcome refuge. As we wake in the morning we are greeted by the sound of coo-coos in the valleys. At first we thought we were hearing ourselves crack up! Washington should import a few to go along with the atmosphere.

His return to the Division CP after the journey just described was reported in a letter containing the following:

The weather has turned precipitously, if I may play on words. Roads have become greasy, dangerous ways, topped by a few inches of what resembles melted chocolate ice cream. [He then reported accidents to Chaplains Jones and Mendonsa.] Both are with outfits on the line, but we have plugged the gaps by having a couple of the Padres triple in brass. They have already been doubling in brass.

On 1–2 August the Division was visited by Dr. Stewart Robinson, Chairman of the General Commission on Chaplains. After protests from Slattery his visit had been extended from the few hours which I Corps, in charge of arrangements, had first allotted. Accompanied by Chaplain Morse of 8th Army and his own son, a lieutenant in Combat Service Group, the visitor was given the plush treatment by General Selden, who ordered 'copters to hop Dr. Robinson about. Included in the itinerary were two visits to General Harrison at Base Camp and a tour to a front line company in Chaplain McCabe's sector. The details of the visit here were handled most efficiently and courteously by Chaplain Prickett.

(Maj. Gen. William K. Harrison, an Army officer with a long record of interest in the work of chaplains, had succeeded Adm. C. Turner Joy on 22 May as senior delegate of the United Nations Command at the Panmunjom truce talks.)

Chaplains' Chaplain

Among the standard items of social small talk to which chaplains are routinely subjected is the tired old question, "Say, 'padre,' who do you take your troubles to?" No chaplain will, of course, give the answer that rises first to his mind, for such occasions are hardly appropriate for a serious rejoinder. The answer ought to be obvious to anyone who knows what a chaplain is; like all sincerely religious men, he takes his troubles to the Lord. Still, human mediation is as frequently helpful to the servant of God as it is to his lay brethren. The ideal supervisory chaplain is one who can be at the same time firm enough not to overlook the needs of the service and sympathetic enough to be of aid and comfort to his colleagues. He should be, in the traditional sense of the term, the "bishop" of his brethren.

Three chaplains in the Division were called upon to face difficult personal situations during the summer of 1952. Early in May Chaplain B. N. Wolfe was informed that his father was in the terminal stages of a grave illness. He requested information via the Red Cross and asked for emergency leave. Slattery wrote to Chaplain Salisbury:

Commission Visitor.

Dr. Steward Robinson (center, first row), Chairman of the General Commission of Chaplains meets with the Protestant chaplains of the 1st Marine Division in Korea. Standing (left to right): Chaplains Oscar Weber, First Medical Battalion; Robert H. Willets, 1st Battalion, 7th Marine; Ernest A. Wolfram, Jr., 1st Engineer Battalion; Alexander W. Boyer, 1st Motor Transport Battalion; Alla W. Robertson, 1st Tank Battalion; Thomas A. Newman, Jr., 1st Service Battalion; and Carl W. Herrick, 2d Battalion. Sitting (left to right) Ward D. McCabe, 2d Battalion, 1st Marines; F. E. Morse, deputy Army chaplain (EUSAK); Dr. Robinson; A. D. Prickett, assistant chaplain of the division and John H. Muller, 1st Shore Party Battalion.

Leave requests are extremely tight here. In the event that he is granted leave our G–1 intends to request his detachment. We have orders for his detachment in July; his reporting date here was 20 December 1951. Will you be kind enough to alert the proper desk for such a contingency and perhaps send out a replacement for him quicker than anticipated? We will be able with a little juggling to cover the Protestant services he has been handling.

Wolfe's leave was denied, but upon further assurance from Slattery that the situation in the Division could be adequately covered, Salisbury ordered him detached on 23 June. Wolfe left, as Slattery wrote, "deeply grateful for your consideration in sending orders for detachment earlier than July."

On 5 August he wrote: "Perhaps you have heard that Chaplain Callahan's mother died on 26 July." In accordance with policies then in effect the chaplain was denied emergency leave.

On Saturday, 2 August, the Catholic chaplains went to Callahan's battalion where we sang a Solemn Requiem Mass assisted by Pat Adams and Gus Mendonsa. The rest of us sang the Mass and were a little bit pleased with our memory of the music, as many of us have not been at a Solemn Requiem in some time and had neither notes nor organist to accompany.

The results were neither lugubrious nor ludicrous and I am sure Chaplain Callahan's spirits were lifted considerably. Due to Dr. Robinson's tour our fellow chaplains were not able to attend. One consoling note was the turnout of enlisted men of the battalion. Protestant lads stood the outposts for the Catholic lads who came to kneel in the rain and mud, garbed in full battle dress of helmet and armored vest.

A month later Slattery was writing to the Chaplains Division, "Chaplain Weber's father died on 10 September. He received the telegram notifying him of the death but no further details have arrived as yet." Unless the serviceman's presence was adjudged positively necessary that he might attend to family matters, emergency leave was not normally granted in the case of the death of a parent.

On this entire matter Slatery wrote on 17 October:

Speaking of morale, we have a new directive from the Marine Corps Commandant, which is much more "humane," on emergency leave requests, and a new Chief of Staff who is not quite so adamant as was the former Chief of Staff.

The proper balance beween a man's own assessment of his personal needs and the command's judgment concerning his usefulness to the military service is not one always easily arrived at. At this point chaplains often are able to be of service both to the command and to its members; and sometimes, as this account shows, a chaplain was himself involved in the dilemma.

"Bunker Hill"

Reduced for the most part to "trench warfare" this summer's fighting was only occasionally punctuated by violent combat. Such were the furious episodes which occurred in August over two hill outposts, dubbed by the Marines "Bunker Hill" and "Siberia." Directly involved in both were units of the 1st Ma-

Prelude to Bunker Hill.

Chaplain Oscar Weber holds communion services for marines before they join in the fight for Bunker Hill.

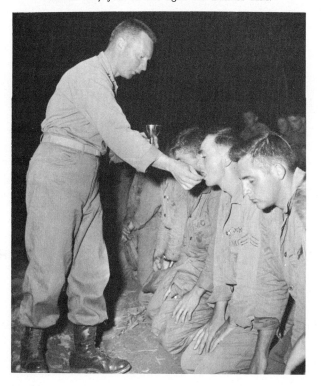

rines. Writing soon afterwards, on 17 August, Slattery told the Chief:

Two of your chaplains distinguished themselves by their devotion to duty. . . . Chaplains McCabe and Callahan stood by their men through the long nights. At one time McCabe was at an aid station which was surrounded. . . . Neither suffered any wounds, though both looked extremely weary when I went up to see them on Wednesday.

And he went on:

Chaplains Weber and Guillaume backed up their efforts by working at the front, although both their battalions had been in reserve. Tex Robertson followed his Tankers right into the thick of it too.

At the medical companies an outstanding job was done by Chaplain Barlik, who shifted from the Operating Room to the Admission Ward, saw wounded off in the 'copters and at the same time managed to sandwich in his services with the Korean Marine Corps unit nearby. The Korean Marines, incidentally, expect the assignment of a Korean Catholic chaplain shortly, which will relieve us of the responsibility.

Flying over the 3d Battalion, 1st Marines, command post during the "Bunker Hill" holocaust was a green brocade banner depicting the Archangel Michael, his feet resting on the vanquished hammer and sickle of Communism. Lt. Col. G. T. Armitage, battalion commander, deciding that his men needed to be reminded of the dependence of their cause on God, secured permission from Headquarters, Marine Corps, to fly the banner. Designed by Capt. J. B. Ord, a company commander, it was embroidered by Korean children in the Star of the Sea Roman Catholic orphanage at Inchon. On 25 July the Roman Catholic personnel of the battalion were dedicated to the protection of St. Michael, and each company furnished a burgee of the banner. Capt. H. J. O'Conner, a company commander, commented: "Regardless of their creed, our men felt the banner to be a very personal incentive." Flown for the first time at "Bunker Hill," the flags accompanied the battalion in subsequent actions and were still flying when the guns at last grew still across Korea. When the original had become battleworn beyond repair, it was duplicated by wives of Korean Marines and the tattered relic sent to Marine Corps Headquarters.

"Siberia"

"Siberia" was a hillcrest in the Panmunjom corridor where a terrible, indecisive 24-hour battle took place. During the darkness a United Nations outpost manned by ten Marines was overrun by a reinforced company of Chinese; two were killed and seven of the remaining eight wounded. An undersized platoon attempting a counterattack was quickly beaten back. With morning close air support was brought into play

International Chaplains' Conference.
Chaplain Ward D. McCabe is host to visiting chaplains. Left to right Chaplain Roy H. McKenzie, Unit No. 16 Field Regiment, Royal New Zealand Artillery, 1st Commonwealth Division, Chaplain McCabe, and Chaplain Roy Liddell, 1st Battalion of the King's Own Scottish Battalion.

and a reinforced platoon charged the hill, but after an hour and a half ordered to withdraw, so devastating was the opposition.

Air strikes were made on "Siberia" all afternoon and at first dark, as a ripple of rockets hit the hill, the Marines moved out once more. By midnight the battle had become, as Marine Corps Combat Correspondent T. Sgt. Jim Coleman put it, a "hand-to-hand slugging match." Although driving the Chinese down the reverse slope the Marines were finally unable to hold the hill and were ordered to withdraw. Throughout the fight Chaplains McCabe and Callahan stayed with their Marines, helping the wounded and acting as stretcher bearers when not attending to their religious duties.

Both chaplains were subsequently given the Letter of Commendation award. That of Chaplain Ward

D. McCabe covered the period 28 April–31 August 1952. "During periods when the regiment was engaged in combat against the enemy," the citation read in part, "he worked long, tedious hours, with no concern for his personal safety, to aid and comfort the sick and wounded. His courage and initiative in helping to evacuate the wounded were an inspiration to all who observed him." Chaplain James T. Callahan was cited for services from 22 March to 26 September, the citation reading in part:

During periods when the regiment was engaged in combat against the enemy, he devoted long, arduous hours, with complete disregard for his personal safety, providing aid and comfort to the sick and wounded. . . . His cheerfulness, sympathetic understanding of individual problems and his ever ready willingness to offer advice and comfort to all were outstanding.

Mass on the Western Front.
Chaplain James T. Callahan holds mass for the 1st Marines immediately behind the frontlines.

Combat Footnotes

A realistic picture of what actually went on in Korea must sometimes be obtained from what appear as merely "footnotes to history." Incident upon incident would be needed to fill in with meaningful detail what often appears in an historical account as only a bare outline. Many such were reported, often full of courage, sometimes of pathos and not seldom of humor also. Chaplain Slattery once wrote:

One lad stopped me and asked if I would hear his confession, as his company was moving out. I squatted on the hillside and suddenly had a line of forty or more waiting to be "shriven." With all due respect to the seriousness of the sacrament and the occasion, I couldn't help chuckling when one lad knelt down and said, "Father, I haven't been to church in a long time; may I have another chance?"

He added: "They are fine lads. I suggested to each one that a clean conscience is like a clean weapon, invaluable in battle."

On one occasion Charlie Company, 1st Battalion, 7th Marines was moving up. S. Sgt. E. A. Seneri, heavy machine gun section leader yelled to his men, "No matter what happens up here, I don't want any man leaving any weapon or part behind. When we move out, leave nothing!" That night a fierce battle took place; next morning, the action over, the sergeant took inventory and found a machine gun barrel and accessory parts missing. Shouted the sergeant, "No man leaves here until those parts are produced!" That afternoon Seneri sheepishly accepted the parts

from Chaplain Prickett. Pfc. L. E. House, Jr., had been wounded and on being evacuated had refused to leave behind his spare machine gun parts. About to be sent to a hospital ship, he was still clutching them when the chaplain came along and promised to see that they were returned to the careful sergeant.

Concerning Chaplain Samuel Sobel the Division Chaplain once wrote, "He sparkles as does the Star of David we have on the chapel here." (The Division chapel was embellished with a glistening white cross and six-pointed white star on its front wall.)

Sam suggested that he would take a picture of the crowd leaving a Sunday Mass as "proof" of fine attendance at the "Synagogue." I agreed to line up some likely candidates and have two fine young Marine officers—O'Hara and O'Brien—who could pass for Cantors to flank the good Rabbi.

During a bit of fierce fighting in October the Reverend Wynn Rhys of the British Commonwealth Division came over to offer Slattery the loan of some of his chaplains if the Marines became short-handed. As they stood talking the two chaplains witnessed an awesome scene.

One of our Marine pilots was caught by antiaircraft fire. He was too low to bail out and fought to bring his crippled plane back over our lines. But he could not land safely and went in with a crash, the plane a blazing inferno. Wynn and I prayed from the distance for his soul. . . .

Religious Ministry

More important in their own eyes than all their other work was the chaplains' religious ministry, which under the circumstances presented its familiar aspects not only to the chaplains but to their military "parishioners" as well. Rarely, even in the most stable units, with chapel facilities somewhat approximating those back home, did Divine Service fail to seem different from worshiping in the familiar, hallowed surroundings of one's own church or synagogue. Knowing that, the chaplains helped to bridge the difference. They tried to make real to their congregations, large and small, in open-air or log-buttressed bunker or Quonset chapel, the Presence of God. As they knew or sometimes rediscovered, and as their Marines often learned for the first time, a man is never nearer home than when he prays.

Statistics give at least a skeleton outline of the chaplains' ministry. The May figures below were taken from a report made by the Division Chaplain to the conference of chaplains held in June, where they were listed individually after each chaplain's name. Slattery thought this would "help keep the boys on their toes." The September figures have been taken from the semimonthly reports submitted by the Division Chaplain to the Division G–1.

	May 1952	September 1952
Sunday services conducted......	309	351
Attendance...............	15, 532	18, 505
Daily services conducted.......	493	607
Attendance...............	9, 022	9, 758
Special Services, etc.[1]..........	358	540
Attendance...............	9, 736	14, 466
Visits to hospitals, aid stations....	403	501
Patients visited............	3, 057	3, 528
Letters written...............	840	807
Counseling interviews..........	8, 401	5, 794
Visits to Brig................	Not listed	9
Prisoners interviewed.......		59

[1] Including Bible classes, rosary devotions, character guidance lectures, and other special or supplementary services.

The chaplains of course had no control over weather, strategic moves, tactical situations, or other influencing factors, but the fact that, as they held more services, the men generally attended them in larger numbers would seem to bear out Slattery's expressed hope in May that, while they were already doing a good job, the chaplains could "step up production" somewhat.

During June Chaplain Willets conducted 29 Sunday services and 57 daily services, for a total of 86, topping the list. The Roman Catholic chaplains had each conducted 15 Sunday masses (3 on each of 5 Sundays) and a Mass daily, plus usually some other service, such as a rosary devotion or catechetical instruction.

During October the following chaplains each conducted over 50 services, as indicated:

	Sunday	Daily	Total
A. D. Prickett................	18	62	80
C. H. Elliott.................	16	38	54
R. H. Willets................	24	27	51

Five others had conducted 40 or more services each during the month, including Sunday and daily: W. Rowland, 45; J. H. Muller, 44; O. Weber, 43; and A. F. Mendonsa and E. A. Slattery, 40 each.

The chaplains too were often in need of spiritual refreshment. A retreat (or as Slattery wrote, since "Marines never retreat," a Recollection) for the Roman Catholics was held in August at the Columban Fathers' House in Seoul, the chaplains going in two shifts so as to keep the Division covered for emergencies. The Protestants also planned a retreat at Seoul.

The weekly Roman Catholic newspaper *Our Sunday Visitor* carried in its 5 October 1952 issue a digni-

Anointing With Oil.
Chaplain August F. Mendonsa anoints a candidate for baptism with oil.

fied spread on the work of Navy chaplains in Korea, featuring A. F. ("Gus") Mendonsa in a generous number of field photographs engaged in typical chaplain activities: hearing confessions and celebrating Mass, typing letters (to parents or wives of wounded Marines, to bereaved relatives of those killed in action or to anyone else to whom it was a service to a Marine to have a letter written), visiting in hospitals and engaging in counseling in all sorts of situations, even distributing cakes and cookies sent over by a women's church group in the United States. The text read:

Like anyone else in the United Nations Military Forces he finds that there are no set hours of work. On the battlefield, especially, the call to duty is frequent and the hours long and arduous. At all times of the day and night, the wounded and the dying cry out for the chaplain. And the men of all faiths who serve God by ministering to His people are always there to heed the cry.

So, too, in the rear echelons and the base camps, the chaplains are ready to serve the men. While their first duty is to care for the men's spiritual welfare, there are many times when they take a hand in material things.

The serviceman's family, his pay worries, his entertainment and general welfare, all these are often the province of the chaplain. He must be the priest, the confessor, the counsellor, and the brother of those he serves.

Reminiscent of the Old Testament story of Moses and the Exodus was the Ark that "went to war" in Korea. When Chaplain Sobel was slated for the Division, he had the Ark constructed in Honolulu and brought it out with him. An upright chest of Philippine mahogany, its opened doors revealed superimposed upon them hand-carved candelabra, gilded to symbolize the Golden Candlestick of the Jerusalem Temple and fitted with flame-shaped bulbs. Veiling the parchment scroll of the Torah there hung a handsome curtain embroidered with a crown and a Star of David. The two Tables of the Law affixed at the top were surmounted in turn by a burning light symbolizing the Eternal Light which is the Word of the Lord. Used in Jewish services in various chapels, the Ark was so compact that the chaplain was able to carry it in its specially made canvas case to front line units as well.

As summer turned into fall Sobel made plans for observing the High Holy Days, beginning with Rosh Hashanah (New Year) and ending with Yom Kippur (Day of Atonement). An accompanying photograph shows the chaplain with the *shofar* (ram's horn) raised to his lips, sounding the age-old call that brings

Israel to the sanctuary of her God. Services were held not only in the Division chapel, but also in smaller units. (Wrote Slattery, "Sobel went on Friday to conduct services at the Shore Party Battalion, where Chaplain Muller had gathered about 30 Jewish personnel.") On occasion, as conditions allowed, the Jewish chaplain would fly to the 1st Marine Aircraft Wing to hold services there.

This history cannot and indeed need not detail the activities of each individual chaplain; from the material available accounts have been selected which were either unusual or else typical enough to illustrate the work of all the chaplains. We should like to echo a word included in FMF Pac Chaplain M. H. Twitchell's quarterly report of 2 May 1952.

The pointing out of certain outstanding work on the part of particular chaplains named in this report is not intended to reflect in any way on the quality of performance by the other chaplains. The . . . monthly statistical reports, and

Jewish Services.
Chaplain Samuel Sobel conducts Jewish services for 1st Division Marines.

Mural Dedication.

Maj. Gen. Edwin A. Pollock, Commanding General, 1st Marine Division, and Private Sedney S. Levy, the artist, stand by a mural dedicated in the Division Chapel on the 177th anniversary of the founding of the U.S. Marine Corps. The mural depicts the work of the chaplains among marines.

---

reports received from other sources, reveal that the chaplains are giving an outstanding performance of duty in their ministry with the personnel they serve.

And in one of his letters to Chaplain Salisbury, Slattery wrote:

In reviewing some of my letters, I noted that I have not made mention of Chaplains Muller and Strumski. Both are working in rear area billets which are both demanding. They are two unsung heroes, in the sense that their work is not of the "headline" variety.

Both chaplains were not only working faithfully with their own Marine charges, but were busy in helping the civilian populace, in leper colonies, orphanages, schools, and local churches.

Chaplain Muller was attached to the first shore party, located in an area known as Ascom City. There he had the use of a handsome chapel built in 1945 by American troops on occupation duty in Korea following World War II. An all Korean choir trained by M. Sgt. P. C. Payne and Pfc. Fred Bussa under the chaplain's guidance sang at numerous service functions and broadcast weekly in the Seoul-Inchon area from the Segaly Methodist Church in Bupyong.

Muller wrote of preaching in a former Buddhist temple which, with its attendant buildings, had been previously turned into an orphanage caring for 350 children, its main shrine now a place of Christian worship. Wrote the chaplain:

We have preached the unsearchable riches of Christ in mess halls, a maintenance shop, movie theaters, the open air, in classrooms, and in our lovely chapel, and in Korean schools, orphanages, and churches. We average seventeen services a week.

Included among his "converts to Christ" were American servicemen, ROK soldiers and wounded veterans, and personnel from the Korean Service Corps—the civilian laborers attached to military units; and the chaplain added, probably remembering by contrast most civilian parishes at home, "The majority of them are men!"

The Chaplain Section had an appropriate gift for the 177th Marine Corps Birthday celebrated, as it is annually, on 10 November. Two large murals for the Division CP chapel, painted by Pfc. Sid Levy, were dedicated in a service led by the Headquarters Battalion chaplains, with Maj. Gen. Edward A. Pollock, new Division commander, giving the address.

The general commended the artist for having caught the "religious spirit of the fighting Marines who dedicate themselves daily to a cause of justice and honor." He continued:

As we observe Marines worshiping in the field, we forcibly realize that in their hearts there is a fervent, undying faith which blood and death and the clamor of battle cannot suppress. . . . The hundreds of thousands who have attended various services since the Brigade first came to the shores of Korea will be as lasting a contribution to the redemption of this country as the blood shed and the lives given.

A handsome bulletin carried photographic reproductions of the murals under the legend "My house shall be called a house of prayer for all people." Each mural was composed of montage arrangements of small scenes of chaplains engaging in their combat ministry, dominated in the upper section by helmeted faces, in one mural two representing the Army and the Air Force, in the other, two representing the Navy and the Marine Corps. Included in the responsive reading were two intensely compelling verses: "Behold how good and pleasant it is for brethren to dwell together in unity" and "Except the Lord build the house, they labor in vain who build it; except the Lord keep the city, the watchman waketh but in vain."

From January to November inclusively the chaplains conducted 3,662 Sunday services with 193,787 attending and 5,513 daily services with 101,180 attending. Special services (Bible classes, etc.) totaled 3,852, with 100,630 in attendance. They had held

56,857 counseling interviews, made 4,475 visits to the sick and wounded, and written 8,522 letters.

Chinese Upsurge

During October and November action at the front was stepped up; more frequent clashes were marked by extremely bitter fighting. On 9 October Chaplain Slattery wrote,

As you have gathered from the news reports, we have had an extremely busy few days. Chaplains Jones and Barlik, at the medical companies, went sleepless a few nights due to patient load.

And on 27 October:

Once again we had a busy night on the front. The Chinese Communists seem to be celebrating their second anniversary of entrance into the Korean War by pushing hard against outposts of ours.

The next day he reported on the action in a long letter to Chaplain Salisbury.

The Marines have won another great battle. The papers are probably calling it the "Battle of the Hook." As usual your chaplains performed well, which is expected of them now.

Chaplain Prickett spent the first night of the battle at a forward aid station. I went up to see him yesterday and he was pretty tired. . . . Chaplain Guillaume had spent the night at the battalion aid station, and Chaplain Pat Adams came up for last night. When Guillaume went to the forward aid station, Prickett and Adams took care of the evacuees at Battalion. I went to see Prickett again this morning. He was much refreshed and spent the day visiting his unit casualties who had not been already evacuated to the hospital ship.

As usual the medical companies are rushed. Moore teamed up with Jones and Lane and they did a wonderful job at Charlie Med. Barlik and Herrick teamed up at Easy Med.

Incidentally Barlik received some garbled publicity, a United Press report which states the chaplain has a medical degree. It was one of those wrong slants that eager journalists get. Barlik has given unselfishly of his strength and the medicos really have words of high praise for his assistance in the OR [operating room]. I have seen him work there and he does have pretty good technique. I want to assure you, however, that he is *not* "practising medicine and surgery."

Barlik was consequently awarded the Letter of Commendation, which cited among his other ministries his help to the surgeons: "Performing in the capacity of an assistant at surgical operations, he contributed materially to the success of more than 75 surgical cases." The award was for the period 30 March–3 November 1952.

Savage as it was on occasion, the fighting continued to be sporadic. In the intervals and in those units not directly engaged, life went on much as usual. On 18 October Slattery wrote that 1st Aircraft Wing Chaplain Parker had flown up "to see how we were caring for two of his 'chopper' units. We gave him the $64 tour of the front lines, which he enjoyed tremendously."

On 26 October Chaplains Weber, P. Adams, and Sobel held a Memorial Service for Marine and Navy personnel of the 1st Marines and attached units lost in combat from 26 -July to 12 October 1952. The cover of the service folder displayed a bronze plaque affixed to a stone building, with the shadow of a Marine in combat dress falling across the inscribed words:

THAT THE BEAUTY OF
HIS COUNTENANCE BE
NOT HIDDEN FROM
HIS OWN

THAT HIS WOUNDS
AND WOE WHEREIN
HE WROTE HIS LOVE
BE KNOWN TO
ALL THE PEOPLE
HE REDEEMED

Chaplain T. A. Newman, Jr., a former Navy hospital corpsman and according to Slattery a man of "naturally sympathetic disposition" was able to render exceptional service in motivating Marines who had developed "nerves" to return to the lines. On 10 November his battalion commander authorized him to go to one of the forward outposts, carrying a Marine Corps birthday cake. "Chaplain Newman said some prayers for the lads on the outpost, then all hands sang the Marine Corps Hymn and they all sat in a cave to feast." Slattery added:

Incidentally, I have a standing agreement with all battalion commanders that chaplains will not go forward of the MLR [main line of resistance] to OP's [outposts] without specific authorization. "Real estate" forward of the MLR is under hot dispute too often for the Padres to tour without a special visa.

Concerning this point Chaplain Mannion wrote in reply:

I certainly agree with [your policy]. . . . The unnecessary exposure to danger may be commendable to a limited degree, but certainly our chaplains should not be foolhardy, exposing themselves to unnecessary danger and running the risk of cutting off their services to God and country.

As November drew to a close, after appropriate Thanksgiving services everywhere throughout the Division, the men's thoughts began turning toward Christmas and home. Ten boxes of gaily wrapped Christmas gifts arrived in the Division chaplain's office from the employees of the Kiplinger Organization in Washington, D.C. Writing to them on 3 December

Slattery said, "Even though it seems as though we are rushing the season a little, the packages have been distributed to the men on the line."

Bronze Star Awards

Four chaplains received the Bronze Star for services in the 1st Marine Division during the 8th Korean Campaign or for periods whose terminal dates fell within that time. Chaplain James C. Moore was awarded the Bronze Star for "meritorious achievement . . . while serving with a Marine infantry battalion in Korea from 12 February to 5 July 1952." After citing his initiative, courage, and industriousness in providing a ministry to his men, Moore's citation continues: "He was consistently present in the front line trenches when friendly patrols and raids returned from making contact with the enemy."

Chaplain Noah L. McDowell was cited for courageous action on 13 September 1952. The Fire Direction Center, Battery C, 159th Field Artillery Battalion received an intense concentrated shelling by hostile fire, one shell scoring a direct hit on a squad tent, killing four men and wounding five others. Chaplain McDowell, who was with the 4th Battalion, 11th Marines, when word was received of the situation in the Army unit, immediately made his way there. His citation continues the story:

Entering a gun section tent where a direct hit had killed or wounded the occupants, he bravely remained with the men in the face of grave danger to render spiritual comfort and to administer first aid. After helping to move the wounded to nearby sheltered bunkers for further medical treatment, Lieutenant McDowell remained with them until they were evacuated.

Chaplain Robert H. Willets, who received the Purple Heart after being wounded on 12 June, was also awarded the Bronze Star for his service as regimental chaplain, 7th Marines, covering the period 2 May–20 September 1952.

Although frequently exposed to enemy mortar, artillery and small arms fire and wounded in action on one occasion, he persevered in his efforts to aid and comfort the men of the regiment, constantly leaving sheltered positions and moving through interdicted zones to minister to the spiritual needs of the stricken men. By his marked coolness under fire, strength of faith and unswerving devotion to duty, Lieutenant Willets served to inspire and encourage all who observed him. . . .

The fourth was Chaplain Lionel A. Guillaume whose Bronze Star award for the period 29 April–8 November 1952 cited his untiring labors in the face of enemy fire.

Despite extremely adverse conditions, he constantly moved among the wounded Marines with words of encouragement, attempting to make the casualties as comfortable as possible and, in many instances, administering first aid to the stricken men.

Letter of Commendation Award

Nine chaplains serving in the 1st Marine Division received the Letter of Commendation for duty during the 8th Korean Campaign or for periods whose terminal dates fell within that time. Those of Chaplains McCabe, Callahan, and Barlik have been noted.

Chaplain Alan R. Gibbons was cited for service from 15 October 1951 to 7 May 1952, almost all of it within the 7th Campaign. His citation notes that "his courageous and selfless actions were directly instrumental in saving the lives of several wounded Marines." Chaplain Henry C. Duncan's award covered the period 18 January–29 May 1952, noting that "working under hazardous conditions, he was constantly at hand to administer spiritual guidance and assistance to the men. . . ."

Chaplain Jonathan C. Brown, Jr., was cited for excellent service from 30 May to 4 November 1952; Chaplain Alla W. Robertson for service with the Tank Battalion from 2 March to 7 November 1952; and Chaplain Oscar Weber, for the period 2 August–30 November 1952, the latter part as regimental chaplain, 1st Marines. All three were commended for their devotion and courage in providing a religious ministry to men in combat, earning by their attitude the respect and gratitude of the men they served.

The ninth chaplain to receive the Letter of Commendation was Ernest A. Wolfram, Jr., for service in the 1st Engineer Battalion from 15 January–1 September 1952. His citation read in part:

Lieutenant Wolfram conducted services for all units of the battalion and planned services to meet the religious needs of all faiths. With no concern for his personal safety, he went to companies in direct support of front line units to hold church services, although often subjected to enemy sniper, mortar and artillery fire. On one occasion, while visiting members of the battalion working on a road within close proximity to the enemy, he was pinned down an hour by enemy mortar fire. . . . His conduct throughout was in keeping with the highest traditions of the United States Naval Service.

Chaplain Wolfram died on 30 July 1955, while serving in the cruiser MANCHESTER.

Air Wing Chaplain Parker

Joseph F. Parker had reported on 18 April 1952 as Wing Chaplain. Something of his activities at the outset of the 8th Korean Campaign can be described by means of excerpts from the Historical Diary submitted by him for inclusion in the Wing's Historical

Wing chapel with newly constructed front.

All Hands Evolution.

Even the generals turned out when Chaplain Parker called for volunteers to help paint the newly constructed chapel of the air wing. Pictured here wielding paintbrushes are Brig. Gen. Clayton C. Jerome and Brig. Gen. Frank H. Lamson-Scribner, commanding general and deputy commander respectively.

Chapel Painting.

Seabee Lawrence Schoenrock puts the finishing touches on a religious painting for the MAG 33 new chapel as Chaplain Gerard J. Clark looks on.

Korean Painter.

Jung Na Vi is shown with his painting of Christ executed for the MAW Chapel. The artist was an art professor at the University of Seoul.

Report, which in turn became part of the official records of the Marine Corps' participation in the Korean War. (The selected entries are here paraphrased.)

1 May. Distributed clothing. Wrote to theological schools stateside asking for Greek New Testaments for seminary professor in Pusan.

4 May. 0900, Communion at MAG 33 in absence of Chaplain Seymour, on leave in Japan. Communion at 1015 in Wing Chapel. Drove to MGCIS–3 for Communion at 1300. 1500, another service and Communion at MAG 33. Brief devotional, MAG 33, 1800. Preached to Korean Presbyterians at Do Koo through interpreter at a night service.

8 May. Visited Orphanage, taking scrap building materials and clothing.

11 May. Mothers Day. Twenty children from orphanage sang at 1015 service in Wing Chapel; large congregation. Children ate with the men in the mess hall. 1300 service at MGCIS–3 and 1800 service at MAG 33.

13 May. Received overstocked dry cereals and powdered milk from station and divided it in equal parts for Catholic Orphanage, Pohang City Orphanage, and Marine Orphanage.

19 May. Two loads of scrap lumber with no salvageable value to the Armed Forces given to Chung Nim Dong Church.

28 May. Attended dedication of Chung Nim Dong Church. Donated 600,000 *won* from Protestant Chapel Fund. Gave the sermon and conveyed best wishes from the Staff.

30 May. Spent morning with aid of interpreter examining account books of the U.S. Marine Orphanage. Books in good order.

Other entries in the same Historical Diary indicate that the chaplain was busy with the more or less routine duties of his office. In the absence of the American Red Cross Field Director he acted in cases requiring Red Cross assistance. Meanwhile he was holding choir rehearsals, consulting with men who came to him for help, visiting Sick bay and brig, securing and distributing supplies to his Wing chaplains, attending Staff meetings, and in other ways supervising the overall moral and religious ministry of the MAW.

Improvements on the new Wing Chapel continued. On 6 May a new altar was installed, behind which were painted three murals by L. F. Schoenrock, a Seabee BU2 stationed with the Marine Aircraft Wing, who gave his spare time to the project. On Sunday, 18 May, some 200 officers and men gathered at 1300 and within 2 hours the exterior had been painted. Among those wielding paint brushes were Brig. Gen. C. C. Jerome, Commanding General of the Wing, and his deputy, Brig. Gen. F. H. Lamson-Scribner. "The band furnished music, hot dogs and cokes were served and all hands had a good time." Later in the month

Choir Robes.
Here is shown the choir of the 1st Air Wing dressed in their new choir gowns made of parachutes.

brass candelabra were secured from the Army Chaplains Warehouse, and 20 small trees were secured and planted around the chapel.

Deciding that the new chapel warranted a properly vested choir, the chaplain went to the parachute packers of the Air Wing, who dug up several parachutes which could not be salvaged. Half of the nylon material was dyed black at a native dyeing establishment, the rest left white; a local Korean tailor turned the 'chutes into choir robes. Marine personnel wore the black robes over their green dungarees; the white robes were worn by Korean girls, employed on the base, who participated in the chapel services.

Parker wrote later, "We are proud of our chapels. The one at the Wing is being constantly improved and is now the best in Korea, though I may be a little prejudiced." Both Marine Aircraft Group 12 and Marine Aircraft Group 33 were enlarging and beautifying their chapels and a new one was built at MGCIS–3, although it had no chaplain aboard. "We have developed a friendly competitive spirit as to who is going to have the best chapel."

On 5 May the Wing was visited by Chaplain H. E. Austin, formerly attached to 1st Marine Division, then assigned to Air, FMF Pac, Marine Corps Air Station, El Toro, Calif. Austin had been delegated to speak for the Chaplains Service Corps, a voluntary group in Los Angeles, offering welfare items and religious equipment for the use of chaplains.

Parker issued regular memorandums to the Wing chaplains. That of 7 May, for instance, requested an inventory by each chaplain of the religious supplies and recreational gear in his possession, together with a reminder on accountability procedures where appropriate. Other items concerned chapel funds, expendable altar supplies and monthly reports. The chaplains were advised of the Wing Chaplain's planned itinerary for the forthcoming month.

The Memorandum of 13 June reminded the chaplains that according to the 1949 Geneva Convention their ID cards should be stamped with a red cross; they were referred to Bureau of Naval Personnel letter 31–52, dated 29 February 1952. There were two other reminders: that chaplains' records are retained in a Marine unit's Medical Office and that the Chaplains Division expects to receive direct from each chaplain concerned a complete set of any change of duty orders, with all endorsements.

Chaplains Aboard

From Chaplain Parker's roster submitted on 8 July the following distribution of chaplains in the 1st MAW appears:

Wing	J. F. Parker	CDR	BAP (S)
Wing	E. C. Mulligan	LCDR	RC
MAG 33	H. A. Seymour	LCDR	METH
MAG 33	E. M. Lynch	LCDR	RC
MAG 12	E. R. Lineberger, Jr.	LTJG	LUTH
MAG 12	P. J. La Duca	LTJG	RC
MWSS–1 (Itami)	W. B. Conn	LT	METH
1st 90 AAA	C. R. Harrison	LTJG	DISC

Welcome and Farewell.

Orphans and Christians from a Methodist Church hold a dinner for Chaplain Edwin R. Weidler who was returning to the United States, and for Chaplain Ernest R. Lineberger, Jr., who is Weidler's relief.

Lynch had reported on 7 April relieving Chaplain Sullivan. Lineberger reported on 15 May relieving Chaplain Weidler. Chaplain Conn reported on 22 May and was assigned to Itami relieving J. C. Brown, who was transferred to the 1st Marine Division after 2 months duty in the Wing. Mulligan arrived on 14 June, replacing Chaplain Horvath. Only Seymour had been with the Wing longer than 8 months. Parker wrote to the Chief: "The average tour of duty is seven (7) months for aviators and ten (10) months for line and staff. I understand the present policy of the Bureau is to keep chaplains in Korea for the same length of time as other officers." Parker asked for a Roman Catholic when Harrison should be relieved; Conn could then be assigned to the AAA Battalion and the Catholic assigned at Itami, where the Air Force already had a Protestant. Chaplain Mannion replied for the Chief of Chaplains concerning the matter of chaplain rotation:

It is our intention to make the tour of duty with 1st Marine Air Wing in Korea 12 months; however, if other officers remain there only 10 months we feel that we should fall in line. Let us put it this way: The duty will be 12 months but we will attempt to relieve chaplains at the end of 10 months.

Chaplain Lynch was hospitalized in Naval Hospital, Yokosuka, in June. He returned to duty after a month but, not recovering satisfactorily, was detached to the States. In October Chaplain Conn also became seriously ill and was transferred stateside. The roster of 1 October showed the following:

Wing	J. F. Parker	CDR	BAP (S)
Wing	E. C. Mulligan	LCDR	RC
MAG 33	E. R. Lineberger, Jr.	LTJG	LUTH
MAG 33	G. J. Clark	LT	RC
MAG 12	J. H. Lampe	LCDR	PRESBY (USA)
MAG 12	P. J. La Duca	LTJG	RC
MWSS–1 (Itami)	J. W. Paul	LCDR	METH

Lampe had reported on 7 July, Clark on 10 September and Paul on 11 September. Chaplain H. F. Fenstermacher reported on 18 October and was assigned to the AAA Battalion at Pusan.

The 1st Marine Aircraft Wing was thus better supplied with chaplains than at any previous time. Its complement was actually six, but having to cover the AAA Battalion (which had no chaplain allowance) and the Service Squadron at Itami (which ordinarily might have been expected to be with the Wing headquarters) raised the requirements.

Concerning Itami Parker wrote on 28 October:

MWSS–1 has an average strength of 600 officers and enlisted men permanently attached and in addition is the unit through which all replacement and rotation personnel are processed. Itami Air Force Base is also the facility used as a meritorious rest and recreation center for personnel of the First Marine Aircraft Wing. Approximately 65 officers and 385 enlisted men from units in Korea are temporarily attached at all times in addition to the regular complement. In view of these factors it is highly desirable that proper religious guidance be available. The situation is aggravated by problems involving relationships with Japanese women.

Since the Air Force chaplain aboard was also a Protestant, Roman Catholic ministrations continued to be furnished by American missionary priests.

Relief Work

With the Wing headquarters now located near Pohang, Chaplain Parker took an active hand in the affairs of the Marine-supported orphanage begun there with the help of Chaplain Cleaves. Cleaves had joined with American Presbyterian missionary William B. Lyon and the Pohang Presbyterian ministers to initiate the project. With money given by Air Wing Marines some land and a few buildings were purchased, a board of directors organized, and the institution incorporated in the name of the Presbyterian holding body as the Marine Memorial Orphanage. After a few months 50 children were being cared for.

The directors were soon faced with a choice between seemingly endless expansion on a day-to-day basis or an attempt to make the home self-sustaining while caring for fewer children. The solution was a compromise: limited expansion little by little, and at the same time the purchase of productive rice land. Less than a year after its start, the orphanage owned over 2,000 *pyong* (a plot 6 feet square) of rice land. On one occasion, as he presented the latest Marine contribution—four and a half million *won* ($750)—Chaplain Parker commented, "Much of the food on which orphans will live this winter will be harvested by the older children off their own paddies. By this time next year, if donations do not fall off, there will be enough rice to feed them all year and perhaps some left over to market."

MAG 12 moved to Pyongtaek, on the west coast, some 250 miles from the Wing headquarters and MAG 33. There Chaplain E. R. Weidler was instrumental in establishing a new orphanage. In his reply to the Corps historian's questionnaire of March 1954 he noted that before the home was set up, children had been living in caves and trenches. He added that Commander Lederer had contributed $550 from what he had received for the story he had written about the work of MAG 12 with Korean orphans.

Three chaplains of the 1st Marine Aircraft Wing were cited during the period under review, one receiving the Bronze Star and two, Letters of Commendation. Chaplain Edward M. Lynch was awarded the Bronze Star for service from 9 April to 15 August

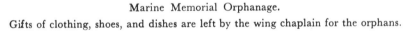

Marine Memorial Orphanage.
Gifts of clothing, shoes, and dishes are left by the wing chaplain for the orphans.

Visit to Buddhist Temple.

Chaplain Stephen G. Horvath talks to a Buddhist priest at a Korean temple a few miles from a forward airbase of the 1st MAW.

1952; his citation mentions his faithfulness in ministering to the spiritual needs of his men and cites his outstanding work with the orphanages in the Pohang vicinity. "A diligent and tireless worker, he traveled regularly to hold services and consultations with men stationed at a remote camp."

Chaplain Stephen G. Horvath's Letter of Commendation, covering the period 19 July 1951 to 18 June 1952, noted that "his excellent cooperation with chaplains of other faiths was such as to gain him respect and popularity." The chaplain was commended also for work with orphanages at Pusan, Kangnung, and Pohang; he had raised over a thousand dollars for the Roman Catholic orphanage in the latter place.

The Letter of Commendation awarded Chaplain Edward R. Weidler for service from 22 August 1951 to 19 May 1952 singled out for special praise his work with Korean civilians, including North Koreans "who were enduring the hardships of a severe winter with inadequate means of subsistence." The citation concluded:

Lieutenant Weidler's activities throughout were completely dedicated to the humanitarian principles embodied in the precepts of Christianity and in the Charter of the United Nations and were in keeping with the highest traditions of the United States Naval Service.

Chaplain Parker was cited by the Republic of Korea. This citation in part reads,

Despite the tremendous hardships Chaplain Parker devoted much of his time to organizing specific aid projects and allocating the vitally needed relief goods for those "lost children." The sympathetic concern exhibited through the establishment of an orphanage at Pohang on May 10, 1952, for alleviating the suffering orphans confronted with the threat of disease, starvation, and exposure has made substantial contribution to our relief works and has materially raised the standards of care in the institution.

USS HAVEN

In addition to these individual awards, the hospital ship HAVEN, which has figured in our account on several occasions, received the Presidential Unit Citation of the Republic of Korea for distinguished service from 18 October 1950 to 25 June 1952. Chaplains serving in the HAVEN during those dates were the following:

Paul K. Potter.....	METH	September	1950–December 1951
John J. Reardon ...	RC	September	1950–September 1951
Edwin R. Howard..	CONG	December	1951–October 1952
Francis J. Klass....	RC	October	1951–December 1952

Perspective on Korea

At the invitation of the Chiefs of Chaplains of the Army, Navy, and Air Force the Reverend Dr. Joseph R. Sizoo, professor of religion, George Washington University, and formerly minister of St. Nicholas Collegiate Church, New York and dean of the New Brunswick Theological Seminary, made a month's visit to Japan and Korea in October 1952. He held conferences with line and staff officers and with chaplains, met the troops and talked with them and in other ways attempted to study American involvement in the Far East that he might help the churches interpret it back home.

The following lengthy quotations are from a digest of the address that he gave to denominational representatives at the General Commission on Chaplains "Chaplains' Memorial Building" in Washington soon after his return.

What I saw and heard has deeply moved me. I'm not here as a lecturer reciting a travelogue. I'm here as a minister to read you a footnote to the "Acts of the Apostles."

There is much we shall have to learn and unlearn. I learned that this is no "phony war." I had to unlearn that this is just a regrettable, unfortunate minor holding operation which we had to go through with until, sooner or later, when they got around to it, the political leaders of the world would declare peace on earth, good will toward men.

That's not true. It's war! I was in an area where there were 1,200 casualties in 1 day. I talked to a general who had just come down from a hilltop where they had counted 2,000 enemy dead. I've been on the side of a ridge when a helicopter came down out of nowhere and men strapped the wounded in baskets on both sides and flew them back to the hospital. I've been in a hospital where there were 1,500 of our wounded men. When you have 125,000 casualties in our ranks and over a million casualties in the enemy's, you can hardly speak of a minor holding operation

. . . . .

You get a feeling that our men are embittered. After all, so much of what is happening should not have happened, could have been otherwise. The truce talks have left them bitter. We kept our word and didn't build up our army except to provide replacements for those who returned. The enemy built up an army of one million who've had military training for a whole year. What's more, these million men have had a year to be indoctrinated. The old army was often glad of the chance to surrender. That's no longer true. There were on one occasion, when I was there, something like 1,800 casualties of the enemy—and we took only 8 prisoners.

. . . . .

Although this is a war that is grim and cruel and costly, our army is an army of peace, and our soldiers are men of compassion.

To understand this you really have to see Korea: The most tormented country you can possibly imagine. Twenty-two million people go to bed hungry every night. Since I've been back, sometimes I think of it and I can't swallow. . . . General Van Fleet told me the day that I saw him that we were feeding that day 2 million Koreans to keep them alive. There are three scourges in Korea today: tuberculosis and cholera and smallpox. Our doctors and medical corps, when they are through with their chores, will go out to some nearby village and they'll vaccinate 700. They'll build little hospitals.

I've seen what the enemy did to Korea. But our men are not plunderers. Our men are helpers. They are not destroyers, they really are saviors.

I preached in a chapel one Sunday morning with a handful of men. The chaplain told me they were accustomed to take up a voluntary collection and send it to some Korean enterprise. For many months at the end of a month they had sent a check for $500. Just a handful of men! I was with a certain Corps where they took up a collection of $84,000 for the hospitalization of Korean refugee children.

. . . . .

You can't explain our army and you can't explain its expression of compassion without talking about the chaplain. After all, because he is what he is, that army is what it is. I've met with chaplains in groups. I've walked with them, slept with them, eaten with them, prayed with them; and I've come to know them as men. They are a very superior corps.

One thing which impressed me was the way the Protestant and Catholic and Jewish chaplains worked together, with a great sense of comradeship of the Spirit.

Now I want to make a few observations about these chaplains:

1. They preach what is central in our religion and they stick to it. They do not indulge in trivialities. They do not take the thing that is in the center and push it beyond the circumference or take the thing that lies on the circumference and put it in the center.

2. These chaplains practice what they preach. They live it. They don't give men an argument; they give them the example of a Christ-filled life. I have never . . . seen anywhere a more completely dedicated group of men.

3. These chaplains have quickened the sense of compassion. They keep alive in our troops a concern for the people in whose land they are fighting. Wherever you go in Korea,

if you see a little hospital or clinic or asylum, you just know there's a chaplain behind it.

4. These chaplains are true missionaries of the Christian faith. . . . The great missionary enterprise in East Asia is being carried out by our chaplains, and I hope that the missionary world will capture something of their imagination.

5. These chaplains are going to be the leaders of the church of tomorrow. Some day the soldiers are coming back with their frustrations and bewilderment and embitterment, and they are going to ask some uncomfortable questions. They will say to us, "Brother, where were you when we were in Korea?" But when the chaplain stands there with them, they will believe him and follow him.[5]

Stalemate

The Department of Defense would later designate 30 November 1952 as the end of the 8th Korean Campaign. The date itself meant next to nothing. The front lines remained substantially where they had been at the beginning of the campaign. The peace talks continued, but an impasse seemed to have been reached on the issue of involuntary repatriation of prisoners of war. The end for which the United Nations had gone to Korea—to counter Communist aggression and to bring peace as quickly and permanently as possible to that devastated land—remained after twenty-nine months unaltered but unaccomplished. Men continued their monotonous vigils in outposts and bunkers, and occasional outbursts of violence added to the already long roster of the wounded

and dead.[6] And now the raw winds began to sweep down from the North, bringing the first snows of winter. Navy chaplains, ministers of the peace of God, prepared themselves and their fellow-countrymen to celebrate a third Korean Christmas.

The Corps

Thus far in the Korean War another splendid chapter had been written in the annals of the Navy Chaplain Corps. By 1952 some 800 regular and reserve chaplains were on active duty, approximately 130 of these assigned duty at Marine stations and with Fleet Marine Force units. From 30 to 35 chaplains were on duty with Marines in Korea, and others serving in ships or stations in the Far East area. Though new conditions frequently demanded unusual initiative and flexibility in the performance of duty, the mission of the Corps remained the same: to protect, encourage, and train personnel of the naval establishment in the realization and development of moral and spiritual values consistent with the religious beliefs of the individual concerned.

Unfortunately the number of chaplains available was not sufficient to enable the Bureau of Naval Personnel to fill all billets.

---

[5] *The Chaplain*, vol. 10, No. 3 (June 1953).

[6] Total United States casualties through 24 October 1952 were 123,395, of which the Navy had suffered 1,679, the Marine Corps 23,193. There had been 21,471 deaths; 91,260 personnel had been wounded; and there were 12,868 missing. The Marines alone had suffered 20,218 wounded and 2,928 dead (*Britannica Book of the Year*, 1953; article, "Korean War").

CHAPTER NINE

THIRD KOREAN WINTER

1 December 1952–30 April 1953

Once again winter descended upon Korea and with it an accompanying decline in military activity. For over a year the conflict had been in a state of stalemate. During this period both sides had so reinforced their positions that they could be captured only at great cost to the attacker.

On 5 December President-elect Dwight D. Eisenhower left to visit the forces in Korea. A number of other visitors were to pay a call upon the military forces before the New Year.

The truce talks had been indefinitely suspended in October and many men looked quizzically at the beam of the searchlight at night and the balloons at day which marked the location of Panmunjom, the site of the negotiations. They were wondering "when will it all end?"

Naval action was confined to minesweeping, blockade escort duty, carrier strikes, surface and aerial patrols in the Yellow Sea, the Sea of Japan, the Korean straits and the coastal waters of Formosa. As early as October the "Cherokee" plan was developed, which was defined as a plan "to destroy enemy's logistics at the battle line." [1] A number of sorties just behind enemy lines were made by the planes of KEARSARGE, PRINCETON, and ESSEX. These were referred to by pilots as *hot* strikes because of the amount of flak which was encountered on these missions.

November 18 marked the first encounter with Russian MIGs. The three American pilots who participated in this engagement were interviewed by Eisenhower during his December visit.

January saw a few meetings between liaison officers at Panmunjom. February marked an upsurge in the Cherokee strikes. The following month, March, was the one well remembered by Marine chaplains. On the 5th Stalin died; the month also saw riots by diehard Communists, this time on Yongcho and Koje Islands, but it was the activity on the front held by

the 1st Division which the Marines remembered best. On the 26th a sector of the I Corps was under attack and lost ground. This attack included the battles of HOOK, VEGAS, RENO, and CARSON. By launching a strong counterattack the Marines in this sector were able to regain their positions.

April brought a more hopeful outlook at Panmunjom. On the 6th talks began which led to an agreement on the 11th to what was called "Operation Little Switch." This operation consisted of the exchange of prisoners which occurred on the 20th when 6,670 Communist personnel and 684 UN prisoners were exchanged. Of the latter 149 were U.S. personnel. Finally, after a suspension of 199 days, the armistice negotiations were resumed.

1st Marine Division

Chaplain Lonnie W. Meachum reported as the Division Chaplain of the 1st Marine Division on 10 December. Chaplain Slattery wrote to the Chief of Chaplains on the 17th indicating that a painting of Christ is to be presented to General Pollock for his promotion of chaplains' activities. In this same letter he mentions that Billy Graham is expected to preach at a pre-Christmas Service on Monday the 22d, and that Cardinal Spellman is to celebrate Mass on Christmas. Chaplain Meachum's reaction to his new duty assignment is revealed in his letter of the 30th to the Chief of Chaplains in which he says in part,

This has been a madhouse since the day I arrived. Chaplain Slattery said that the pace is normal procedure.

The office is like 42d and Broadway with "visiting firemen" from UN outfits, our own chaplains, and VIPs from the States. It seems that everyone coming to Korea wants to visit the Marines.

We had Billy Graham on 23 December. About 1,000 Marines gathered to hear him. Approximately 200 stood when he challenged them to rededicate and consecrate their lives to Christ. At first the General was not going to stay for his sermon, but upon meeting him he (the General) was charmed with Graham's personality. General Pollock was

---

[1] Cagle and Manson, *op. cit.*, p. 462.

Christmas Visitor.
Billy Graham chats with Maj. Gen. Edwin A. Pollock, commanding general of the 1st Marine Division during Graham's visit to Korea during the Christmas season, 1952.

New Chapel.
A new chapel is erected near Wosanri by the 1st Engineer Battalion to which Chaplain Karl H. Ernest is assigned. The chapel was dedicated 4 January 1953 with General Pollock and Chaplain Meachum participating in the service.

Mural.
This painting is the work of artist, Sgt. Russell Vickers, and was given to the 1st Engineer Battalion Chapel where it was placed over the altar.

Chaplains.
General Pollock has his picture taken with the chaplains of his division. The photograph was taken 19 December 1952 at Yongji-ri.

The Predecessor.
Here is pictured the chapel formerly used by the 1st Engineering Battalion. Note the stacks which indicate the presence of an underground heating system fashioned after the Koreans.

Stateside Christmas Gifts.

Children of St. Paul Orphanage receive Christmas gifts sent from the States and delivered by the 2d Battalion, 1st Marines. Their chaplain, Gerald E. Kuhn, is seen on the right holding one of the orphans.

Chaplains' Conference.

The chaplains gather for a conference at the 1st Marine Division Command Post. In the front row (from left to right) are Chaplains A. W. Boyer; E. A. Wolfram, Jr.; Oscar Weber; R. F. Barlik; J. T. Callahan; (in the second row:) N. L. McDowell; J. C. Brown, Jr.; B. N. Wolfe; R. Siegel; C. E. Elliott, Jr.; P. Adams; (in the third row:) A. F. Mendonsa; W. P. Lane; A. D. Prickett; E. A. Slattery; W. D. McCabe; R. H. Willets; V. J. Lustig; B. J. Nowakowski; (last row) E. S. Jones; F. J. Forney; G. W. Herrick; A. W. Robertson; L. A. Guillaume; C. T. Duggan; H. C. Bowling, Jr.; and J. H. Muller.

one of those who stood to rededicate himself. We would have had more to attend if I Corps had not changed the day and hour at the last minute. We were told at first that he would be here on the 22d.

Cardinal Spellman's Mass was at 0830 on Christmas Day. About 2,000 attended. He preached a fine sermon and shook hands with about 1,000 men. Strumski developed a good choir for the Mass.

Our own services were "out of this world" on Christmas. One's limit in Spiritual Ministry here is his physical stamina. I preached six times the first Sunday. However, I am arranging for church parties to come in to headquarters so I can visit more. For instance, I have been to one chapel dedication and General Pollock and I are to go to another [2] next Sunday.

Chaplain Slattery came to my candlelight service and I went to his Mass. I accused him of stealing my "thunder" in his sermon. Then Spellman stole from both of us.

Ed was a very popular Division chaplain. He received the Legion of Merit on Christmas night. He left on Saturday with tears in his eyes and joy in his heart.

Chaplain Slattery's Legion of Merit was awarded by General Pollock. The citation reads in part as follows:

Commander Slattery displayed outstanding ability and foresight in caring for the spiritual welfare of all the Marines in the division. An understanding, capable, wise, and persevering leader, he organized his section in such a manner that spiritual services and guidance were always available. Frequently making journeys throughout the division, in the most adverse weather and terrain conditions, he expressed little concern for his personal welfare in order that all the Marines might receive the opportunity to attend services of their own particular faith. Commander Slattery's perseverance, friendly manner and selfless devotion to the men he served were an inspiration to all who observed him. His skilled service and exemplary conduct throughout this period were in keeping with the highest traditions of the U.S. Naval Service.

Combat "V" was authorized.

With the approach of Christmas other Marine chaplains were busy with holiday projects. Chaplain G. E. Kuhn worked with the 2d Battalion, 1st Marines, in distributing gifts sent by the Telephone Employee's Volunteer Service of San Francisco. Visits were paid to orphanages operated by the Yong Nok Presbyterian Church and the Sisters of St. Paul. Once again children were happy because Marines had played Santa Claus.

Another such project was described by Chaplain Thos. Allen Newman of the 2d Battalion, 7th Marines. Because of the scarcity of material a small Santa Claus suit was constructed. "Toys were a must, for children had to have toys at Christmas . . . The supply system of a Marine battalion does not have

such items in stock so many Marines were enlisted in the search for candy and toys. Where all the materials and toys came from is a mystery left unsolved." Forty foster fathers were selected from the Marines. Children were found in a refugee village. In fact there were over a thousand there. The ones doing best in school were selected. The mess hall was decorated with real trees. Christmas cards were on each table with plenty of candy for the children.

At the appointed time a truck picked up its colorful and unusual cargo. The children, ranging in age from 8 to 11 but looking much younger, were dressed in bright Korean costumes and as they traveled along they sang Korean songs for their escorts. Their arrival was eagerly awaited by all who wanted "a kid of his own." Bashful and a little frightened the children climbed down from the truck into the many pairs of outstretched Marines arms. Rivalry was keen to get a particular child and cries of "that one is mine," started a small "discussion" in several cases. The foster father secured food for the child and assisted in the cutting and eating of it. Some children were too frightened by the mass of men to be very hungry while others didn't care for the food. The bolder ones ate with complete disregard for the huge group of interested spectators. Peculiar appetites soon became evident, for some children would eat only bread and jam while others would only eat potatoes. One thing that all enjoyed was the candy; no one had any trouble feeding "their kid" candy. Several Marines insisted that their charges take home vast numbers of candy bars which they placed in the pockets and hands of the little ones. Impromptu singing would start in one corner of the hall and all would stop to listen as one small girl would sing the Korean love song A Arirang; joining in all the children would sing with her. This pleased the Marines and resulted in loud cheers and applause.

Santa Claus was next on the program. Outside the mess hall beside one of the Christmas trees St. Nick sat with his bags of toys. Each child got the presents which were intended for him or her and then with the help of the foster father they would play with them. These were toy trains, clowns, Santa Clauses, and dolls. The children received gum and candy again and again as Santa Claus emptied his bags. Several hundred onlookers crowded around the activity taking pictures; holding the children or playing with them. Each man wanted his picture taken with one of the children. The 1st Marine Division Band was there to play for the affair. Seated in the outdoor movie area with their guardians the children listened to the American music. They in turn sang in Korean for all the Marines such songs as Silent Night and other Christmas carols. The Marines, not to be inhospitable, responded with a loud rendition of Jingle Bells.

As the children began to get restless and tired, the signal was given for all children to be returned to the truck. Their hands full of candy and toys each child was tenderly lifted up into the truck by strong hands. A count was made and it was discovered that two children were missing. Two of the Marines had taken their "offspring" to answer the call of nature. Even in Korea the duties of a "parent" never change. The farewell was very different from the welcome.

---

[2] Chapel for 1st Engineering Battalion.

Now the boys and girls were happy and few were afraid. Singing as they left, the children made their mark upon the Christmas of a battalion of Marines; made it one they would never forget! Santa Claus had been there that day!

Another Christmas project was that undertaken by the chaplains of the 11th Marine Artillery Regiment, Chaplains William P. Lane, Catholic, and Noah L. McDowell, Southern Baptist. Through the courtesy of Minnesota Mining & Manufacturing Co., and the Revere Camera Co., 5,000 recording tapes were flown to Korea. Brief messages were recorded by thousands of Marines and mailed to their loved ones back home. In addition the "homefolks" could record and return reply messages to the Marines.

Just prior to Christmas Chaplain Charles T. Duggan completed his tour of duty with the 1st Division. He was subsequently awarded a Commendation Medal with Combat "V". The citation read in part,

> During an intense barrage of enemy mortar fire, he unhesitatingly went to the forward area to give spiritual guidance and aid the wounded. On one occasion, he voluntarily went to a forward aid station to be with the wounded during a period of intense enemy action.

The new roster of the 1st Division for January included a number of new chaplains. These were Chaplains G. E. Kuhn, Lutheran; W. Rowland, Episcopal; K. D. Killin, Presbyterian, USA; J. C. Moore, Methodist; R. W. Shreffler, Presbyterian, USA; K. H. Ernst, Presbyterian, USA; A. S. M. Kirkland, Nazarene; J. P. Byrnes, Catholic; R. L. Crabtree, Methodist; R. G. Hutcheson, Jr., Presbyterian, US; L. W. Meachum, Southern Baptist; E. J. Kelly, Catholic; W. H. Vinson, Southern Baptist, and J. T. Moore, Catholic.

In a letter of the 29th Chaplain Meachum indicated that another visitor was expected on the 31st, Bishop Austin Pardue, Episcopal, from Pittsburgh.

Also things were about to happen in Washington. After a long and fruitful period as Chief of Chaplains, Chaplain Stanley Salisbury was turning over the helm to Chaplain E. B. Harp, Jr. This transfer occurred on the 1st of February. Chaplain Salisbury had had more than 30 years of naval service. He entered the naval chaplaincy in 1921, but he had served in World War I as an Army chaplain. He served as Chief of Chaplains from 1 September 1949–1 February 1953. His new position was in the service of his denomination in a new post as chairman of a special committee of chaplains and service personnel (Presbyterian Church, USA).

The ninth Chief of Chaplains, Rear Adm. Edward B. Harp, Jr., was a clergyman of the Evangelical and Reformed Church, and came to his new position with a wealth of naval experience, having served in a number of billets during the course of 23 years. His most recent assignment had been Assistant for Planning in the Chaplains Division.

To return to the 1st Division, in February Chaplain Calvin H. Elliott was detached from the Division but not without recognition by the Commanding General. His citation reads in part,

> During periods when the unit was engaged in extensive combat against the enemy, he provided moral and spiritual guidance to all men of the regiment. Expressing complete disregard for his personal safety and comfort, he aided in the evacuation of the wounded.

The following month saw the detachment of another chaplain, Albert D. Prickett, who was awarded the Bronze Star medal. Of the deeds of this chaplain the following are among those listed,

> Through his profound sincerity and unerring skill in the administration of the spiritual needs of the command, he was a constant source of inspiration and comfort. Despite the extreme danger of enemy mortar and artillery fire, he expressed complete disregard for his personal safety and made repeated trips to the front lines in order to aid the men. During one engagement, he unhesitatingly directed armored personnel carriers loaded with wounded Marines through impact areas to a place of safety. As a result of his personal courage and selfless devotion, he was instrumental in saving the lives of several wounded Marines.

For something on the lighter side as reported by Chaplain Homer L. Schnick, Southern Baptist, of the 1st Service Battalion, who at least on one occasion went on a tour of the various shower units attached to the infantry battalions, he states,

> It was amusing to think about how men were required to wear helmets and flack jackets to the showers and then take their showers, *sans* everything. In connection with the shower units, it is well to point out that the shower units in operation near the front line positions where the men could clean up occasionally and exchange their dirty clothes for clean ones (even if they didn't always get the proper sizes!) were among the best morale boosters the men had. Men came from the muddy trenches and bunkers covered with mud and dirt, and left clean and considerably braced up. Sometimes rear area units may not be credited properly for the part they had in supplying gear and services, but having served with such a group, I believe that they deserve a pat on the back for a job well done. From showers to bread to ice cream (one assistant I had stated that the first meal that he had in Korea after he got to the front lines in the month of February 1953, he had ice cream, among other things, for breakfast!) to shoe, tent, and flack jacket repair the services of the 1st Service Battalion ran. Morale was not as good in the rear areas probably because the sense of mission and glory was not as keen, but they served as did the front line riflemen.

During its stay with the Division, Chaplain John P. Byrnes reports that he administered the Sacraments for the Army detachment at Panmunjom once a week, and Chaplain Karl H. Ernst reports that he never worked so hard in his life in the holding of services. Chaplain Ernst also reports on the value of tours to Seoul that gave his men an opportunity to see another side of the Korean people and their culture.

It was about this time that some consideration was given to an extension of the period of a tour of duty for the chaplains to 12 months instead of 10. On 26 February Chaplain Meachum wrote to the Chief of Chaplains stating, "I am glad that you decided to keep it at 10 months. This is tough going in the dust, cold, heat, mud, 'incoming,' and what with one and two services a day and all a man can stand up to on Sunday."

A glance at the roster of February indicates the following new chaplains, J. B. Conlon, Catholic, A. J. Barry, Catholic, R. E. Brengartner, Catholic, E. V. Lyons, Presbyterian (USA), L. F. Rice, Catholic, T. V. Edwards, Catholic, and W. H. Nordby, Lutheran.

In March the Division Chaplain indicates that there is a concentrated effort in the promulgation of Character Education Programs underway. In a personal letter (entered in his file) dated 20 March we also read for the first time of retreats being set up for chaplains. He writes,

All of our chaplains are invited to meet Chaplain Bennett at I Corps Chapel on 8 April. In lieu of this trip to I Corps we will not have our regular monthly Protestant retreat in April.

We have had fine fellowship at these meetings since I came. Our fellows did not pay much attention to the retreat before the January meeting. They do not feel that they should leave their outfits. However, I am going to insist that they go. We get a chance to meet the chaplains in the Commonwealth and 2d Divisions. They secure an outstanding missionary or native to speak in the morning and the divisions rotate with the devotional period after lunch.

He further mentioned action on the front 18 March; he says,

We had 89 casualties the night of the 18th, 9 KIA's with superficial wounds accounting for the most of the others. Our boys (CHC) are doing a wonderful job.

The battles which took place this same month caused a number of chaplains to record their experiences. One such account was entitled "On a Hill Far Away" and was written by Chaplain Allen Newman. Because it vividly describes a chaplain in action it is recorded in full as follows,

I couldn't get any closer to the ground which I hugged with all my body. The enemy mortars and artillery shells were landing and whistling around us. How did I, the chaplain, ever get way out here was the question I kept asking myself? It all happened so fast! It wasn't planned that way! The plans were for a show the next Sunday; a choir that was to sing for Easter; a series of Lenten services. A nice and quiet weekend. The men had been rehearsing for the Palm Sunday variety show during the past 4 nights. The choir just 2 nights ago had practiced for Sunday services. Then last night in the middle of rehearsals the 30 minute alert was given to all troops of the 2d Battalion, 7th Marines. There was trouble on the lines; several outposts were under attack. With rapid and precisionlike movement the 2d Battalion began to ready for battle.

The trucks started arriving during the night, their engines roaring out the noise of their coming. In the darkness of the early morning the men climbed into the trucks bound for a destination unknown. There were no bands to cheer them, only the voices of the platoon sergeants and officers piercing the night with curt cries, "all right keep moving." There was excitement in the air and anticipation made many a heart beat faster. One company, then another, pulled out toward the front line in the direction of the 5th Marines sector and away from the security and peace of our reserve camp. We had been in reserve for just 2 weeks and expected to stay there for at least 2 more weeks but the enemy wasn't cooperating with our plans and hopes. All that night the sound of artillery and the light of flares reminded us that there was crisis ahead—a dangerous opportunity for the battalion.

With the coming of daylight the flares and artillery shells stopped their ceaseless flow. Quiet became the early morning hour's song. I tried to take stock of all my men; to locate all the widely scattered companies. All the companies were still waiting the word as to what they were going to do. The outposts Reno and Carson had fallen to the enemy during the night. Rumors were making a rapid tour of the companies—"Easy Company is going to take Reno back"—"Dog Company was to help." No one knew just what was going to happen. Easy Company was in a position to move out at any moment. I walked among these men that I knew and loved, talking, joking, just being with them as they worried and wondered what was in the future for them. I wondered too. The morning passed quickly with Easy Company. Early in the afternoon word came that Fox Company had been committed to recapture outpost Vegas from the enemy. They had already started up the hill and were in close range fighting with the enemy.

The battle was on! There were four chaplains besides myself in the immediate vicinity. They were seeing the wounded and dead as they came through the medical aid stations. My men were fighting for their lives. I had to go with them. And there I was in the advanced Fox Company C.P. which was set up in a gully at the closest tip of Vegas. It was 1630 on Friday, 27 March when I got out there. I had gone out with a platoon of Weapons Company men who had been organized into stretcher teams and supply carriers. We were waiting for darkness to come so that we could remove the many wounded men who were still up on the hillsides. It was too hazardous to attempt relief during the daylight hours. Bad news travels fast and

Christmas Day on the Front.

Chaplain Allen Newman offers a prayer for all fighting marines at Christmas Day services at the front.

I was told that one of the men who was a soloist in the variety show and was to sing for Easter services had been killed early in the fighting. His name was Matthews, Sgt. Daniel P. Matthews. That was the first of much sad news that came to me. The battle was more personal than before. Since there was nothing I could do but wait for darkness, I began to make the rounds of the men who were crouching in the gully. There were men from the 5th Marines waiting to help remove the wounded to the main line of resistance. I talked to as many of the men as possible in between the enemy mortar barrages. During one heavy attack a cry went out behind me, "Help me I'm hit." And the word "corpsman" echoed from man to man in the gully. The man just a few feet in front of me was moaning. A piece of an enemy shell had hit him in the head. Rapidly the corpsman, James McCrabe HM3, and I dressed his wound. Quickly we placed him on a stretcher and started across the rice paddies that separated Vegas from the friendly lines. I had known this particular man for several months as he had often attended church services. He was

afraid that something like this would happen to him—and it did. As fast as was possible we rushed him to the doctor, but in spite of using eight men and the speediest route, he soon gave up the fight for his life. More and more of my men were coming back that way.

With darkness came the wounded, carried by their buddies who stumbled in the darkness. Eager hands reached down to pick up stretchers for the long and wearisome trip back to the lines. Names were called out, "Smith! Wooten! Ward!" as attempt was made to find out who was on the stretcher. Strong and then sometimes feeble voices answered back, "I'm all right, one of my buddies is still out there; take care of him first." I could hardly recognize any of the forms or faces as men I had known before and yet they were the same men who had climbed into the trucks just a few hours ago. They were surprised to hear my voice. The word was soon passed that the chaplain was "out here." A few asked me in weak voices to write their mothers. Others were too far gone to say anything. One boy who had his chin hanging far below its normal place needed another bandage, and as I placed a new battle dressing on his damaged chin, he kept saying he was O.K. I hadn't even recognized his face at all. No tears were shed by those whose bodies ached with pain; no words of self-pity or complaints were said that night.

The long trains of men carrying stretchers—four men carrying one wounded began the many journeys that were to continue during the night. Back and forth went Marines and Koreans carrying supplies out to Vegas and the dead and wounded back in again. Word was passed that there were 16 seriously wounded up in the lowest trench line. A group of stretcher bearers, enough to carry back 12 wounded, under the leadership of Sergeant Schrum started out to make this journey. I went with them to help and encourage the tired and weary men. We traveled the three or four hundred yards to the place where the men were waiting. There in a shallow trench were the men who had been waiting for hours for us to come and get them. They were *all* seriously wounded. We had to decide which ones we could take and which ones would be left until the next trip. A decision like that might mean the difference between life and death for some of them. There was never a word or outcry from any as we quickly and painfully lifted them onto the stretchers we had carried out. Broken legs, missing legs, torn bodies, dirty wounds, all were common to those who depended upon our skill and judgment for some chance to live. Those who had cared for them told us that there were six more seriously wounded farther up the trench line. We had to leave some so we picked the ones we thought needed to get back quickest. One after another the stretcher teams of four would leave with their burden and start the hazardous and difficult journey through darkness to life and safety. I left with the last team. Our stretcher was a broken one so that delayed us until we could find another out there on the hill. By that time all of the other teams had disappeared into the night and we had to find our way alone. We lost our way once, but soon found the gully where the other teams were waiting to make the last leg of the trip.

Fox Company made one more assault on the outpost early Saturday morning. They refused to allow anyone to leave the lines during the attack to go to Vegas so I decided I had better see what had happened to Easy and Dog Companies. Finding that they were not committed to action, I returned to the Battalion Command Post to eat and wash. Early Saturday afternoon Dog Company started out to Vegas to assist in the fighting. Enemy artillery caught them in one of the valleys beside Vegas and they sustained 40 casualties. Returning to the lines again Dog Company brought back the dead and wounded. The men worked frantically to bind up the injuries and evacuate the casualties. It all came so quickly and was such a surprise that most of the men still didn't realize what had happened. I walked around the group of dazed men who still remained in Dog Company talking to most of them. Many were in a state of shock or stunned by the sudden attack which struck them. It took several hours to clear the wounded and take them to the field hospitals. Once again an ache was in my heart and a wound in the side of the battalion.

Night brought sleep for me and a few other fortunate men who did not or could not stand a watch that night. The first rays of sunshine brought Palm Sunday to Korea. As I climbed Vegas hill to see the men of Easy Company I thought, "What a different Sunday this was than the one that had been planned." No human choir was to sing for my men that day, only the chorus of enemy shells singing around them. No sermon telling of Jesus' entry into Jerusalem filled their hearts. But they were to feel the eternal Presence of God as they crouched in the trenches or hid in their rabbit holes for hours during the nights and days ahead. No one had to ask them to pray. They did it naturally as a man would cry out for help if he were helpless. Easy Company that Palm Sunday morning was digging into the debris-filled mountain top. The sun was warm and kindly

---

Chaplain Gives Lecture.
Chaplain Matthew J. Strumski delivers an educational lecture on character to marines in Korea.

Preparation for Vegas.

Chaplain James Kelly prays with marines from the 2d Battalion, 7th Regiment as they stand by to move out to hit the enemy.

to those who still felt and saw its radiance. There were those men who had grown cold with death and now only felt the warmth of heavenly sunshine. We began the slow and difficult task of bringing the dead down from the top trenches. Every man in the trench would help as the stretcher was carried down the trench line. In the trench I saw faces I had known before—men of Easy Company— tired, dirty, afraid, and heart-sick from the loss of friends and buddies. When 1030 came I thought of the church service that I should be conducting back in the reserve area for the 3d Battalion, 7th Marines. These men on Vegas needed the reassurance that God hadn't forsaken them. They needed so much that only God could give.

Sunday morning and part of the afternoon we searched the hillsides of Vegas looking for the dead who had been left behind in the excitement of the fighting. I collected men who were not busy fighting wherever I could find them and formed them into stretcher teams. My friend Sergeant Matthews was still lying out there somewhere and I wanted to bring him back again. We failed to find any trace of his body. More than a week later he was found and recommended for the Medal of Honor for his heroic deeds. We found other men, broken bodies sprawled behind bushes in hideous ways hardly recognizable as men we had once known.

Since we were under enemy observation, we worked rapidly and in small teams of four. The hill having been cleaned of its burden of human flesh as far as we could go, our sad procession started in with our heavy loads. Once again the church music was lacking—only the voices of tired men calling out commands or cheering each other on. What an entry was being made by these men who had found the eternal peace that they had fought to gain. If only the world could see the sorrow in this scene!

The light melted into another period of darkness again and with the night came increased enemy activity. Death and injury once again touched the hilltop of Vegas. It was late that night before I found my way out to the hill. Stretcher teams were going back and forth between the hill and the wire which marked the main line and safety. Most of the Marines were exhausted from the days without sleep and the emotional strain of the battle. Finally an opportunity to help presented itself—they needed someone to show a group of 48 Korean stretcher bearers the way to Vegas. One Marine thought he knew but wasn't certain. Quietly I offered him my services and stepped in front of the long line of men to start the journey out to pick up 12 wounded Marines. The Marine asked me where my weapon was; my comment was, "I have none.' He said no more but still

— 169 —

didn't realize that I was a chaplain. I didn't disclose my identity since he might be embarrassed to let a chaplain lead him out to Vegas. We crossed the rice paddy which divided the outpost Vegas from the check point and friendly forces. Breaking the group into two equal parts, I instructed the second half of men to come up Vegas hill after the first group had reached the top and had started down with their cargos. Flares lighted the area around the outpost so that it seemed like daylight. It was easy to find the trail which led to our goal. The men followed with silent steps. Upon reaching the trench line of Vegas the wounded and dead were quickly placed on stretchers and started toward the main lines. There was no need to tell the Koreans to hurry; they moved as fast as they could. Occasionally enemy mortars reminded us that it was unhealthy to spend much time there unprotected by any trench or cover. "Doc" Minter, the corpsman, moved through the trench line calling out, "any wounded up there; anyone who needs a doctor?" The word went from tired and trembling lips to all who could still hear and understand. There was one Marine who crawled down the trench line, dazed and quiet. He was suffering from concussion. We told him to follow the stretcher which contained a wounded Marine. Back to the peace and safety of the aid station started the small groups of four carrying their precious burdens away from the mess and chaos of that hill.

Most of the men had to remain on Vegas. They were held in fixed positions by duty and valor. Their only question was, "when do you think we'll get off this hill?" They had a job to do, but they still wanted to taste the fruits of victory. They wanted to live just as I wanted to live. That was the last time I walked up Vegas hill where the "valley of the shadow of death" was a reality to all who passed by. What heroes were left out there the world will never know. When the next afternoon brought relief to Easy Company the men returned to camp without a complaint, too tired and weary to act like the returning conquerors that they were.

That night after showers and the first warm food for days the men began to talk in small groups gathered together in their tents. As I moved from tent to tent I could hear the retelling of a hero's deed, or softly the mentioning of a buddy's name and then the deep silence that comes when death has passed that way. Empty cots and empty hearts were silent reminders of friends who had gone their way. Lives were changed [in] those past few days. God had made His Presence felt to men who never felt they needed Him before. A trench became for some the stepping stone to heaven while to others it was the beginning of a new life with God. None were ashamed to admit their need of God—none held back a word of praise about Him.

In one group a reporter was gathering details for a story. He was going to tell the world about Vegas. Man after man gave him bits of battle news; told of friends who were brave and true. With eager and professional hands the reporter recorded dates, times, and facts in his notebook. Later he would weave into words the meaning of their actions. However, no written or spoken word could ever tell the thoughts of men who had fought and won a battle for an unknown outpost. How could anyone explain what was in their souls; these men who had seen the agony and pain of friends whose lives were touched by war? These men who

had lived in the hands of God "on a hill far away . . .?" God alone was the recorder of their lives.

Chaplain Newman was awarded a Silver Star for his part in the engagement from 26–27 March. His citation reads as follows and includes the fact that he courageously gave up his armored jacket, which was a very scarce item.

For conspicuous gallantry and intrepidity in action against the enemy while serving with a Marine infantry battalion in Korea on 26–27 March 1953. Serving as a chaplain, Lieutenant (jg.) Newman displayed outstanding courage, initiative, and devotion to duty. During the assaults on vital enemy held outpost positions, he continuously exposed himself to devastating enemy mortar and artillery in order to assist the stretcher bearers and comfort the wounded. *Expressing complete disregard for his personal safety, he courageously gave his armored vest to a Marine whose vest was unfit for wear and for the remainder of the 2-day period he went without this added protection in an area interdicted by hostile fire.*[4] During the reorganization phase when the enemy was only fifty to one hundred yards away, he fearlessly walked about the trench line offering words of encouragement and spiritual guidance to the men. His presence was a distinct comfort to the men and contributed in great measure to the maintenance of spirit and high devotion to duty among them. Lieutenant (jg.) Newman's outstanding actions and indomitable spirit served as an inspiration to all who observed him and were in keeping with the highest traditions of the United States Naval Service.

Chaplain Newman described the activity of a chaplain on the line. He said,

When the battalion is on the line, he trudges the ridgelines to hold services with a different company every day. He writes to the family of every new man who joins the battalion, regardless of faith.

He keeps a note pad full of requests to purchase things for the man when he goes to Seoul twice a month. He goes down with a jeep and trailer loaded with candy, clothing, and other supplies for orphans.

He comes back loaded with candles, radio tubes, gasoline lanterns and anything else his men have requested. Some of this he can get from the Army post exchange.

Chaplain Newman's devotion to his men and the Marine Corps is demonstrated by the occasion of the birthday of the Marine Corps. One is told that Chaplain Newman

. . . managed a cake and took off, unarmed and on foot, along a trail leading to the most extended outpost of the battalion.

Shells were landing on the position when Newman jumped into the main bunker with the cake. The handful of men holding the lonely post were cheered for days by his act.

Chaplain Nordby gives a general picture of the area occupied by the Division at this time,

---

4 The italics are the historian's.

A chaplain recalled to duty from his civilian parish finds that there is little here in Korea to remind him of the vast sweep and scope of the fast moving actions of World War II days. The front lines facing no-man's land extend for miles up and down hills, winding like the Great Wall of China across rolling terrain, rice paddies and great jagged peaks. The men live in sand bagged bunkers; two, three, and four to a bunker. The architecture and innovations in these dwellings depend upon the ingenuity of the occupants— and the American young men have never lacked in originality and imagination. Some of the bunkers are veritable bear traps and pitfalls of gadgets, latches, stoves, collapsible bunks, pinup pictures and the ever present supply of C-ration cans mixed with a ready stock of hand grenades. Practically all bunkers have some type of stove for heating and coffee making. In most cases one hot meal a day is carried up to the lines or troops are brought down in reliefs to advance mess tents.

The chaplain finds that his congregation on the line does not lead a safe and comfortable life. These men are harassed by rats and insects to say nothing of mud or the reddish colored Korean dirt. In spite of all this the morale of the troops on the front lines is the best in the service. It is here that one enjoys that peculiar feeling only experienced, unfortunately on the field of battle; the feeling that everyone is concerned with taking care of the other person. Such great passages as "Greater love, hath no man than this: that he lay down his life for a friend," becomes a beautiful common experience. Marines will not be stopped from going out under fire to get a buddy. None complain if they have to carry a friend a great distance to the forward aid bunker.

As for the battle actions, they are usually localized struggles involving squads, platoons and companies, sometimes battalions. However, the size of the units fighting is not a measure of their bitterness as far as the individual is concerned. The actions that carry up steep, 60° slopes in face of artillery and mortar fire and the desperate last stands of small units on outposts are as grim in their ways as anything the Marines witnessed on Guadalcanal, Tarawa, or Saipan. Many of the actions consist of night patrols and ambushes well forward of the lines, fought out in the dark at conversational range with both sides making desperate attempts to capture prisoners. Then again there are the quiet periods of waiting, listening, but little action for days or weeks at a time, and then it may break wide open.

Chaplain James C. Moore, Methodist, describes his experiences in the Reno and Vegas operations by saying,

The Chinese began an assault on these positions just at dusk, preceded by a tremendous artillery and mortar barrage which was to be numbered in the thousands of rounds. Such an assault meant casualties, so the chaplains gathered in the aid station at 1st Battalion.

The first casualties were already there, having been hit in the battalion command post itself. Shells were still coming in intermittently, so each man had his eye on the nearest hole. The wounded were taken care of, put on ambulances, and sent back to the medical companies in the rear. The doctors, the corpsmen, and the chaplains, settled down in foxholes to wait for the first load of casualties to come from the line. Everyone knew that the night would not be used for sleeping.

Those waiting at battalion aid pieced together what news they had. Outpost Reno had been overrun, and all the men on it were lost—Vegas had been taken—all the men were lost or captured—"Fox" company, from the 2d Battalion, was going out to Reno—the outposts must be retaken— there were many casualties. And so they waited.

The first wounded from the line came in. Bodies torn and bleeding—minds shaken from the incessant pounding they had received. The doctors worked quickly—putting on bandages—giving life-saving albumin—directing the corpsmen. The chaplains knelt over the men. The priest heard confessions and gave absolution—the Protestant chaplains prayed with them—all trying to comfort men whose bodies were suffering.

And the casualties continued to come.

Some of the men had no wounds on their bodies, their tags having only one word—"concussion." These men were wounded in their minds. They needed rest and sleep to wipe away the shock which had numbed their minds to reality. Some were shaking uncontrollably—some muttered words without meaning—but most just sat and stared—their eyes blank—seeing nothing.

The doctors asked the chaplains to take care of the men suffering from concussion, for the seriously wounded were demanding all their attention and skill. Then, the chaplains began a process which became all too familiar in the days which followed. The less serious cases were led away to places where they could sleep; the more serious were taken to one side and held for the doctor's examination when the rush slackened. The human mind can take great pressures, up to a certain point, and these men had passed that point.

On the outposts, the fighting continued; while in the rear areas, all efforts were turned towards assembling enough men and material to drive the Chinese from our old positions.

The coming of day brought to light many things. The supply tent near battalion aid, had received a direct hit from an enemy shell, but of all the medical supplies stored there, only a bottle of poison ivy lotion was broken. Around the aid station was the evidence always left by the wounded; blood-soaked clothing—torn and muddy—gaping helmets— empty boots, all bearing the individual imprint of their former owners.

The Marines began to send more men out to Vegas, so the chaplains had another task to perform. They hurried to the areas where the men disembarked from trucks, before beginning the long trek out to the hill. There, if time allowed, short services were held, and at the very least the Navy padres had prayer with the men. Whatever hour the men went out, the chaplains tried to be there—from early in the morning, until late at night.

One day ran into another, the fight went on without let up. All through the days and nights, the wounded continued to pour in. Men became groggy from lack of sleep, and the few minutes they managed to spend napping, only served to emphasize their need for real rest. The infantry went out to Vegas, were relieved, only to go out again. Men lost all sense of time.

You know the rest of the story. Vegas was retaken, and

Memorial Service.

A battalion commander in the 5th marines calls off names of men killed in the "Vegas" operation who were members of his unit at a regimental memorial service near the front.

---

is now held by the forces of the United Nations. The men who fought so hard for those hills are not there now. Some of them have gone home; some are resting, in reserve areas; some are still in hospitals; and there are many who are gone forever.

Chaplain E. Vaughan Lyons, Jr., Presbyterian, USA, adds the information that he and Chaplain Edward J. Kelly, Roman Catholic, were with Chaplain Moore. He adds,

It seemed as though the stream of wounded and dying would never cease. All night long the chaplains knelt beside the steady flow of litters, sometimes to repeat a passage of scripture, sometimes to give words of reassurance or comfort, sometimes to hear confessions or to administer the last rites, sometimes to merely joke or light a cigarette, but always they knelt beside each man to pray. For 5 long days the chaplains kept their vigil beside the wounded, while nearly 1,000 men passed through the aid stations. Thanks to the heroic and tireless efforts of doctors, corpsmen, and litter bearers hundreds of them are alive and recovered today. Few of them were evacuated without the ministry of a chaplain.

When it was over three weary chaplains tired, hungry, and dirty, returned to their tents to face the grim task of writing the heartbreaking letters informing the next of kin that the battle is forever ended for their husband or son. Not until this was done was there time for reflection. What about those who live through such an experience? What happens to them?

Combat is both a terrifying and an exhilarating experience. The pressure of combat intensifies the whole range of human emotions. Men in the strain of battle hate intensely, love intensely, fight intensely, and at the same time exhibit intense compassion for their buddies. Friendships are forever solidified. A spirit of camaraderie develops which is unlike anything else.

No one thinks of himself as a hero. Afterwards, each one thinks only of how much more he could have done or should have done. Whatever he did, it was not enough. He was there to do a job and at the time he did it as best he knew how. Riflemen, mortar men, wiremen, machine gunners, corpsmen, platoon leaders, doctors, chaplains accepted their role with only one thought and prayer. "Lord, give me the strength to do my job as well as possible." Afterward, whatever was done never seems to have been sufficient.

Chaplain Lyons said concerning the evacuation of the dead and wounded from Reno, "It was like the blind leading the blind. Some could not see, so others carried them along and held them up. Many of the men couldn't bring their stretchers off the hill." An observer says that "through the maelstrom of flying metal and destroyed life went the chaplain and his 20-man "crew"—cooks, clerks, radiomen, messengers, supplymen, truck drivers, and mess waiters, but all Marines." It was their job to save the remnants of the unit that had faced a thousand Chinese troops.

Chaplain Edward J. Kelly, Roman Catholic, is reported[5] holding the services on Palm Sunday for the veterans of Outpost Vegas by John Casserly. The reporter records.

I looked about the small, windblown tent at the faces of these young men. Some of their lips trembled out swift, short prayers. Others had their heads bowed, almost resting them on the backs of crude wooden benches . . . A young leatherneck's field pants were ripped down the left leg from the hip to his ankle. The back of his right boot was cut away. He wiped bleary eyes on a sleeve that had hit the dirt many times.

He walked to the Communion rail with a limp. Others followed. . . . After the service a sergeant asked, "What about the men on Reno?" . . . He quickly added: "What about the last few men?"

"They're all gone," I said.

He looked away and put his helmet on and began walking down the steep hill . . .

Shortly after the battle a Marine correspondent, T. Sgt. Bill Daum, described a memorial service con ducted by a chaplain,

With the First Marine Division in Korea—"Greater love hath no man than this; that a man lay down his life for his friends."

The words echoed between the brown hills and were swept away on a chill spring wind.

This was Korea. The men assembled with bowed heads were Marines—members of the 5th Regiment—gathered in a memorial service for buddies killed in action on bloody Vegas.

Most of these men had lost someone during the 3-day siege which saw first Chinese, then Marines, holding the battered knob. Anyone watching the hundreds of battle-hardened Leathernecks would find it hard to believe that 10 days before, this silent, prayful group had shattered one Red assault after another in a life and death struggle.

Battalion commanders called off a somber roll: Marines who would never again answer up at a muster. These were the dead.

Three volleys rang out and were lost on that same chill wind which took the chaplain's prayer.

Then came "Taps"; the finale in this drama of battle, its emotions and men.

Two chaplains were released from duty with the Marines in June and were presented with awards.[6] The first was Chaplain John P. Byrnes who w a s awarded the Bronze Star with a Combat "V." His citation reads in part,

When elements of the regiment were committed to the main line of resistance and subjected to intense enemy action, he traveled over roads that were under constant enemy observation administering both spiritual and physical aid to the wounded. Disregarding his personal comfort, he made continuous daily visits to men on the front line exerting every effort to render spiritual guidance to those in need of his services. Often, whenever patrols and raids were conducted forward of the main lines, he would spend long hours awaiting their return to be of whatever assistance he could.[7]

The second was Chaplain Gerald E. Kuhn who received the Commendation Medal with the authorization of a Combat "V," concerning this award was the following statement in part,

He provided moral and spiritual guidance and comfort to the personnel of the regiment and during periods when the unit was engaged in extensive combat operations, he disregarded his personal safety and comfort in order to assist in caring for the sick and wounded. Although frequently exposed to the hazards of enemy small arms, mortar and artillery fire, [he] helped evacuate the wounded and tendered spiritual consolation and peace to the severely injured.

Chaplain Walter Nordby, who was involuntarily recalled to active duty, wrote,

I have learned much more during this tour in Korea and Pendleton than I did all during the last war. I am sold on the Marine Corps 100 percent. My ministry has surely been a rich one with the Marines. In reserve my Character Guidance lectures were very well received with good discussions following. After the word got around that I wasn't trying to deliver sermons I even had the company commanders and platoon leaders attending. Things like that made me feel like a part of the fighting team.

It was at Easter time that Chaplain Matthew J. Strumski crusaded for Peace in Korea by traveling with an officially consecrated Pilgrim Virgin Statue sent from the Bishop of Fatima, Portugal.

Chaplain Samuel Sobel, Jewish Chaplain, was detached from the Division on 13 April. He was awarded a Bronze Star for his activity. His citation states in part,

Carrying out frequent trips to the front lines, he imparted strength and peace of mind to the troops throughout many days and nights while under heavy enemy artillery and mortar fire. Conscientious in his devotion to the fulfillment of his mission, he ministered to the spiritual needs of the wounded and dying at the front lines, forward aid stations and medical companies of the division. His inspiring efforts, resourceful initiative and unswerving devotion to duty throughout reflect the highest credit upon Lieutenant Sobel and the United States Naval Service.[8]

---

[5] In the *Philadelphia Inquirer,* 30 March 1953.
[6] These awards are noted here because of their application to this period.

[7] This chaplain was also awarded the Purple Heart for wounds sustained 27 February 1953.
[8] The Purple Heart was also awarded for wounds sustained on 29 March 1953.

Rainbow Village—Site of Little Switch.
An overall view of the village set up by the 1st Engineers Battalion. The main entrance is on the left.

Chaplain of the Year—Reserve Officers Association

The Reserve Officers' Association chose Chaplain Sobel as the "Chaplain of the Year" (1955) noting his work with Marines in Korea. The Four Chaplains Award was made by the Department of the District of Columbia at the dedication of the $100,000 Four Chaplains Memorial Fountain at National Memorial Park, Falls Church, Va., on 25 September 1955. Chaplain E. B. Harp, Jr., Chief of Chaplains accepted for Chaplain Sobel who was stationed overseas at the time. In part the citation read,

As the only Jewish Chaplain in the Marine Division he, without regard to his own personal safety, made frequent trips to the front lines and spent many days and nights with the men under heavy artillery and mortar fire in order to bring them the strength and consolation of their faith as well as many physical comforts and food.

Disregarding his personal comfort, he ministered to the spiritual needs of the wounded and dying at the front lines, forward aid stations, and medical companies of the Division. As a result of his spirit of self-sacrifice he was wounded in action.

Truce Talks

The resumption of the truce talks in April which were to lead to "Little Switch" focused world attention upon the participants in the true talks. Some indication of the character of the chief U.N. negotiator may be gained by the comments of two chaplains. Chaplain Newman stated that he served as Protestant Chaplain in the United Nations Peace Camp, conducting services for the delegates at Munsan-Ni. He testifies that Maj. Gen. William K. Harrison was a frequent attendant at these services and that he gave encouragement to the chaplain in his work. Chaplain Schnick while serving with the 1st Service Battalion also conducted worship services at the United Nations Base Camp. He tells of General Harrison, as he was leaving one of the services, taking the hand of the chaplain and saying, "Chaplain, you believe in the Bible, don't you?" Chaplain Schnick replied "Yes, sir, I do." The chaplain states, "He then said, in a way I won't forget and with feeling 'I do too.' This was one of the most memorable experiences that I had while serving in Korea."

Little Switch

Finally on 20 April the day had come when the prisoners, some of them after long periods of captivity, were to be returned. The Division Chaplain writes to Chaplain Harp concerning the exchange of prisoners, commonly called "Little Switch," which occurred on 20 April,

Today was a day of liberation for some of our prisoners of war who came through Panmunjom into open arms and warm hearts at Freedom Village in the 1st Marine Division sector. Everything possible was done to welcome them and make them comfortable.

This event marked one of the greatest opportunities for chaplains in the U.S. Naval Service. We were standing in our section of the processing lines by our altars ready to extend the hand of Christian fellowship to soldiers and Marines of many nations. They were eager and happy to receive our spiritual ministry. Many wept with joy in their hearts. We had prayer with them. We served Holy Communion; gave them New Testaments, Missals, and rosaries.

We made our sections as attractive as possible by getting flowers from the hillsides. We pinned the religious posters, church pennants, and spare altar cloths to the walls of the tents. The impression on the prisoners was terrific—as well as on generals, newspaper men, photographers, and all hands who were engaged in the processing work. I was never so proud and humble in trying to minister as a military chaplain.

I remember one man who wanted me to read a few verses from the Bible. He had been a prisoner for 29 months; I read the 23d Psalm. If I had not known it from memory I would have stalled on the verse: "Though I walk through the valley of the shadow of death, I will fear no evil, for Thou art with me." Both his and my eyes were full of tears. Then I read the Beatitudes and a part of I cor. 13.

It seems that they were allowed to conduct church services by holding prayer meetings and singing a few familiar songs from memory while prisoners. The ones with whom I talked said that they did not have any clergyman or priests to help them.

Tomorrow we will be back. Our chaplains in the lines and medical companies are ministering to battle casualties every day and night. Every chaplain I have is doing a wonderful job.

This letter speaks for itself, and bears eloquent testimony as to the work of the chaplains on this memorable day. Chaplain Meachum's own activity was pictured in a number of press releases.

There are other accounts of "Little Switch" as given by participating chaplains. The chaplains had arranged folding altars at the exchange site for Protestants, Catholics and Jews in one of the long rows of hospital tents erected by the United Nations. Their part in the operation became quickly apparent when the first 50 American prisoners arrived and sought first of all spiritual comfort after their long ordeal of sickness, pain, and captivity. Of those first 50, 35 took communion as their first act of freedom.

A number of the chaplains state that much of the credit for setting up the program should go to Chaplain Meachum. The men were brought in ambulances from the Panmunjom exchange point and unloaded. They were separated into four lines which went through two tents each. In the first tent Chaplain E. Vaughan Lyons, Jr., states that, the returnee

... was given a physical examination, preliminary medical treatment, and a new issue of clothing. He was then taken to the records section to establish identity and clarify his status. From there he was ushered into the press tent for interviews by representatives of the press, provided the returnee was willing for such an interview. From the press he was taken to the nourishment section where he sat down and was given a cup of soup or coffee.

It was at this stage that chaplains talked with the men. Chaplain Leo F. Rice, Roman Catholic, de-

---

Freedom Sign

A marine of the 1st Engineer Battalion puts the finishing touches on the sign to be placed at the medical camp where the prisoners will be received.

Released POW Pfc. Billy Brown talks with Chaplain Andrew J. Barry, Jr., upon arrival at Freedom Village.

Scenes From Little Switch

Chaplain Lonnie Meachum serves communion to Billy Penn shortly after his repatriation from the Communists.

Chaplain Richard W. Shreffler prays for Pfc. Reggie A. Sullivan shortly after the latter's release and arrival at Freedom Village.

---

scribes his experiences in a paper entitled "Rebirth in Freedom Village." He affirms that,

In the Marine tents we chaplains were placed in an ideal location. After the men had been given a military briefing, had been interviewed by the press, had changed from their blue Chinese uniforms of repatriation into the uniforms of free peoples, they were brought to the nourishment section. Here we chaplains were invited to meet them. In the four lines of tents each line was terminated by a visit to a little chapel. In this part of the tent a Protestant altar was set in one corner, a Catholic altar was in the other corner, and the Jewish chaplain was called when needed.

The men with whom I talked touched me deeply. They came in various conditions: some healthy and trim looking (with a wind burn from their long ride of several hundred miles), some just skin and bones. Some had stumps of legs left, some had withered arms. . . . Some looked as though they were TB cases, some looked emotionally aroused and confused. In some cases their hearing was impaired.

Our job as chaplains was not so much to question them on what had happened in general but to make them feel at home, to get them to relax a moment, to direct their thoughts along a religious line, and then to see if they wanted to make an act of thanksgiving to Almighty God. In general, most of the men did want just that, ASKED for it, and the greater majority of them wanted to receive Holy Communion.

When we met them at the coffee table usually a Catholic priest and a Protestant chaplain seated themselves with the man. We asked if they had been to church. They usually said: "On Christmas and Easter yes, but not most Sundays." One man showed us some pictures he had taken with a camera up there—and some pictures of what he said was

a religious ceremony. They told us that sometimes a man was allowed to keep his New Testament with him. I know of only one Catholic man who had an English missal with him on his return—although they had them when captured.

Chaplain Lyons records,

A very large percentage of the returnees requested communion; it was the first time that some of them had received the sacrament for 2 or more years. While prisoners they were permitted to hold religious services. At least that was true in the later months of their imprisonment. In the early days of the war, services were prohibited.

Since there were no chaplains in the camps the men organized their own services of worship. They sang hymns which they remembered. A few of them managed to keep New Testaments or Bibles, but most of them were confiscated when they were taken prisoner. The men reported that Chinese guards who understood English were present for each service and the scripture lesson as well as the hymns and sermon had to be cleared in advance of the service.

Chaplain Lyons gives testimony to the fact that,

The privilege of distributing the sacrament to these men will long live in my memory as one of the great thrills of my ministry in the service. Participating in these individual communion services I gained a new appreciation of the meaning and significance of the sacrament.

Chaplain Rice speaks of the reports concerning worship,

Some Protestant men told me the Catholics would gather for devotions. Other men tell us that when the rosary was said the Communists would break up the meeting because

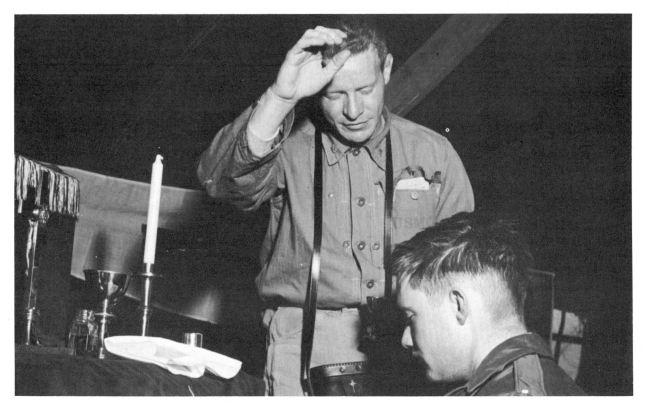

Thomas H. Waddill is given communion by Chaplain Vaughan Lyons at Freedom Village. Waddill was captured by the Communists in the Reno action.

they said "we don't know what you are doing." Since there are captive priests admittedly, and these could have been made available to the Catholic men, it is apparent that these men were deprived of an essential element of their religion—namely, the administration of the sacraments by legitimately ordained priests.

Some of the men made their own crosses and crucifixes by melting down the metal from their toothpaste and shaving cream tubes. There are a number of personal accounts given by chaplains. Chaplain Rice tells how,

One man really touched me. He sat down at the coffee table. I introduced the Protestant chaplain and then myself as the Catholic priest. He told us that he had not been to the Sacraments the whole 2 years in prison. He said his rosary had been taken from him. He asked for a rosary and also to go to confession and communion. He then looked around, his eyes twinkled and he said: "Gee, I'm free." And then he filled up, sobbed heavily, and after a few sobs said "Gee, Father, I'm sorry I'm crying." I said "That's all right—I'm with you." And I'm sure those others sitting at the table with him were crying too. The Division chaplain, Chaplain Meachum, stepped up behind the man, braced the man's shoulder and said: "All right son, come along and you'll be all right." We all stood up and directed him to the chapel. I took him by the arm and led him to the chair

for confession. He was then ready for communion. As he sat down to make his thanksgiving I gave him a rosary. He asked me to put it around his neck. I suppose his feeling was: On my neck it's more my own." Also, the rosary is another one of the signs we use to indicate the members of the union of communion of saints. As he stood up I put my arms around his shoulder and led him to the man who was to take him to the Army hospital just outside our tent. "I hope to see you back in the States," I said in farewell.

Other Roman Catholic Chaplains were also serving. Chaplain Elmer F. Ernst was with Chaplain Rice. Chaplain Andrew J. Barry was on hand to assist where the British Commonwealth men were being processed. Chaplain Thomas Edwards assisted with other UN troops. Two other chaplains, Edward J. Kelly and John T. Moore participated. The Jewish chaplain attached to the Division at this time was Chaplain Murray I. Rothman. He worked along with the other chaplains in both "Little and Big Switch."

Chaplain Lyons adds this story,

About a month before Marines of the 5th Regiment were engaged in a heavy battle for three forward outposts. Outpost Reno and Vegas were completely overrun by the Communist forces. A few Marines were recovered from Vegas, but there was no indication of what had become of the men on Reno. It was known that many of them had been killed and that perhaps a few had been captured. Among the men on Reno was a Navy Hospital corpsman from Fort Worth, Tex., named Thomas Waddill. About 2 weeks after the engagement Mrs. Waddill wrote to the regimental chaplain of the 5th Marines stating that she had received a telegram from the Navy Department informing her that her son was missing in action. Since there were no survivors from Reno it was not known what had become of any of the men. It was believed that most or all of them had died, although this information was not conveyed to her. The chaplain's closing sentence of his reply was, "We unite with you in our prayer for peace and for safety of your son."

Again Mrs. Waddill wrote a beautiful letter to the chaplain in which she said, "While we still hope, it is good to know too that Tom enlisted in the Navy, and also volunteered to go with Marines to Korea because he considered it his duty, that he had hospital training to offer. He believed the war worth while." In closing she stated, "Our faith is in God, and in the ultimate goodness of his plans."

The chaplain was amazed to see Corpsman Thomas Waddill walk through the line on Thursday as a returned prisoner of war. Even though Mrs. Waddill was immediately informed that her son was returned, the chaplain wrote to assure her that he was well and on his way home for a happy day of reunion. Such are the experiences of the chaplains at Freedom Village. Each man has his own story to tell.

Chaplain Rice concludes,

To hear them tell that they did try to gather for Divine Service, that many of them did pray every day shows that these men have the elements of free men in them. They have initiative in them: for even now they feel that others worse off than they should have been released before them (and they so told the Commies); that they wanted to make use of confession and communion, receive a new rosary, say a psalm of thanksgiving, or pray with their Rabbi— these are real men . . . These are the men whose eyes lighted up when the chaplain would tell them: "This is 'Operation Little Switch'—We hope it is the start of 'Operation Big Switch'—and the still bigger switch to the ways of Peace."

Chaplain Rice seems to express it for all the chaplains when he says, "It was the most touching thing in my life."

Chaplains of the Division observe the Sabbath on every day of the week. Among the accounts of "Continuous Sabbath" is the one given by Chaplain Richard G. Hutcheson, Jr., which he calls "Sunday Comes on Wednesday in Korea."

Sunday comes on Wednesday at Easy Battery. The Protestant chaplain is a jeepborne circuit rider, with scheduled services at 13 different places each week. So Protestant church-goers at "E" Battery, 2d Battalion, 11th Marines, congregate at 3 o'clock on Wednesday afternoons. It makes little difference to them. Manning the 105-mm howitzers, light artillery workhorses of the 1st Marine Division, is a 24-hour-a-day, 7-day-a-week job. Days pass in nameless succession for men at war.

A jeep, identified as that of the chaplain in appropriately ecclesiastical Old English script, rolls into the Battery area. The time is 1415 on Wednesday, 22 April 1953. For Chaplain R. G. Hutcheson, Jr., one of the four chaplains serving the 11th Marines, this is the fourth stop of the day. He started the morning with an early, unscheduled visit to a Rockets Battery, where night before last one man was killed and several others injured in an operational accident. From there to "D" Battery for a 10:30 service and for lunch in the new mess tent (incoming enemy artillery rounds showed an uncomfortable liking for the vicinity of the old one a couple of weeks ago!). Then on to "F" Battery for another service right after chow. And now "E." This will be the chaplain's last service of the day, but there is a Bible class tonight at the CP of another battalion.

Easy's guns are quiet now, but the first glance shows that everyone is hard at work on the parapets and bunkers. Winter weather took its toll of sandbags. They were serviceable as long as they stayed frozen, but now spring has thawed them and the rotten ones must be replaced quickly, the bunkers rebuilt. It is hard, backbreaking work. The chaplain makes the round of the gun positions, stopping briefly to chat with the men as they work. If someone has a problem to talk over with him an appointment is arranged after the service. At Gun No. 1 work on the parapet has been completed and several of the men are taking a break. The chaplain sits down to visit. S. Sgt. Stuart H. Floyd of Chester, Ga.—a member of the First Baptist Church there— wonders if the chaplain has heard how many sick and wounded Marines have been returned at Panmunjom so far. What about their physical condition? What have they said about the treatment they received from the Chinese? The talk goes on from there to a discussion of the possibility of a truce, and then to rotation. All topics lead eventually to rotation!

It is 10 minutes till 3, and the chaplain walks up to the mess tent, now converted into a chapel. Sergeant Floyd, a regular churchgoer, says he will be on up in a few minutes. A look inside the tent shows that everything is ready. Pfc. Kenneth L. Terrell of Des Moines, Iowa, a future Baptist minister and now a very capable chaplain's assistant, has been hard at work. The portable altar kit has been brought in from the jeep and arranged on a mess table at one end. Benches have been placed in front of it, between the tables. The folding organ is open, in its place to the left of the altar. Hymnals are on the benches.

Pfc. Edward J. Evans, of Trenton, N.J., has arrived early for a few words with the chaplain before the service starts. Last Wednesday Eddie was baptized, and a letter is now on the way to Ewing Township Presbyterian Church in Trenton, asking that he be received into membership. His wife is already a member, and he hopes, sometime after next October, to walk into that church with a brand new baby to be baptized! Eddie has been reading his Bible regularly, and he has come across a passage in St. Matthew that he doesn't entirely understand. After a few minutes' discussion its meaning is cleared up.

The congregation is arriving now. As the men take their seats rifles are laid aside, but kept close at hand as regulations require. Attendance is small today. Most of the regulars are present, though. S. Sgt. Philip L. Foss, of the Elm St. Methodist Church in South Portland, Maine . . . Phil was very active in his home church. President of the Youth Fellowship at one time, and secretary-treasurer of the Sunday School. Cpl. Allen N. Turner, of Statesville, N.C.—former Sunday School superintendent at Pleasant Grove Presbyterian Church. Cpl. Samuel M. Baer, member of the Lutheran Church in Watsonville, Calif. Cpl. Samuel B. Fielder, Jr., of Bel Air, Md., where he belongs to Mount Zion Methodist Church, Cpl. Gayle E. Bracken of Mundy's Corner, Pa., member of Pike Brethren Church. Pfc. Harrison C. Grimes—not a church member at present, but thinking of joining—a future Baptist.

The service opens, as usual, with hymns requested by the men. Today the first request is for "Jesus Calls Us, O'er the Tumult." Then "Stand Up, Stand Up for Jesus"; "I Love to Tell the Story"; "Holy, Holy, Holy, Lord God Almighty"; and "Rock of Ages, Cleft for Me." Nobody asks for "The Old Rugged Cross" today, although that one is seldom overlooked!

Time for hymn singing is about up, and the more formal part of the service begins with a responsive reading. Today's selection is entitled "Trust in the Lord"—part of the 63d Psalm. During the reading the guns of the Battery, silent until now, open up with a "Battery one." Temporarily the voices are drowned out. The worshipers are conscious of the fact that outside the tent their buddies in the parapets are still fighting a war; that a few thousand yards to the north are the Chinese Communists who will be on the receiving end of the rounds that just left the guns; that a few miles to the west sick and wounded prisoners are being exchanged at Panmunjom; that truce talks will reopen there on Saturday, in a renewed attempt to end the war which is all around—which, in this service of worship to Almighty God is so far away, yet so very close. The service continues with prayers, a Scripture reading from the Book of Job. The chaplain, in his sermon, talks about the way Job met tragedy and suffering in his life. He knows that one of the buddies of the men present was killed 2 weeks ago and that they felt it deeply; he knows that before rotation date rolls around others may be touched by tragedy. The sermon is designed to show that in a firm faith men find their greatest strength to meet life's hardships. The men sing "Faith of Our Fathers" as the service closes, and as always they sing heartily. After the benediction they pick up their rifles, shake hands with the chaplain, and return to the guns. Sergeant Foss sticks around for a minute. He has just received the first pictures of his brand new daughter—taken 12 hours after she was born, on April 3d—and he wants the chaplain to see them. He is very proud of her, and he has a right to be.

A few minutes and the church is folded up, packed away in the jeep. The tent is once more a mess hall. Sunday is over, and it is Wednesday again at Easy Battery. But for a short time 11 men, from 10 States, from 7 denominations, have been a Christian Church. It happens hundreds of times every day, in the 1st Marine Division and all across the Korean front. It is a commonplace, a normal part of service life. But it is a source of pride, too, this knowledge that wherever the American Soldier, Sailor, Airman, or Marine is, there the Christian Church is.

About this time Chaplain Kenneth D. Killin was awarded a Letter of Commendation for the period 26 November to 20 April 1953. Chaplain Killin is described as one who constantly disregarded his personal safety and comfort "in order to minister aid and comfort to the wounded . . . His determined efforts and selfless devotion to duty served as a constant inspiration to all who observed him."

The 1st Marine Air Wing

The chaplains continued their fine work at the 1st Marine Air Wing. There were few changes in the Roster of Chaplains. Chaplains F. P. O'Malley and J. F. Cloonon, Roman Catholics, were

MAG 12 Chapel (Exterior).

This chapel was located at K–6, south of Seoul. Note the sandbags on the roof placed there to protect the roof against high winds.

MAG 33 Chapel.

Using flat stone from the ocean floor on the east coast of Korea this chapel located at Pohang (K–3) has a striking appearance. The bell was specially cast in Taegu and was paid for by selling fertilizer bags from the air strip.

Monthly Meeting.

Chaplain Parker dressed in Korean garb welcomes Brig. Gen. Alexander W. Kreiser, Jr., assistant commanding general of the 1st MAW. The other chaplains do not appear to be overburdened although they are equipped to "carry the load." Other than Chaplain Parker and the general those pictured here are: Chaplain J. H. Lampe; Col. Samuel S. Jack, Chief of Staff; Chaplains G. J. Clark; E. C. Mulligan; E. R. Lineberger; and J. W. Paul.

on board prior to 6 January. They were assigned to MAG 12 and Hedron 1 respectively. Publicity and citations acknowledged the accomplishments of the chaplains. Noteworthy is the award of the Bronze Star to Chaplain Paul J. La Duca covering the period 29 January to 21 December. Besides traveling over hazardous terrain in subzero weather to minister to his own men, the chaplain

directed the members of his congregation in helping the orphans of the area and assisted in providing aid to 2 destitute orphanages with a total enrollment of approximately 250 children, thereby implementing the work of agencies concerned with creating a strong feeling of friendship to those in need.

Chaplain Parker wrote on 6 December referring to the Marine Memorial Orphanage at Pohangdong and of the Eden Marine Orphanage at MAG 12. He also stated that during the 8 months that he had been in Korea that he had distributed 24 tons of clothing from the States. "The Post Office men are often angry because of the weight of the packages. The Commanding General has requested me to keep his jeep loaded with bundles of clothes so he can pass them out to the Korean naked." He further stated that a film called "Operation Orphans" was made for TV. "At no other time in my naval career have I had such an opportunity to help suffering humanity," he affirmed.

Visitor.

Francis Cardinal Spellman with Chaplain Mulligan and Chaplain Parker during his Christmas visit to K–3 in 1952.

Christmas Scene.

Chaplain Twitchell, FMF, Pac, Chaplain, stands with Chaplain O'Malley and Chaplain Parker beside the wing chapel nativity scene.

Chaplain M. H. Twitchell, FMF chaplain, visited the Wing and the Division the last of December and the first of January.

It is noted in the later award of his Commendation Ribbon that Chaplain Edwin C. O'Malley was responsible "for the inspirational appearance of His Eminence, Francis Cardinal Spellman before Wing personnel on 31 December 1952."

Chaplain J. H. Lampe cites the Christmas party of 1952 as an outstanding experience. MAG 12 had on board, 400 orphans from 4 different orphanages, which they supported. They each received gifts and saw Santa, but ". . . the tremendously important thing was that the men got to see or care for these children as if they were their own . . . and these children had a firsthand experience of being cared for by someone who, for the moment, was a real "daddy." It was more than the giving of gifts—it was the giving of themselves and their love that made the experience a vital, living thing for all concerned."

Articles appeared in the *Ladies Home Journal* [1] and the *National Geographic Magazines* [3] concerning the work of the unit with orphans. The former article described "Operation Kidlift" and told about the work of Marines at Kangnung, and presented the part played by Chaplains—Weidler and La Duca. [9] A TV film was produced to present the story of the MAG–12 orphanage at Kecksa-ri. By this time the Marine Memorial Orphanage at Pohangdong has 6 buildings and 5,700 pyong of ricelands (a pyong is 36 square feet). The MAW also took over the support of an orphanage at Pyongtaek, 40 miles south of Seoul. Chaplain O'Malley noted on 3 March that a number of the Roman Catholic chaplains were about to go on a retreat to Seoul for a Day of Recollection.

Chaplain Fenstermacher, assigned to the Gun Battalion and the H&S Battery in Pusan, found that it was much better to have services on weekdays rather than to try to serve all batteries on Sunday. It ". . . permitted me more time (for) visiting and counselling with the men at the batteries both on Sunday and weekdays."

By this time the Wing has five chapels constructed.

Forces Afloat

No vessels of our forces were sunk during the period under consideration, although previously, in August, the tug SARSI, was sunk by a mine resulting in nine casualties. There was an increase in antiaircraft fire

---

[1] *Ladies Home Journal,* December 1952.
[3] *National Geographic Magazine,* February 1953.
[9] Cp. p. 227f.

and for the period 1 June 1952 to 31 May 1953 Marine and naval units lost 170 aircraft from that source, but only three were lost in aerial combat. There was enough action on ORISKANY for the chaplain to have the problem of where Mass should be held. Chaplain G. J. Barras states, "The wardroom was used for the first Mass at 0800 to the accompaniment of launching planes and bouncing bombs." They moved below to the crew's lounge for the remaining two masses though at times they moved down even one more deck.

Chaplain Warren L. Wolf was cited (in lieu of a Bronze Star) for his work aboard the BADOENG STRAIT. Many fine things are said about this chaplain including "While in the Yellow Sea, this officer conducted services on numerous United Nations ships of the screening element in addition to those on his own ship, which services . . . were invariably well received by his hosts." Chaplain Wolf indicates that he felt like "the Bishop of the Yellow Sea as I serviced Canadian, British, and American Destroyers. The Dutch could not use me as my German was too out of date." He also indicates an improvement at the staging area, Sasebo, and states that Chaplains Lonergan and Brink, who were stationed there, were very helpful. Chaplain Walsh relieved the former 1 April.

A number of chaplains in the Fleet note the zeal of their personnel for religious administrations. It is evident that the chaplains were doing a great deal to accept the challenge thus presented. As in previous periods the ships' companies were awake to the needs of others and contributed generously to worthy causes both in America and in Korea.

The hospital ships the REPOSE, HAVEN, and the CONSOLATION continued to carry out their missions of mercy. They too expressed an interest in the orphans in Korea.

MSTS

A number of chaplains continued to serve with MSTS. Their reactions to their duty is of great interest. Chaplain John W. Robb pointed out that the ship's primary function was transporting troops to the war area. He felt the importance of not "preying upon the fears of the men, but rather in making a constructive religious appeal."

Chaplain Reginald A. Berry tells of the cooperation of the Commanders of the Military Departments aboard the ships on which he had served. He tells how the executive officer of the Military Department of the USNS Gen. D. E. AULTMAN held Roman

Catholic Rosary Services when Catholic Chaplains were unavailable. Chaplain James R. Spaid tells of the reaction of some commanding officers to the work of chaplains. He affirms that several commanding officers stated that until they came to transport duty and saw the program of chaplains working under them, they had not realized the importance of the chaplains in the military organization and have thus given them including himself, their full and complete cooperation.

Chaplain Spaid also tells of an Army lieutenant who had come

. . . aboard for a voyage to Korea who had no use for the Church and anything it stood for due to some unfortunate experiences his family had had in his younger days. He stated that he had given chaplains a "hard time" at every opportunity. Upon his seeing our full schedule of daily services for almost every faith, the schedule for Bible classes, choir practices etc., he decided to check in on a few and talk a little with the men hoping to aggravate them a bit and knock the program apart. About half way out from the States this officer took sick for the first time in his life and called for me and in the course of our conversation he uncovered his plan, but he admitted it had utterly failed for he said he had absolutely no success in discouraging the men attending these various activities; in fact, he felt himself being influenced by the services. So he saw me each day for a period of instruction and I don't believe he missed a single daily service after that for the balance of the trip. I wrote his wife at the officer's request, in relation to his decision which made her most happy and inspired her to get back in active work in her former church. I thought it might be a temporary thing, but I have the word of the Port Chaplain at Pusan, Korea that this officer during his entire stay in Korea was one of his most loyal supporters and was very active in assisting the chaplain there. The officer now has returned to the States and now I have had several letters from them stating that they feel that their decision has brought a closeness in their lives they have never before experienced.

Each voyage of an MSTS ship is a new experience. New leadership is sought and found. Chaplain Spaid speaks of his volunteers, saying,

. . . the most glory is due those many young men who volunteered their services to assist me in the entire program. Those men who played the organ, directed our many choirs, those who sang solos, who did the ushering, who assisted in the libraries as well as the religious services as well as those who actually conducted rosaries, Bible classes etc., did a magnificent job in the making of our program possible. Without them we would never have been able to have such a complete program. On transports, we have a very minimum of our own personnel and as a result our congregations are different each trip; these volunteers did an invaluable piece of work and certainly should be recognized for their most unselfish efforts.

Chaplain Nelson speaks of the Bible study class as the best source for Sunday School teachers and choir members.

Chaplain Spaid says concerning the variety of services,

It was nothing unusual to have Protestant, Catholic, Jewish, Latter Day Saints, Christian Science, Pentecostal, Seventh Day Adventist (and even Mohammedan on one trip) and others . . . held on one day. Catholic and Protestant services are held daily and many of the other groups especially the L.D.S. had services on a daily basis. In addition to the services, Bible classes and instruction classes were conducted daily along with daily choir practices.

Chaplain Nelson reports on counseling stating that it varies greatly, depending on whether a person is going to Korean waters or away from them. Sex education, marriage, and family life were the emphasis on the way out. On the way back the main emphasis was on civil readjustment. He also speaks on counseling men who are interested in full time or part time religious vocations. Chaplain Jesse D. Harder also confirms the latter stating that "Several men have indicated their desire to become chaplains. A number of men want to become chaplain's assistants." From the reports of the chaplains it would appear that character education lectures were held aboard MSTS vessels and were well received. Collateral duties were as numerous as ever. Chaplain Nelson says that in the Special Services program alone, "On some trips we have as high as 50 members of ship's company and troop personnel under our supervision." From the listing of activities aboard his ship it would appear that Chaplain Peter J. Marron would need as much help as Chaplain Nelson had.

Chaplain Rauzelle M. Johnson tells of a voyage on an ocean that was "pacific" in name only. In fact he was packing his congregation in. He recalls that,

The chapel area was filled. The ship took a roll while we were reading the responsive reading; we had to stop the reading. A crowded chapel was about half full since the men were sliding from side to side. When the reading was resumed the chaplain read: "Arise, O Lord." And the congregation read: "And save me, O, my God." And they meant every word of it. The normal trip took 12 days; this one took 19 days.

Chaplain Norman B. Holmes calls attention to his 2-year shipboard duty serving the Korean theater as marking "the first time in more than 25 years that a Christian Science Navy Chaplain has served afloat and in combat waters." It also appears that Chaplain Holmes was the second chaplain of his affiliation to serve in the naval chaplaincy. Concerning services aboard his ship, Chaplain Holmes reports,

Aboard each ship my primary duty was to provide for the spiritual welfare of all embarked personnel. To this end I conducted Sunday and daily Protestant Church services underway with one Communion service each outbound and inbound voyage. In addition Sunday and daily Roman Catholic Rosary services were arranged for personnel of that faith whenever there was no passenger Catholic chaplain available to hold Mass. Furthermore, services were arranged weekly for personnel of the Latter Day Saints and Jewish faiths. Finally, since I am a member of the Christian Science Church, I also conducted Sunday and midweek Christian Science services.

Chaplain of the Year, B'nai B'rith

On 12 February 1953 Chaplain Robert D. Goodill was serving on the GEORGE CLYMER when 75 miles away the SS PRESIDENT PIERCE was shaken by a blast after which fire broke out on the vessel. While the CLYMER was hastening to assist the stricken ship the chaplain asked for and received permission to board the vessel upon arrival. It took 5 hours to arrive on the scene. Meanwhile some of the injured had been transferred to the BARRETT. The PIERCE was determined to continue on course but requested a fire-fighting party. At 0300 Chaplain Goodill was the first to board the vessel. He headed to the scene of action where a hatch had been blown completely open. He assisted in fighting the fire which was consuming part of the cargo of oxygen tanks, rubber tires, and other inflammable material. Learning of casualties he went to minister unto them. Later he attempted to go to the BARRETT as he was informed that one of the men taken aboard had died. He notified the Captain of the PIERCE of this loss and returned to the wounded. He "offered spiritual consolations to the sufferers regardless of their religious affiliations." He subsequently was designated as "Navy Chaplain of the Year," for 1953 by the Chaplain A. D. Goode Lodge of B'nai B'rith.

CHAPTER TEN

KOREAN DEFENSE

Summer and Fall 1953

1 May–27 July 1953

After the prisoners had been exchanged in the "Little Switch" Operation the UN representatives on 26 April began full negotiations for an Armistice. The problem had been made difficult by the refusal of 114,500 Chinese and 340,000 North Koreans to return to their homeland. It was further complicated by the Communists insisting that they be returned to them even if force had to be used.

The war was "stepped up" late in May and by the first of June whenever truce prospects brightened the enemy would increase his efforts to gain ground along the MLR (Main Line of Resistance). A number of outposts changed hands with no appreciable change occurring in the territory held by either side. The attacks ranged from company to division size with the heaviest concentration located in the eastern sector. Anchor Hill and Hill 812 passed into enemy hands in late May and early June. Heavy action followed in the central sector. The ROK forces were pushed back in several areas, and the Fleet was called to support them. The ships involved in this support action were the BOXER, LAKE CHAMPLAIN, PHILIP-PINE SEA, and the PRINCETON. One of the heaviest bombardments of the war occurred in the effort to recapture Anchor Hill. The NEW JERSEY, BREM-ERTON, MANCHESTER and the ST. PAUL assisted in this action.

It was evident as early as the end of the first week of June that the anticipated terms of the Armistice which involved a divided Korea did not please President Rhee. He asserted that the South Koreans would fight to the bitter end for a United Korea. This feeling of discontent erupted in demonstrations staged by the South Koreans on 26 June. Seemingly in reply to these demonstrations the Communists launched one of their heaviest attacks of the war. They struck with 6 divisions on 13 July using 80,000 troops against 60,000 ROK soldiers on a 20 mile front. The South Koreans were pushed back as much as 7

miles. In support of the ROK forces over 500 sorties were flown daily by the Fleet aircraft.

The "East Berlin" attack occurred on Sunday night, 19 July. It was preceded by a Communist concert of Chinese and American music after which at 2030 the Chinese attacked with 1,500 troops. Rather bitter fighting followed. On the 24th "Boulder City" was under attack. The next day what was called a "flare-up" took place at Outpost Esther and at the Berlin complex. It was on this occasion that the 5th and 7th Marines repulsed a 3,000 man attack.

Fleet action continued until the cease fire with the ST. PAUL firing the last round of the war at sea at 2159, 27 July 1953. Peace had come but only after 136,862 American casualties of which 24,386 had been killed or died of wounds. A bugler sounded "Taps" at the 1st Marine Division.

The 1st Marine Division

The 1st Division was removed from the line 4 May 1953 after 20 months of fighting. On the 29th they returned to repulse a 2-day attack by the Communists. They were again returned to reserve on 5 June and remained there until 8 July when they were ordered into the sector previously manned by the 25th Infantry and in time for "Berlin." It was about 2 weeks later that "Boulder City," the last major action of the war, took place.

The Chief of Chaplain's Visit

One of the important events during this period of "Korean Defense" was the visit of the newly appointed Chief of Chaplains.

On 16 May Chaplain Edward B. Harp, Jr., Rear Admiral, left Washington for the Far East. He was accompanied by Chaplain Joseph P. Mannion, Assistant Director of the Division. At Pearl Harbor Chaplain Warren F. Cuthriell, Fleet Chaplain, joined the group. Most of the 200 chaplains in the Pacific Ocean area were visited. Chaplain Harp brought the Me-

Chief of Chaplains Visits.

A number of chaplains accompany the chief of chaplains on his visit to the 1st Marine Division, on 29 May 1953. Pictured here are (left to right) Chaplain Bak Jong Won, Korean Marine Corps; Chaplain W. F. Cuthriell, Pacific Fleet; Rear Adm. E. B. Harp, chief of chaplains; Chaplain J. P. Mannion, assistant, Chaplains Division; Chaplain Kim Dok Son, Navy chaplain with Korean Marines; Chaplain D. J. Silvers, COMNAFE; Chaplain J. A. Whitman, COMNAFE; and the division chaplain, L. W. Meachum.

morial Day Message at the 1st Marine Division. These words of Chaplain Harp deserve attention:

. . . let me hasten to say that there is ample justification for your presence here in Korea. No—it's not for political or economic reasons, as we might be tempted to feel at times. This conflict here is not an isolated incident far removed from the rest of the world. On the contrary, this might be one of the last bastions upon which hangs the very fate of our western civilization.

You are here because Communism is endeavoring to engulf the world. It is no more or less than that. For a long time too many of us have maintained a stubborn blindness—too many have gravely underestimated the diabolical forces which the Communists have let loose upon our world. It's hardly necessary for me to tell you that we are not up against something superficial, but something that is critical and profound. We are up against a way of life, a philosophy, yes—a religion, if you will—which seeks to destroy the very concept of God—all personal freedom and thereby enslave the whole human race. And no where are we in closer grip with this force than right here in Korea.

What happens here and the ultimate decisions that will be made, may very easily determine the very fate of our civilization—of our way of life, possibly for generations to come. It is for this that our departed heroes—those whom we are now honoring—have fought and have died.

Chaplain Harp was told by General Pollock, the commanding general, that the chaplain is one of the most important persons in the Division.

The Chief of Chaplains returned to Washington on 10 June, expressing his gratitude for the fine work of the chaplains he had visited and for the keen interest in and support of the programs of chaplains on the part of commanding officers. He found an increased emphasis being placed upon the Character Education program. He felt that the morale of military personnel was excellent.

"Battle Reports"

Chaplain Meachum in a letter of 23 June notes that General Pate cut the ribbon and made a speech at the dedication of the new division chapel the previous Sunday. On 25 July he writes:

We hope we are just through winding up another hassel [1] that started early last night. The 7th Regiment took another beating, along with some elements of the 1st and the 5th Regiments. I was up all night visiting the medical companies and supervising the assignment and work of chaplains. A few casualties were expected to arrive late at the medical companies when I left at noon.

The infantry chaplains are doing a superb job in their battalion aid stations. Chaplains attached to separate battalions are relieving the medical battalion chaplains to give constant coverage in the medical companies. These are the worst "clobbered" of any hassel since I've been out here. We are having many head and chest casualties, and many arm and leg amputations.

The last accounts of the battle action are given by several chaplains. Chaplain Peter J. Bakker, American Baptist, tells something of the fighting as seen in his sector:

On the 7th of July we moved on the line in the Chang Dang sector, just north of Seoul, and had our camp at the foot of Hill 229. Berlin and Esther were on our right flank. My opportunities were practically limitless. I held two or three services a day with the men right on the Main Line of Resistance, and in front of it on the Outpost. This required a good deal of hiking, but that never hurt anyone. The services were small, but very profitable.

The enemy—Luke as we call him—3 years ago we called them—"Gooks" apparently did not always appreciate the services. We had just finished a service in the Easy Company area when 13 or 14 76 shells came flying in on us. The men holler: "Chink on the way", and everyone ducks into a bunker, and it is quite an experience . . . especially with a large quantity of Napalm stored near by.

Some may say that it just happened that way, but I believe it was God's guidance and protection. Early one afternoon my driver, Pfc. B. Holloway, and I were on our way down the Panmunjom road for a service when I noticed an outpost some distance in front of the MLR, and wondered who was up there. We investigated, and found a group of Korean Marines, and a group of Marines from another regiment. They said that they did not have a service for 3 months. We had a wonderful time—including songs by the Koreans, and preaching to them through an interpreter. We then proceeded to our original point, and found that while we were at the service, many "rounds" landed on and around the bunker where we were going to hold our service.

Our first Marine to be hit last month was the result of a mortar blast—hitting the man, Private (First Class) Hansen in the chin, neck and left arm. One of our corpsman was hit about the same time by a mortar. Our first KIA (killed in action) was a Lieutenant Stumbo from Lancer, Ky. A mortar blast hit right over him, and a deep gash right behind the ear did the damage. I had a memorial service for him by the Battalion Aid Station, just after he was hit, with his commanding officer and fellow officers paying their last respects to a fine Marine.

[1] Boulder City.

Land mines proved to be a continual source of trouble. Our patrols were continually stepping on them, and the terrific blast that it gives a man in the legs is anything but pretty. We lost quite a few legs because of them. I had the opportunity on several occasions to help carry some of these men back up the hills after they were wounded. God was merciful in particular with two of these men—one Alfred Kalinowski, sergeant, had his leg in a horrible condition. The corpsman did a wonderful job in stopping the flow of blood, and even though he lost a leg, he is coming along nicely. Another lad, a big colored boy, stepped on a mine, and has lost both of his legs, but is coming along in good shape.

One of our patrols going out to hill No. 90 was ambushed about 10 p.m. Reinforcements were sent out, and another group had to be sent out to retrieve that angel squad. We were busy ministering to the wounded all that night, and on through the morning. We only were able to get two of the KIA's, and I had the privilege of taking them back to our C.P. During the next day we spotted five more dead lying on the hill, but were unable to go out and pick them up as Luke had the entire area zeroed in. That evening the funeral procession went to pick up the fallen Marines. We plastered the surrounding area with outgoing of various kinds. The men made a sweep of the hill, picked up seven valiant Marines. I proceeded with a squad of men to the bottom of the hill and helped carry those seven out to the Panmunjom road and safety. As you may observe, we were right adjacent to the Panmunjom area with its no fire zones, etc. As I rode back to our Command Post in an APC (armored personnel cargo) vehicle, I prayed for the next of kin of each one, and remembered that each one was dear to God, and to an entire circle of loved ones at home. Right behind our procession, Luke was blasting our trail with mortars.

Late one evening we received the word that some men on our left flank had received some mortar blasts. I carried one, George Hallabaugh, Jr., from Billings, Mont., into the aid station. He had just received a chest wound, and Dr. Roger Milnes asked for a copter to take him to the Medical Battalion. We carried George up the hill to the copter strip and waited for the helicopter. I was holding George's hand, talking to him, and praying for him. After assisting him in the copter I gave him a parting prayer, and told him everything would be all right, and closed the door. We all skooted down a small bank, hid our eyes from the dust and heard the copter take off, only to sputter and then saw this horrible crash with several flashes of light. We raced the 20 yards to the copter, and I saw three people—two inside the plane, and one pinned underneath. I asked where the third man came from, and someone said, "He's one of the guards." Two guards, who had just joined the outfit, were guarding the road, and the crash caught both of them, killing them instantly. We got George and the pilot, who were both unconscious, out of the copter. George now had his forehead split somewhat. Another copter was ordered and George was flown out to Able Med. for treatment, and the pilot who was all right was sent out by ambulance (crackerbox). We had a memorial service for the two men killed: Pfc. Floyd McCoy and Pfc. Delton McInnis, the next morning which was Sunday.

Concerning the helicopter accident and other inci-

Worship on the Front.

Chaplain John T. Moore who is pictured here states that this picture was taken during the bitter fighting for "Berlin and East Berlin" outposts just before the truce in Korea. Several of the marines who received communion were killed the same day. 3d Battalion, 7th Marines, suffered 450 alone.

Chaplain and Men Before Battle.

A chaplain and marines pause for a moment of prayer before going to battle during the fight for "Boulder City."

dents, Bakker's citation for a Letter of Commendation has this to say about the chaplain himself.

Exhibiting personal courage and initiative, he conducted religious services in front line trenches, bunkers and platoon areas. Expressing complete disregard for his personal safety he frequently exposed himself to enemy mortar and artillery fire to conduct religious services on the main line of resistance for the marines manning combat outposts. On one occasion, when a helicopter evacuating a seriously wounded marine crashed, he personally removed the wounded man, the injured pilot and the bodies of two sentries killed in the crash.

Chaplain John T. Moore, Roman Catholic, sent some action photographs of the fighting around the "Berlin and East Berlin" outposts. He stated that some of the Marines who received Communion were killed the same day. He states that the ". . . 3-7, 1st Mar Div suffered 450 casualties alone."

Chaplain Homer L. Schnick, Southern Baptist, has this to say:

With Chaplain Paul C. Hammerl, I visited the wounded at "E" Medical Company during the last serious fighting before the truce in July 1953. A sober sense of the awful reality of war surrounded the room where the men were being brought in—ambulatory and stretcher cases. One young fellow I'll never forget. He was muddy and wet and in considerable pain and discomfort. Being thirsty, he asked for a drink. After a corpsman got some wet pads for me, I cleaned around his mouth, eyes and ears (the mud was caked in his ears) and applied the pad of water to his lips. In talking with him, I learned that after he was wounded, he had been dragged up and down the muddy trench line by the Communists before being rescued by men of his outfit. The shock was most evident as the men were first brought in, but it was amazing to see the men return to normalcy so rapidly in the succeeding days that we visited them. One felt a real sense of mission as he assisted the doctors and corpsmen in their busy times. Once, when talking with one of the doctors, he said that he didn't know whether he could take much more or not. It was good to be able to be there just to talk with them. No door was closed to the chaplain. He was well received and was an integral part of the team.

Chaplain Robert E. Brengartner tells of a Navy Chief Corpsman who was so impressed by the peace and joy which the Sacraments brought to the wounded that he himself took instructions and was received into the church.

Chaplain Brengartner is later awarded the Letter of Commendation with "Metal Pendant and Combat Distinguishing Device" authorized. In the citation are found these words:

During the period when the battalion was engaged in extensive combat operations against the enemy, he continuously worked long and arduous hours, frequently under intense enemy shelling in order to provide comfort and aid to the sick and wounded. His courage and determination in helping to evacuate and in tendering spiritual consolation to the severely wounded men won the admiration and confidence of all who served with him.

The following incident demonstrates the type of work done by the chaplains,

Assisted by a four-man Marine squad Lt. Robert E. Brengartner, CHC, USN, led in the dramatic rescue of a wounded Puerto Rican Marine left in no man's land, Korea, by Chinese Red captors.

After a Chinese loudspeaker boomed to United Nations forces that a "squad would be allowed to remove the soldier without being fired upon," Chaplain Brengartner led the Marines toward the victim. Despite his wounds the Marine tried twice to walk to the Allied line, but collapsed.

On reaching the man, Father Brengartner gave him Absolution. The Marine, clad only in winter underwear and a sweater stuffed with Red propaganda leaflets, was clutching his Rosary Beads. The Chinese covered the area with their rifles but did not fire as the rescuers took him to the Allied line.

The Truce

Chaplain Bakker [2] writes concerning the last day of the war:

I WAS THERE—THE SIGNING OF THE TRUCE

On Monday morning of 27 July at 10 o'clock General Harrison walked into the Truce Pagoda which we had watched during its construction from our outpost, sat down, and signed the truce. Folks—I was there. I decided that two-fifths ought to be represented, as I came over with the brigade 3 years ago, and so was present. I sat in the chair that the general sat in, and had my picture taken. I also got shots of the general, the pen he used (a Parker 51), and surrounding areas. It was quiet, semitense, nondramatic and yet deeply historical. When our grandchildren study about it in school—you tell them, Uncle Peter, and Grandpa Pete was there.

The look, and feeling of utter contempt that the Chinese Communists have for us is something to see. I felt like decking the entire group of them. The hatred in their eyes seems to stem from the bottom of their high top boots.

Chaplain Hutcheson states that "Three out of four 'Services of Thanksgiving for Peace Restored,' conducted on the day the Korean Armistice was signed (during 12-hour period between signing and effective hour) were interrupted by incoming artillery fire!"

Chaplain Meachum was asked for a statement for the press:

He wanted my reaction to the truce which had been signed a short distance up the road at Pan-Munjan. My first reaction was: Thank God this "Meat grinder" has stopped. The more I thought, the harder it was for me to give a short concise statement.

Briefly I would like to write a few thoughts and reactions.

---

[2] Chaplain Bakker is known among other things for his ability as a wrestler. He at one time asserted that he found a better counseling relationship after wrestling with a man.

First, I thought of our front line troops who have been fighting in the Division in Korea since August 3, 1950. Of course, many who fought with this Division have gone home. Such places as Inchon, Chosen Basin, Seoul, Pusan Perimeter. In these places the Marines fought a moving war, but on March 15, 1952, this Division moved from the east coast to the west coast of the 155 mile battle front and relieved the ROKs about 30 miles north west of Seoul with Pan-Munjan located in the center of our front.

Here we have fought a bloody, vicious, trench, bunker, and outpost stalemate. Patrols went out in front of the Main Line of Resistance each night. Artillery pounded and planes rained fire on the enemy around the clock until 10 p.m., July 27, 1953. The last 27 days of fighting were as vicious as any battles previously fought.

I went to a battalion command post on the 27th to visit Chaplain E. O. Floyd. While talking to him, a young Marine who was muddy and tired walked up to us and asked for communion. His request was from a heart of gratitude that the firing had stopped.

At another battalion, I found Chaplain C. P. Hoff wet with perspiration at the close of a thanksgiving service. In the same chapel where he had conducted his service, Chaplain R. E. Brengartner was holding Mass. And so it was with other chaplains all along the line.

For the officers and men there was rest and sleep—a chance to bathe and wash clothes. Yet they know that the job here is not over until the terms of the truce have been effected.

Second, I thought of answered prayers. Here is a quote from a letter which I picked up on the battle front: "I would love to see you tonight. Well, Ray, you be good and pray. I am praying for you every day and night for the dear Lord to watch over you and take care of you and bring you back home safe and all right. The dear Lord is good and He will hear and answer prayers if we have faith in Him and put our trust in Him. Love, Mother."

The above statement is virtually the same thing that Lt. General William K. Harrison, the head of our truce delegation, said to me on Monday when I commented in his quarters at Base Camp that I know he is happy that the pressure on him will be relieved now that a truce has been signed.

Third, I thought when I heard the last firing mission of our 155-mm howitzer—the battery fired about an hour before the flares were fired over the battle lines signaling cease fire—How long will our guns remain silent in the face of our enemy? I hope that I will never have to hear them "bark" again. When will human beings stop trying to destroy each other?

One fact remains evident. We must be alert and on guard until the Communists show good faith in trying to bring about peace.

Fourth, the Christian and charitable relations cultivated between the officers and men of the 8th Army and Koreans make this beautiful country one of the most promising mission fields in the world. The old oriental religions are empty and do not hold inspiration, hope, and salvation. Koreans are turning to Christianity. Conditions here are as they were in the Greek and Roman culture during the 1st century when Christianity overcame paganism.

Awards:

A number of chaplains were recognized for their fine work during this period. Chaplain Newman was again decorated. This time it was the Bronze Star. Concerning his work the citation informs one that:

Working long hours under adverse conditions, he personally met each casualty as he arrived at the aid stations, regardless of the hour, both day and night. He wrote to the realtives of each man, regardless of the seriousness of the disability and followed the initial correspondence with progress report letters. He spent countless hours traveling to various aid stations and hospitals where casualties of the battalion had been evacuated for treatment. Despite the extreme danger, he often held religious services on the main line of resistance and voluntarily advanced to the outpost positions forward of the main lines in order to be of service to the Marines in these exposed areas. Through his determined efforts and understanding attitude, he restored confidence in many of the battle weary Marines who had been sent to rear areas as a result of excessive front line duty.

The other Bronze Star was awarded to Chaplain Elmer F. Ernst

. . . he frequently made visits to tank crewmen who were manning positions on the main line of resistance. Expressing complete disregard for his personal safety, he repeatedly exposed himself to murderous hostile mortar and artillery fire in order to reach the tank crewmen and offer them spiritual guidance. He voluntarily and habitually was aboard armored vehicles when they were employed in the evacuation of wounded Marines and so was enabled to render aid, spiritual assistance and consolation to the many wounded.

The "Commendation Metal Pendant" with Combat "V" was awarded to Chaplain John B. Conlon, Roman Catholic, Chaplain Roger L. Crabtree, Methodist, and Chaplain Samuel D. Chambers. Chaplain Conlon

. . . displayed outstanding ability and professional skill. His highly commendable ministrations to the wounded and sick aided immeasurably in the excellent morale sustained among the patients. When heavy casualties arrived, he demonstrated outstanding attention to duty and personally rendered spiritual guidance and advice to those in need. Throughout the entire period, he diligently brought to each wounded Marine consolation and spiritual comfort which contributed materially in the treatment of pain and suffering.

It is said of Chaplain Crabtree that

. . . he exhibited tireless efforts and outstanding attention to duty as he regularly visited the widely scattered elements of the battalion, as well as the provisional regiment of which the battalion was a part, in order to minister to the needs of the men. Sustaining an exceptionally vigorous schedule, he normally conducted 14 religious services each week. These included services at the forward elements of the unit where he was sometimes exposed to enemy artillery and mortar fire.

Of Chaplain Chambers it is said that

On numerous occasions, he disregarded his personal safety and visited the main line of resistance units in order to render

Flying Chaplain.

Chaplain Leo F. Rice adjusts his parachute in preparation for a takeoff in a Marine aerial observation plane. His destination is the camp of a Marine observation squadron and his mission is to hold mass.

counsel and words of encouragement to Marines during intense enemy mortar and artillery fire. On one occasion, ignoring his own safety, he skillfully assisted in the evacuation of one wounded and two dead Marines. During a critical 3-day period when a strategic position was being subjected to vicious hostile attacks, he continually attended to the spiritual needs of wounded Marines brought to the battalion aid station.

Although the citations may sound repetitious, it is a repetition which brings great glory to the U.S. Naval Chaplain Corps. Attention is called to Chaplain Crabtree's work with civilians in his citation.

His effective personal contacts with the large Korean civilian population throughout the sector and his support of Korean religious and charitable organizations established cordial relations which assisted materially in the successful accomplishment of the unit's assigned mission.

Chaplain Rice writing on 20 July concerning his return from the front, tells of his work with the Combat Service Group in Masan. He states that the "big problem here is to keep the men busy on the compound so that the moral problems can be licked." Academic work and vocational courses were offered and plans were laid for hobby programs. A citation in connection with the award of a Bronze Star on October 1953 states that he continually demonstrated

. . . Exceptional ability in dealing with the most difficult religious, morale and personal problems. His skillful coordination and efficient administration of the charitable efforts of

the command increased the prestige of the United States Forces in the area. Disregarding his personal fatigue, he conscientiously worked extremely long hours in order to effectively discharge his responsibilities.

Concerning his previous work the citation has this to say:

. . . he frequently went to the scene of battle to administer last rites to the dead and offer prayers for the wounded. He diligently visited the sick and wounded in hospitals and regularly visited refugee villages in the vicinity of the regiment to offer religious guidance to the predominantly Christian population. In the absence of chaplains in other United Nations units, he visited those units to conduct services and attend to the religious needs of the personnel.

Another Roman Catholic Chaplain, John T. Moore, received the Bronze Star for the period 2 April–1 August. One learns that:

When the infantry companies and other elements of the regiment were committed to the main line of resistance and subjected to intense action, he expressed complete disregard for his personal safety and traveled over roads that were under constant enemy observation and frequent mortar and artillery fire in order to carry out his duties. He was continuously on hand at forward aid stations administering both spiritual and physical aid to the wounded men. He made daily visits to the men on the main line of resistance, holding services in bunkers and exerting every effort to administer spiritual guidance to the men.[3]

"Sunday Routine"

A Marine Correspondent, M. Sgt. James F. Frye writes of the Chaplain's Sunday activity. He followed Chaplain Homer L. Schnick, Southern Baptist, of the 7th Regiment. There were four services that day. The regimental service consisted of Marines and a British Commonwealth Division. Late in the afternoon there was a visit to the MLR, ". . . the busy chaplain climbed precipitous hills to reach defensive positions sprinkled over rugged countryside so he could spend time with those in need of his advice and counsel."

The 1st Marine Air Wing

Most of the information on the work of the Chaplains of the Wing comes from their citations. Mention has been made of Chaplain E. C. Mulligan's Commendation, but it should also be noted that he was instrumental in the establishment of a special Catholic Orphanage nursery for destitute infants at Pohang, Korea.

He enhanced goodwill for United Nations forces through his ceaseless endeavors to aid needy civilians and by main-

[3] Chaplain Moore was wounded the day before the truce was signed, and thus became the last naval chaplain casualty of the Korean conflict. Chaplain Willetts was wounded about 2 weeks earlier.

taining liaison with the Korean Catholic Bishop of the Taegu Diocese . . . Dedicated to the humanitarian principles embodied in the precepts of his faith, Commander Mulligan's activities resulted directly in greater comfort and welfare for hundreds of helpless Korean families and orphans and enhanced the morale and efficiency of the 1st Marine Aircraft Wing.

He was detached in June.

Chaplain Parker was relieved as Wing Chaplain in May by Chaplain Allen Jones, Presbyterian, US. On 25 June Chaplain John J. Burns relieved Chaplain Mulligan. Chaplain Gordon Griffin reported aboard in May. Chaplain Lineberger left in May. He had been cited by the Korean government and also had been awarded the Bronze Star. For the latter it was said that he

. . . supervised the construction and furnishing of [a] chapel where he instituted regular classes in religious instruction, and often led services for congregations of other religious denominations when chaplains for those faiths were committed elsewhere in the forward area. Sparing no efforts to aid the less fortunate in the war-torn country, he participated in the establishment of two separate orphanages for helpless Korean children and was largely responsible for the creation of the United States Marine Memorial Children's Clinic designated to provide advance medical care for destitute women and children in the vicinity of Pohang. In addition, he was instrumental in the purchase of rice land for hungry Koreans and in the delivery of tons of clothing and toys to needy civilians in the combat zone. By his inspiring efforts, resourceful initiative and unswerving devotion to duty, Lieutenant, Junior Grade, Lineberger directly aided in increasing the health, comfort, and welfare of hundreds of helpless Korean families and orphans and contributed materially to the overall morale and efficiency of the two Marine Aircraft Groups.

The citation by Korea was like the one received by Chaplain Parker. It concluded,

His demonstration of energetic efforts and generosity in working for the betterment of the Korean war orphans left homeless in the midst of the war in which the peace-loving people stand firm in the path of aggression to safeguard freedom and human dignity has elicited the highest possible praise from all those cognizant of his fine spirit.

Chaplain Fenstermacher tells of his contacts with the Korean chaplains,[4]

In Pusan I had contacts with the chaplains of the Republic of Korea Navy Chaplain Corps. Their Chief of Chaplains, Cmdr. D. B. Chung, ChC, ROKN, had his offices there. My first contact with the ROK Navy chaplains, however, came through their Senior Chaplain of the Korean Marine Corps, Lt. Cmdr. C. S. Park, who visited me at our Battalion Headquarters early in January 1953. Chaplain Park and I discussed the work of a chaplain in general, as well as the language barrier . . . I helped him out with quantities

of chaplain supplies . . . I met the Chief of Chaplains, as well as all his chaplains who served the ROK Navy and Marine Corps, nine altogether. All are men consecrated to God as far as I could see, serious about their work, and hard workers.

On 14 June 1953 I was guest preacher at a Divine Service in which we commemorated the Fifth Anniversary of Chaplain activities in the ROK Navy. I preached in English and Chaplain Chung interpreted what I said in Korean. The service was held in the Korean Navy Church in Pusan, the church being set up in the well deck of an LST which is tied up to the dock at Pier No. 1 in Pusan and used for church services every Sunday. Nearly 500 attended this anniversary service, including high-ranking ROK Navy officers, the ROK Navy Band, and a large well-trained choir.

"MSTS"

One chaplain[5] submits a very interesting account of a draft of Marines arriving in the Far East just after the truce had been signed.

The fighting in Korea was very fierce last summer and replacement drafts from Camp Pendleton were seriously training for combat. I was given the task to accompany the July 1953 replacement draft to Korea. We were to travel on the USNS GEN. NELSON M. WALKER and there was a Protestant chaplain aboard. I was to conduct Catholic services for the men.

It was a noisy group of Marines that I joined in San Diego, on July 16, 1953. The next afternoon we were given quite a farewell with the Marine Corps band and three generals to see us off. The approaching dangers of combat were forgotten for the moment as the ship sailed out of the harbor. Most of the men were looking at the pier for a last glimpse of a relative or friend. Others just gazed at the city and wondered when they would see San Diego again. The older men realized that some of these men would probably never see the United States again for they would be in combat in a few weeks.

As we neared Japan the tension mounted and the men spent more time at church services, preparing their souls should they be called upon to sacrifice their lives. The news dispatches were avidly read daily. The mail boxes were always crammed with letters to mothers and fathers, to wives and sweethearts.

But it was a wonderful feeling when the news of the truce reached us three days out of Japan. The carefree attitude of the young men returned and a prayer of thanksgiving was sent heavenward. We all looked forward to Japan and Korea confident that the danger of death was passed.

The conditions of the truce made it impossible to enter Korea immediately and we went from Kobe, Japan to Sasebo, Japan where we spent 5 days. It gave us an opportunity to see a bit of the Japanese people and customs. Finally on August 7 we arrived at Inchon, Korea, and were put ashore. Again the conditions of the truce changed our plans. We were not allowed to bring any weapons ashore with us and all rifles and pistols were collected. [A] provision of the truce specified that we could not add to our forces in Korea. So before we could land, troops to be taken to the United States, had to be taken aboard. We used a shuttle system. First

[4] Cp. pp. 107ff.

[5] This account is credited to Chaplain Normand A. Ricard.

a boatload of men would board the ship and would return with their replacements. As I was in the liaison group that was on T.A.D. orders I was in the first group to leave the ship. But it was a happy, excited group of Marines, to whom I waved goodby.

As we approached the landing at Inchon, I thanked God that the truce had been signed and prayed that the peace would be permanent and that no more lives would be sacrificed for the preservation of freedom.

Forces Afloat

During this period a variety of items of iterest come from the Fleet. Chaplain Ralph Handran, Roman Catholic, speaks of the transporting of prisoners. He states that the ANDERSON usually carried 45 prisoners from the Far East. For the most part they were men who had gotten into difficulty in Korea and had been sentenced by courts-martial. They were very bitter and the chaplain held services for them in the brig on Sundays because they did not want to appear on deck.

Work aboard the hospital ships continued. Chaplain Luther E. Olmon, Lutheran, in the REPOSE wrote,

At present we are in Korean waters supporting the Marines. The Korean truce talks seem to be at a standstill at this time. Our patient load has kept about the same. The chaplains have a fine opportunity aboard a hospital ship.

Circuit riding was rather commonplace. Chaplains Andrew J. Grygiel in the ORISKANY, and Lawrence R. Phillips in the ESSEX speak of transfers by highline and helicopter to other ships in the task force. Chaplain Gordian V. Erlacher tells of being transported from the NEW JERSEY to Wonsan Harbor to conduct services on the Island of Yodo. Where circuit riding was not possible Lay Leaders are reported doing a fine job. For example, on the JOHN R. CRAIG, Catholic Services were led by the Executive Officer and Protestant Services by the First Lieutenant. The destroyer MOALE had an ordained Baptist minister in the Gunnery Department who not only had held services all around the globe on naval vessels, but on this ship he found time to mimeograph bulletins for all Catholic and Protestant services held aboard ship and to broadcast his own religious program over the ship's PA system each Wednesday. On one cruise he organized a choir of 45 voices consisting of officers and enlisted men.

It is encouraging to find that some of the ships during the Korean conflict found room enough aboard ship to set up a chapel. This has been something of an accepted custom in the British Navy. Chaplain B. E. Heuer, Lutheran, reports that the CORREGIDOR set up a permanent chapel in the quarters formerly used as a Pilot's Ready Room.

Chaplain George W. Thompson, who as an enlisted man in World War I rose to Quartermaster Second, was doing a fine job on the VALLEY FORGE. His Sunday starts with

. . . a Communion service, includes Sunday School classes and two regular church services, and ends with a Protestant Fellowship and Evangelistic Service. During the week, he leads a Bible class which meets three times a week, and holds Protestant Devotional Services twice daily—in the early morning and late evening. He is continuing a tradition carried out by his predecessors on the ship by pronouncing a short prayer for all hands at "Tatoo" over the ship's public address system.

In summary it is seen that this period began with the conflict still in progress. Several bitter battles were fought. Once again the chaplains had acquitted themselves in a manner to deserve high praise. The truce was signed and with it were to come different problems to surmount; different victories to be achieved.

CHAPTER ELEVEN

ARMISTICE AFTERMATH

27 July 1953–27 July 1954

It was an uneasy truce but peace had come to a war torn area. The United States, as did the United Nations, recognized the Korean campaign as active for the campaign ribbon could still be earned for the period ending 27 July 1954.[1] It is this date that has been considered as the end of the Korean Police Action.

The summer was best known for "Big Switch" and then inevitably there was another Korean winter. By this time there were a number of shifts in personnel.

The 1st Marine Division

On 1 August the Divisions withdrew to lines stipulated by the Armistice agreement. Soon thereafter there began a very busy period for the Marines for on 5 August "Operation Big Switch" was set in motion. This return of Allied prisoners of war began at "Freedom Village" which was located in the 1st Marine Division sector. On 4 September the 1st Provisional Demilitarized Zone Military Police Company was activated from 1st Division troops, for the purpose of enforcing the neutrality of the buffer zone between the territory of the United Nations and North Korea. "Operation Big Switch" was completed on 6 September. The Division now devoted most of its time to training and position improvement and in the program of Armed Forces aid to Korea for reconstruction and rehabilitation of that war torn country. There was a short period ending on 21 January 1954, when the last of the prisoner exchanges took place with the transfer from the Division's area of those prisoners of war who refused to return to their lines.

It is evident that many units held memorial services. The 2d Battalion, 5th Marines, had theirs on 9 August at which General Pate dedicated the memorial wreath. It was about this time that the commanding general also presented to the 30 division chaplains the new altar kits. These were described as

. . . resembling a woman's large shoulder pocketbook, are made of canvas and contain vestments, altar linen and all other necessities for conducting church services in the field. Eventually, they will be issued to "Padres" serving with all Marine divisions and to a few on small naval craft.

Big Switch

"Now hear this. Now hear this." Over the loudspeaker comes an authoritative voice. "Serial Two passed Check Point Five at one—zero—three—two hours. Approximate time of arrival, 3 minutes. All processing personnel man your stations."[2]

Marine M.P.'s, Navy corpsmen, Army and Marine personnel men, Chaplain Meachum accompanied by four Protestant and four Catholic chaplains together with all others concerned with the reception of American repatriates move quickly to their posts. On a platform overlooking the entrance to the building, press photographers ready their cameras.

Into the enclosure moves a line of ambulances, their great red crosses bright against squares of white. From them emerge young Americans of all sizes and shades of color, most of them in the shapeless blue cotton outfits furnished by the Chinese Communists but some stripped to their white cotton shorts, clutching ditty bags with their few personal belongings. Strong hands help them down from the vehicles; warm smiles greet them. Some shout "Freedom! Freedom! Wonderful Freedom!" Some hop out of the ambulances without saying a word; their eyes and expressions bespeak a new life and a new hope. A few are brought out on stretchers, but the greater part walk eagerly and unassisted through the wide doorway under the red and gold sign "Gateway to Freedom."

At the first station the returnees are dusted with disinfectants to reduce the possibility of disease. Next they are given a preliminary medical check. It is determined whether they are physically fit to continue the rest of the processing which includes among other things an interview by the press and regular chow. Tags are given noting these facts. At the third station they are registered with representatives of the Adjutant General's Corps of Marine personnel and the names of their next of kin are checked. The Adjutant General will notify their next of kin regarding their recovery and general physical condition. Then, tagged

---

[1] No engagement star was authorized as the actual fighting had ceased.

[2] This account is a compilation of various chaplains' accounts.

and clutching numerous papers as well as their ditty bags, the repatriates meet the chaplain at the fourth station.[3]

Chaplain Meachum says,"We were standing in our section of the processing lines by our altars ready to extend the hand of Christian fellowship to soldiers and marines of many nations." The room was dominated by a large mural depicting the varied activities of chaplains with the 1st Marine Division. Chaplain Meachum describes the setting

We made our sections as attractive as possible by getting flowers from the hillsides. We pinned the religious posters, church pennants, and spare altar cloths to the walls of the tents. The impression on the prisoners was terrific—as well as on generals, newspaper men, photographers, and all hands who were engaged in the processing work.

The chaplain extends his hand in warm welcome to the serviceman. After a brief get acquainted period, the chaplain determines the religious affiliation of the man. If not of his own faith the man is introduced to a chaplain who is. The chaplains claim the men

Memorial Services.

The National Colors are carried to the 2d Battalion, 5th Marines Chapel as the memorial services begin in memory of the men in the battalion who have lost their lives in Korea.

[3] NOTE: Chaplain William H. Vinson tells us that "as planning for 'Big Switch' came into its final stages, the many lessons learned during 'Little Switch' were applied. One of these lessons had to do with the chaplains section in the processing line. It was decided that food for the soul should come before the food for the body. In the previous operation, the chaplains section was set up behind the nourishment section and offered very little privacy or atmosphere of reverence to the worshipers."

Rollcall.

In a service conducted by Chaplain Peter J. Bakker the names are read of those who gave the supreme sacrifice and who were members of the 2d Battalion, 5th Marines.

Altar Kit.

Chaplain John T. Moore shoulders the new compact altar kit provided by the Chaplains Division. It is designed to make it easier for chaplains of all faiths to bring church services to marines in the field.

A closeup of the contents of the kit.

of their own faith and sit down with them for a friendly chat. The Catholic chaplain dons a violet stole, hears confessions, administers communion, and presents rosaries, medals, prayerbooks, and missals as desired.

Chaplain Rice. says,

Because we were not certain of the physical condition of the returning PW's at Freedom Village the priests of the Marine Division were ready to give the sacraments to any requesting them. The idea caught the imagination of the PW's and a great percentage wanted communion after confession. Having chapels at Freedom Village turned out to be a big consolation to men of all faiths. One correspondent said to the Catholic Far East news representative: "How come the priests are administering confession and communion to the PW's? After all you don't meet people with the sacraments coming back from a trip." I proposed this to one of the returning prisoners. He answered: "I spent 3 years in prison and I examined my conscience all the time. I sure want to go to confession. I'm starting in a new life right here."

Another Roman Catholic Chaplain, Paul C. Hammerl, has these incidents to relate,

. . . listen to some of them at Freedom Village. "I never prayed before at home but, I prayed up there and I don't see why I should stop now." "My girl tried to get me to go to church, but I couldn't see why then, but now I know

better." "I didn't have many instructions in the faith, but I will learn all I can in the future."

If you may think God isn't in the hearts of our young men, listen to their stories and see how they formed study clubs, how they exchanged thoughts of God as often as they could. It would do many a doubter good to see the crosses they molded out of toothpaste tubes so they could have a reminder of Christ about their person. Some had Bibles they received years ago from their pastor, now worn and well used. Others on their own, bound up their Bibles to make them last and treasured them above everything else. Our men came back with little in the way of material goods, but if they had salvaged and saved a medal, a Bible, or a rosary, they took it along to bring back home. One lad carried a Bible of his buddy who died. "I want to give it to his mother to show her he prayed and used it regularly." What a consolation such will be for the brokenhearted mother.

For adherents of Judaism, Chaplain Murray I. Rothman was present to take them before the Ark with its sacred scrolls of the Torah (Law) for the traditional prayers of Israel. Protestant chaplains held services of thanksgiving and served communion to those who desired it. Chaplain William H. Vinson affirms that over one-half of the men did receive Communion. Chaplain Walter H. Nordby tells of some of the experiences of the men,

One prisoner looked at you and in reverent tones slowly

Big Switch.

Chaplain R. N. Stretch, 11th Marines, holds service for two repatriated POW's at Freedom Village Chapel.

Chaplain Paul C. Hammerl counsels with a returned POW at Freedom Village.

Division Chaplain Francis T. O'Leary administers communion during a mass celebrated at Freedom Village for UN POW's repatriated from North Korea on 6 September 1953 at Munsan-ni.

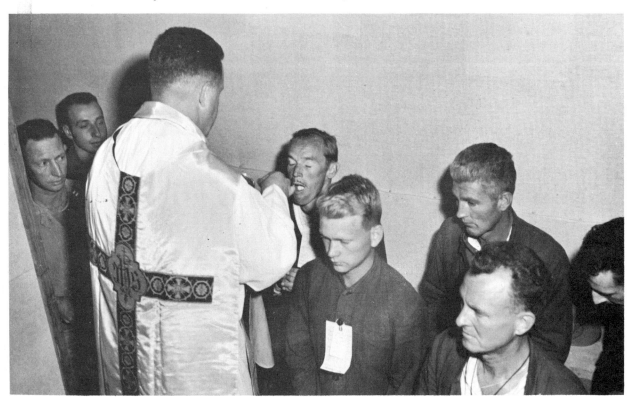

said, "Thank God I am here able to experience this moment of freedom after 32 months of living hell."

Another rather thin, but sun-tanned southern soldier quietly stated, "We had a couple of good fellows who held services for us whenever possible." One tall Texan said, "They took our Testaments away and only let us have short supervised services on Christmas and Easter."

A great number of the returning Americans wore lead crosses made from melted toothpaste tubes. Catholics and Protestants alike possessed them.

As you looked into the eyes of these men you felt proud of them. Think of what they had endured for their country. Think of the one named Valdery who showed you a torn bit of scripture he had carried all the way. He said, "The Lord has been with me through two death marches, first Bataan and now this past one. I want to thank Him now."

. . . You can't help but remember the proud Marine who came through the gate that separated the Americans from the Commonwealth and other U.N. troops. The officer asked, "American?" The reply was, "Yes, Sir!" Not this fellow, he replied, "Marine, Sir!" He was courteous and you immediately liked him—you were proud he was a 7th Marine—your outfit.

. . . There were some sad moments, men on stretchers, some men with Chinese symbols like the dove of peace of Chinese numbers tatooed on them like medieval prisoners . . . Life would hold great moments ahead for all, even the sad. As one man said, "Today it is like I have been born all over again."

Chaplain Robert W. Smith tells the story of an Air Force sergeant who was shot down while making a bombing raid over North Korea. He descended by parachute into the midst of enemy troops. He resigned himself to immediate death or torture. He was overwhelmed by a longing to live. As he walked off toward prison he could hardly believe his ears for he heard North Korean children singing, "Jesus loves me. This I know, for the Bible tells me so." This one song changed his outlook "and he felt if these children can sing about Jesus then surely they do have respect for life." He

. . . came back to tell that story. He wasn't a church member, he seldom went to church, he had taken Christianity for granted and now he realized that America's greatness was not in her tanks, planes, or bombs but in her God, in Jesus Christ, her Freedom, everything revolved around Him, and it took that simple little Sunday School song, "Jesus Loves Me" to awaken him.

. . . I have seen them accept Jesus Christ as their Saviour as they knelt at the altar here in Freedom Village, I have heard them tell me how Christ saved them at the prison camps, how they were "Born again"—a spiritual birth into God's Kingdom. I have watched tears roll down sunken, sun-tanned cheeks as we talked about our Lord. I have heard men tell me that if God calls them they will become missionaries.

Chaplain Vinson states,

In the early months of the war, no religious services were permitted in the camps. Some few loyal Christians began to request permission to hold services. One lay preacher, Alfonso Johnson, from Columbus, Ohio, likened his experiences to those of the Apostle Paul, as he too, was jailed for attempting to hold services. I asked where he found words of comfort and encouragement in the time of trials. He replied, "I just kept reading more about Paul, finding that he met the same problems as I, and was triumphant, many years ago." In later months the prison officials permitted the men to hold religious worship services in small groups under the watchful eye of an interpreter. On occasions like Christmas and Easter, large services were held with excessive photographic coverage for propaganda purposes.

Most of the men desired to stop for a moment of prayer in thanksgiving to God for their freedom and His ministry to them during the long prison months. We retired to one of the small chapels, located adjacent to the waiting room, to bow in a moment of prayer. It was indeed a privilege to kneel there before the altar and pray with these men. More touching was the occasional man who desired to lead in prayer himself. These men poured out their hearts to God in joyful thanksgiving at their first opportune moment after coming back to freedom.

Some stories were elicited by the question put by Chaplain Vinson, "Do you have your New Testament with you?" Many said,

. . . that their Testament was taken from them along with other possessions when they were captured. Some lost them in the hospitals. Some reached down in their personal effects bag and brought out their prized possession, a well worn dog-eared Testament. Many had crude canvas backs; the result of a prison camp rebinding to try to preserve the book. On the pages of these testaments were marked the favorite passages that had brought comfort in the time of misery, hope in the time of despair, light in the time of darkness. All the men liked to tell about the place the New Testament had played in their lives. Each man was presented with a fresh, new Testament to carry with him on his journey back home.

Chaplain Bakker said that the men told him, "You couldn't get my New Testament from me" and showed him copies well worn and somewhat frayed.

After a final blessing the man next goes to the Refreshment Section. The procedure for the rest of his time at Freedom Village is described by Chaplain Stretch,

In the Refreshment Section is usually a general of the Army or the Marine Corps to greet and chat with his men. From here those who wish to be interviewed by newspaper and magazine correspondents are taken into the Press Section. Then come ditty bags of toilet articles handed out by an attractive Red Cross girl, the shedding of prison clothes and hot showers. In pajamas, bathrobe, and slippers the man proceeds into the Army Evacuation Hospital set up alongside the warehouse, for chest X-ray and thorough physical examination. Here he has his dinner and receives any mail which awaits him. Later, returning to the warehouse, he is issued new clothing of his own branch of service and waits for further transportation to Inchon and the ships which will take him to the United States. His waiting is in a comfortable lounge maintained by the Red Cross, where light refreshments are served and the scenes and events of home are presented in posters, photographs, magazines, and newspapers.

Chaplain Bakker also has this general note,

On Wednesday, 5 August at 9 a.m. we started receiving our POWs. I was on hand to shake the hand of nearly all our UN personnel, and many of the South Koreans. The number of Marines returned was very few. The first one of our men that I welcomed there in the shadow of the Truce Pagoda was Pfc. Francis E. Kohus, Jr., from Cincinnati, Ohio. He was captured on Warsaw in 52. One of the lads returned was captured in March of this year on Vegas, where this outfit suffered many casualties. I had a service with his company last week, and will have another one there every Thursday.

As you have read in the papers, the men were not too emotional—they looked as though they had all the stuffings beat out of them. By contrast—these Communists come by singing and shouting and waving their flags—there goes another truck load of them. Of course our men have been beaten down for a long time, without proper food—they told me that two of our chaplains starved to death—one of whom was repeatedly kicked in the stomach. The commies never had it so good with food, medicine, etc.

On the 10th of this month I saw the men being loaded on an LST, awaiting transportation out to the GENERAL WALKER for passage home—they still looked somewhat gaunt, peaked, and washed out. The trip home with good food, etc., should do them a world of good.

Chaplain Meachum concludes with this statement,

When the gate swung wide on 5 August at Freedom Village, ambulances, 4 to 6 in a serial, came through 3 or 4 times a day with returning POW's to be processed, 341 Americans were received. Approximately 90 percent of these were Negroes. This week was a "field day" for me as a Baptist chaplain, because most of these men were Baptists. They greeted me, one after another, with a big smile, "Chaplain, I've been waiting many months to talk to you!" Whereupon they would pour out their hearts in relating their religious experiences during the long months of their imprisonment. They were permitted to gather in large numbers for religious services on special occasions, such as Christmas, Easter, and Thanksgiving. Many of them related that they had gathered in small groups regularly to worship. The first man with whom I talked, by the name of Dobbins, told me from his stretcher that he conducted services until he became ill and was sent to the hospital.

The chaplains of the 1st Marine Division were designated to minister at Freedom Village under the Detachment Command of Colonel Metz, USMC. The 25 chaplains of the division will participate in the entire processing with groups of 8 working 1 week at a time. At the end of this first week, every chaplain who participated, including Protestants, Catholics, and a Jewish chaplain, had a rich experience in

his religious ministry . . . For all these returned, we chaplains thanked God that these have been able to endure the awful hardships of the Chinese Communist's imprisonment.

. . . One said that he was a Christian before being captured, but that while he was in prison God laid His hand on him, calling him to become a minister of the Gospel, and so he will go to school in Atlanta, Ga., to prepare himself.

It is in order here to quote Chaplain John W. Berger, Methodist, who was in the GEN. N. M. WALKER,

While aboard the GEN. N. M. WALKER (T–AP125) the first group of returning prisoners in Operation Big Switch were brought aboard at Inchon. Chaplains at Freedom Village had evidently done an excellent job of ministering to the immediate needs of these men. It fell to us (Maj. Henry Durand, USA, Roman Catholic, and myself, Protestant) to accompany these men back to the States.

The constant interrogation to which these men were submitted left little time for planned religious activity. Consequently, while we had two services daily (one each), most of our time with these men was spent regularly at irregular hours. We spent this time in their berthing compartments talking both with individuals and groups as the occasion presented itself. However, I did not once leave a compartment without one man asking, "Chaplain, could I talk with you a few minutes?"—and often it was two or three asking.

All the 300 plus men certainly knew there were chaplains aboard during those 2 weeks enroute home. But some in particular sought us out. My memory still vividly recalls the confidences brought to me by men who now had a new fear—of their own companions. There were at least a half dozen with whom I counseled that had yielded to the pressure of prison life and availed too much of enemy propaganda.

But it was not ours, as chaplains, to investigate. For such matters we urged re-counsel with the CIC team aboard. As such, we, as chaplains, acted in the true and accepted capacity of letting the confessor think out loud and begin that period of catharsis which would in some measure bring him back into harmony with his prior environment.

In addition, there were all the rest who reflected their months in prison with that noticeable reticence to converse with anyone. And I think this is where we did our best work—by simply being among them hours at a time, working quietly, slowly, in Christian love and fellowship. (My own particular interest in the returning prisoners lay in the fact that somewhere among them was a young man who had been a part of my young people's group, and because of a broken home, also a part of my own home. I looked anxiously for him, but he was not among this first group.)

Besides the above mentioned "progressives," I had particular fellowship with one Negro sergeant. He had led many of the religious services while in prison camps and had a particular ministry through music. He provided three quartets while aboard ship, indicating that that was one of their means while in camp to revive their spiritual needs. The two of us worked together in the compartments.

While much will be written about these men, more will be left unsaid. God only knows how so many men survived the ordeals reflected in their thoughts and bodies. It seemed a little out of place to have such a grandiose welcome by television, bands and speeches upon arrival in the States—these men who simply wanted to return to the peace and quiet of their homes.

Chaplain Bakker tells of the return of General Dean, stating that he

. . . was returned just like the rest of the officers and men. He rode in the same ambulance, went through the same line, and knelt in prayer in the same chapel for a prayer of thanksgiving. He wanted everyone to know that, "I was not hunting tanks with a bazooka when I was captured."

It was during "Big Switch" that Chaplain Meachum was relieved by Chaplain Francis T. O'Leary as Division Chaplain of the 1st Marine Division. As a result both participated in the program. Both were cited for their work. Concerning the work of Chaplain Meachum, for which he was awarded the Bronze Star, one reads,

. . . Frequently making trips throughout the division area, in most adverse conditions, he expressed complete disregard for his personal welfare in order that all the Marines might receive the opportunity to attend services of their own particular faith. During the repatriation of United Nations personnel from enemy prison camps, he was constantly present to insure that the men who had undergone the hardships of prison life had every opportunity to receive, upon their return, the spiritual guidance they so eagerly sought. Commander Meachum's highly competent leadership, organizational ability, and tireless efforts served as an inspiration to all who observed him.

Chaplain Meachum summarized the Big Switch Operation by saying that

. . . of the 3,600 prisoners passing through to Freedom, at least 95 percent sought religious assurance and comfort as their first act; from the chapels they went on to those other comforts of the American way of life—ice cream and fresh milk. To the 3,600 freed prisoners the chaplains gave out 1,800 new testaments, 500 rosaries.

Some of the Participating Chaplains in Big Switch.

A photograph taken at the time of the relief of Chaplain Lonnie Meachum by Frank T. O'Leary as division chaplain. Pictured are (first row, left to right) W. H. Vinson; F. T. O'Leary; Major General Burger; Major General Pate; Colonel Nelson; L. W. Meachum; E. V. Lyons. (Second row, left to right) P. J. Bakker; L. F. Rice; S. D. Chambers; E. F. Ernst; R. N. Stretch; J. B. Conlon; M. I. Rothman.

"It was the men who had good religious and home training who stood their ordeal best," the chaplain said.

General Mark Clark states, "We have solid evidence after all the returns were in from Big Switch that the Communists still held 3,404 men prisoners, including 944 Americans."

In September Chaplain O'Leary issued the following roster of Chaplains of the Division:

Name	Rank	Assignment	Church affiliation
O'LEARY, F. T.	CDR	Div Chap	RC
MOORE, J. T.	LTJG	Hq Bn	RC
ROTHMAN, M. I.	LTJG	Hq Bn	JEWISH
EDWARDS, T. V.	LT	Sh Pty Bn	RC
HAMMERL, P. C.	LTJG	"E" Med	RC
PIEPER, P. F. W.	LTJG	Sh Pty Bn	LUTH
RICE, L. F.	LCDR	1st CSG	RC
SCHNICK, H. L.	LTJG	1st Svc Bn	BAP (S)
SCHROERLUKE, H. P.	LTJG	1st Arm Amph	EVAN& REF
SMITH, R. W.	LTJG	7th MT Bn	BAP (S)
TACKETT, J. H.	LTJG	1st Eng Bn	METH
VINSON, W. H.	LTJG	1st Ord Bn	BAP (S)

1ST MARINES

HOFF, C. P.	LCDR	1st Bn	LUTH
CHAMBERS, S. D.	LT	2d Bn	PRESBY
BRENGARTNER, R. E.	LT	3d Bn	RC

5TH MARINES

LYONS, E. V.	LCDR	1st Bn	PRESBY
BAKKER, P. J.	LT	2d Bn	BAP (A)
ERNST, E. F.	LTJG	3d Bn	RC

7TH MARINES

NORDBY, W. H.	LT	1st Bn	LUTH
FLOYD, E. O.	LTJG	2d Bn	BAP (S)
BARRY, A. J.	LTJG	3d Bn	RC

11TH MARINES

STRETCH, R. N.	LCDR	Hq Btry	PE
BASSETT, W. T.	LTJG	....	BAP (S)
CONLON, J. G.	LTJG	4th Bn	RC
DOWD, F. A.	LT	....	RC
KANE, J. A.	LTJG	....	RC

Awards

Two chaplains were given Letters of Commendation. Chaplain E. Vaughn Lyons as regimental chaplain

. . . displayed outstanding ability and professional skill. Throughout the period, he diligently provided moral and spiritual guidance and comfort to the men of the unit. During periods when the regiment was engaged in combat, he devoted extremely long hours and disregarded his personal fatigue in order to aid and comfort the wounded Marines. On numerous occasions, he rendered invaluable assistance in evacuating the casualties. His outstanding attention to duty, initiative and resourcefulness served as an inspiration to all who observe[d] him.

Similarly, it is said of Chaplain Richard G. Hutcheson, Jr., that he

. . . displayed outstanding ability and professional skill. When the battalion was deployed in support of the main line of resistance, he labored unceasingly in ministering to the moral and spiritual needs of all Marines in his care. He made himself constantly available and sought opportunities to counsel and aid those in need. Despite heavy artillery and mortar fire, he could always be found in an endangered area rendering medical and spiritual aid. His outstanding example of integrity and physical and moral courage served as an inspiration to men of all faiths and contributed materially to the high morale of the battalion. Lieutenant Hutcheson's indomitable spirit and conduct throughout were in keeping with the highest traditions of the U.S. Naval Service.

With the cessation of fighting on the front there was an accompanying increase in attendance at Divine Worship in the Division.

Chapel & Worship

A great deal of interest was paid to the construction of houses of worship by the various units. Winter would arrive all too soon and buildings would not only provide shelter but would also enhance the spirit of reverence at the services. One such project was that of the 2d Battalion 1st Marines. Chaplain Chambers states that,

The last engagement of the war before the ceasefire had been very intense, fraught with heavy casualties on "Boulder City" and "East Berlin." Consequently, when we moved off of the MLR on the appointed day after the truce, the men were anxious to have their own chapel of more permanent construction than merely a tent or a cleared spot on the side of a hill; and they wanted a memorial chapel to the memory of those who were left behind. What they turned out was a prize of ingenuity.

The MLR had to be vacated within 72 hours, as I recall, and a demilitarized zone established. That meant that whatever was to be salvaged from the line bunkers had to be brought south quickly. The men of the battalion worked around the clock to dismantle and save the tremendous amount of wood, metal, and other construction items stowed up forward. Captain Paul Reigert, our S–4 officer, provided one truck for the chapel and into it went a load of the huge timbers used in the bunker construction. The beams were 12 x 12 x 16 feet long. They were taken right out of the front line fortifications. Our problem, however, now was to get these into usable timber for a chapel. Three cartons of cigarettes did the trick. An old Korean with a sawmill worked feverishly to cut these monsters into 2 x 4's and 4 x 4's.

We selected the highest hill of our new encampment for the chapel site. A dozer cleared a level plain and the construction began. The beams cut by the Korean provided the framework and skeleton of the chapel. It was 24 feet wide and 70 feet long with a 10-foot chancel area. Around the frame we stretched chicken wire 3 feet high on both sides

Conference.

A conference is held at the 5th Marine Regiment's officers mess. Left to right: Chaplain F. T. O'Leary; Col. E. D. Martin, Jr.; commanding officer, 5th Regiment, Chaplain S. D. Bennett, FMF Pacific chaplain, and Chaplain R. E. Jenkins.

of the chapel's length. A good mixture of mud and straw was applied to this to make a very substantial wall. The upper area of about 3 feet was left open since the weather was still exceedingly hot.

The roof posed the next problem, but a carton of soap was traded for a truck of straw and a thatched roof took shape. We gave it a "haircut" and it looked as shipshape as any Korean dwelling. A steeple topped the front of the chapel and we capped that with straw too. A Major Young, our S–3 officer, ran across a bell in a neighboring community. I never did learn what the barter price was but he donated that and every week thenceforth it woke him up for Divine Services.

. . . a 16-foot white cross on the hill overlooking the camp made this the most significant sight for miles around. It was not long until the steps up the side of the hill were worn smooth by those who came to worship in the 2d Battalion's Memorial Chapel.

One distinctive feature of the chapel was a picture which was hung over the altar. This was a print of a likeness of Christ composed of over 86,000 Korean letter characters made by a prisoner behind the bamboo curtain. The ideograms were quotations from the Gospel of Matthew by the artist which he had recalled while in prison. This picture was donated to the chapel by the Young Nak Orphanage.

It is partly this work in building the chapel that is cited in the award of a second Letter of Commenda-

tion to Chaplain Chambers. His additional work in the field of relief is noted,

. . . he contributed immeasurably in the construction of a modern battalion chapel. Constantly aware of the problems of the men whose moral and spiritual guidance was his primary goal he was sympathetic, realistic and always helpful. He earned the confidence and loyalty of the officers and enlisted men with whom he was associated. On another occasion he cheerfully worked long and arduous hours in preparation for a series of Christmas parties held for Korean children and residents of the refugee center. His thorough planning and sound supervision were evidenced by the great volume of contributions received and the ultimate success of regimental area Christmas parties. His steadfast devotion to duty and dedication to a worthy cause maintained a better understanding between the Republic of Korea and United Nations Forces.

Another chapel built and dedicated to those lost in the unit was that constructed by the 11th Marine Artillery Regiment. It was called the St. Barbara Chapel. Col. Manly L. Curry, Commanding Officer, presented a bell to the chapel. The first services were conducted by Chaplains R. N. Stretch and J. A. Kane. The latter was assisted in the celebration of the Mass by Chaplain O'Leary. The cost of the chapel was defrayed by offerings of members and friends of the regiment. The stonework was

Dedication Day.

Church Call is sounded announcing the dedicatory service for the chapel of the 2d Battalion, 1st Marines. Chaplain Chambers led the men in the building of this place of worship.

---

designed and built by men in the unit. This chapel was also built in the center of the 11th Marine Command Post. It was completed and dedicated on Thanksgiving Day, 1953. Chaplain S. B. Bennett, chaplain, FMF, Pac, writing later about the chapels as he saw them on an inspection made in May, had this to say,

I recently visited these chaplains serving with the Marines in Japan and Korea. The effective work they are doing is exemplified by the large church attendance in their beautiful chapels. The most conspicuous and the most central spot was selected for the location of these chapels. No other building in the area is photographed as often as they are. They stand as a constant reminder of God and His everlasting presence. There is an atmosphere of reverence and appreciation wherever they can be seen. The commanding officers and the men are proud of these monuments of joy

and beauty because they made them possible by various means of forethought and labor. Of course they require constant vigilance for cleanliness and upkeep. The new men soon feel these chapels belong to them.

About this time Chaplain Murray I. Rothman was awarded the Letter of Commendation. Concerning this chaplain it is noted that

. . . His personal warmth, initiative and keen understanding of the fighting men and their problems made his presence an important factor in maintaining the high morale of the division. As the only chaplain of his particular faith in the division, he made weekly visits to each front line regiment and battalion conducting religious service, personal consultations and spiritual ministration. Expressing complete disregard for his personal safety, he once visited the personnel on an outpost located far forward of the main line of resistance for religious consolation and ministration despite

Saint Barbara's Chapel.

Chaplain E. J. Nerthling, left, chaplain with the the 11th Marine Regiment shows Chaplain S. B. Bennett, FMF Pacific chaplain, the memorial plaque on the new chapel.

Chaplain Bennett Pays a Call.

Chaplain Bennett talks with the chaplains in front of the 5th Marines Memorial Chapel. (Left to right) Pictured here are P. A. Johnson; Chaplain S. B. Bennett, FMF Pacific chaplain; R. F. Jenkins; and F. A. Dowd.

Another Meeting.

Chaplain C. E. Rains meets Chaplain Bennett in front of the chapel of the 2d Battalion, 7th Marines.

the fact that he was subjected to hostile mortar and small arms fire. His regular visits to the hospital ships were of great comfort to the wounded Marines of all faiths within the division. He was selected and served commendably as chaplain during the repatriation of prisoners of war.

Chaplain Rothman was released from active duty on 27 November 1953. The new Jewish chaplain was Richard Saul Sternberger, who reported 17 November.

Another chaplain receiving the same decoration was Chaplain Emmet O. Floyd in which it is stated that

. . . During the last days of bitter fighting he frequently disregarded his personal safety by exposing himself to heavy concentrations of enemy artillery and mortar fire to aid the wounded and render spiritual comfort to the personnel of the regiment, regardless of faith. During the period of reorganization and development of the main battle positions following the cessation of hostilities, when the situation was tense and the troops performed hard physical labor under extremely adverse field conditions, he continued to circulate amongst the men delivering spiritual solace to those who requested it and by his personal example contributed materially to the successful accomplishment of the regiment's assigned mission.

Clergy Visitations

Two distinguished visitors paid visits to the forces in Korea during the Christmas Season. One was Bishop William C. Martin, President of the National Council of Churches of Christ in the U.S.A. and President of the Council of Bishops of the Methodist Church, who returned from his trip commending the commands for their interest and concern in moral and spiritual matters. He praised the work of the chaplains and was especially impressed with the 1st Marine Division. Bishop Martin said,

Thousands of them came during that snowy, freezing Christmas week, to bow in prayer in the chapels they had built with their own hands. As we reached the front lines, where they look across the 2½-mile-wide No-Man's Land of the demilitarized zone to watch the enemy digging in, many hundreds of them came to services, their guns in their hands.

Cardinal Francis Spellman, a perennial [4] visitor of the troops, reported that he had his largest congregation since making these trips.[5] He stated that more than 6,000 men attended one of the services held for the 1st Marine Division. It was also about this time that Rabbi Eichhorn conducted a series of retreats for Jewish chaplains in Japan and Korea.

Chaplain Cameron P. Hoff tells about the first Christmas after the truce. He says,

We heard the bells at Christmas. Over the frozen rice paddies they pealed their joyful song. Salvaged from some

---

[4] This was his third Christmas tour of the Korean area.
[5] His visit was from 22 December–4 January. Chaplain Giles Webster was his personal escort.

ruined temple where once a pagan god was worshipped their melodic voices now praised the Living God. From the thatch-roofed native dwellings bright-eyed babies and wrinkled, old, "papa-sans" watched in wonder as the graceful, lighted Christmas tree shed its colorful radiance upon the frozen parade ground. Where only a Christmas ago the sullen throb of bombers filled the air now the heavens were glad with the sound of carols.

We heard the bells at Christmas as we gathered in our chapel on the hill. A hundred candles spoke softly to the night, and we remembered when lights were afraid to shine as we listened in the unrelieved darkness and sirens shrieked their warning. We know the meaning of a silent night. We have lived through other nights made hideous by the shriek of shrapnel, the deadly chatter of machine gun and rifle, the dull crash of enemy mortar and artillery. Now in a silent night "all is calm, all is bright."

We heard the bells at Christmas while we remembered those for whom the bells tolled not many months ago. They

---

Christmas Vistor.

Bishop W. C. Martin looks through a B.C. Scope at an observation point overlooking Panmunjom, on his visit during the Christmas holidays. Bishop Martin was the president of the National Council of Churches.

were among the worshipers last Christmas, meeting in tiny groups wherever the chaplain could call a congregation together. They gave their lives on the treacherous raids and patrols in "no-man's land." They died valiantly on savage Korean hills in a war-spawned hell of steel and flame and fanatic enemy hordes. Now the bells are singing "sleep in heavenly peace, sleep in heavenly peace."

We heard the bells at Christmas and they brought to mind the church bells which ring out in country and city and town back home. Some of our men are spending their first Christmas far from their homes and loved ones. There are lonely hearts in Korea at Christmas. Many of the familiar Christmas customs are missing. All but the simplest holiday trappings are absent. The mission of American forces in Korea cannot pause even for this Holy Day. The lonely outposts overlooking the demarcation zone must be manned. The fortified bunkers and the long main battle position must be occupied. Even in the various command posts there are security tasks and essential services which must be performed. Still the bells are singing a glad song at Christmas. The glory and wonder of the Saviour's birth lies upon the earth this night. Over the still-broken native villages, over the shell-cratered hills, over the silent wasteland where the enemy keeps his careful vigil the bells are sounding. As the chaplains go from chapel to mess-hall to crowded bunker the carols follow and the Christmas Gospel gladdens the hearts of men.

One problem was created when Chaplain Sternberger was released from active duty about the middle of May and the Division was left without a Jewish chaplain. He had stayed until after the celebration of Passover. Chaplain O'Leary wrote in July, "We run into trouble every Sunday in our attempts to 'chopper' an Army Jewish chaplain for services. Please rush the new rabbi to us as fast as practicable." Due to the scarcity of Jewish chaplains Chaplain H. T. Miller did not arrive until 24 September to represent that faith.

Chaplain O'Leary was detached as Division chaplain the 1st of July. He was relieved by Chaplain L. M. C. Vosseler. He was awarded a Letter of Commendation, the citation of which reads in part,

He demonstrated a remarkable foresight and determination in caring for the spiritual welfare of all the Marines in the division. An understanding, capable, and persevering leader, he skillfully organized his section in such a manner that divine services were conducted within all the units of the division and spiritual guidance was available to all. Despite the most adverse conditions of terrain and weather and with complete disregard for his personal comfort, he repeatedly traveled long distances to the most remote units in order that all Marines might have the opportunity to attend services of their particular faith. He was constantly present during the repatriation of United Nations prisoners of war to ensure that the men who had so recently undergone the hardships and deprivations of prison life had every opportunity to receive immediately on their return the spiritual consolation and guidance they so eagerly sought.

By the time of the change of divisions chaplains so many changes had been made in the roster that the list for 1 July 1954 contains nearly all new chaplains.

Name	Rank	Assignment	Church affiliation
O'LEARY, F. T.	CDR	Div Chap	RC
TUXBURY, V. W.	LCDR	Hq Bn Chap.	BAPT (A)
BARRENGER, A. N.	LTJG	1st Ser Bn	PE
HEIM, R. L.	LTJG	1st MT Bn	RC
JONES, W. L.	LTJG	7th MT Bn	BAPT (S)
KENNY, T. A.	LTJG	1st SP Bn	RC
KUHLMANN, J. L.	LTJG	1st Eng Bn	AofG
MARSH, H. J.	LTJG	1st Tk Bn	L. D. S.
JOHNSON, D. A.	LTJG	1st Ar Am Bn.	EvMiss-Cov

1ST MARINES

MARTINEAU, E. R.	LCDR	H&S Co	RC
CANFIELD, R.	LTJG	2d Bn	PRESBY (U)
FAY, C. I.	LTJG	1st Bn	METH
HITCHENS, W. C.	LTJG	3d Bn	METH

5TH MARINES

JENKINS, R. W.	LCDR	H&S Co	BAPT (A)
ELWOOD, C.	LT	1st Bn	LUTH
IVERS, V. J.	LTJG	3d Bn	RC

7TH MARINES

THEOBALD, D. K.	LCDR	H&S Co	PRESBY (USA)
KIEFER, R. W.	LTJG	1st Bn	LUTH
RAINS, C. E.	LTJG	2d Bn	BAPT (S)
GIBBONS, M. F.	LTJG	3d Bn	RC

11TH MARINES

NETHERLING, E. J.	LT	HqBtry	LUTH
QUISENBERRY, J. W.	LTJG	2d Bn	Chr. SC
KANE, J. A.	LT	4th Bn	RC

3d Marine Division

Mention should be made of the reactivation of the 3d Marine Division which took place on 7 January 1952. This division was moved to Japan on 3 August 1953. It included 25 chaplains of whom Chaplain I. W. Stultz was the Division chaplain. He wrote in December about the ministry in Korea and Japan saying,

In a sense our ministry in Japan and Korea is more important now than under combat conditions. We are up against all the problems that are created when troops are garrisoned in a foreign country. We are fighting monotony, immaturity, moral illiteracy, and every factor that makes a contribution to moral degeneracy.

He then speaks of the chapel centered programs and moral leadership programs which were geared to meet the situation. In June 1954 Chaplain Maurus F. Cook relieved Chaplain Stultz.

The 1st Marine Air Wing

For the most part the recognition given to the chaplains of the Wing was for their participation in

JONES, A.	CDR
BURNS, J. J.	LCDR
LAMPE, J. H.	LCDR
FENSTERMACHER, H. F.	LCDR
O'MALLEY, F. P.	LT
SMITH, J. R.	LT
CLOONAN, J. F.	LT
STROMAN, H. W.	LTJG
McKNIGHT, P. G.[1]	LTJG

[1] McKnight was Paul's relief.

In September Chaplain Paul was detached. His Letter of Commendation includes the following comments,

He continually gave his attention to sick and wounded patients who were flown to Japan at all hours of the day and night, and greatly assisted the medical officers by maintaining an exceptionally high degree of morale among the patients. Lieutenant Commander Paul met and assisted all replacement drafts reporting for duty in the forward area.

Chapel—Third Division.

A view of a chapel used by marines of the 3d Division. This chapel is located at Camp McNair, Japan, where the 12th Marines was located. Mount Fuji is shown in the background.

relief work. This will be more fully considered in a subsequent chapter. The roster of the command was as follows,

Wing Chap	PRESBY (US)
FMAW	RC
MAG–12	PRESBY (USA)
1st90MMAABn	EVAN & REF
MAG–12	RC
MAG–33	CHRISTIAN
MAG–33	RC
	NAZARENE
MAG–16	PRESBY (USA)

It is evident from this that the Wing participated actively in the movement of the sick and wounded and of replacements.

Chaplain Lampe was awarded a Bronze Star about this same time. His citation emphasizes the work which was done for needy civilians,

Continually seeking ways to aid Korean civilians, he instigated and supervised the construction and furnishing of a new orphanage building to house 150 destitute Korean children. His ceaseless endeavors permitted the purchase of rice land for hungry Koreans and the delivery of tons of clothing and toys to needy civilians in the combat zone. Dedicated to the humanitarian principles embodied in the precept of his faith, his activities resulted directly in greater health, comfort and welfare for hundreds of helpless Korean families and orphans, and enhanced goodwill for all United Nations forces.

Before the change of Wing Chaplains, Chaplain Bennett, FMF Pac chaplain, on his visit in September 1953 noted the high morale of the chaplains, the new chapels under construction, and other aspects of the command.

Chaplain Paul of MSWG–17 had been detached without a relief at Itami. Chaplain McKnight was selected to go there. It would appear that, like other areas where troops were stationed in Japan, problems of morality and intermarriage were present at Itami so that a chaplain was essential. Chaplain McKnight was to continue covering MAG–16 (at Honshin which was about 15 minutes away by helicopter). Chaplain J. D. Gould, Southern Baptist, arrived October 1953.

Upon the detachment of Chaplain Allen Jones, Wing Chaplain, he was awarded the Legion of Merit. Concerning his work one reads,

Thoroughly understanding the problems confronting men in a combat zone, Commander Jones capably administered to the spiritual needs of military and civilian personnel of

Gift From the Fleet.

Chaplain John J. Burns, left, and Chaplain Allen Jones both of the 1st Marine Air Wing exhibit money orders received from the VALLEY FORGE for the Memorial Orphanage.

all faiths. Handicapped by the widespread dispersion of Wing units, he traveled throughout the combat area to establish a close and effective liaison between the chaplains of outlying units and the Wing chaplain's office . . . His talks to civic organizations in Korea and Japan promoted good will and mutual understanding between the Wing command and the populace of these two countries. Dedicated to the humanitarian principles embodied in the precept of his faith, he was instrumental in the purchase of rice land for undernourished Korean orphans and the delivery of tons of clothing and food to needy civilians in the combat zone. His untiring efforts resulted directly in greater health, comfort, and welfare for hundreds of helpless Korean families, thereby greatly enhancing indigenous friendship for all friendly forces in Korea.

With the departure of Chaplain Jones the new Wing Chaplain, Jeremiah F. Gearan, Roman Catholic, took over the spiritual leadership of the command.

Another chaplain decorated with the Bronze Star at this time was Chaplain Harry F. Fenstermacher. It is recognized that

His endeavors permitted the purchase of rice land for hungry Koreans and the delivery of clothing and toys to needy civilians in the combat zone. Working in close liaison with Korean military personnel, he was instrumental in helping to establish the Chaplains Corps for the Republic of Korea Navy. Dedicated to the humanitarian principles embodied in the precept of his faith, his activities resulted in greater health, comfort, and welfare for helpless Korean families and orphans and enhanced goodwill for all United Nations forces.

A Letter of Commendation was awarded Chaplain Joseph F. Cloonan calling attention to the fact that he

. . . provided inspirational guidance in ministering to the spiritual needs of men in the forward area. He was instrumental in the direction of the successful operation of a special Catholic orphanage at Pohang, Korea. Enhancing good will through his ceaseless endeavors to aid needy civilians, he personally delivered hundreds of packages of food and clothing to destitute Korean families. Dedicated to the humanitarian principles embodied in the precept of his faith, Lieutenant Cloonan's activities resulted directly in greater comfort and welfare for many helpless Korean families and orphans, and enhanced the morale and efficiency of the 1st Marine Aircraft Wing.

One other award of the Commendation Ribbon was made to Chaplain Francis P. O'Malley which noted that his

. . . endeavors assisted in the construction of a school for a Korean orphanage and the delivery of clothing, food, and milk to needy civilians in the combat zone. He gave valuable and untiring assistance as a member of the Korean Rehabilitation Board which controls the building of schools, milk stations and sanitation facilities for Korean refugees and orphans. Dedicated to the humanitarian principles embodied in the precepts of his faith, his activities resulted in greater health, comfort, and welfare for helpless Korean families and orphans and enhanced goodwill for all United Nations forces.

The wing also built chapels. As Chaplain James B. Martin expressed it,

Our Marine Air Group has been working its way out of the mud. Fortunately, in 3 months we were able to give the men a newly painted and 100 percent enlarged chapel, seating 154. It is converted to two small chapels for weekly and private devotions. No one under the same circumstances has a nicer religious arrangement, anywhere in the 1st Marine Air Wing.

Chaplain Samuel B. Bennett had previously stated that this Chapel—MAG–11—was too small, but plans were being made to enlarge it.

Forces Afloat

The continual problem for chaplains afloat was the matter of coverage. During October through December, at the invitation of RADM, W. D. Johnson, Chaplain Herbert C. Albrecht of the KEASARGE functioned as coordinator for all the ships in Task Force 77. Dispatches were sent out to the ships inviting them to send in requests for services prior to 1200 Friday. Chaplains were then scheduled for the extra services.

. . . the admiral issued a regular operational plan for Sundays to move chaplains around in the task force mostly by helicopter. Chaplains were "hopping" all over the task force in accordance with this "Sky Flight Plan."

The Flag PIO issued this communique:

From CTF 77

FOR PIO X RELIGIOUS SERVICES ON SUNDAY ARE A USUAL ROUTINE FOR FOLKS WHO LIVE ON LAND BUT TO SEAGOING MEN, SCATTERED IN FORMATION WITH A NAVAL TASK FORCE THEY ARE SOMETHING SPECIAL X PARA X TODAY, WITH TASK FORCE 77, OPERATING IN THE FAR EASTERN WATERS ON TRAINING EXERCISES, NEARLY EVERY SHIP IN THIS UNIT WAS AFFORDED AN OPPORTUNITY TO PASS THE WORD THAT RELIGIOUS SERVICES WOULD BE HELD X MANY OF THE SMALLER SHIPS DO NOT HAVE A CHAPLAIN ABOARD AND HELICOPTERS WERE USED TO FLY 6 NAVY CHAPLAINS FROM CARRIERS AND A CRUISER TO DESTROYERS OF THE FORCE X THE AERIAL "SKY PILOTS" CONDUCTED 19 SERVICES FOR THEIR SEAGOING CONGREGATIONS IN MESS HALLS, RECEPTION ROOMS AND ON HANGAR DECKS X

Admiral Johnson stated that the willingness of the chaplains concerned to travel by helicopter and high-line in order to conduct services has been an inspiration to all hands. Chaplain Joseph M. Broadley reports on his circuit riding during this period

While attached to the Staff of Commander Landing Ship Flotilla ONE, and in the Far East, I followed the practice of riding on different ships of the Flotilla (LST, ARL, LSMR). During October 1953, I spent 2 weeks on the LSMR 401 while it was on patrol along the west coast of Korea. To my knowledge this type ship had not had a chaplain aboard for duty, other than to conduct Divine Worship, prior to this time.

Chaplain Kenneth D. Killin of the BATAAN carried a small kit which he had made himself for the purpose of holding services for small groups.

A number of chaplains assisted the fleet as they had in the past. Chaplain Thomas D. Parham is mentioned as conducting Character Education lectures for Destroyer Squadron 22. Chaplain Daniel J. Silver reports that he conducted Jewish services over a territory extending from the Formosa Straits to Korea. He also found time to coach a football team, the Yokosuka Seahawks.

Chaplain Hedges Capers in the SICILY tells of the fine group of Christian laymen which he had on board

The active participation of the men on the USS SICILY was unusual. We had a group of approximately 15 who consistently took part in all worship services. For the Sunday services, one man would read the scriptures, another would lead in the responsive reading. This same practice prevailed in the Tuesday night Bible class. The Thursday night fellowship hour was conducted exclusively by the men with previous assistance by me. I used to end this meeting with closing remarks. The Saturday night prayer meeting was conducted solely by the men. The Sunday evening service was conducted by the men. My only contributions took the form of advice and coaching beforehand. This entire program was carried on while we were at sea and in foreign ports.

Hospital ships continued in the area. Chaplain O'Leary in the HAVEN indicates that he aided a number of servicemen of different nationalities.

MSTS

Chaplain James R. Spaid speaking of the daily newspaper aboard his ship had this item of interest,

On a number of occasions we have carried United Nations troops (Puerto Ricans, Ethiopians, Greeks, French, Turks etc.), and in each instance a special effort was made to condense the world news, [draw up] schedules of religious and other activities that would be of interest to these men and published [them] in the regular daily paper in their own respective languages. While on board the GEN. WM. BLACK (T–AP135), we carried the French Battalion from Inchon, Korea to Saigon, Indo-China (during the last week of October 1953). Since these were the only troops aboard we published the entire paper in French and English in columns side by side. In this way the French troops had an opportunity to pick up a little English and our Military Department and Crew were able to study the equivalent in French. The men seemed to appreciate this effort on the part of the newspaper staff which also happened to be staffed by Frenchmen with the exception of my yeoman.

Chaplain Russell A. Cervin wrote a lengthy picture of the work of the MSTS Chaplain called "To Korea and Back." The closing paragraphs capture the feeling of the troops as they went to, or returned from Korea.

Early in the summer of 1951 a process of rotation of troops in Korea began. Prior to that time many of our ships returned to the United States without passengers. Before that time everything was going the other way. Since that time we have carried full loads both ways.

Embarkation of troops leaving the States for Korea has its sorrows. I've seen women cling to their men and have to be forcibly pried loose from them so they could board the vessel. Just after pulling away from the dock an officer of many years in the Army said to me one day, "After being in the Army as long as I have you are supposed to be tough. But I'm not very tough right now." A tear glistened on his cheek as his wife and child were standing on the dock straining for a last glimpse of husband and father.

The attitudes of men going to combat are different from those of the men returning from it. On the way over they are somewhat tense as they face an unknown future. There is a certain amount of effervescence in church going which is sloughed off on the way home. Outbound church services are crowded with habitual churchgoers plus those with "foxhole religion." On the way home the men who have always gone to church are present plus a number of others who have found a vital religious experience on the way over or on the field of battle. Though the attendance going home is not quite as large, it is often more stable.

When leaving the States for Korea the men are more serious in attitude than the men returning, though those coming home are more mature. Especially is this evident in the harbor at Inchon. Going down our gangway headed for a long period of duty in Korea the men are serious and quiet. But when the LSU's pour out the homecoming troops on the floating dock there are wild shouts of joy and a great deal of joking and laughter. I took some pictures of the dock full of happy soldiers waiting to climb our gangway. Everyone yelled and waved and wanted to get into the act. They were filled with relief and joy at leaving Korea.

Rest and Rehabilitation

One of the problems that existed among troops should be mentioned. This had to do with R and R (Rest and Rehabilitation). Chaplain James A. Whitman, Bapt(A), ComNavFe Chaplain, writing in March states that the 1st Division and the 1st MAW send men to Japan for R and R continually. Chaplain Whitman insisted on the necessity of the proper briefing of newly arrived chaplains because of this problem.

This R and R situation is a most serious problem effecting American prestige in the whole Far East. I feel this briefing is very vital and most important to the moral welfare of the men the chaplain will serve in Korea. Part of the briefing process is to encourage the chaplain to go to Tokyo where he contacts chapel centers, religious leaders and tries to get a fair picture of what worth-while things servicemen can do in a city like Tokyo. (Most men gravitate to Tokyo no matter where their R and R transportation drops them off.)

The Far East Command Chaplains' Committee, of which I am a member, is trying desperately to determine how to improve the R and R program and how to help servicemen better use their time spent in Japan, especially those who come for 8-day periods from Korea.

Far East Chaplains of Army, Navy, and Air Force are all sure that much of the problem must be solved through the leadership and "on the spot knowledge" of chaplains serving units in Korea; and this character training must be done largely before the briefing given to men just before jumping to Japan for leave.

End of Campaign

The campaign was over. Many of the Reserve chaplains had already or were planning to return to civilian activities. As has been noted most of the men now with the divisions and the airgroups were new. An audit of the Korean conflict reveals that out of

. . . the nearly 950 chaplains who were on active duty during the time of the Korean hostilities—i.e., from June 1950 to the cease-fire agreement of July 1953—166 Navy chaplains had served with the Marines in Korea and approximately 150 others served aboard U.S. ships in Korean waters, making a total of about 316. This was 35 percent of the total Corps.

Chaplain Samuel B. Bennett answers the question that many people in the United States were asking, "What are the chaplains doing now that hostilities have ceased?" It is not a difficult question to answer, because it is what they always do in peace time. Chaplain Bennett's reply was

They are ministering to the needs of the men. These needs are not peculiar to Korea and Japan. Perhaps there is more sensitivity toward God and our homes because they are so far away. I know there is a constant hunger for companionship and fellowship. This gives the chaplain an opportunity to be close and offer guidance and give assurance that God cares and that each person counts.

Korea must still be occupied. The needs of the civilian population were crying to be met. The problems of all occupation troops were now to descend upon the chaplains. In most cases a great deal of the attention of the men was directed toward helping others and in the process their own problems faded into insignifiance, something of the magnitude of these projects is now to be considered.

CHAPTER TWELVE

CIVILIAN ASSISTANCE

Civilian Assistance

"I have given it to . . . the sojourner, the father-less, and the widow according to all the command-ments which Thou hast commanded me." Deut. 26:13.

No history of naval chaplains in Korea would be complete if it were confined purely to chaplains' activi-ties in assigned military units. It is essential that one have at least a partial picture of the deeds which the chaplains accomplished in other areas. Nationals came out of the hills on numerous occasions to at-tend the divine services held by chaplains. Through the chaplains' examples at Inchon the Korean Marine and Navy chaplaincies were established.

Korean service troops worked and died beside the Marines and were ministered unto by Navy chaplains. Through chaplains working among civilians, churches were rebuilt, sermons were preached and sacraments were administered even for those confined to leper colonies. Hospitals, schools, and clinics were aided and even at times established to care for the needy. The greatest accomplishment was found in the con-cern the chaplains, and the personnel of their units, had for the "little hungry ragged beggar orphans who roamed the streets and fields," and what they did for them.

In recounting this saga, due to lack of information, many groups and individuals will not be given their full credit but the true recognition of the deeds of men are best written in the hearts of those whom they aid. However, it is hoped that this account will at least, in part, pay tribute to one of the truly great achievements of Navy chaplains in Korea.

Previously in this work certain individual projects have been noted, but it is felt that special attention should now be called to these projects collectively.

The problems of Korea were felt all during the con-flict, but they did not end with its cessation. With the complete destruction of one-half million homes and an equal number damaged, the primary task was to assure the survival of a good percentage of the population. In fact 9 million people were homeless or refugees. Though 80 percent of the hospitals were demolished even more destructive was the loss of both parents on the part of 100,000 children.

The chaplains' story of participation in the civilian projects began virtually when the first chaplain ar-rived and continued as long as a charitable man of the Armed Forces remained. It did not include just Korea but it extended throughout the Far East. Many ships, stations and units not only assisted in this program, but also continued to remember charities at home with additional donations to Red Cross, March of Dimes, Navy Relief, and in the case of the WIS-CONSIN participation in the Madison (Wisconsin) Community Chest. A lengthy catalogue could be drawn up of all the benefactors and their recipients. And even that would only begin to tell the story. It has been estimated that in services and supplies al-most $365 million for relief had been given by the end of 1953, and there are still agencies today who continue the work.

As most of the Christian population of Korea was Presbyterian much of the relief work was done among members of this denomination. Someone has ranked the religious groups according to numerical strength in the following order: Presbyterians, Roman Cath-olics, Methodists, Korean Holiness (not to be confused with the Holiness groups in America) and the Sev-enth Day Adventists.[1] One of the wonderful things

---

[1] Muller gives estimates in his book:

Presbyterians_____ 650,000
Methodists_____ 200,000
Korean Holiness_____ 50,000
Others:
    Baptist, Church of Christ, Salvation Army,
      Episcopal, Seventh Day Adventists_____ *50,000
    Roman Catholics_____ 250,000
*President of Korean National Christian Council gives a total of a million and a half Protestants.

was the fine spirit of cooperation among the diverse groups of Christianity. Where the need was, attempts were made to meet it by everyone irrespective of religious affiliation. Pictures and articles show Protestant Chaplains helping Roman Catholic institutions and vice versa. When human beings needed clothing, food, and shelter or else they would die, chaplains did not pass by on the other side. America can well be proud of the Good Samaritans of all rates and ranks in the Armed Forces of Korea.

Pusan

At the beginning one should start with Pusan. It was about the closest to Japan and it was here in the early days of the conflict that many of the refugees gathered. As has been noted seminaries moved here from Seoul. Even today refugee problems remain in this city. Chaplain Henry F. Maxwell, of the USS THOMAS JEFFERSON, states that in 1950 he had only brief contacts with the Korean Christians at Pusan, but already he was encouraging the sending of money and clothing to the destitute. Chaplain Edgar A. Day tells of the evacuation of Chinnampo and transporting the refugees to Pusan in December 1951. He says,

We had been at Yokosuka, Japan, only a few days when we received urgent orders to proceed to Chinnampo to evacuate refugees and ROK soldiers. We arrived there December 4. We worked all night taking those poor people aboard; men, women, and children. The saddest thing was bringing the ROK soldiers aboard. Over 600 were wounded, 500 being stretcher cases. Their wounds had been unattended for 10 days. They were hungry, cold and in great pain. Yet, few of them moaned or complained of their pain. They are rugged people with seemingly a stoical approach to pain and disaster. Of course, I was at a disadvantage not speaking their language. Our ship wasn't prepared to care for so many people, especially so many wounded. We had our ship's doctor, two South Korean doctors, one South Korean nurse and woman chemist. We never did get to change all the dressings or do the necessary surgery that many needed. They were aboard 2 days. I spent my time carrying water and emptying urinals, etc. Yet there were rewards.

Very few spoke English. Most who did were Christians. One young man who spoke fair English asked me one day, "Why are you so kind to poor Korean soldiers?" I told him I was a Christian and a minister. He then told me that he was a Christian also. The Korean doctor and nurse who were with me at that time said they were also Christians. They didn't understand English but seemed to know what the word "Christian" meant. Out of the 600 men I had several expressions of appreciation, if not in words, in the expression of their faces.

I mention the above because I got disgusted several times at the lack of concern for each other among the soldiers. Few indeed, would carry water and care for the physical needs without direct orders and careful supervision. We would get some able-bodied soldiers to work carrying refuse up and out of the compartment. Then they would disappear. We then had to round up more men and watch them most of the time to see that they, too, didn't take off.

We had five men who were "YMCA men" from Chinnampo. They had their English-Korean Dictionary and phrase books. Hung Seek Ann was the son of a Methodist pastor in Chinnampo. His father was murdered by the Communists as they fled northward. As the Communists were now threatening the city all Christian leaders were forced to flee to save their lives. Kee Taik Bak was a pastor of the Duk Lunk Ree Church. He also was studying at a seminary in the city. I couldn't quite understand all the details of his life. He said he had a large family of little ones and property in Chinnampo. Therefore, he couldn't take them with him. Since he was a pastor he would be immediately shot. I suppose he feels that his family would be reasonably safe since it was the leaders who would be in danger. He came to my room and wanted to sing. He hummed the hymn, "My Country 'Tis of Thee." So we two sang the entire song through. He sang in English most of the time, occasionally lapsing into his native tongue on a word or two. Then we sang all the Christmas hymns we could locate. I tell you it was a lovely duet. Then we had prayer. He prayed fervently. Seldom have I heard a more sincere prayer. I reached over and placed my hand on his knees to show I understood. Hot tears washed my hand literally in a stream. Later on he and three buddies came back and we duplicated the service. They loved "My Country 'Tis of Thee." After seeing the country I would say it applied to Korea as much as to America. It was a great experience. We left the refugees at Pusan.

Chaplain Charles E. Webb tells of another group of refugees from the other side of the peninsula. They were brought back by Chaplain John Murphy from the North Korean city of Hungnam and were classified into two groups, "one consisting of a Catholic priest and six nuns in charge of a large number of small Korean orphans and a small contingent of aged people; the other was a group of sick adults between the ages of 20 and 50." In order to make these groups at least partially self sustaining a laundry was set up in their dwellings and the Marines of MAG 12 gave of their dirty linen to be washed by this grateful group. The second group was supplied with items needed to make clothing. Many of these items, including a sewing machine, were secured by the chaplains from Japan.

Chaplain Wendell C. Wheeler on MSTS duty reports bringing clothing, powdered milk, and vitamins to Inchon and Pusan which had been donated by a west coast group. Chaplain Barnes notes refugees from Seoul in Pusan and the fact that assistance was rendered to Chosen Theological Seminary.[2] As has been

---

[2] See pp. 99, 101, 112.

Ewha University.

Dr. Helen Kim, president of Ewha University expresses her appreciation for the aid given by U.N. troops in Korea at services at the 1st MAW.

Dedication of the 11th Marine Memorial School for Girls.

Bishop Choi delivers a brief message during the dedication of the school at Masan to which the 11th Marine Regiment contributed $12,000.

noted the seminary had only two squad tents and nondescript shacks constructed of surveyed material given by the military. It was here that they lived and studied. Offerings were taken at the services of the 1st MAW and given to the president of the seminary. As the only institution licensed by the government to grant a B.D. degree, they continued under these adverse conditions to turn out ministers for work in their country.

Another institution that had moved to the Pusan area from Seoul was Ewha University, one of the oldest institutions of higher learning for women in Asia. It, too, was aided by the Marines. Later the *New York Times* in an editorial of 18 June 1956 called attention to the 70th anniversary of the university and stated that it had an enrollment of 5,000 students. It further stated that gifts from the United States made possible the dedication of a new building and facilities "this week" at Seoul.

Clothing was given to orphanages and "Lighthouse"—the Korean organization for work with the blind. The existence of the Korean Blind School in Pusan has previously been noted.

The USS BATAAN delivered 4 tons of clothing to a transport for transshipment to Korea. Chaplain John J. Coffey was among those who accompanied the shipment to Pusan. It was thought that this ship was the first to collect and deliver a large load of clothing to Korea. Distribution was made to the Maryknoll Sisters Clinic, the Sae Dul Children's Home and the Central Presbyterian Church. The REPOSE gave $2,000 to Pusan Orphanage the winter of 1952.

Chaplain Fenstermacher tells of the situation in Pusan during his stay there,

There was no combat in the Pusan area during the period I was there. It was a rear area, and since it is a large city it became one of the main havens for refugees and was filled to overflowing with people. The overflow built themselves makeshift shacks of any kind of scrap materials they could gather—wood, tin, discarded beer cans—in any open spaces they could find in alleyways, along the edges of fields or the banks of the river, and on the hillsides. Then came the problem of making a living for the family in a city already overstaffed with employable people. The orphans took refuge in the many orphanages which had been set up in and around the city. These were filled, but they always seemed to be able to make room for more. Some orphaned children roamed the streets and slept wherever they could find room, such as at the railroad depot or under the piers along the waterfront. On inquiry I found that many of these did this by choice; they had been admitted to orphanages, but would not submit to the discipline and attendance at school demanded by the orphanages, or else felt they could get more food by begging or by some other means of their own. So they left the orphanages.

Anything we could do would be only a drop in the bucket among so many poverty-stricken people. But as a battalion we tried. We had our personnel write home to ask for used clothing to be distributed to help keep these Koreans warm during the winter. The response was very good. Packages of clothing began to arrive within several weeks, and continued to arrive from then on. As much as possible I had the men themselves deliver the clothing for distribution to the needy. Since all the firing batteries were located near some village, some of the clothing went to these villages to be given to the needy in the villages, the deputation of Marines often consulting with the "head men" of the villages to determine the needy. Other clothing went to the Baptist,

Methodist, Presbyterian, Seventh Day Adventist, and Roman Catholic Missions. They had constant calls for clothing, never seemed to have enough to go around; and they either knew the people asking for clothing or else often investigated the family before giving (an important point, since Koreans have been known to feign extreme poverty, accept clothing, and then sell it at the market). Other clothing we took directly to orphanages and to the Old Folks' Home at Tongnae, near Pusan.

. . . H and S Battery held a Christmas Party to which 60 orphans from the Cross Orphanage were invited. In addition to clothing, canned and packaged foods, candy, and toys were given to the orphans. At the same time, all the firing batteries held parties to which they invited the children of the villages located near them and gave them similar gifts. The children of the Cross Orphanage were trained to put on a show consisting of tumbling, singing, and skits. They staged their show at each of our batteries at least twice, always receiving an offering in Korean money for the support of the orphanage besides other gifts.

Not all of the relief items necessarily arrived at their destination. Chaplain Philip P. Shannon, Roman Catholic, states that several cases of powdered milk,

. . . destined for an orphanage in Pusan and transported from the States aboard the GENERAL STURGIS, were seized by Japanese sentries in Yokohama as possible black market merchandise. The reporting chaplain was "simply" attempting to leave the milk with the port chaplain, Yokohama, for the first available shipment to Pusan. Since the GENERAL STURGIS was departing immediately for Inchon, a frantic call was made to the port chaplain's office. However, time did not allow the "black marketing chaplain" to see the outcome of the incident nor has he ever found out what became of the skimlac.

Chaplain Preston C. Oliver, Presbyterian (US), in the USS VULCAN met a young Korean who was attending the seminary in Pusan who became his interpreter. Later the chaplain arranged for the man to attend seminary in the United States.

There were a number of recipients of relief goods. These included the Christian Social Service Center (Methodist), the Chief of Chaplains of the ROK Navy for further distribution and others. The CONSOLATION aided the Maryknoll Clinic. One of the relief projects was "Operation Goodwill" which was put on by the MT. McKINLEY. Her Chaplain, Thomas M. Gibson, reports that clothing was collected on the west coast and delivered to the Hope Hospital in Pusan, a hospital sponsored by the Reformed Church of Holland, Mich. Chaplain Kenneth W. Carlson tells of ships making contributions to Pusan after her disastrous fire.

Masan

About 30 miles to the west of Pusan there was another city which was assisted by our forces. It was the city of Masan. Chaplain William A. Rennie tells of the winter of 1950–51. The Medical Battalion was invited by the neighboring Presbyterian Church to use their sanctuary for worship.

For the Christmas Eve service, one of the Catholic corpsmen volunteered to create a manger-scene tableaux with about 10 of the children of the church. Everything went off fine, as by candlelight, with the Korean congrega-

---

BATAAN Delivers Clothing.

Crates of clothing are brought on Navy trucks to the Maryknoll Sisters Clinic at Pusan.

Lt. (jg.) Joseph Holtzer (left); Chaplain John J. Coffey (center), and Cmdr. Ralph W. Arendt of the BATAAN pose with children at the Sae Dul Children's Home in Pusan. They helped deliver over 7,500 pounds of clothing brought by the ship from San Diego to the Far East.

Marines Discuss School.

The future of the 11th Marine Regiment Memorial School in Korea is discussed by, left to right, Lt. Col. R. D. Heinl, Jr., executive officer; Chaplain Leo F. Rice; M. Sgt. J. D. Sharpe; M. Sgt. R. M. Tarlton; and Col. James E. Mills, commanding officer of the regiment.

tion as our guests, the choir sang "Silent Night" and the lifelike tableaux was posed in a corner of the church. Corpsmen and Marines placed their gifts at the foot of the cradled-babe. A very effective service of worship and dedication was the result.

Incidentally, a few days later, the pastor of the church, in order to show the appreciation of his people for the gifts given to the church, presented me with about 180 pounds of roasted peanuts for the "church men and sick patients."

Chaplain Bingaman [3] affirms that the offering taken from January to May 1951 resulted in the eventual establishment of a Catholic parochial school. The Protestant offerings were distributed to the seven native congregations. It was through these offerings that the Methodist and the Presbyterian congregations were enabled to renovate the interior of their sanctuaries. The parochial school referred to above was built by the 11th Marines and was called the 11th Marine Memorial School for Girls, (or St. Joseph Catholic School) "in memory of our Regiment's dead and disabled." Chaplain Kulinski credits the building of the school to the desire of the Marines to make amends for the devastating artillery damage suffered by the city. It is interesting to note that some of the funds contributed to this school came from the contri-

bution of refunds on "coke" bottles. Chaplain Rice writes,

The education problem is great. The children love to learn. There is a big beautiful school built by the 11th Marines in town: It is a middle school, for girls, and trains 500 girls between 12 and 17.

There are several other middle schools and many grammar schools. But some of the classrooms are made of salvage tenting. One principal had a plan for a good school. The people were willing to help—but a hill occupied the spot. The Marines sent out bulldozers and leveled the place that would have taken several months by Korean methods.

In another note Chaplain Rice states that the girls of the school put on "a parade to show their appreciation of the $12,000 contributed by the 11th . . . Marines."

This chaplain also tells of

. . . a village of some 7,000 people right behind the stay-back-line. The interpreter helped us when we distributed candy and clothing. When I asked him if the people had any religion, he said: "We are all Episcopalians." Monsignor Carroll at Pusan was able to send me a hundred bags of clothing from the NCWC.

Chaplain Waters tells of aiding a seminary in Masan,

In May 1951, I [surveyed] eight "shotup" tents and gave

[3] See p. 62f.

[them] to the Masan Seminary which was forced to leave Seoul. There were about 90 students and 10 teachers and they were attempting to carry on their classes in various homes and churches. In order to realize any shelter from these eight tents, we placed four tents over four in such manner that the bullet holes would not be in the same places. Under these the seminary was able to carry on its work for another month until it was moved to a former Japanese Temple.

He also tells of the remodeling of the churches mentioned above but states that the Methodist Church had been destroyed by fire. "We gave an offering to either one of the churches, the orphanage, the seminary, a kindergarten, or the Korean hospital." He states that his unit, the 1st Amph. Traction Battalion raised $1,396 for these causes.

In Chaplain Austin's monthly report of 30 July 1951 of the Chapel Fund it was indicated that the offerings were given to the Reverend Kim Chang Ho, president of the local pastor's organization, for distribution among refugees, school children, and orphans.

Chaplain Rice adds color to ones view of Korean life by telling of the

. . . festival of the eighth moon and the town of Masan—like other towns in Korea—would celebrate the harvest with 3 days of festivity.

To us Americans it seemed strange to see this type of Thanksgiving Day. The fields of grain were ready for cutting. The stems of high grass weighted with grains of rice waved gently in the paddies. Sorghum stood, with bent tassle, like the blossoming corn at home. Children stood guard over every terrace—acting as live scare crows. Here was a harvest yet to be taken.

Masan has something to be grateful for. The path of war has not shattered the mud walls of its homes. The guerillas are not active in this area. The military salvage points give the refugees a great deal of work. The people seem ever to be on the go—either to market or home again—but they realize little for all their work.

Problems face this harbor town. Sewage and garbage disposal seem to be nonexistent—or perhaps it is that the open sewers were adequate when the town was smaller.

. . . To make the festival of the eighth moon a better day—to show that we Marines noticed their sorry plight—a group of Marines decided to do something. We could brighten the day for the most abandoned at least on this festival.

Clothing had been sent from the States and

By this time we knew fairly well the need of the people. The directors of the homes of old ladies, for orphans, for the refugees, know that the chaplain will listen to their requests. By this time we had a list of all the asylums in town. So one fine day off we went.

Captain Davis, six Marines and the chaplain headed for the neediest "homes." Under the bridge there lived some 38 women, as many men again, and children. In all about 80 people lived under that bridge. The roof was good, if a little damp: it was a concrete bridge. The floors of the shacks underneath were more scanty: they were drafty, and would let in the flow of water when the stream would rise. The Marines went to each woman and presented her with a bundle of clothing—trying meanwhile to avoid a stampede. Then we went off to the refugee centers. They live in tents. By now the tentage has faded under the sun and has been beaten by the weather. No longer does it keep out the rain. In an area 20 by 20 there will be 8 families housed. We brought the truck in close to a building allowing room for a single lane of persons. When the women came through that lane they could not stampede the Marines. By the time we had given out the bundles a few had caught on to the idea that they could crawl under the truck and beat the line.

Next we went down to the beggars' center. Before we reached this place we sent our interpreter ahead to speak to the boss and tell him what would happen. One Marine spotted a dirty old beggar, crouched against a fence. He brought her a bundle. She took it with joy and sorted its contents. Right before our eyes she changed into the clothing. She was very modest about the whole thing. A person in the latest beach tent could not have changed clothing better. One Marine said: "I'll never forget that sight till my dying day."

At the old ladies' home the poor old folks came out to meet us. These little people greet you like grandma on Mother's Day. They will work these pieces of clothing over. At the end this clothing will meet the Korean size and style. We did not hesitate to leave old overcoats and those old kimonos, night gowns and house dresses here. They will all be used. The old ladies once asked for a sewing machine. Now I see why.

Up to the orphan asylums we drove. The collections donated at the Catholic and Protestant services on Sundays had helped these places. In one place the Sunday collection was enough to put in a radiant heating system (for $50 the Koreans can install such a system: they merely have a small stove at a very low angle on one end of the house. As the flue rises, it proceeds diagonally upward under the floor, so that the flue rises at the other end of the house. Meanwhile the heat of the flue will heat stones under the floor and provide the heat.) As a result of our visits to these orphan homes the children knew us. They put on a little show for us. We left them sweaters and whatever little bit of children's clothing we had.

The festival was a happier day—for the orphans, house girls, people living under the bridges, beggar centers, refugee centers and many more. In all, some 750 bundles were given out—clothing for an estimated 2,000 people. And the Marines were happy in this task. When asked why his eyes were so red one Marine said: "I'm allergic to the dust we pick up in the warehouse when we opened those bags: but I love this job."

Most likely these poor people we helped were amongst the people who could not afford to buy a ticket for the arena. That afternoon we saw a thousand people or more peeping over the fence watching the ox fight, a mild Korean custom.

Another city in this area was Chinhae. It was here that the PIEDMONT left gifts of money and clothing according to Chaplain Harold F. Symons.

Visitors on the PIEDMONT.

Chaplain James F. Heffernan is host to a group from the Sacred Heart Kindergarten, Chinhae, Korea. The children put on a show in Korean dress for the ship's company.

Inchon

Chaplain Rennie writes that

A few days after going ashore at Inchon with the 1st Marine Division, through one of the Korean workers, I made contact with a local Methodist Church on the outskirts of town. The church had sustained some bomb damage. The pastor of the church would not accept help but rather offered a choir for the Sunday services at the Division hospital.[4]

Chaplain Wylie R. Bryant tells a story of refugees in this area while he was serving aboard a MSTS vessel. He writes,

On a bitter, cold night of early January 1951, the watch officer of the USNS MARINE ADDER, anchored in Inchon Harbor, Korea, heard cries for help coming from the sea. The searchlights revealed a 20-foot wooden boat filled with Korean refugees sinking some 100 yards off starboard of the ship. Life boats were immediately launched and the refu-

gees were brought aboard the ADDER. There were 27 people, 18 of whom were small children. These Koreans had left their home in Seoul to escape the Communist invasion, and with the last money they had they had purchased this decrepit boat in an attempt to escape by sea to a refuge in South Korea. Only a few miles from shore the boat began to sink.

When we brought them aboard they were sick, hungry, and very frightened. Medical care and food was immediately given to them. The crew and military personnel of the ship gave items of their own personal gear to supplement their clothing. They were bedded down in one of the compartments for the night, and were transferred on the next morning to a Destroyer of the South Korean Navy which took them to a safe refuge.

Somewhat later a MSTS Chaplain, William J. Trower, Roman Catholic, learned of the Tabitha Home for Widows and Orphans, which included women who had lost their husbands as a result of the war; some had been soldiers but others had been purged by the Communists. They needed a sewing

---

[4] Cp. p. 21.

machine. The crew of his ship heard of this and *four* machines were obtained in Japan together with 19 bolts of cloth. Over and above this, materials were brought back for the use of missionaries. Chaplain Richard J. Holmes in the ELDORADO spent many months at Inchon during which time he states that a great deal of work was accomplished among the refugees and the orphans. Food, clothing, and toys were supplied to two orphanages in Seoul, two in Inchon, and two in Pusan. In addition assistance was given to a hospital. The hospital ships, REPOSE and HAVEN, brought food, milk, sewing machines, spoons, bowls, etc. Chaplain O'Leary states that the HAVEN brought about 10 tons of supplies in January 1953 including in addition to the above: medicines and bedding. Forty boxes and burlap bags of supplies were brought over in 1954. Surveyed medicines were given to the clinics.

A number of ships contributed to the Woman's Police Orphanage. Some of these were the GEORGE CLYMER, CONSOLATION, and the LOS ANGELES. Letters of appreciation were received from many groups of which the one from this institution is typical,

this civil war has made plenty of poor orphans who are lost their parents and warm cradle, they were wandered on the cold street during cold winter night, but now this orphanage fortunately have men like you who are very kind helper in the world especially UN force, We have feeling very thankful day and night (English translation of the Korean).

In addition Chaplain Black of the CONSOLATION speaks of interest in the work of the First Presbyterian Church of Inchon among widows and unwed mothers. A number of the chaplains of the 1st Division speak of aiding Inchon orphans.

Most of the ships mentioned above and units of the 1st Division supported the Star of the Sea Orphanage and hospital operated by the sisters of St. Paul. Parentless babies were cared for here. Most of the major equipment had been destroyed by the Red troops, but an up-to-date dispensary was able to care for most medical needs. The Catholic institution also cared for many older children.

The story of a foundling is interesting. He was found on the dusty, war-torn streets of Inchon. He was temporarily cared for at the dispensary of the Army Service Command headquarters, commonly called "Ascom City," from there he was transferred to The Star of the Sea where Chaplain Edward O. Riley became interested in the lad. Chaplain Riley of the POINT CRUZ brought the child aboard the CONSOLATION for a physical examination. It was after the examination that the examining doctor told the chaplain he wanted to adopt the child. Arrangements were made. The child was brought aboard the chaplain's ship for transportation but was suddenly transferred to the transport GENERAL GAFFEY to go to Seattle, much to the consternation of the carrier's personnel. Father Riley was temporarily detached from his ship to escort the baby to Seattle. Because the child was nameless he was called George Cruz Anscom.

It was also at Inchon that St. Paul's Cathedral, which was badly damaged by the North Koreans when they occupied the city, was redecorated by the voluntary contributions of money and labor by UN forces.

A unique establishment was that of Inchon Sungyuk, on the island of Fushi (Fussito, Fusshi-do). When the Communist invaders entered Inchon they took over the buildings of the Inchon Christian Orphanage, which had been established in 1946 by Holiness Church Missionaries. The children were left to fend for themselves. Kwak Sun Yong, a Holiness missionary, picked some of them up, but he was caught between enemy fire. He finally brought them to the island where he and his wife took on the responsibility of caring for the group which consisted of 34 little boys in addition to his own family. The children learned gardening and fishing, both of which are important vocations on the island. They also were given basic education by their "parents." The "Family" was found and mentioned aboard ship by a working party of the ST. PAUL which was sent ashore to set up a navigation marker. It was nearly an "all hands evolution" in an attempt to aid the orphanage.[5] Chaplain Faber H. Wickham lists the work done by the ST. PAUL for this group during the winter of 1950–51. Housing facilities were rebuilt; food, clothing, and money were donated. Requests made to U.S. families for help, as in other instances, met with a fine response. The LOS ANGELES, in which Chaplain Organ[6] was assigned, took over the project[7] from the ST. PAUL. There was also an assist from the TOLEDO according to Chaplain Vosseler. By this time the number of orphans had risen to 42.

---

[5] See article entitled "Armed Forces Care Through CARE," *U.S. Naval Institute Proceedings.* August 1955, vol. 81, No. 8, pp. 897ff.
[6] An interesting side note concerning this chaplain is that he repairs watches as a hobby. His repair equipment was so bulky that when the question of his detachment came up, his commanding officer requested that he be retained until the ship came back to the States so that the equipment could more easily be removed from the vessel. This was granted.
[7] This ship reports having aided 10 orphanages and hospitals in Korea.

Korean Lepers.

One hundred forty of the 300 patients of Son Ke Won Leper Colony crowd into their small church for Sunday services conducted by Chaplain Muller. The girl on the left is collecting the church offering.

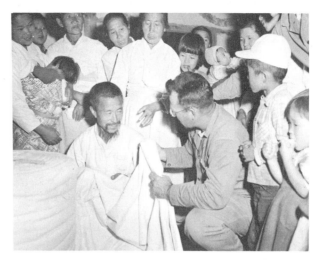

Operation Love.

Chaplain Martineau shows Whang In Sun a part of a bolt of white English wool sent by the BOXER as a part of Operation Love which brought over 30 tons of clothing to Korea.

Chaplain Muller tells somewhat in detail his work at Ascom City and environs in his book "Wearing the Cross in Korea."[8] He restored the brick chapel there for worship which he calls "second to none in Korea." Through the contributions of an aunt, Della Muller, the first Christian church was erected in a Korean Veterans' Camp (Wha Rang). Chaplain Muller tells of the new building constructed for the Yaktai Church and a framed tent church for the Sixth Presbyterian Church at Inchon, and also for a new church at Ta-nam-lee.

Chaplain Muller performed outstanding work with the leper colony at Song-Ke-Won, about 2½ miles from Ascom City. At his first service he had 150 present. Through gifts of the men at Anscom Chapel and a group of Army personnel at Inchon Chapel and friends in the United States, together with a small gift from the lepers themselves, a chapel was constructed and dedicated on 23 November 1952 with an attendance of 405. Chaplain Muller also conducted a successful work in the Prisoner of War prisons. Kim (Mok san-nim), Muller's interpreter, planned to become a minister and it was the ambition of the Marines of Muller's unit to help him do so.

Chaplain John W. Robb, when he went to Memphis from duty with MSTS, showed colored slides and because of the interest created in that U.S. city money

was sent to the Kae Sung Orphanage. The LOS ANGELES also contributed to the Sung Kwang Orphanage which was established by Capt. Joseph Bolan, Jr., UNCACK representative in Inchon. One of the cleverest young hoodlums of the city was persuaded by Bolan to recruit other boys to clean the ground for this orphanage and thus aided in its establishment. Also noteworthy was "Operation Good Will" which brought assistance to the Star of Hope Orphanage (Catholic).

Chaplain Edward R. Martineau, Chairman of the Armed Forces Assistance to Korea Program, spurred by the success of his 1953 Christmas party set in motion his "Operation Love" with mimeographed letters being sent to the United States. Beginning on the east coast with 60 barrels of clothing the operation ended in the fall with over 30 tons at Inchon harbor for distribution by the chaplains of the 1st Marine Division.[9]

Seoul

Chaplain Theobald, who had sailed into Inchon Harbor on the flagship of the 7th Fleet for the liberation of Korea in 1945, states concerning the capital city, after seeing it again in 1955, "Now, the streets and buildings of Seoul bore little resemblance to the ones I saw in 1945. How could this little country ever recover from such complete destruction?"

Because of its size and importance Seoul had many

[8] The Society for Reformed Publications, Grand Rapids, 1954. See also p. 260.

[9] See also p. 64.

Severance Hospital.
Chaplain Kenneth D. Killin visits the orphaned sick and crippled children at Severance Hospital.

relief problems. There were many institutions that tried desperately to cope with the needs. One of these was the Sam-Ae Children's Home. This orphanage had 365 children many of whom came from North Korea. It was located in an old Japanese Buddhist temple. The 1st Division gave this group assistance.

Severance Hospital was a recipient of aid from the MAW. Comdr. Calvin T. Doudna, chief medical officer, took a special interest in this institution, which had been founded in 1884 and is partially church supported. It had trained almost one-third of the doctors in Korea (1,300) and 500 nurses. Three invasions of the city had left its first modern hospital in shambles. Wiped out were the maternity ward, three nurses' residences, the auditorium, the main

classroom of the medical school and other buildings. The situation was further complicated by the scarcity of usable equipment. The prewar bed capacity of 150 had been built back to accommodate 66, but crowds, mostly destitute, appeared daily for help since the reopening of the facilities in 1951. Dr. Florence J. Murray stated "nearly 125 patients are treated daily at the clinic. No one is turned away without aid . . . although we cannot afford all the medicines and supplies needed and considered necessary in a modern hospital." Some supplies were delivered by Commander Doudna and Chaplain Kenneth D. Killin.

A number of the 1st Division chaplains speak of contact with Methodist missionaries. One was Dr. W. E. Shaw whose son had been a Naval Intelligence officer and had lost his life while serving with the Marines.

Chaplain Rennie found a prospective Methodist minister among the Korean workers following the 1st Medical Battalion and had the satisfaction of seeing him make a start in that direction. Chaplain Hoff organized aid for a building program of a Methodist church. Chaplain Prickett enlisted help for the Nam-Buk Orphanage.

The 7th Motor Transport Battalion assisted a Methodist Orphanage, and their Chaplain, Robert W. Smith, delivered money to Korean pastors to be used to build a church. This same unit sponsored the procurement of weaving machines which would produce rice bags. The plan was to purchase enough material to make 1,000 machines. The recipients were to be the people of Puja-Gun County. The first machine was presented by General Pate to Lee Chong Song. "Gun-Su" or chief of the county. Chaplain Smith indicated that the machines would produce six bags a day and increase the villages' monthly income by $20,000.

Chaplain Patrick Adams speaks of monthly visits to Seoul for a Day of Recollection whenever it was feasible. As a result of these visits liaison was established with the priests and nuns of Seoul which resulted in quantities of supplies being directed by the chaplains to Catholic orphanages and other institutions serving the needy. Chaplains Kuhn and Duggan are known to have worked for St. Paul's Catholic Orphanage in Seoul.[10]

The largest church in Korea was the Young Nak Presbyterian Church. It would be assumed that this church operated the Young Nak Presbyterian Orphanage, which was under the supervision of the Reverend and Mrs. Edward Adams, and which cared for about 130 children most of whom were under 6 years old. Chaplain E. V. Lyons, in reporting the nature of the assistance program of the regiment, points out the value of having servicemen see the way missionary work is carried out and in having them take a part in it themselves. Chaplain McCabe, as well as Chaplain Lyons, also speaks of helping the Young Nak Orphanage.

There are many accounts of Christmas parties being given for children. As Chaplain Newman indicates, for the first time, the children had an opportunity to meet Santa Claus. Wounded children were among those brought aboard the HAVEN for a visit, with Chaplain Tufft acting as host.

Bishop Ro of Seoul was presented with money for the needy of South Korea by some units.

Pyongteck

Chaplain O'Malley writes about the two orphanages, the Catholic and the Episcopal, at Pyongteck. Two thousand dollars was raised to purchase 500 sections of rice land to support the orphans when the

10 P. 164.

Nam-Buk Orphanage

Chaplain A. D. Prickett and Cpl. John A. Buxton visit the orphanage to bring clothing for the children. The institution is located in Seoul.

Gift.

Chaplain Robert W. Smith is shown giving money to the pastors of the Korean church at Kumchon-ni. A Korean Army chaplain is pictured on the right. The money was donated to help complete the church building which is under construction in the background.

Leathernecks left. The contributions were made by MAG–12 and other interested people. In a recent letter Chaplain O'Malley states that the name of the Catholic Orphanage was Holy Angels. He also states

The orphanage building we put up was a two story affair. The marines had donated approximately $1,000; then the Army allowed the orphan youngsters to salvage loose cement from broken bags in boxcars. There were close to 130 orphans at this location. The kids lived in squalid hovels prior to the erection of the building. Clothes wise and for food we relied on help from the States, and also "garbage" from the marine kitchens.

Chaplain O'Malley was not earth bound in his relief work for he relates that

. . . being with an air group I did have access to the use of a helicopter. Maj. John Lavoy did the piloting and we wandered far and wide around the area giving help to refugees. Our method of delivery was simple. Our engine noise flushed refugees out of their caves; then we dropped food and clothing. We also used the helicopter to take serious medical cases back to our base for emergency treatment by our doctors. Major Lavoy and his 'copter certainly were angels of mercy to thousands of refugees.

Chaplain Paul J. La Duca also aided the Catholic institution mentioned above which cared for 125 orphans.

Chaplain Joseph H. Lampe appears to have spearheaded the creation of the Eden Orphanage at Pyongteck.[11] MAG–12 bought and helped to build the facilities. Here the Marines housed, clothed, and fed 150 orphans with a strong assist from the folks back home. Other clothing was made available and Chaplain Lampe states that it was distributed through the local Presbyterian Church.

. . . to some of the more than 50,000 refugees which were in the area; always the pastor made the recipients realize that it was out of the Christian love of the American people which prompted the sending of the clothing, resulting in a new respect for the Christian way of life. Some helicopter pilots came in to get clothing, then go off on a trip, watching for small refugee groups where they could land and distribute the clothing to the very needy. Preaching in Korean churches, sometimes 35 miles or so away from the base, helped us to come close to the people and let them know we were concerned about them.

Chaplains La Duca and Lampe worked hard to meet the needs of the poverty stricken people, faced with another Korean winter. Lampe wrote,

The situation here is very critical. Unless we can get much more clothing and provide more food and shelter, thousands of Koreans will die as the treacherous winter takes its toll of the homeless and the hungry. It is hard to describe the suffering of these people.

[11] On p. 157 Chaplain Weidler is mentioned as being instrumental in establishing a new orphanage at Pyongteck.

A playground was constructed by the Marines and through their gifts a $2,000 brick western style dormitory was constructed with housing for about 150.[12]

Pohangdon

Chaplain Webb once again entered the laundry business. This time it was

. . . in a small village about 8 miles from K–3 (Pohang). It had been reported that a French bishop lived outside the village, caring for a group of women and orphans. With a guide I found the Most Reverend Germaine Mousset of the Paris Foreign Mission Society and former Ordinary of the Diocese of Taegu in charge of a small number of Korean women who had been on the verge of being instituted as a religious congregation just before the war began and lines of communication had been temporarily severed. Although in the clothing of laywomen they maintained a religious discipline and way of life which was remarkable. And there were, of course, the ever present orphans of war, sickly and hungry. Again a laundry was set up on a fairly large scale, vehicles commandeered for transportation, word-of-mouth publicity effected, and the same successful results achieved.

I should like to add here that the Marines of MAG–33 were very generous to this orphanage. Not only did they bring their laundry there (when it could have been brought to other and nearer laundries) but when I requested donations of money these were given willingly and freely by Marines of all sects, both officers and enlisted men. During a period just less than five months which I spent at K–3 Bishop Mousset reported that he had received in actual American money (changed into Korean won) a sum slightly more than $2,000. This splendid generosity is indicative of American charity for the unfortunate everywhere and is one of my warmest memories of the men of Marine Air Group 33.

Chaplain Webb tells of overcoming the language barrier through the use of Latin. But he still felt handicapped for according to him,

. . . I told Bishop Mousett that my lack of remembrance of many words severely restricted my sinning for I could only commit those sins for which I knew the words; otherwise in my confessions to him I would be making sacrilegious confessions and adding another burden of sin.

In the course of the war at Pohangdon the Catholic Orphanage[13] was damaged by Communist artillery. This institution had been directed by Father DesLandes of Vichy, France, for 31 years. He had also established an old people's home and an institute for the blind and crippled. A number of tiny refugees from Seoul, Chongju and Suwon and from all parts of Korea found their way to this center. The Pohangdon Catholic Orphanage feeds and clothes about 150 children from 3 months to 17 years of age. A number

[12] This evidently has reference to Eden Orphanage mentioned above.
[13] Also called Po Hang Catholic Orphanage and Little Flower Catholic Orphanage.

Orphans Will Keep Warm.
Chaplain Lampe distributes clothing to orphans of Eden Orphanage.

MAG Eden Orphanage.
An interior view. Note the American newspapers used to cover the ceiling.

of gifts were presented to the orphanage one of which was a late model station wagon presented by Chaplain J. F. Gearan.

In 1952 MAG–33 gave enough money to build the first Catholic church in the town, St. Michaels. It was well constructed and met a great need. The first pastor was Father Aloysius Kim Dou-Ho.

Later, on 19 September 1952, Gen. Clayton Jerome received a very gracious letter from Father Kim expressing appreciation of clothing distributed by Chaplain Parker. In it he says that the clothing was distributed to "over 300 poorer houses."

They have been deprived of their estate, family, and everything comfortable by this war, accordingly they were so starvating, desperate, and degraded that they might be inclining their mind to communism.

But those who have never touched were receiving your gifts, fruit of your love, in tears from deep emotion from no their own neighborhood, but American marine corps who are fighting for us. Seeing these scene, I could find again the Christian love which they had been lost, and through which they can see our Lord in their warm hearts that made their tears shed.

Therefore we must notice that your American young men at active services are the combatants who kill the Red by the bullets, in contrast with this, your people in the relief work are the crusader of love who protect these people from the Communists by the Christian love (English translation of the Korean).

The Wing also was instrumental in the construction of a Protestant church called the Ochun Protestant Church, at Ochun, Korea. On 29 October 1952 Jung Duck Soo wrote a letter to Chaplain Cleaves thanking him for "relief goods" and signing the letter "Clergyman of the Ochun Church" which would indicate that the church was well established by the autumn of that year.

Another recipient of aid from the 1st MAW was the Agapei Orphanage near Hunghei.

The Marines left their name attached to two institutions in Pohang, the U.S. Marine Memorial Children's Clinic, and the Marine Memorial Orphanage.[14] Chaplain James R. Smith, who served as a director of

---

[14] Cp. p. 157.

both in 1954, states that two Korean doctors and three registered nurses served the clinic. He also says that there were 112 children and a staff of 11 at the orphanage.

Discussions concerning the orphanage began in November 1951 under the direction of Chaplain Cleaves of MAG–33. Three thousand five hundred dollars was contributed by the 1st MAW for the initial site which was purchased on 28 November 1951 and which consisted of 15 acres of land. W. O. Philip Slocum was one of the leaders in the campaign. The actual construction began in February 1952 under the direction of Chaplain Seymour. The orphanage was completed 1 month later and housed 12 children. This number was increased to 35 by the end of March 1952. By the end of the first year the number was 66 and still later the number was reported as 109.

The institution was officially dedicated as the U.S. Marine Memorial Orphanage on 16 March 1952.

Less than a year later it had six buildings and rice land valued at more than $38 million won or $6,500 and was incorporated by the Presbyterian ministers of Pohang. Chaplains Parker[15] and Lineberger, through an extensive publicity campaign, continued to collect clothes, raised money to buy land, and constructed three additional buildings. It appears also that a rice mill was purchased. Improvements continued to be made until the orphanage was called the newest and

the most modern in Korea. The orphans were taught to farm the land and harvest the crops, so that when the Marines should leave, the institution would be able to continue its work. Chaplain Gould reported a campaign to set up a TB sanitarium at the orphanage to isolate and treat cases of this disease among the children. A new kitchen was also in the plans. Since 1956, total support of this orphanage has come from funds through World Vision Inc.

In June 1953 the second phase of the project was begun with the dedication of the Marine Memorial Children's Clinic. It also was a project of the Protestant Men of MAG–33 and Headquarters Squadron–1. Two large Japanese constructed two story buildings had to be obtained about a quarter of a mile from the Marine Memorial Orphanage. There were two purposes in mind in the establishment of the clinic. One was to give free medical care to all orphans and the secondary one was to offer prenatal care for expectant mothers.

The clinic started in a small downstairs room, but with the addition of new floors on the second floor, wards were set up there and plans were underway for "in-patient care." At the time of its inception the clinic was the only one of its kind in South Korea.

Both Catholic and Protestant personnel aided another institution in Pohang, the Pohang City Orphanage,[16] which was partially supported by the citizens of the town. It was said to care for 130 children.

[15] Cp. pp. 180–2.

[16] Also known as Po-hang Orphanage and Eden of Angels.

Eden is Paradise.
The marines of MAG 12 feed and clothe 150 Korean homeless children, but most of them give credit to their families back home for much needed packages of clothing.

Orphanage at Pyongtaek.
A group of the orphans is shown with Chaplain Paul J. LaDuca, Kim Soon Nam, teacher, and Father Lee Su Yung, who combine their efforts to manage the orphanage. The orphanage is aided by MAG 12.

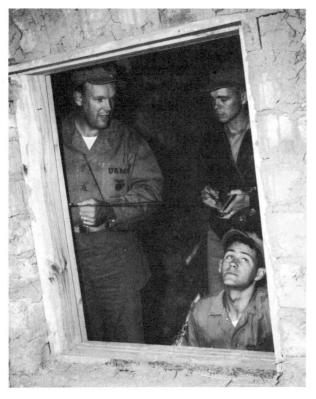

Eden Orphanage.

Chaplain Joseph H. Lampe is shown putting the finishing touches on the first permanent building of the orphanage which was built by men of the Marine Air Group 12 on land which they purchased for that purpose.

Say It With Flowers.

The Korean lass is doing just that. The recipient is Chaplain Stephen G. Horvath of the 1st MAW in gratitude for his work for the Saint Michaels Church in Pohang-dong. The church was built with donations from his unit and this is the occasion of the dedication of the church.

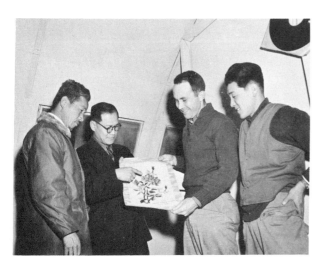

Gratitude.

A hand woven tapestry is presented to Chaplain Richard D. Cleaves for his assistance to the Ochon church.

Visiting Orphans.

Pohang Catholic Orphanage is visited by Force Chaplain S. B. Bennett and other chaplains. Pictured here are (left to right) Father Lois Leo DesLandes, who is in charge of the orphanage; Chaplain John D. Gould, Chaplain Jeremiah F. Gearan; and Chaplain Bennett.

Ochon Church.

Chaplain Richard D. Cleaves stands in the pulpit of the Ochon Church which he helped build with donations from the Marines. With him, on the right, is the Reverend Teun Byung Sik, of Pohang, and on the left is Elder Jeung Duck Su of the Ochon Church. An interpreter stands on the far side. The church is filled to capacity twice on Sundays.

A Memorial Check.

Chaplain Allen Jones gives a check sent by Mrs. O. P. Higgins as a memorial to her son, who was a Marine pilot killed in action in Korea, to a representative of the Agapei Orphanage near Hunghei, Korea. The son's name was Capt. William Higgins.

St. Michael's Church.

A view of the Catholic church to which the 1st MAW contributed $4,000 for its erection.

U.S. Marine Orphanage.

An aerial view of the orphanage. The section in the back was the first section. The section on the left was built later. Interestingly, it has a roof made of beer cans. The land which was purchased for cultivation was to the right of of the photograph.

The Eden of Angels.

This city operated orphanage extends helping hand to all orphans. It is supported for the most part by donations from the 1st MAW and feeds and clothes about 150 children from 3 months to 17 years of age.

U.S. Marine Orphanage—1959.

The institution is still in need of help. Here is a view of the section built during the Korean conflict.

Visiting Chaplain at Clinic.

Chaplain Bennett, force chaplain, pats a child on the head which is strapped to the back of the mother, as a group of of patients await their turn at the U.S. Marine Memorial Children's Clinic, Pohang, which welcomes all Korean babies and children for treatment. Chaplain Bennett visited the clinic during his tour of the 1st MAW.

U.S. Marine Orphanage—1959.

Chaplain R. W. Aldrich meets with the superintendent of the orphanage who is holding one of his charges. His name is Chung Jin Yurl. His assistant who is also pictured on the left is Su Tu Po. The plaque reads "Marine Memorial Orphanage, Founded by First Marine Air Wing, USMC", and contains the Marine insignia. In the background one sees a present day picture of what was the first buildings of the orphanage somewhat improved.

Wonsan

Although American troops were only in North Korea for a brief time they gave as much aid as they could to the civilians they found there.

In Wonsan as has been noted [17] Chaplain Murphy of 1st MAW reorganized the Catholic group and in addition formed the North Korean Catholic Relief Society. He arranged for captured grain and beans to be rationed daily to the poor of the city. The Tuck Won Monastery which had been razed by the Communists was repaired by UN forces. Chaplain Carr and Chaplain Kenneth W. Carlson, Baptist (Gen. Conf. of America), tell of the need of the medical facility at Wonsan, speaking of the limited inventory consisting of a bottle of pills and a snake bottled in formaldehyde. Both appear to have used a Korean priest and Latin to translate the names and usages of the drugs surveyed by the ships' medical officers and given to the facility.

In the winter of 1951–52 the WISCONSIN picked up a North Korean in Wonsan harbor who had been fired upon when he evidently was attempting to swim to an UN occupied island. He was given blood transfusions and every effort was made to save his life. He died and both chaplains, H. W. Buckingham and E. J. Kapalczynski, participated in the committal service.[17a] Chaplain John H. Shilling, Methodist, in the PHILIPPINE SEA tells of planes taking supplies obtained from the states to Koreans on Wotje Island, in Wonsan Harbor, who were cut off from a normal source of supply by Communists.

Chaplain Garson Goodman assisted in the project of helping a Korean YMCA in Hamhung to reestablish itself. But, of course, all these activities in North Korea soon again came under Communist control.

Kangnung [18]

Much has already been written about "Operation Kidlift" which brought 139 children, who had come

---

[17] Cp. pp. 34f.

[17a] Cp. pp. 116f.

[18] See also pp. 114, 130, 158, 182.

through the front lines on the east coast from North Korea, by plane to Kangnung. During that winter of 1951–52, 450 [19] orphans were cared for in four different orphanages. Over 40 tons of clothing were received from the churches in America for the children. Chaplain Weidler describes K–18 (Kangnung), where MAG–12 was located, as ". . . the most advanced aviation unit in Korea. The installation here is of a semipermanent nature." He added,

The work with the youngsters has provided an activity for the men, whereby they can convert some of their spare time to a worth-while cause. This work together with the contact with church groups, here at our chapel services, has provided more acceptable contact with Korean civil life than would normally be possible.

Among the orphanages at Kangnung there was the Kangnung Columban Fathers Orphanage with which Chaplain Horvath worked devotedly. Photographs show the dedication of a Methodist orphanage in Korea "which was founded by Chaplain Weidler with the help of marines stationed nearby." This orphanage appears to have been in or near Kangnung.

Refugee Camps

A number of refugee camps were set up in Korea. One of these was at Munsan-ni.[20] Chaplain Billy N. Wolfe describes what he saw,

---

[19] Other sources give a smaller figure.
[20] Cf. p. 126.

I witnessed the heartache of South Korean families being evicted from their houses in the front line area. In "No Mans Land" I counted 74 orphan children, as our convoy moved along the road [from] Munsan-ni to Panmunjom. They held out their hands begging for food, many of our G.I.'s tossed candy and C-rations to them and they lined the road each day looking for and expecting the food.

Chaplains Hammerl, Rice, Nordby, J. Brown, and Stretch distributed relief items to refugee camps. The KEARSARGE contributed 1,200 pounds of clothing for children abandoned at the front. Chaplain McDowell tells of sending trucks for children from the refugee village for a Christmas party and when they did not return he went to the village for the children himself. His unit ended up with twice as many children as planned. Many other units had Christmas parties. Chaplain Rains tells of one for 2,000 refugees which must have been one of the largest. Perhaps the biggest project in Christmas parties was that of Chaplain Bakker who was cited for conducting Christmas parties for ". . . 2,800 needy Korean children . . ."

One of the great projects in relief occurred during the winter of 1952–53 when the 1st Engineer Battalion *adopted PaJu, a refugee village* of 1,500 people. Chaplain Ernst affirms that an offering was taken in order to buy food on the native market. "Once a week men of the battalion visited the village and

---

A Baby Doll.

Chaplain R. N. Stretch of the 11th Marines gives a doll to a Korean girl at Munsani Refugee Camp.

Distribution.

Aside from clothing and food there was also candy for the children. Here Chaplain Leo F. Rice is seen handing a Korean boy a bar of chocolate.

This Is School.

It looks like tent city but it is part of the Kumchin Primary School. The school was composed of but two small permanent buildings and the rest of the classes were normally held in these unheated tent-classrooms. As many as 80 children attend classes in each of these tents. Marines of the 5th Regiment and Korean school officials are inspecting the school with a view toward improvement of facilities.

---

brought food, clothing, firewood . . . [The] project lasted 14 weeks."

Kumchon

The 1st Marine Division occupied the Kumchon area on the west coast from March 1952 until August 1953. Of the 112,701 civilians in the area 69,369 were refugees and "19,755 suffering from causes other than land losses." The Civil Affairs group organized a 4–H Club, PTA, and Korean Young Men's Association. Aid was given in getting basic industrial plants into operation. Orphans were processed through the Civil Affairs Section and turned over to the Po Wha Orphanage at Seoul. The Division maintained seven refugee camps with the total population given as 14,355. The two main relief organizations were the Federation Farmers Association, which was Korean and distributed grain for seed and relief, and UNCACK, which was the UN agency for the distribution of grain and supplies for relief. This gives some idea of the broader relief program.

More specifically Chaplain Vinson tells of the work which was done with the Presbyterian Mission of Kumchon. Particular interest was shown in its school which grew from 75 in January to 225 pupils by August. The Marines gave surveyed tents and fixed "ammo box decking" for additional school rooms. Some civilians were treated at the 1st Corps, Civil Affairs, 1st Marine Division Kumchon Hospital. Another source tells one that the 7th Motor Transport Battalion donated and erected the Presbyterian Church at Kumchon.

Toward the end of 1954 it was stated that 1,500 students were to be taught that year in the 3 buildings of the Kumchon Primary Schools constructed under the sponsorship of 1st Battalion, 5th Marines. The school was said to be the largest of any of the Armed Forces Assistance to Korea Schools (AFAK) to date.[21]

Others

The Nam Buk Orphanage in Yongdongpo, and the Christian Children's Home in Anyang were aided by the 2d Battalion, 7th Marines and the 1st Service Battalion.

There were numerous institutions that were aided by the Marines but not a great deal of information is available concerning them. Among these were the Catholic Orphanage at Anchoong, which cared for 125 children, St. Camellia's orphanage operated by French nuns, Children's Garden of Holy Mind at Bup Yong, an Orphanage at Wonju, and at Kecksa-ri and the Dong Dwang Orphanage which was almost fully supported by the 1st Division.

"Operation Uncle" was a program led by the chaplains of Marine units which had as its goal the "adoption" of 3,000 orphan boys.

Inactive Reserve Chaplains in the Far East

Chaplain Whitman notes the presence of three inactive reserve chaplains in the Far East. At least two of

---

[21] See p. 234.

these were active from time to time in the program of the chaplaincy. Chaplain C. E. Blackler, Baptist (N), performed training duty at Yokosuka as did Chaplain Worth C. Grant, Baptist. In addition to these, Chaplain Stanton R. Wilson, Presbyterian (USA), began serving as a missionary in Korea at Andong in January 1953.

Orphans Adopt Marines

There were some children that did not want to stay in an orphanage, but persisted in staying at Marine encampments. Chaplain Fenstermacher tells of such a case,

One cold night in December 1952 several of our hospital corpsmen heard someone crying outside the fence around our compound, near the sick bay. They called the officer of the day and me, and we went out to investigate. It was a small Korean boy, barefooted, bareheaded, and with only an old burlap bag covering his body for clothing. We took him into the sick bay for examination. No part of his body was frozen, but his body temperature was a great deal below normal. The corpsmen fed him and kept him over night in a warm bed, and in the morning my clerk, Sergeant Tracey, and I found him a home in one of the orphanages. He was a refugee from the combat area and didn't know what had happened to his parents or where they were.

Later on, but still during the winter, another small Korean boy was taken in under similar circumstances at one of our firing batteries. The Marines kept him and cared for him for a few days, and liked him so well that they wanted to adopt him as the Battery Mascot. However, it was against the policy of the command to have Koreans as mascots. It was felt that if we opened the door to one, more would surely follow and the practice might get out of hand; and that it actually would be a disservice to the mascot in the

long run, since living with the Marines would make him become used to a way of life and a standard of living which would make it extremely difficult to readjust to the Korean way of life after the Marines were gone, and would tend to keep him from attending school.

Accordingly, I was called upon to find a place for the boy, now known as "Sammy" to the Marines, in an orphanage. This I did. But within 3 days Sammy was back at the battery. Upon questioning him through an interpreter we found that he didn't care for the meals served at the orphanage nor did he appreciate the discipline and the attendance at school required of him. The diet at an orphanage hardly could compare with the menus served in our mess halls nor did it include the large amount of American candy and chewing gum which Sammy received as mascot. As for discipline, by comparison there was none for Sammy with the Marines. So he ran away from the orphanage to return to the battery.

Two more times I took Sammy to an orphanage, and each time he returned within a few days. Finally, I made arrangements for the boy to be taken to the headquarters of the 1st Marine Aircraft Wing, about 90 miles from Pusan, there to be taken in by the Marine Memorial Orphanage which is supervised by and supported by Marines. There Sammy made his adjustment, and seemed to be content to stay. He was still there and doing well when I left Korea.

Naturally by the time we found Sammy a home where he would stay, everybody in the Battalion knew him or at least about him and was interested in the final disposition of the case. So we ran an article in the battalion newspaper entitled "Sammy Adopts the Marines," in which we covered the history of his case.

A number of chaplains tell similar experiences.

Distribution

It was not always easy to get supplies to the needy; Chaplain Ralph H. Walter, Presbyterian (USA)

Chalice for Korean Church.

Maj. Joseph P. Cushing, Commanding Officer of the 2d Motor Transport Battalion, Camp Lejeune, presents a gold chalice to Chaplain Martineau to be delivered to the Immaculate Conception Church which he helped to rebuild in KalkO-ni, Korea.

MAG—Marine Orphanage—Keoksa-ki, Korea.

An aerial view of the building and grounds of the orphanage supported by the Marines.

Chung Im Protestant Church.

This small church at Chung Im, Korea, was financed with gifts of marines. The Koreans spoke of it as "Parker Memorial Church."

Distribution of Scripture.

Chaplain E. R. Barnes is pictured with Korean children who have just received a copy of the scriptures.

states that "many times I have lugged gear over the side only to have to lug it back to another port until I was able to find some kind soul who would deliver it to Korea."

In addition to food and clothing there was the distribution of the Scriptures. Chaplain Taylor tells of giving Korean New Testaments to civilians and to Korean Marines serving with his unit. Chaplain Barnes distributed Bibles to Korean children. There was a call for Greek New Testaments by refugees on an island who had established a Bible class.

Building Churches

As has been mentioned before, a number of churches were built.[22] It should be noted that Chaplain Rains helped in the design and building of a church, Chaplain Horvath worked to open a Korean chapel and Chaplain Spohn lent a tent to a young minister so that he could organize a new church in a nearby community. And so it goes, some were temporary structures, others were rather impressive. One of them was the Chung Im Protestant Church which was financed by Marine gifts.

Civilian Worship

There were any number of contacts which chaplains made in the conduct of worship services. To cite a few, Chaplain Mulligan visited another island, Cheju-do, where prisoners were kept, and held serv-

ices. In the case of Chaplain Martineau, he was adopted by a refugee group as their priest, since the regular came to them only twice a year.

The Interpreter

Very few chaplains could speak Korean; as a result great use was made of interpreters. One chaplain in answering his questionnaire spoke of his "interrupter." Although this is probably a misspelling it is all too true. One preaches for a minute or two and then waits for the translation, and so it goes. Chaplain Wolfe used a Korean Marine Chaplain; Chaplain Capers had the services of a son of a Methodist Korean pastor named Pak.[23] Chaplain Forney states that his civilian interpreter was introduced to Christianity, accepted Christ and was a great help to him. Almost entirely on his own the Korean learned to play the pump organ. Chaplain Crabtree says that it was the work of the Marines at an orphanage in Kang Wha Do that won his interpreter to Christianity. Were all the facts available, the story of winning Koreans, interpreters and others, to Christianity by the chaplains would be quite revealing. For example, in the case of Koreans, Chaplain Muller lists 1,256 conversions [24] during his tour of duty.

On Land and Sea

Chaplains were in touch with Koreans aboard ship as well as on land. Chaplain Symons writes of two

---

[22] The work of Chaplain Muller and others has been previously mentioned.

[23] Cp. pp. 232f.

[24] In addition 106 American servicemen conversions are listed by this chaplain.

Interpreter.

Kim Hae Jong interprets for Chaplain John H. Muller as he delivers a Monday night sermon to his congregation of 200 at the Song Won Leper Colony.

Joint Sunday Service.

A Korean and an American Navy Chaplain join in conducting religious services for American and Korean marines in Korea.

ROK ensigns who were aboard a destroyer for training. They expressed an interest in his religious ministry "as it might pertain to them" and requested assistance in English grammar and speech. For 2 months they met and discussed these subjects.

Chaplain Crabtree tells of meeting Lieutenant Colonel Choi, who was in command of a battalion of the Korean Marine Corps and who was a sincere Christian. In March 1953 Lieutenant Colonel Choi invited the chaplains and the commanding officers of the units in the area to attend a Korean Memorial Service. "This service generated unity, understanding, and good will among Koreans and Americans . . ."

Chaplain Robertson for a time conducted services for the Korean Marine Corps Tank Company before they were assigned a Korean Chaplain. The services of Chaplain Ruleman held for an attached Korean Marine Tank Company are described as follows:

. . . Seated cross-legged on immaculate mats with shoes removed and carefully lined along the center aisle, were 75 Korean Marines, among the toughest fighting men in the world. Captain O, commanding officer, had told them all men should be present and should remain quiet. He remained for the service and joined in the warm hearted singing from the United Nations Hymnals printed in both Korean and English.

. . . Lt. Hong, the interpreter, was raised as a Presbyterian Christian who hopes to study in America after the war and return to Korea to build a new school.

Chaplain E. F. Ernst made a trip of 160 miles by jeep twice a month to visit the island of Kangkwa to preach to the American troops attached to the 2d Guerilla Partisan Pact which was composed principally of North Koreans fighting on the side of South Korea.

The Korean Service Corps

The Korean Service Corps was a quasi-military body consisting of inducted laborers organized in 1951 under the control of the ROK army. Prior to that time Koreans were hired directly for certain tasks in the U.S. military installations. The men of the Corps generally worked 10 hours per day and in emergencies 14 hours. A rest period of 24 hours was given every 15 days. The period of enlistment was for 6 months. The Corps was composed of men who failed to qualify for the armed forces of Korea because of age or some other disability. Some remained in the organization after the 6 month's period because of the scarcity of employment on the outside. The 1st Division had about 5,000 of the Corps attached to it and in addition hired 650 civilian workers. The main tasks of the members of the Corps were to carry supplies, evacuate the wounded, and to do general police or manual labor about the camp.

Chaplain Capers in his work with the Corps secured hymn books with parallel English-Korean. Through the aid of Pak [25] a large church attendance was attained. Chaplain Muller notes the large percentage in his group that had not attended a Christian service

[25] Cf. p. 231.

before.[26] Chaplain Uber tells of good attendance from the 120 men attached to his unit. Chaplain Brosius tells us of Pak and Lee. It is presumed that it was the same man to whom Chaplain Capers made reference. The first mention of these two civilian laborers was when they volunteered to leave North Korea and embarked with the 1st Division from Hungnam in December 1951. Chaplain Brosius "spotted" Lee in his first service with the group because of his beautiful baritone voice. He was used in the choir henceforth. Pak repaired an old smashed Japanese organ which he practiced upon assiduously. Both managed to be assigned to work in sick bay.

Pak gave much of his life's blood for an American marine. In September 1951, during the battle for Hill 749, one of our men tripped off a Communist shoe box mine just a short distance from our battalion forward aid station. The enemy spotted the explosion, and began dropping mortar rounds into the general area. Without stopping to think twice of their personal safety, Pak and Lee grabbed a stretcher and ran through a mined area ahead of a corpsman. They began evacuating the marine, and in so doing Pak also set off a mine and was critically wounded. He lost a leg, was partially blinded and received many severe wounds in his efforts to assist one of our men. Lee remained with us as a faithful

---

[26] In Ch. V of his book "Wearing the Cross in Korea."

assistant up until the time I left the lines. These two men were truly "God's own," serving to the best of their ability where their duty called.

Chaplain Felder obtained a series of phonograph records in the Korean language. These records include hymns, scripture passages and sermons. As a result of these records several men volunteered to conduct further Korean services.

As a result of these services, other Korean services were started in other units. Two of these units were "C" and "D" Company of the 1st Engineer Battalion. These were two outlying companies serving the infantry regiments on the lines. These services brought about a better understanding between the Koreans and the American servicemen as was evidenced in their contacts with one another.

On Christmas at

Midnight 1951 the Koreans worshiped at the midnight services with American personnel. At the conclusion of the midnight services practically all personnel in attendance walked to the side of a mountain where a public address system had been rigged previously. From here the Americans and Koreans sang Christmas carols together. They sang carols alternately, that is the Americans would sing one in English and the Koreans one in their native tongue.

A solo was sung by a Marine major and a solo sung by a Korean Christian. A truly inspirational Christmas Serv-

Final Tribute for a Korean.
Taps is sounded at a funeral service conducted by Chaplain Joseph Gallagher for a member of the Korean Service Corps who was killed in action while carrying supplies to frontline infantrymen of the 1st Marine Division.

Crazy Man, Crazy.

This "real gone" troupe of pint-sized song and dance men is celebrating the dedication of Bong III Chon Primary School, one of the 14 projects completed by the 1st Marine Division under the Armed Forces Assistance to Korea Program.

ice. In the valley below were located several thousand American personnel among whom were patients in two forward hospitals.

Schools

Interest in the education of the children of Korea was doubtless the concern of many from the beginning of the conflict but it was not until 1953 that the Marines appear to have been able to set up a constructive program of action. It was during this period that M. Sgt. John T. Cain became so touched by the needs of the children for education that he determined to investigate the matter. After talking with officials at a school near his air base he attempted to change military funds into Korean currency to spend for children's school expenses. Not only was he able to convince the paymaster to exchange his money, but he also enlisted a few other contributors. Thus he was able to have three boys and six girls enrolled that had not been in school since 1950. The tuition was $6 per year per child.

The idea caught fire and Cain had to put some Marines on the waiting list until he had screened more children. The second month Cain flew 30 missions and yet worked at his investigations. He said, "I plan to put five or six more children back in school next week, as soon as I can sandwich in trips to the schools between flights." Shortly thereafter he was shot down over North Korea and listed as missing in action. Lt. William P. Lane picked up the leadership of the project and the number of children being educated in this manner rose to 20. It was the hope

of Lieutenant Lane to add 100 more pupils to the program before Christmas. It was grand news when "Big Switch" brought the return of Sergeant Cain to the Marines.

The Marine program had so developed that in November of 1954 members of the 1st Division Headquarters and the 5th Marines joined villagers in dedicating four new schools. The projects had cost about $30,000 and would provide facilities for 3,742 students. These schools brought to 14 the number of AFAK projects completed in the division area. The new schools included three primary schools at Chugwon-ni, Bong Ill Chon, and Kumchon. The latter was the largest with 1,500 students. The fourth school was the most advanced institution of learning sponsored in the division area up till that time. It was the Munsan-ni Agricultural High School.

It may be assumed that many other schools were assisted directly or indirectly. One such project was to help the Chosen Theological Seminary to reestablish itself in Seoul. Books for the library and other items were sought and given according to Chaplain Schroeluke.

It is recognized that this chapter gives but a glimpse of what was done for Korean civilians. Only time will tell how lasting and how valuable the work of the American servicemen has been. It is beyond contradiction that it can not help but have its impact not only in Korea but throughout the Orient. America will fight for freedom, but America also will lend a helping hand to those who suffer from the ravages of war.

EPILOGUE

Redeployment

In a sense the Korean situation is still an active one. The MLR is quiet. There are few UN or American troops there. After 27 July 1954 the military continued the relief program. Gradually the troops were relieved by fresh replacements. During the early part of March 1955 the redeployment of the 1st Marine Division to Camp Pendleton began. Gen. John E. Hull, UN Far Eastern Commander, paid tribute to the Division on the 3d saying, "You have added a new chapter to the already proud history of the Corps and it is with a sense of regret that the United Nations Command and the Far East Command mark your departure from this theater of operations after four and one-half years in Korea."

Special Emblem

The preceding November a special ceremony was held in Washington by Gen. Lemuel C. Shepherd, Jr., Commandant of the Marine Corps, in which the first of the new emblems, authorized for the service ribbons of naval personnel who have had combat with the Marines, was awarded. Among the first three men to receive the emblem was Chaplain John H. Craven.

Operation Glory

The ceremony held on 20 January 1956 associated with the removal of the first 50 of approximately 850 bodies of unknown servicemen to their final resting place in the National Memorial Cemetery of the Pacific in Honolulu began what was termed "Operation Glory." The impressive ceremony was held alongside the MANCHESTER and honored all the unknown who had fallen on the field of battle on Korean soil. General Lemnitzer, CinC of the Far East and UN Commands, paid tribute to the Korean dead saying, "Their sacrifice has given reality, meaning and purpose to the guarantees inscribed in the United Nations charter that all peoples of all nations . . . may live securely in dignity, in freedom, and in justice."

Summary

No adequate summary will ever be written of the work of the naval chaplains in Korea. Their contribution may be considered as dual in nature for they gave unstintingly to their military personnel but also found time to heed the cry for help from a civilian population.

The courage displayed on the battlefield by the chaplains as they ministered to the spiritual needs of their men will go down in history as one of the greatest epics in the existence of the Corps. Almost without exception the Marine Corps recognized this in the awards which they gave to the chaplains concerned. Their extraordinary devotion to their men and tireless work among the wounded, their ceaseless visitation on the front in the face of incoming shells were noted as in the "highest tradition of the naval service" but they also came to be so universal that they were expected of every chaplain as normal procedure.

The Marines had increased the number of chaplains in a Division after World War II which was tacit recognition of the value of having chaplains with their units. Now with this display of sacrificial service the chaplains were not hampered by collateral duties. They were working day and night at their own appointed tasks. Daily worship services in the bunkers, administration of communion, holding confessions, praying for and with the wounded or dying completely eclipsed lesser things. These and many more activities endeared the chaplains to the fighting men. The lasting influence of these representatives of God upon the men as they make their contribution to American life may be incalculable, but it cannot help but be great.

Certainly in the Chaplain Corps a standard has been set that will be hard to maintain and certainly will be extremely difficult to excel. It is only hoped that chaplains in the future, if they have to serve on the field of battle, will measure up as well as have these in Korea.

Not all the battles were on the main line of resistance. As one chaplain puts it

Many chaplains fought a desperate battle against the immoral influences that would destroy the moral fibre of the young men who served tours of duty in the Far East. These chapters of heroic Christian effort cannot be written but the results of these battles have saved many a sailor or marine from disgrace and shame.

It is expected that in a subsequent volume of the history the development of the Moral Leadership

Protestant, Catholic, and Jewish chaplains head the procession of pallbearers as the four caskets, containing the unidentified American servicemen, move toward the prow of the MANCHESTER.

Pallbearers from the Tokyo Tri-Service Honor Guard stand at attention as final rites are performed under the 8-inch guns of the MANCHESTER.

Program will be traced, but with troops in far away parts of the world, "eternal vigilance" is still the watchword in this program.

The chaplains, who were not with their men in combat but had to wait until they flew back on missions, worked just as faithfully with their men but whether aboard a vessel or at an air base they were able to devote more time and effort to care for the needs of the refugees. This does not mean at all that the infantry did not also work in this area, for all participated. The hospital ships, the MSTS, the battleships—all answered the call for help. The whole effort in restoring or establishing schools, hospitals, and churches was a gigantic one, and one which appears unique in the annals of history. Armies are considered in the destructive sense. Whoever heard of an army taking time to rebuild what had been torn down by the shells of their own or their enemy's guns? Since when had it been the concern of the fighting units to care for the widows, orphans, the sick and the destitute? And yet here it happened—in a section of the world where life had been considered cheap. Suddenly a western nation had shown compassion, had cared. Back of it all was the chaplain giving leadership and guidance to these projects.

A number of practical improvements came out of the conflict. Better combat altar kits, better methods and techniques in implementing the Moral Leadership Program were among these. But in the words of Maj. Gen. Clayton C. Jerome, Commanding General of the 1st Marine Air Wing, as he spoke of the relief work of this command

The men of this command have undertaken completely on their own a tremendous project worthy of our finest Christian traditions, and it should be an inspiration to the millions of Americans who have loved ones here . . . Here is democracy as it is throughout the free world.

It is this great display of humanitarianism that stands out so vividly as one looks at Korea.

Thus one leaves the story of the naval chaplain in Korea. A story of bravery beyond the call of duty, a story of caring for one's fellowmen but as the history closes the fighting man was to remain still in Korea. On bleak austere mountains he would watch across the neutral zone, but he would not be alone.

God Is With Him.

Silver Star

Bonner, R. A., USNR, BIBLE PRESBY
Griffin, C. J., USN, RC
Newman, Thomas A. Jr., USNR, BAP (A)
Sporrer, O. E., USN, RC

Legion of Merit

Craven, J. H., USN, BAP (S)
Ingvoldstad, O., Jr. (LUTH)
Jones, Allen, USNR, PRESBY (US)
Peck, W. S., USN, PRESBY (USA)
Slattery, E. A., USN, RC

Bronze Star

Austin, H. E., USN, BAP (A)
Byrnes, John P., USN, RC
Cleaves, R. D., USNR, BAP (A)
Craven,* J. H., USN, BAP (S)
Cummins, G. W., USNR, BAP (A)
Edwards, Thomas V., USNR, RC
Ernst, Elmer F., USNR, RC
Fenstermacher, Harry F., USN, EVAN REF
Ferris, J. S., USN, METH
Fitzgerald, J. C., USN, RC
Gallagher, Joseph P. F., USNR, RC
Groover, H. H., USNR, DISC
Guillaume, L. A., USNR, RC
Hayes, H. H., USNR, DISC
Hickey, B. L., USN, RC
Hoff, Cameron P., USNR, LUTH
Ingvoldstad, O., USN, LUTH
Jones, G., USN, BAP (A)
Killeen, P. A., USN, RC
La Duca, P. J., USNR, RC (OFM CAP)
Lampe, Joseph H., USNR, PRESBY (USA)
Lineberger, Ernest R., USNR, LUTH
Lynch, E. M., USNR, RC (OMI)
Markley, J. H., USN, METH
Meachum, Lonnie W., USNR, BAP (S)
Mendonsa, A. G., USNR, RC
Moore, James C., USN, METH
Moore, John T., USNR, RC (CSP)
Murphy, J. P., USN, RC
McDonald,* J. D., USN, RC
McDowell, N. L., USNR, BAP (S)
Newman, Thomas A., USNR, BAP (A)
Peeters, R. T., USNR, RC
Prickett, Albert D., USNR, BAP (S)
Quirk, J. M., USNR, RC
Reilly, G. J., USNR, RC (CP)

*Received two Bronze Star medals.

Rice, Leo F., USNR, RC
Schwyhart, R. M., USN, BAP (A)
Sobel, Samuel, USN, JEWISH
Sporrer, O. E., USN, RC
Tennant, W. G., USN, METH
Trodd, J. P., USN, RC
Van Antwerp, E. I., USNR, RC
Willets, R. H., USNR, BAP (S)

Air Medal

Fitzgerald, J. C., USN, RC
O'Neill, J. J., USNR, RC

Letter of Commendation Awards

Adams, Patrick, USN, RC
Bakker, Peter J., USNR, BAP (A)
Barlik, R. F., USNR, RC
Brengartner, Robert E., USNR, RC
Brooks, W. E., USN, BAP (A)
Brown, J. C., USN, BAP (S)
Callahan, J. T., USNR, RC
Capers, K. H., USN, PRESBY (USA)
Chambers, Samuel D., USNR, PRESBY (USA)
Cloonan, Joseph F., USN, RC
Conlon, John B., USNR, RC
Cook, A. R., USN, METH
Crabtree, Roger L., USN, METH
Cummings, H. H., USNR, PRESBY (US)
Duggan, Charles T., USNR, RC
Duncan, H. C., USN, METH
Elliott, Calvin H., USN, PE
Ernst, Karl H., USNR, PRESBY (USA)
Fenning, R. C., USN, LUTH (MoSy)
Frame, Clovis A., USN, METH
Gallagher, J. P. F., USNR, RC
Gibbons, A. R., USNR, RC
Hayes, H. H., USNR, DISC
Hearn, W. M., USN, BAP (A)
Hollingsworth, J. E., III, USN, BAP (S)
Horvath, S. G., USNR, RC
Hutcheson, Richard G., Jr., USN, PRESBY (US)
Jolly, D. W., USN, PRESBY (U)
Keaney, K. J., USN, RC
Killin, K. D., USNR, PRESBY (USA)
Kirkland, Albert S., USN, NAZARENE
Knapp, P. J., USNR, RC (OFM)
Kuhn, Gerald E., USNR, LUTH (MoSy)
Kulinski, A. M., USNR, RC
Lane, W. P., USNR, RC
Lonergan, V. J., USN, RC
Lyons, Earle V., USN, PRESBY (USA)
Lyons, W. N., USNR, BAP (A)

Chaplain Otto E. Sporrer.

Chaplain Robert A. Bonner.

Chaplain Thomas A. Newman.

Chaplain Cornelius J. Griffin.

Chaplain Orlando Ingvoldstad, Jr.

Chaplain Allen Jones.

Chaplain Edward A. Slattery.

Chaplain Walter S. Peck.

Chaplain John H. Craven.

Mahler, W. A., USN, RC
Meade, H. E., USN, RC
Meehan, Daniel F., USN, RC
Mulligan, Edwin C., USNR, RC
McCabe, W. D., USNR, PRESBY (USA)
Nordby, Walter H., USNR, LUTH
O'Leary, Francis T., USN, RC
O'Malley, Francis P., USNR, RC
O'Neill, J. J., USNR, RC
Patton, R. L., METH
Paul, James W., USNR, METH
Peeters, R. T., USNR, RC
Pigott, C. S., USN, BAP (S)
Reaves, J. E., USN, METH
Robertson, A. W., USN, BAP (S)
Rothman, Murray I., USNR, JEWISH
Ruleman, R. N., USN, METH
Salyer, O. B., USN, METH
Seymour, H. A., USNR, METH
Smith, James Rex, USNR, DISC
Sullivan, J. A., USN, RC
Szczesny, C. A., USN, RC
Taylor, W. A., USNR, BAP (A)

Weber, Oscar, USNR, LUTH
Weidler, E. R., USNR, EVAN & REF
Wolfram, E. A., Jr., USN, LUTH (MoSy)
Wright, George Arthur, USN, EUB

List of Purple Heart Medals

During the 3-year Korean War, no Navy chaplains were killed in action. The following 15 received Purple Heart medals for wounds as they were received:

Orlando Ingvoldstad, Jr	15 September 1950
William G. Tennant	22 September 1950
Robert A. Bonner	27 September 1950
Kevin J. Keaney	29 November 1950
Cornelius J. Griffin	6 December 1950
Eugene I. Van Antwerp	26 January 1951
Charles S. Pigott	26 January 1951
John M. Quirk	4 June 1951
Joseph P. Trodd	8 June 1951
John E. Hollingsworth	20 June 1951
James S. Ferris	14 September 1951
John P. Byrnes	27 February 1953
Samuel Sobel	29 March 1953
Robert H. Willetts	11 June 1953
John T. Moore	26 July 1953

APPENDIX A

UNIT CITATIONS

PRESIDENTIAL UNIT CITATION

1st Provisional Marine Brigade _____ 7 August–7 September 1950

1st Marine Aircraft Wing
  One award covering three periods _____ 8 March–30 April 1951
  18 May–30 June 1951
  3 August–29 September 1951

1st Marine Division (Reinforced):
  (1) First PUC for action in Korea; the Division's fourth PUC. Includes Marine 15 September–11 October 1950
    Aircraft Group 33 and other supporting units.
  (2) The Division's fifth PUC _____ 27 November–11 December 1950
  (3) The Division's sixth PUC. One award covering three periods _____ 21–26 April 1951
  16 May–30 June 1951
  11–25 September 1951

A number of smaller commands, to which no chaplains were attached, also received the Presidential Unit Citation. (See Cagle and Manson, *The Sea War in Korea*.)

NAVY UNIT COMMENDATION

1st Marine Division (Reinforced). One award covering two periods _____ 11 August 1952–5 May 1953
7–27 July 1953
1st Marine Aircraft Wing _____ 1 August 1952–27 July 1953

SHIPS*

BADOENG STRAIT	3 August 1950–1 August 1951
BON HOMME RICHARD	22 June–18 December 1952
ESSEX	21 August 1951–5 March 1952
LEYTE	9 October 1950–19 January 1951
PHILIPPINE SEA	4 August 1950–30 March 1951
	31 March–31 May 1951
	31 January–27 July 1953
PRINCETON	5 December 1950–10 August 1951
	15 April–18 October 1952
	13 March–15 May 1953
	11 June–27 July 1953
SICILY	3 August 1950–1 August 1951
VALLEY FORGE	3 July–18 November 1951
	1 January–5 June 1953
	11 December 1951–11 June 1952

ARMY DISTINGUISHED UNIT CITATION

1st Marine Aircraft Wing _____ 22 November–14 December 1950

---

*Except in the case of BADOENG STRAIT and SICILY the award covers appropriate embarked air groups.

A number of smaller commands, to only one of which was a chaplain assigned, also received the NUC. That was USS HENRICO (APA 45), for the period 15 September–25 December 1950. (See Cagle and Manson, *The Sea War in Korea*, app. IV.)

1st Provisional Marine Brigade	2 August–6 September 1950
1st Marine Aircraft Wing	3 August 1950–26 February 1951
1st Marine Aircraft Wing	27 February 1951–11 June 1953
1st Marine Division (Reinforced)	15 September–27 September 1950
1st Marine Division (Reinforced)	26 October 1950–27 July 1953
Hospital Ships:	
USS CONSOLATION	11 August 1950–31 August 1951
USS HAVEN	18 October 1950–25 June 1952
USS REPOSE	16 September 1950–31 July 1951
7th Fleet	1 July 1950–27 July 1953

Plus certain Task Force commands, certain Fleet Activities commands, Fleet Air Wing SIX, certain Surgical Teams, and other smaller and specialized units, for specified dates.

(Sources: *U.S. Navy and Marine Corps Awards Manual* (NAVPERS 15,790. Revised 1953, and further revised by current Official Change Memoranda.); Cagle and Manson, *The Sea War in Korea* (1957); Montross and Canzona, *U.S. Marine Operations in Korea* (1954–   ).

APPENDIX B (1)

FIRST PROVISIONAL MARINE BRIGADE

FLEET MARINE FORCE (REINFORCED)
C/O FPO, SAN FRANCISCO, CALIF.

14 JULY–12 SEPTEMBER 1950.

14 July 1950—Embarked aboard ships with 1st Marine Brigade. Chaplains and assignments for shipping:

Lt. Comdr. Otto E. Sporrer, Catholic, 11th Marines. Aboard USS PICKAWAY.

Lt. William G. Tennant, Protestant, 3/5 Marines. Aboard USS PICKAWAY.

Lt. (jg.) Bernard L. Hickey, Catholic, 2/5 Marines. Aboard USS GEORGE CLYMER.

Lt. Comdr. O. Ingvoldstad, Jr., Protestant, 1/5 and HS/5 Marines. Aboard USS HENRICO.

The faith of ship's chaplains was taken into consideration so that, as far as possible, a Catholic and Protestant Chaplain were in each transport. The HENRICO was the only ship that had no Catholic chaplain for the trip, but when it was forced to stop in San Francisco for emergency repairs, Comdr. D. F. Kelly, Catholic, of Alameda Naval Air Station was invited aboard on 17 and 19 July to hear confessions and say Mass.

During the remainder of the trip on the HENRICO daily Protestant Vesper Services were conducted by the chaplains and daily Rosary Services were conducted by two of the Marine Catholic officers. This latter was done with the assistance of the chaplains.

On the PICKAWAY and CLYMER daily Mass was held and Protestant Services were held on Sunday. On the PICKAWAY the chaplains initiated and assisted in conducting several Happy Hours.

All ships arrived in Pusan, Korea, the evening of 2 August 1950.

COMMENTS REGARDING CHAPLAINS WITH TROOPS AND ON TRANSPORTS

1. Protestant chaplains, in the main, should be more aggressive to conduct daily devotions, vespers, or Bible studies. Under proper leadership Protestant men respond well.

2. Determined effort should be made to see that chaplains are either placed in rooms with fewest possible room mates, or are afforded a place for consultation, because of the number of men who desire to talk in private.

3. Chaplains should "advertise" their presence aboard. A temporary cardboard sign in the passageway outside their room is a great help.

4. Transport chaplains should carry all types of religious material far above their normal needs to accommodate troops and troop chaplains whose gear, of necessity, must be placed in holds. They should anticipate needs of embarked troops. One ship was completely out of New Testaments before the trip was completed.

Immediately after arrival in Pusan, troops debarked and made a night movement to Changwon. At this time chaplains were assigned and made movements with:

2/5 Marines—Lt. (jg.) B. L. Hickey.

3/5 Marines—Lt. W. G. Tennant.

Brigade Rear Echelon—Lt. Comdr. O. Ingvoldstad, having been turned in to Sick Bay, which remained in Pusan.

1/11 Marines—Lt. Comdr. O. E. Sporrer.

During the period 3–6 August the chaplains rendered services with the units to which they were attached and also other units in the bivouac area.

On 7 August the troops went into their first action south and west of Masan, Korea. At this time chaplains were assigned as follows:

3/5 Marines—Lt. (jg.) B. L. Hickey.

1/11 Marines—Lt. Comdr. O. E. Sporrer.

"B" Medical Co. at Masan—Lt. W. G. Tennant.

Rear Echelon, at Pusan—Lt. Comdr. O. Ingvoldstad.

First casualties were received and chaplains were under fire for the first time. This engagement continued for the period 7–13 August.

During this period Chaplains Hickey and Sporrer covered the forward aid stations; Chaplain Tennant covered the Navy and Army evacuation centers and cemetery at Masan; Chaplain Ingvoldstad covered the Army evacuation hospital at Pusan, through which all of our patients passed on their way to the hospitals in Japan. Chaplain Ingvoldstad was released from medical treatment on 12 August and that day joined the forward aid station, having made arrangements with the Army chaplains to conduct Catholic and Protestant and Jewish services for the Rear Echelon in Pusan.

1. While chaplains in the field are, and should be, given great freedom of movement in order to render services where most needed, they must, at all times, keep their immediate command informed with up-to-the-hour information as to their whereabouts. Practical knowledge of various types and means of communication should be had and utilized.

2. Protestant chaplains should be more alert to conduct worship services whenever opportunity affords, without waiting for Sunday.

3. It is valuable to have a chaplain at each battalion aid station, the collecting and clearing station, and the hospital. This would have taken six chaplains in this operation. Where a choice must be made, it is preferable to have a chaplain with the forward aid stations, not only for the wounded but the morale of the troops who are entering the engagement and see the chaplain up close with them.

4. Chaplains must give an air of calmness and assurance, give of their faith and courage, give their church's ministry and beware of asking operational questions, repeating ill-founded rumors, and becoming "amateur strategists." A chaplain in combat must give, give, give of the best he has!

5. Where chaplains must cover much mileage to reach separated units, a jeep of his own is invaluable. However, alertness and initiative can get him around much also, although not with much, or any, church gear.

6. Chaplains should know the location and activity of units other than their own and think of chances for services of worship for them. Use of operational maps and communications makes this feasible.

7. Chaplains should be cognizant of the duties of the Graves Registration Office and alert to check on the accuracy of their records. Chaplains should maintain their own record of burials for future reference in letters to next of kin. They should ascertain the *official* dates of death so that no discrepancies occur between their letters and the official death notice.

8. Chaplains should have a note book for jotting down names and services rendered, especially to seriously wounded or dead, in aid stations. Slips of paper with checkoff list of services rendered and placed in patients' pockets are not practical.

9. Chaplains should remember that, in a way, they are personal representatives of the next of kin and act accordingly.

10. Navy chaplains are not able to conduct funeral services for all of their own men because Army chaplains cover Army cemeteries and also operational demands delay their return to the cemetery. However, they can secure the records of which chaplain and when the funeral services were conducted for their own men.

.   .   .   .

On 14 August the Brigade was ordered to proceed as quickly as possible to Miryang for assistance in the Naktong breakthrough. They arrived at Miryang 15 August.

Chaplain Ingvoldstad, having been assigned a jeep and trailer, traveled independently via Pusan where additional Catholic and Protestant religious supplies were obtained from our reserve and the Army.

Two Protestant and Catholic services were held on 16 August and at 2000 the troops began to move forward.

17 August. 2/5 Marines went into attack at 0800. In the afternoon 1/5 Marines continued the attack. During this day over 300 casualties were handled in the forward aid station. Chaplains Ingvoldstad and either Sporrer or Hickey were in the forward aid station all day, with Chaplain Tennant at the Regimental Collecting and Clearing Station. That night Chaplains Tennant and Hickey were in the forward aid station, Chaplain Ingvoldstad at Regimental Collecting and Clearing, and Chaplain Sporrer with 1/11 Marines.

18 August. 1/5 Marines continued the attack and later in the morning 3/5 Marines went into attack, taking the third and final objective with light casualties. 2/5 Marines in late afternoon moved forward through 1/5 Marines and secured objective two. During this day and and night chaplains were placed as follows:

Chaplain Ingvoldstad—1/5 aid station, 3/5 aid station, 1/11 Marines for church 2/5 aid station for night.

Chaplain Sporrer—1/11 Marines and visited all aid stations.

Chaplain Tennant—Regimental Collecting and Clearing Station.

Chaplain Hickey—visited all aid stations; mostly with 3/5 aid station.

19 August. The Brigade was relieved by the Army and returned to Miryang. Chaplain Ingvoldstad visited the Army cemetery at Miryang and obtained records; also visited the Army hospital and Naval Operating Unit and patients there. Chaplain Ten-

nant returned with Regimental Aid, Hickey with 3/5 Marines Aid, and Sporrer with 1/11 Marines.

20 August. Protestant and Catholic services were conducted for Brigade and also Engineers. The Army hospital and cemetery were again visited. In the evening the Brigade began to entrain for return move to Chang-won-Masan area, arriving the next morning.

COMMENTS REGARDING PERIOD 14–20 AUGUST

1. With two Protestant and two Catholic chaplains and only one battalion at a time in the attack it was possible to have both a Protestant and Catholic chaplain in the forward aid station at all times and also to cover the Regimental Collecting and Clearing Station with a chaplain.

2. Chaplains can and should judiciously exchange places so that a continued chaplain's ministry is available and the physical demands are evenly distributed.

3. Under fire and being close to the front lines chaplains may be tempted to go forward of the aid station to do the job of a front line corpsman. A chaplain should refrain from this because while he is assisting 1 or 2 and exposing himself to enemy fire, 8 or 10 may have been brought into the aid station from other sectors and his services may be permanently lost as a chaplain.

4. Funeral and Memorial Services were again not conducted by Navy chaplains as we departed the area prior to burial of all of our men and the cemetery was in no condition for the holding of a large service.

* * * * *

From 21 August to 31 August the Brigade was in Army reserve status bivouac area. During this time it was possible to hold daily Mass, and Protestant services were often conducted. Arrangements were made for funeral and Memorial Services at the 25th Division, U.S. Army Cemetery, Masan, Korea, for all of our men buried there as a result of our first action 7–12 August. This was attended by the Brigade General and Staff and 500 men and all chaplains participated. Pictures of this service are on file in

Commandant of Marine Corps (Code AO)
Washington 25, D.C.

It was the general's desire that an individual picture of each grave with the appropriate chaplain standing by in benediction be taken so that families could secure copies if they so desired. Such pictures were taken during this period at Masan and also at Miryang

Cemetery for deaths resulting from 17–19 August action.

Protestant and Catholic services were conducted for the first time at the Brigade air component located at Chinhae.

Sunday, 27 August, the greatest number of services in one day (eight) were conducted: Protestant and Catholic services at bivouac area for all of Brigade there, at Masan for Medical Detachment and Service Battalion, at Chindong-ni for 11th Marines who were on detatched duty in support of Army, and at Chinhae for the air components.

COMMENTS REGARDING PERIOD 21–31 AUGUST

1. While the physical strain of combat, travel, and diarrhea causes a chaplain to want mainly to rest and write personal letters in bivouac, he should move about among his troops. This can be done, with chaplains attached to a regiment, by eating each meal with a different battalion. It also helps the troops to understand that the chaplain does not belong to only one particular battalion or only to Regimental H & S. A chaplain attached to a regiment should be able to feel at home in any battalion and should use time in bivouac area to help the troops understand this fact.

2. Facts concerning next of kin, official dates, and burial records can and should be compiled during this bivouac time, even though letters cannot now be written.

.   .   .   .   .

The morning of 1 September 1950 a warning order to return to Miryang for assistance in another Naktong breakthrough was received. In the afternoon the move began and was completed early the next morning. The afternoon of 2 September Brigade moved forward close to Yongsan. Sunday, 3 September 1950, 2/5 Marines went into attack, followed by 1/5 Marines. This day chaplains were placed thus:

2/5 aid stations, Chaplains Hickey and Ingvoldstad.
Regimental Aid, Chaplain Tennant.
1/11 and 2/5, Chaplain Sporrer.

Monday, 4 September, 3/5 Marines passed through into the attack and Chaplains Hickey and Ingvoldstad moved to 3/5 aid station. That night Chaplain Ingvoldstad moved to 1/5 aid station as they went into attack in the morning along with 3/5.

Tuesday, 5 September, Chaplains were placed:

1/11 and visiting aid stations, Chaplain Sporrer.
3/5 aid station, Chaplain Hickey.
1/5 aid station, Chaplain Ingvoldstad.

Regimental Collecting and Clearing, Chaplain Tennant.

Having again reached its objective, the Brigade that night was relieved by the Army and returned to Pusan on 6 September.

Chaplains returned with their units as follows:

1/11, Chaplain Sporrer.

3/5, Chaplain Hickey.

Reg't/5, Chaplain Tennant.

Chaplain Ingvoldstad returned independently via the cemetery and the hospital at Miryang where burial data was obtained and patients visited.

COMMENTS REGARDING PERIOD 1–6 SEPTEMBER

1. Chaplains again must be warned against going ahead of forward aid stations and also using slack time for exploring and investigating in GI fashion. While all chaplains were under some sort of fire, there is no reasonable excuse for being under fire when away from place of duty. Though a man may be curious to see what is going on and infected with souvenir collecting, a chaplain should hold himself in check because of his value as priest or pastor.

2. Again because of rapid movement we were unable to conduct funeral services at 24th Division, U.S. Army Cemetery, Miryang, Korea.

3. Chaplains, as troops, should keep personal gear at a minimum and in a state of readiness and neatness so that they are not caught unprepared for rapid moves.

.　　.　　.　　.　　.

The period 6–12 September Brigade was in Pusan in warehouses on the docks. For this period chaplains were placed:

1/11, Chaplain Sporrer.

Regiment and 1/5, Chaplain Tennant.

3/5, Chaplain Hickey.

Brigade and 2/5, Chaplain Ingvoldstad.

This period was used in preparing and mailing letters to next of kin, conducting services for all units, and preparing for going aboard ships for next operation.

COMMENTS REGARDING THE PERIOD 6–12 SEPTEMBER

1. Extreme care must be taken in writing letters to next of kin to assure correct official date of death and burial location.

2. With extra effort monthly reports can be accomplished.

3. Use of initiative on chaplains' part in conducting services in smaller ships and other units should be encouraged and used.

4. Chaplains should do the superhuman and refrain from non-constructive recounting of front line and aid station experiences. Much talk on part of chaplain, even though true, has an adverse effect on listeners as regards the chaplain.

The chaplains connected with 1st Provisional Marine Brigade conducted themselves well, gave brave and valuable ministry under fire and in bivouac, and also learned much concerning service with the Marines in attack.

One chief regret was the impossibility of conducting funeral services after the last two engagements, even though graveside services were conducted by Army chaplains.

O. INGVOLDSTAD, Jr.

Enclosures:

(A) Type of chaplain ministration card to be placed in patient's pocket, which proved impractical.

(B) Type of letter written to next of kin by Protestant chaplains.

(C) Type of letter written to next of kin by Catholic chaplains.

APPENDIX B (2)

CHAPLAIN'S OFFICE, 5TH MARINES, FMF 1ST MARINE DIVISION, FPO, SAN FRANCISCO, CALIF.

CHAPLAIN'S SPECIAL ACTION REPORT, 30 AUGUST TO 9 OCTOBER 1950

1. 30 August to 6 September. 5th Marines were in reserve at Masan and in action at Miryang, Korea. This phase is covered in a previous report. During this time the chaplains were informed that there would be an amphibious landing in the near future, and that one chaplain was to accompany each battalion.

2. 6–12 September. Protestant and Catholic services were held at various dock areas at Pusan and on various ships in which our troops were embarked.

3. Chaplains were assigned and accompanied troops as follows:

LT. COMDR. O. INGVOLDSTAD, JR., 2/5 on USS CAVALIER (APA 37).
LT. W. G. TENNANT, 1/5 on USS HENRICO (APA 45).
LT. (JG.) B. L. HICKEY, 3/5 on USS FORT MARION (LSD 22).

4. Services were held aboard ship at sea.

5. At Inchon, Korea, on 15 September 1950 chaplains landed with battalion aid stations. Chaplain Ingvoldstad received a minor shrapnel wound.

6. 15–17 September. Because of rapid advances and separated sectors of battalions, no interchange of chaplains between battalions was possible, nor were services able to be held.

7. 18–19 September. Catholic and Protestant services were held in 2/5 and 3/5.

8. 20 September. The Han River was crossed and the Regiment advanced toward Seoul, chaplains remaining with respective battalions.

9. 22 September. Chaplain Tennant was wounded by mortar shrapnel and evacuated. Division Chaplain was requested to send a replacement.

10. 23 September. Lt. L. R. Phillips, CHC, USN, joined Regiment. Chaplains were then assigned as follows:

LT. COMDR. O. INGVOLDSTAD 1/5 and 2/5 aid station.
LT. L. R. PHILLIPS Regimental aid station.
LT. (JG.) B. L. HICKEY 3/5 aid station.

On this day heaviest casualties to date were received by 2/5, 91 passing through the aid station and many dead were unable to be removed from the field of action. This action continued the following day for 2/5 with 125 casualties, but moderated on 25 September with 65 casualties and advance to outskirts of Seoul.

11. 26 September. Protestant and Catholic services were again held in Regiment, 1/5 and 3/5.

12. 27 September. 3/5 reached Capitol Building in Seoul and mopping up activities continued to 29 September.

13. 29 September. Chaplains were reassigned as follows:

LT. COMDR. O. INGVOLDSTAD, JR., Regiment.
LT. L. R. PHILLIPS, 2/5.
LT. (JG.) B. L. HICKEY, Regiment.

This enabled Chaplains Hickey and Ingvoldstad to work on letter to next of kin while Chaplain Phillips accompanied 2/5 on a separate mission some 10 miles away from Regimental Headquarters.

14. 30 September–4 October. Mopping up in Seoul and advance northwest of Seoul, farthest point being 18 miles, reached by the 3d Battalion.

15. 5 October. 5th Marines moved to assembly area, Inchon, preparing to embark for next operation.

COMMENTS REGARDING THIS PERIOD

1. In spite of the confusion of loading ships, chaplains could and did hold numerous services so that all units had opportunity for worship before being separated on ships not having chaplains.

2. Opportunity was also given so that each man could have his own personal Testament or Prayer Book. The Chaplains Section of Pusan Base Command was very helpful and generous in giving needed supplies. Catholic and Protestant chaplains should be concerned and prepared to offer supplies to men of each other's faith.

3. Assignment of chaplains to definite battalions for an operation seems to be the best way to operate. However, in a regiment going through several operations it is best to rotate the chaplains between the battalions so that men of various faiths in each battalion may have the closer services of a chaplain of their own faith at some time during the campaign.

4. In this operation it was not possible for chap-

lains without jeeps to move to battalions other than their own for services.

5. The system whereby the Division chaplain was able to replace a wounded chaplain in less than 24 hours was very commendable.

6. The Regimental Aid Station also acted as a Clearing and Collecting Section of the Medical Battalion. In this arrangement it is very desirable to have four chaplains to a regiment so that one chaplain could be at Regiment at all times. 762 casualties were handled by Regimental Aid during the period 15–30 September.

7. Burials were accomplished under supervision of the Division chaplain by chaplains of supporting organizations. In a shorter or less extended operation it would be well if chaplains of units to which the deceased belonged could also conduct their funeral services.

8. It was commendable that a Division Memorial Service was conducted prior to departure from the area.

9. The system of assembling all next of kin and burial information by the Division chaplain was of invaluable help to regiments whose personnel records are not available in combat.

10. Chaplains again did their best to conduct themselves and offer their services in a manner of inspiration and helpfulness to the men of this command.

11. During this period the Chaplains Section operated in accordance with the following:

STANDARD OPERATING PROCEDURE FOR CHAPLAINS SECTION

I. MISSION
A. To bring men to God and God to men by:
    1. Providing adequate spiritual and moral leadership.
    2. Making adequate provisions for formal worship services.
B. Under the Commanding Officer to assist in maintaining a high state of morale.

II. ORGANIZATION
A. Table of Organization (* denotes wartime complement only).

Position	Rank/rate	Service No.	MOS	Church
Regimental chaplain	LCDR	....	4100	....
Assistant reg't chaplain.	LT	....	4100	....
Chaplain*	LTJG	....	4100	....
Clerk	CPL	....	5243	....
Clerk	CPL	....	5243	....
Clerk*	CPL	....	5243	....

B. Present Organization

	Rank/rate	Service No.	MOS	Church
Regimental chaplain:				
O. Ingvoldstad, Jr.	LCDR	223739	4100	LUTH
Assistant Chaplains:				
L. R. Phillips	LT	381175	4100	CONG
B. L. Hickey	LTJG	527073	4100	RC
Clerks:				
E. R. Buhman	SGT	1087908	5243	RC
P. B. Barger	PFC	649497	5200	METH

III. OPERATION
A. Regimental Chaplain
    1. The Regimental Chaplain is a member of the Commanding Officer's Special Staff. As such he
        a. Is present at all Staff Conferences which include the Special Staff.
        b. Advises the Commanding Officer in matters relating to the Chaplains Mission.
        c. Acts as representative of the Commanding Officer in those matters relating to the Chaplains Mission.
B. Assistant Chaplains
    1. The duties of the Assistant Chaplain are:
        a. To conduct such religious services and functions as his church requires.
        b. To assist the Regimental Chaplain in the accomplishment of the Chaplains Mission.
C. Regarding Embarkation
    1. Regimental Chaplains should maintain a full supply of consumable, nonperishable church equipment crated and ready at all times for embarkation. This would include:

1,000	New Testaments (American Bible Society preferred because of prayers and hymns inserted which makes it possible to be used for field services).
500	Protestant Prayer Books
500	Catholic Military Missals
500	Rosaries
200	Field Hymn Books
1	Portable Field Organ

    2. The church affiliation of ship's chaplains are then taken into consideration so that, insofar as possible, a Protestant and Catholic chaplain may be on each transport.
    3. Chaplains' office equipment in Line No. 2 material for shipping. As such it may or may not be available during the voyage; but by personally contacting the regimental embarkation officer, certain pieces of equipment can be made accessible for use during the trip and combat loading.
D. Regarding Debarkation
    1. Chaplains debark and go ashore in company with the aid station of the battalion to which they are operationally attached.
    2. Supplies and equipment of minimum nature, depending on operation, accompany them.
    3. Remainder of supplies are to accompany Administrative Section of Regiment.

E. Under Battle Conditions
1. It has been found advisable to have one chaplain and clerk with each battalion. Chaplains and clerks remain administratively attached to Regimental Headquarters and Service Company but are attached to the battalions for operational control. Assignments are made by Regimental Chaplain. At opportune times chaplains are rotated between battalions so that each battalion may have the benefit of each chaplain's particular ministry.
2. Chaplains may, and should, use their initiative to visit other battalions so that both Protestant and Catholic services are frequently in each battalion. If possible the Regimental Chaplain should be informed beforehand, but in any event he should always be informed as as soon afterward as possible, of the services that are held by the Assistant Chaplains.
3. Although there is no Table of Equipment for the Chaplains Section, the equipment necessary for this type of operation for each chaplain is:
   a. Jeep and trailer, in which are carried:
   b. One typewriter, chest, and office supplies.
   c. One portable altar kit (supplied by Navy).
   d. Adequate Testaments, Prayer Books, and religious supplies (supplied from religious sources).
   e. One portable organ and hymn books (supplied by Navy).
   f. Two camp stools.
4. In addition to clerical and musical abilities, chaplain's clerks should be qualified jeep drivers and, as far as possible, be assigned to chaplains of similar faith.
5. The chaplain's base of operation shall be the aid station of the organization to which he is operationally attached and in no case shall he leave the battalion without notifying proper authority in the battalion.
6. It has become a cherished custom and tradition for Marines to hold a Memorial Service for their departed comrades before leaving the theater of action. These and funeral services are normally conducted under the supervision of the Division Chaplain.
   At times the Regiment may be on a separate mission and these services will be conducted by the Regiment. A tested and satisfactory type of combined Funeral and Memorial Service is as follows:
   Setting: One Marine who knew the departed stands at the head of each grave. Funeral party assembles at foot of cemetery, chaplains facing funeral party.
   Service:
   1. Catholic Prayers, Scripture.
   2. Protestant Scripture, Prayers.
   Regimental Chaplain says: "Let us all kneel in honor and memory of our departed comrades while the chaplains go to each grave for the graveside service". (Funeral party and Marines at each grave kneel.)
   3. Chaplains go to respective graves for graveside service. Regimental chaplain says: "Let us stand."
   4. Catholic Prayers, Scripture.
   5. Protestant Scripture, Prayers.
   6. Lord's Prayer by all.
   7. Benediction.
   8. Firing of three volleys.
   9. Sounding of Taps.
   If it is to be a Memorial Service only, No. 3 of the Service may be:
   Regimental chaplain says: "Let us all kneel in honor and memory of our departed comrades while the chaplains lead us in prayer." (Funeral party and Marines at each grave kneel while chaplains turn and face toward graves and offer prayers of intercession and blessing.)
7. Letters to next of kin should be written by the chaplain most closely connected with the deceased. Copies of such letters are sent to the Division Chaplain. Letters are not mailed directly to the next of kin, but are sent, signed and unsealed, in a larger envelope to:
   Commandant
   United States Marine Corps (Code DGU)
   Washington, 25, D.C.
   where they are mailed. This is to prevent letters being mailed to next of kin who have not been officially notified. Extreme care should be taken that dates and grave numbers are the same as the official records show.

F. In Bivouac or Rest Area
1. A Chaplain's Office for all chaplains of the regiment is maintained in a centrally located, easily accessible position. It should be so arranged that each chaplain has a private room for consultation and outer office for clerks. Although there is no Table of Equipment for the Chaplains Section, the equipment necessary includes desks, typewriters, file cabinets, chairs, and book cases sufficient to accommodate the staff. If the bivouac area is unimproved, three storage tents should be provided: one to be used as office and the other two together to form a chapel.
2. The Regimental Chapel should also be located in the central part of the Regimental Area, close to the Chaplains Office, and used only for religious services. These services would include daily Catholic Mass, Protestant Bible classes and week-day services, in addition to the Sunday services.
3. While it is desirable that chaplains are out visiting the units of the regiment, at least one chaplain is to always be in the office during working hours. When battalions have their own Mess Hall, the method of regularly contacting each battalion is for each chaplain to spend the hour or two preceding and following the noon meal with a different battalion each day.

4. General supervision and making of duty and chapel schedules is the responsibility of the Regimental Chaplain, although he may delegate such details as he sees fit.

5. The senior enlisted clerk is in charge of all enlisted personnel assigned to the Chaplains Section and responsible for their performance of duty.

   Assignments to specific duties will be made by him, subject to the approval of the Regimental Chaplain. Such duties include typing, filing, upkeep and cleaning of chapel and offices, music for chapel services, etc.

6. Each chaplain is to conduct such religious services and functions as his particular church requires, but planning and scheduling of same is coordinated by the Regimental Chaplain.

Conclusion

1. *The Chaplains' Manual,* NavPers 15664, 1949 edition, is the guide and authority for the chaplains duties.

2. Common sense in the rapidly changing conditions of battle, remembering to pursue the goal of "Bringing men to God and God to men" under all conditions and at all times is the constant and unchanging form for all chaplains.

O. INGVOLDSTAD, Jr.
LCDR, CHC, USN.

APPENDIX C

HEADQUARTERS
FLEET MARINE FORCE, PACIFIC
C/O FLEET POST OFFICE, SAN FRANCISCO

28 MARCH 1951.

Fleet Marine Force, Pacific
General Order No. 19 } Standing Operating Procedure for the Chaplain Service of the Fleet Marine Force, Pacific

1. The following procedure will be used as a guide by chaplains on duty with the Fleet Marine Force, Pacific.

2. *General:*

a. The Force Chaplain is on the Special Staff of the Commanding General, Fleet Marine Force, Pacific. He shall advise and inform the Commanding General in matters pertaining to divine services, religious activities and interests, and personnel of the Chaplain Corps on duty in the Force.

b. The Division, Air Wing, or Brigade Senior Chaplain is normally assigned as Division, Air Wing, or Brigade Chaplain on the Special Staff of the Commanding General. He shall advise his Commanding General on the assignments and activities of the chaplains within the Division, Air Wing, or Brigade. He will coordinate and generally supervise the work of these chaplains.

c. Unit chaplains have the same functions in their organizations as the Division, Air Wing, Brigade, and Force Chaplains, as concerns the advising of commanding officers about the religious provisions for the unit.

d. Specific duties of chaplains assigned to Marine Corps units are given in the Marine Corps Staff Manual, paragraph 241.

3. *In Bivouac or Garrison:*

a. The functions of the Chaplain Section will be carried out in accordance with the Chaplain's Manual (NavPers 15664); Navy Regulations, article 0807; BuPers Manual C–12202, C–12205, Staff Manual (1948) NAVMC 1022–DPP, and current directives of the Chaplain's Division of BuPers.

b. Chaplains will engage in field training with the organization to which attached.

c. Chaplains will be used in Character Guidance Lectures. They will seek opportunities for showing religious and morality films issued by the Navy Department.

d. Prior to operations in the field, chaplains will procure the portable ecclesiastical equipment issued by the Chaplains Division, BuPers. Care should be taken that each chaplain has enough consumable altar supplies for at least one month's use. The Division or Wing Chaplain will procure replacements through regular supply channels. Arrangements should be made for the following items in the field: a portable typewriter with office supplies, a small 2.9 cubic foot field desk, and two camp stools.

4. *In Combat Operations:*

a. Duties of chaplains between the ports of embarkation and assault beaches:

(1) The Division chaplain will arrange by consultation with the Embarkation officer for at least one chaplain to sail on each ship (transport, LST or LSD) if practicable. Some ships will have ship's chaplains, either Protestant or Catholic, which will be taken into consideration in the distribution of chaplains.

(2) The unit chaplain will schedule religious services and other religious activities after consultation of the commander of troops, commanding officer of the ship and the ship's chaplain, if one is on board.

(3) Chaplains should be placed in rooms with fewest room mates, or be afforded a place for consultation, because of the number of men who desire to talk in private.

(4) Chaplains should make their location aboard known by a sign in the passageway outside their room or office.

(5) Prior to sailing, the troops' chaplain will confer with the ship's chaplain regarding the amount of religious supplies aboard which will be available for his use at sea.

(6) Chaplains will assist, where needed, with the entertainment and recreational program aboard ship for troop personnel.

(7) Troops will expect some special service of worship on the eve of debarkation. Upon approval of the Commanding Officer, and in cooperation with the ship's chaplain, a Mass for Catholics and a Communion or other service for Protestant personnel should be scheduled. A Jewish service should be arranged if numbers warrant.

b. Duties of chaplains in the assault phase:

(1) In an amphibious operation, each chaplain will go ashore with the echelon assigned, usually with the unit Aid Station, equipped for immediate minis-

tration. As soon as practicable after landing, each chaplain of the Division will establish liaison with the unit Personnel Section and Surgeon.

(2) Upon landing, the Division Chaplain establishes liaison with the Division Personnel Officer (G–1), Surgeon, and Graves Registration Officer.

He obtains from the Division G–4 the location of the Division Cemetery.

He establishes and maintains contact with Field Hospitals in Division area.

He coordinates the combat ministration plan for chaplains of the Division, and makes recommendations for replacement of chaplain casualties.

He assists the Graves Registration Officer in coordination of all graves registration and burial activity.

He provides for proper religious rites for burial of the dead in the Division area.

(3) The Regimental chaplain lands with the echelon to which assigned, equipped for immediate ministrations.

He establishes liaison as soon as practicable with the Adjutant, S–1, Regimental Surgeon, Graves Registration Section Chief, and other chaplains of the Regiment.

He obtains information as soon as possible from S–1 as to the location of the temporary Regimental cemetery.

He establishes and maintains contact with the Regimental collecting section, and the Battalion Aid Stations.

He provides for proper religious rites in the burial of the deceased personnel in the Regimental area.

He establishes and maintains contact with Field Hospitals in support of the Regiment. He and the other chaplains should visit daily the Field Hospitals and when required take names of the more seriously wounded, communicating with the parents of the wounded relative to their condition.

He performs Divine Services as prescribed by the Commanding Officer, whenever and wherever practicable.

He will make special effort to insure that chaplains are present whenever companies or battalions come out of the front lines to go into rest or reserve areas and also when reserve companies or battalions are about to move into the front lines.

(4) The unit chaplain's battle station during combat will most generally be the Battalion or Regimental Aid Station.

(5) An additional chaplain will be available from the supporting elements of the Division or the Division chaplain's pool for each infantry regiment during the assault phase. This provides four chaplains, one for each Battalion, and one for the Regiment. Following this, the additional chaplain will resume his previous duty in the Division.

(6) During combat operations, unit chaplains will communicate frequently with the Division chaplain by telephone or guard mail. They will keep their immediate commanding officer informed at all times of their whereabouts.

(7) Unit commanders will provide transportation as necessary to enable chaplains to execute their duties.

(8) When practicable an individual picture of each grave with the appropriate chaplain standing by in benediction should be taken, so that families may secure copies if desired.

c. Duties on Conclusion of Landing and Assault Phase:

(1) At the close of operations unit chaplains will prepare letters of condolence to next of kin of those lost in action. These letters will be properly channeled through the command. The office of the Division chaplain can assist a unit chaplain by looking up the following information relative to each person deceased:

(a) Name, rank, serial number.

(b) Date of death, place of burial, and religion.

(c) Name and address of next of kin.

(d) Name of officiating chaplain at burial service.

(2) At the close of an operation, the Division chaplain, with the approval of the Commanding General, should arrange for a memorial service to be held at the Division cemetery or in other cemeteries where Division dead are buried.

5. *Conclusion:*

Common sense in the rapidly changing conditions of battle, initiative for which there is no substitute, and the reminder to pursue the goal of "bringing men to God and God to men" under all conditions, are the constant criteria for every chaplain.

By Command of Lieutenant General Shepherd:

J. C. Burger,
Colonel, U.S. Marine Corps
Chief of Staff

Distribution:
    Case 1.
    Case 2; A, B, C, D, E, G, X, Y.
    Case 3.
O-F-F-I-C-I-A-L:
    (S) C. C. Henderson,
    C. C. Henderson,
    Major, USMC,
    Adjutant.

APPENDIX D

HEADQUARTERS 1ST MARINE DIVISION (REINF), FMF
C/O FLEET POST OFFICE, SAN FRANCISCO, CALIF.

19/twh
15 Aug 1951

Annex K to
Division General Order } SOP, Chaplains
No. 50

Standing Operating Procedure for the Chaplain Service of the 1st Marine Division, Fleet Marine Force, Pacific.

1. *General*

a. The Division chaplain is a member of the Special Staff, and will advise the Commanding General and staff on matters pertaining to religion and religious activities. He will advise the Commanding General on the assignment and activities of the chaplains within the Division, and will coordinate and generally supervise the work of all Chaplains.

b. Unit chaplains as a member of the respective special staffs will advise the Commanding Officer concerning religious provisions and religious activities for the unit.

2. *In Reserve, Bivouac or Training Area*

a. The functions of the Chaplain Section will be executed in accordance with Chaplains Manual (NavPers 15664); Navy Regulations, Article 0807; BuPers Manual, Articles C12202, C12205, U.S. Marine Corps Staff Manual (1948) NAVMC 1022–DPP, and current directives of the Chaplains Division of BuPers.

b. Each chaplain will arrange to conduct or have conducted Divine Services on Sunday within his own area. The responsibility for the availability of both Protestant and Catholic Services for their personnel rests upon individual unit chaplains. The unit chaplain will also arrange for attendance at Jewish Services when a Jewish chaplain is available.

c. The Unit chaplain will arrange some form of daily Religious Service in his area.

d. Chaplains may be employed in the presentation of Character Guidance Lectures, and will hold themselves available to assist unit Surgeons in preventive lectures on Spiritual and Moral views of V.D. Control.

e. The chaplains assigned to infantry and artillery Regiments will be retained administratively in regimental headquarters, for deployment in accordance with the recommendations of the regimental chaplain.

3. *Chaplain duties in Combat*

a. Amphibious Operations.

(1) The Division chaplain will endeavor, after consulting with the Embarkation Officer, to deploy his chaplains aboard the ships so as to obtain a maximum of spiritual assistance for personnel of all Faiths. He will take into consideration the fact that some ships will have chaplains, either Catholic or Protestant, regularly assigned.

(2) The Unit chaplain aboard ship will schedule services and other religious activities after consulting with the Commanding Officer of Troops, the Commanding Officer of the vessel and the Ship's chaplain. The Unit chaplain will attempt to adhere to any schedule already arranged by the Ship's chaplain.

(3) Unit Commanders will undertake to procure private quarters for the Unit chaplain where practicable or, should that be impracticable, he will provide some place which affords privacy for consultations. Personnel will not discuss private problems in the presence of others.

(4) Once the chaplain has been assigned a suitable location, he should insure that this information be made known to all personnel.

(5) If possible the Unit chaplain should attempt to bring aboard sufficient religious supplies for his troops. This will not be necessary if consultation with the Ship's chaplain discloses that he has an abundance of supplies.

(6) Chaplains will assist, when needed, with the recreational program aboard ship for troop personnel, but not in a degree which will affect adversely the conduct of their spiritual activities.

(7) The chaplain will plan a Special Worship Service on the eve of debarkation, with the approval of the Commanding Officer, and in cooperation with the Ship's chaplain, a Mass for Catholic personnel and a Protestant Service for Protestant personnel. Where possible, and if numbers warrant, a Jewish Service should be arranged.

b. Duties of chaplains in the Landing and Assault Phase and thereafter.

(1) Each chaplain will land with the echelon assigned, usually with the Unit Aid Station. This should be at the earliest moment that his presence ashore is warranted. As soon as practicable after

landing, the chaplain will establish liaison with the Unit Personnel and Medical Sections.

(2) Upon landing, the Division chaplain, will establish liaison with the Division Personnel Officer, the Surgeon, and Graves Registration Officer. As appropriate thereafter he will accomplish the following:

(a) Obtain from Division G–4 the location of the Division Cemetery.

(b) Establish and maintain contact with field hospitals in the Division area and insure coverage for them by chaplains.

(c) Coordinate the combat ministration plan for the chaplains of the Division and endeavor to have available ready replacements for chaplain casualties.

(d) Assist the Graves Registration Officer in coordination of all graves registration and burial activities.

(e) Provide for proper religious rites for burial of the dead in the Division area.

(3) The Regimental chaplain lands with the echelon to which assigned. Upon landing he will establish liaison with the Adjutant, Regimental Surgeon, Graves Registration Section, and other chaplains of the Regiment. At the earliest practicable time he will establish contact with the Division chaplain. As appropriate thereafter he will accomplish the following:

(a) Obtain information as soon as possible from the Adjutant as to the location of the temporary Regimental Cemetery.

(b) Provide for proper religious rites in the burial of deceased personnel in the Regimental area, should a temporary Regimental Cemetery be established.

(c) Establish and maintain contact with medical installations in support of the Regiment, making daily visit to those installations along with other chaplains.

(d) Administer spiritual aid and conduct Divine Services.

(e) Offer assistance to the wounded in communicating with relatives in order to alleviate undue anxiety and worry.

(f) Perform Religious Services where and whenever possible. The approval of the Commanding Officer will be obtained when arranging any Service which would require a gathering of a group of men.

(g) Assure the availability of chaplains for men coming out of action and those about to enter combat.

(4) The Unit chaplain's ordinary battle station during combat will be the Battalion or Regimental Aid Station. Chaplains will not limit their availability by joining any small unit or individual patrol.

(5) Chaplains of supporting Units will be held available by the Division chaplain to be used with forward units or for immediate replacement for chaplain casualties. Chaplains thus used will be returned to their units when no longer needed with combat elements.

(6) Unit Commanders will provide necessary transportation to enable chaplains to carry out their duties expeditiously.

(7) As soon as the opportunity is afforded, Unit chaplains will prepare letters of condolence to next of kin of those lost in action. These letters will be properly channeled through the command. Should the operation be extended over a long period of time, the Division chaplain, when the opportunity permits, will process these letters. The Division Chaplain's Office will assist by obtaining the following necessary information relative to the deceased:

(a) Name, rank, serial number.

(b) Date of death, place of burial.

(c) Religion.

(d) Name and address of next of kin.

(8) At such intervals as are appropriate, the Division chaplain, with the approval of the Commanding General should arrange a Memorial Ceremony at the Division Cemetery or at a site selected by the Commanding General.

4. *Equipment*

(a) Prior to operations in the field, chaplains will procure the portable ecclesiastical equipment issued by the Chaplains Division, BuPers. Care should be taken that each chaplain has enough consumable altar supplies to last for at least 1 month's use. The Division chaplain will procure replacements through regular supply channels. To expedite this procurement a chaplain with a rear Unit should be designated as a supply chaplain. Arrangements should be made for the following items in the field: a portable typewriter with office supplies, a 2.9 cubic foot field desk, and two camp stools.

6. *Collateral Duties*

(a) The primary work of the chaplain is spiritual and moral leadership. He will therefore not be required to undertake duties of any other nature that would absorb the major portion of his time, and thus cause him to neglect his chaplain duties.

By Command of Major General Thomas:

V. H. Krulak,
Colonel, U.S. Marine Corps,
Chief of Staff.

Official:

[S] H. E. Hire,
H. E. Hire,
Lt Col USMC,
DivAdj.

APPENDIX E

OFFICE OF THE DIVISION CHAPLAIN,
1ST MARINE DIVISION, FLEET MARINE FORCE
C/O FLEET POST OFFICE, SAN FRANCISCO, CALIF.

WEBjr:jel
19 FEB. 1952

DIVINE SERVICES
BREAKDOWN BY DENOMINATIONS

*Catholic**

Sunday: 0900—Hamblin Theater (Division Reserve Area)
           1st Motor Transport Battalion
           Headquarters Chapel, 1st Marine Division
     0930—4th Battalion, 11th Marines CP
     1000—Regimental CP, 7th Marines
     1030—1st Battalion Theater (Division Reserve Area)
     1100—1st Engineer Battalion
           1st Ordnance Battalion
           3d Battalion, 11th Marines CP
           Reserve Battalion, 7th Marines
     1300—1st Service Battalion
     1330—"D" Company, 1st Medical Battalion
           1st Battalion, 5th Marines CP
     1400—Regimental Rear Chapel (Division Reserve Area)
     1430—3d Battalion, 7th Marines CP
     1500—"A" Company, 1st Medical Battalion
           Regimental CP, 5th Marines
     1530—1st Shore Party Battalion
     1800—Regimental CP, 11th Marines
     1030—Reserve Battalion, 5th Marines CP
     1800—"D" Company, 1st Medical Battalion (Rosary and Night Prayers)
     2000—3d Battalion, 1st Marines CP (Division Reserve Area)—Rosary and Benediction Service
           1st Motor Transport Battalion (Rosary)

Monday: 1000—"F" Company, 2d Battalion, 7th Marines
     1200—2d Battalion, 5th Marines CP
     1330—"A" Company, 1st Engineer Battalion (Punch Bowl)
     1530—3d Battalion, 1st Marines CP (Division Reserve Area)
     1545—"A" Company, 1st Medical Battalion
     1600—1st Motor Transport Battalion
     1400—"E" Battery, 2d Battalion, 11th Marines
     1800—"D" Company, 1st Medical Battalion (Rosary)
     2000—3d Battalion, 1st Marines CP (Division Reserve Area)—Rosary
           1st Motor Transport Battalion (Rosary)

Tuesday: 1400—"E" Company, 2d Battalion, 7th Marines
     1200—Reserve Battalion, 5th Marines
     1400—4th Battalion, 11th Marines CP
     1600—Headquarters Chapel, 1st Marine Division
     1530—3d Battalion, 1st Marines CP (Division Reserve Area)

---

*Where not otherwise designated, Mass is meant. Editor.

Tuesday—Continued

        1600—1st Motor Transport Battalion
        1800—"D" Company, 1st Medical Battalion (Rosary)
        2000—3d Battalion, 1st Marines CP (Division Reserve Area)—Rosary
                1st Motor Transport Battalion (Rosary)

Wednesday: 1600—Reserve Battalion, 7th Marines CP
        1200—"I" Company, 3d Battalion, 5th Marines
        1400—3d Battalion, 11th Marines CP
        1600—Headquarters Chapel, 1st Marine Division
        1530—3d Battalion, 1st Marines CP (Division Reserve Area)
        1600—"E" Company, 1st Medical Battalion
        1615—1st Service Battalion
        1800—"D" Company, 1st Medical Battalion (Rosary)
        2000—3d Battalion, 1st Marines CP (Division Reserve Area)—Rosary

Thursday: 1030—"G" Company, 3d Battalion, 7th Marines
        1230—"E" Company, 2d Battalion, 5th Marines
        1400—1st Battalion, 11th Marines CP
        1600—Headquarters Chapel, 1st Marine Division
        1530—3d Battalion, 1st Marines CP (Division Reserve Area)
        1600—"E" Company, 1st Medical Battalion
        1630—1st Ordnance Battalion
        1800—"D" Company, 1st Medical Battalion (Rosary)
        2000—3d Battalion, 1st Marines CP (Division Reserve Area)—Rosary
                1st Motor Transport Battalion (Rosary)

Friday: 1000—3d Battalion, 7th Marines CP
        1200—81-mm Mortar Company, 5th Marines
        1400—2d Battalion, 11th Marines CP
        1600—Headquarters Chapel, 1st Marine Division
        1530—3d Battalion, 1st Marines CP (Division Reserve Area)
        1600—"D" Company, 1st Medical Battalion
                1st Motor Transport Battalion
        1800—"D" Company, 1st Medical Battalion (Rosary)
        2000—3d Battalion, 1st Marines CP (Division Reserve Area)—Rosary
                1st Motor Transport Battalion (Rosary)

Saturday: 1230—4.2" Mortar Company, 5th Marines
        1800—1st Tank Battalion
        1100—"H" Company, 3d Battalion, 7th Marines
        1600—Headquarters Chapel, 1st Marine Division
        1530—3d Battalion, 5th Marines CP (Division Reserve Area)
        1600—"D" Company, 1st Medical Battalion
                1st Motor Transport Battalion
        1800—"D" Company, 1st Medical Battalion (Rosary)
        2000—3d Battalion, 1st Marines CP (Division Reserve Area)—Rosary
                1st Motor Transport Battalion (Rosary)

Protestant

Sunday: 0900—1st Signal Battalion
                1st Service Battalion
                1st Battalion, 1st Marines CP (Division Reserve Area)

Sunday: 0900—Continued
                1st Ordnance Battalion
                "E" Company, 1st Medical Battalion
         0930—4th Battalion, 11th Marines CP
                Reserve Battalion, 7th Marines CP
                3d Battalion, 11th Marines CP
                1st Battalion, 5th Marines CP
         1000—Headquarters Chapel, 1st Marine Division
                1st Tank Battalion
                1st Combat Service Group
                1st Amphibian Tractor Battalion
                2d Battalion, 7th Marines CP
                3d Battalion, 5th Marines CP
         1030—"C" Company, 1st Medical Battalion
                Hamblin Theater (Division Reserve Area)
                "A" Company, 1st Medical Battalion
         1030—HMR 161
         1045—2d Battalion, 5th Marines CP
         1100—1st Battalion, 11th Marines CP
                Regimental CP, 7th Marines
                2d Battalion, 11th Marines CP
                "D" Company, 1st Medical Battalion
         1130—4.2" Mortar Company, 7th Marines
         1300—1st Motor Transport Battalion
                Rear Area Chapel (Division Reserve Area)
                "A" Company, 1st Engineer Battalion (Punch Bowl)
                Regimental CP, 5th Marines
         1330—1343 Army Engineer Battalion
                "A" Company, 1st Battalion, 5th Marines
                3d Battalion, 7th Marines CP
         1400—1st Shore Party Battalion
         1500—Regimental CP, 11th Marines
                "H" Company, 3d Battalion, 7th Marines
                "G" Company, 3d Battalion, 5th Marines
                "D" and "C" Company, 1st Engineer Battalion
         1745—1st Shore Party Battalion (Bible Study)
         1815—1st Service Battalion
         1830—1st Combat Service Group
         1900—1st Engineer Battalion (Korean Service)
         2030—1st Ordnance Battalion (Korean Service)

Monday: 0830—1st Battalion, 11th Marines CP
         1830—1st Amphibian Tractor Battalion
         1030—"G" Company, 3d Battalion, 5th Marines
         1745—1st Shore Party Battalion (Bible Class)
         1830—1st Combat Service Group
         1915—4th Battalion, 11th Marines CP (Bible Study)
         1030—"A" Company, 1st Battalion, 5th Marines
         1100—"G" Company, 3d Battalion, 7th Marines
         1330—"I" Company, 3d Battalion, 7th Marines

Tuesday:	1900—2d Battalion, 11th Marines CP (Bible Study)
	1600—1st Battalion, 5th Marines CP
	1915—4th Battalion, 11th Marines CP (Bible Study)
	1830—1st Combat Service Group
	2000—HMR 161 (Bible Class)
	1745—1st Shore Party Battalion (Bible Class)
	1030—"I" Company, 3d Battalion, 5th Marines
	1830—1st Amphibian Tractor Battalion
	1930—1st Amphibian Tractor Battalion (Bible Study)
	0830—1st Battalion, 11th Marines CP
	1300—"H" Company, 3d Battalion, 7th Marines

Wednesday:	1030—"B" Company, 1st Battalion, 5th Marines
	1915—4th Battalion, 11th Marines CP (Bible Study)
	1600—1st Motor Transport Battalion
	1815—1st Service Battalion
	1830—1st Combat Service Group
	1745—1st Shore Party Battalion (Bible Class)
	1900—1st Engineer Battalion (Korean Service)
	1800—3d Battalion, 5th Marines CP
	1830—1st Amphibian Tractor Battalion
	0830—1st Battalion, 11th Marines CP

Thursday:	1900—2d Battalion, 11th Marines (Bible Class)
	1800—2d Battalion, 5th Marines CP
	1915—4th Battalion, 11th Marines CP (Bible Study)
	1830—1st Combat Service Group
	2000—HMR 161 (Bible Class)
	1745—1st Shore Party Battalion (Bible Class)
	1500—"I" Company, 3d Battalion, 5th Marines
	1830—1st Amphibian Tractor Battalion
	0830—1st Battalion, 11th Marines CP
	1100—"F" Company, 2d Battalion, 7th Marines
	1400—"E" Company, 2d Battalion, 7th Marines

Friday:	1030—"C" Company, 1st Battalion, 5th Marines
	1915—4th Battalion, 11th Marines CP (Bible Study)
	1830—1st Combat Service Group
	1745—1st Shore Party Battalion (Bible Study)
	1800—3d Battalion, 5th Marines CP
	1830—1st Amphibian Tractor Battalion
	0830—1st Battalion, 11th Marines CP
	1300—"D" Company, 2d Battalion, 7th Marines

Saturday:	1430—"E" Battery, 2d Battalion, 11th Marines
	1800—1st Battalion, 5th Marines CP
	1915—4th Battalion, 11th Marines CP (Bible Study)
	1830—1st Combat Service Group
	1745—1st Shore Party Battalion (Bible Study)
	1030—4.2" Mortar Company, 5th Marines
	1830—1st Amphibian Tractor Battalion
	0830—1st Battalion, 11th Marines CP

Jewish

Sunday: 1100—Headquarters Chapel, 1st Marine Division
1600—Camp Tripoli
Wednesday: 1000—Regimental Reserve Battalion, 5th Marines
1400—Regimental Reserve Battalion, 7th Marines
NOTE: Plus visit each month to 1st Combat Service Group and 1st Amphibian Tractor Battalion.

Episcopal

Saturday: 0930—Headquarters Chapel, 1st Marine Division

Latter-Day Saint Services

Sunday: 1000—2d Battalion Chapel, Camp Tripoli (1st Marines)
1000—Reserve Battalion, 5th Marines
1400—Reserve Battalion, 7th Marines

BIBLIOGRAPHY

GENERAL SOURCES

Berger, C., *The Korea Knot,* Philadelphia, 1957.

Britannica Book of the Year, "Korean War," 1952.

Britannica Book of the Year, "Korean War," 1953.

Cagle, M. W. and Manson, F. A., *The Sea War in Korea,* Annapolis, 1957.

Clark, Gen. Mark W., *From the Danube to the Yalu,* New York, 1954.

Geer, Andrew, *The New Breed,* New York, 1952.

Goodrich, L. M., Korea: *A Study of U.S. Policy in the United Nations,* New York, 1956.

Gugeler, R. A. (Ed.), *Combat Operations in Korea,* Washington, 1954.

Jones, Ken, *I Was There,* New York, 1953.

Joy, C. Turner, *How Communists Negotiate,* New York, 1955.

Karig, Walter, Cagle, M. W. and Manson, F. A., *Battle Report;* Vol. VI, *The War in Korea,* New York, 1952.

Korea, 1950 (Department of the Army).

Miller, John Jr., Carroll, Maj. Owen J., and Tackley, Margaret E., *Korea, 1951–53,* Washington, D.C., 1958.

Montross, Lynn, *Cavalry of the Sky,* New York, 1954.

Montross, Lynn and Canzona, N. A., *The Chosin Reservoir Campaign,* Washington, 1957; *U.S. Marine Operations in Korea, 1950–53; The Pusan Perimeter,* Washington, 1954—.

Muller, John H., *Wearing the Cross in Korea,* California, 1954.

Ridgway, M. B., *Soldier: The Memoirs of Matthew B. Ridgway,* New York, 1956.

Thomas, Maj. R. C. W., *The War in Korea 1950–53,* Aldershot, 1954.

Vatchee, William, Jr., *Panmunjon,* New York, 1958.

PERIODICALS

Ladies Home Journal, December 1952.

Lederer, W. J., "Operation Kidlift"

Life:

Van Fleet, J. A., "The Truth About Korea," May 11, 1953.

Marine Corps Gazette:

Giusti, E. H., "Minute Men—1950 Model: The Reserves in Action," September 1951.

Montross, Lynn, "Advance to the 38th Parallel: The Marines in Operation Ripper," March 1952.

"Advance to the Punchbowl," August 1953.

"Breakout From the Reservoir: Marine Epic of Fire and Ice," November 1951.

"Buttoning Up the Offensive: The Marines in Operation Killer," February 1952.

"Red China on the Offensive," July 1953.

"The Hungnam Evacuation," December 1951.

"The Pohang Guerilla Hunt," January 1952.

"They Make Men Whole Again: The Medical Battalion and Chaplains in Korea," December 1952.

Nicholson, D. D., Jr., "Their Faith Is Yours," December 1953.

National Geographic Magazine, February 1953:

Mosier, Robert H., T. Sgt. USMC, May 1953, "The G.I. and the Kids of Korea."

Navy Chaplains Bulletin:

Peck, W. S., "The Destroyer Chaplaincy," Fall, 1953.

Silver, D. J., "Chaplain Chung's Corps," Fall, 1954.

The Tidings, Los Angeles, c. 1951.

U.S. Naval Institute Proceedings, "Armed Forces Care Through CARE," August 1955.

U.S. Navy and Marine Corps Awards Manual, NAVPERS 15790; revised 1953.

Stars and Stripes—Korean edition.

UNPUBLISHED SOURCES

J. Floyd Dreith, Chaplain, USN. MS report to Chief of Chaplains on Chaplain Field Training, Marine Barracks, Camp Pendleton, Calif.

Letters of individual chaplains to the Chief of Chaplains. Especially important have been the very frequent letters of the supervisory chaplains (Division Chaplain, 1st Marine Division, and Wing Chaplain, 1st Marine Aircraft Wing). Letters are cited in each case by date, name of sender.

Diary of the 1st Marine Aircraft Wing Chaplain.

Battle Reports by Chaplain O. Ingvoldstad. See appendix B. Copied from Ingvoldstad's personal records, by permission.

Statistical reports of chaplain activities submitted to the Chief of Chaplains, Bureau of Naval Personnel. Normally individual chaplain's reports were combined into more inclusive reports before being forwarded by supervisory chaplains en route.

Questionnaire prepared by the then Historian of the Chaplain Corps, Chaplain C. L. Drury, and distributed throughout the Corps in the spring of 1954. Each reply was numbered as it came in, and the appropriate number placed by the chaplain's name in a master code. Thus it was possible to read each questionnaire without knowing the name of the chaplain who had supplied the answers, if anonymity were wanted; or, conversely, the chaplain's name could be obtained if needed. As is usual with questionnaires, some of the material furnished was of little or no use. On the other hand, a large amount of interesting and sometimes very important data has been derived therefrom. Some material was not included because of the failure to record the date and place of events.

Official Memoranda and Instructions in the files of the Chief of Chaplains, Bureau of Naval Personnel.

INDEX OF PROPER NAMES

COMMANDS, OPERATIONS, SHIPS

GENERAL INDEX

○